TO SAVE AN ARMY

OSPREY
PUBLISHING

TO SAVE AN ARMY

THE STALINGRAD AIRLIFT

ROBERT FORSYTH

OSPREY PUBLISHING
Bloomsbury Publishing Plc
Kemp House, Chawley Park, Cumnor Hill, Oxford OX2 9PH, UK
29 Earlsfort Terrace, Dublin 2, Ireland
1385 Broadway, 5th Floor, New York, NY 10018, USA
E-mail: info@ospreypublishing.com
www.ospreypublishing.com

OSPREY is a trademark of Osprey Publishing Ltd

First published in Great Britain in 2022

A catalogue record for this book is available from the British Library.

ISBN: HB 9781472845412; PB 9781472845429; eBook 9781472845405;
ePDF 9781472845382; XML 9781472845399

22 23 24 25 26   10 9 8 7 6 5 4 3 2 1

Edited by Tony Holmes
Maps by www.bounford.com
Artwork: aircraft profiles by Jim Laurier, air-drop container line
drawing by Tim Brown, © Osprey Publishing
Index by Fionbar Lyons

Typeset by Deanta Global Publishing Services, Chennai, India
Printed and bound in Great Britain by CPI (Group) UK Ltd, Croydon, CR0 4YY

Osprey Publishing supports the Woodland Trust, the UK's leading woodland conservation charity.

To find out more about our authors and books visit www.ospreypublishing.com. Here you will find
extracts, author interviews, details of forthcoming events and the option to sign up for our newsletter.

For Sally, as always.
And to the memory of Jen.
For happy times, love and laughter.

Contents

Introduction

Airlift > **noun** *an act of transporting supplies by aircraft, typically in a blockade or other emergency.*

THE OXFORD DICTIONARY OF ENGLISH

It has become customary – indeed, something of a literary fashion among writers of history – to commence a book with a maxim or axiom from a major historical figure which may assist in contextualising the subject matter or in sharpening a reader's focus.

Some years ago, on a dusty shelf in a second-hand bookshop, I found a worn volume printed on thin British 'War Economy Standard' paper of what were described as 'military classics'.[1] Included within the slender little compendium was a collection of the military maxims of Napoleon, who is considered to be 'the greatest of European soldiers'. Originally published posthumously in Paris in 1827, one of Napoleon's precepts stuck in my mind, and it is very relevant to the subject of this book. It also demonstrates that national leaders and military commanders have ignored history at their peril since it was written, Stalingrad being a classic example of this. As such, I follow the aforementioned literary fashion and quote Napoleon here:

> A fortified place can protect a garrison and arrest the enemy only a certain length of time. When that time has elapsed and the defences of the place are destroyed, the garrison may lay down their arms. All civilised nations have been of one opinion in this respect, and the only dispute has been as to the greater or lesser degree of resistance which the governor should offer before capitulating. Yet there are generals – Villars[2] is one of the number – who hold that a governor ought never to surrender, but that in the last extremity he should blow up the fortifications and take advantage of the night to cut his way through the besieging army. In case you cannot blow up the fortifications, you can at any rate sally out with your garrison and save your men. Commanders who have pursued this course have re-joined their army with three-fourths of their garrison.

This maxim echoes through the years. Napoleon had many eminent military disciples and adherents, among them, for example, the Confederate tactician Thomas 'Stonewall' Jackson, who carried the 1827 set in his haversack throughout his campaigns.

Napoleon's maxim rests on two fundamentals: firstly, that it is militarily acceptable for a besieged force to capitulate at a point in time at which further resistance is deemed by its commander to be futile and/or, in effect, suicidal; secondly, that it makes sense, if possible, for that force to attempt to fight its way out of its predicament in order to save its men so that they may re-join their army.

Some historians have hinted at the influence of Napoleon upon Adolf Hitler. Indeed, during his ascent to power, Hitler himself held an ill-judged and vainglorious sense of comparison with the illustrious French leader.[3] The enforced German halt before Moscow in December 1941 provided some kind of warped sense of connectivity with Napoleon, and thus an implication of strategic justification. But, it seems, Hitler disregarded one of Napoleon's tenets – that a surrounded fighting force should always try to survive, even if the price of survival is captivity, or it should give itself the chance to survive and fight another day by battling its way out of entrapment. As one US Air Force (USAF) airlift expert comments, 'no force can survive behind enemy lines indefinitely'.[4]

Some will question why 'another' book on Stalingrad is needed when shelves already buckle under their published numbers and weight, and when esteemed writers and historians such as Kehrig, Glantz and House, Ziemke, Erikson, Beevor, Hayward and many others have just covered every angle of the epic battle. That is entirely reasonable.

I contend that by far the bulk of the Stalingrad historiography to date has, understandably, focused on the land actions, on the stubborn decisions taken by Hitler, or on von Manstein's efforts to relieve the Sixth Army, and by the vain attempt of its commander, Paulus, to hold out in the shrinking Stalingrad 'pocket' with his diminishing forces. This book will instead view the action from the perspective of the Luftwaffe's enforced and reluctant attempt to supply the Sixth Army from the air so that it did at least have a chance to fight its way out of encirclement – something which would have met with Napoleon's approval, while Hitler's refusal to allow a breakout would not have done so.

Those, however, with a thirst for accounts of air combat and blazing guns may turn away from the story of an operation which they may perceive as being, fundamentally, 'passive' or lacking in action and drama. They would be misguided. This is a colossal story, and it is driven by three dynamics: firstly, the 'ticking clock' which 'ticked' as the approaching and resurgent Red Army closed in on the Sixth Army and the resulting tightening 'noose'; secondly, the feat of human endeavour, on both sides, in the face of appalling and extreme weather conditions; and thirdly, a crisis of command generated by strong, conflicting and competing personalities.

To a great extent I follow in the footsteps of Professor Joel Hayward. His book *Stopped at Stalingrad – The Luftwaffe and Hitler's Defeat in the East 1942–1943* was a revelation when it was published in 1998, and was largely responsible for me deciding to research the life and campaigns of Field Marshal Wolfram *Freiherr* von Richthofen who played a significant role in the airlift, and from whose diaries I quote extensively in this book. Professor Hayward's work is important – and satisfying – as both a broadly sweeping history of the German air campaigns and strategy leading to

Stalingrad, as well as an analysis, in great detail, of the way the Luftwaffe prosecuted its war and executed its regional command and control functions in 1942–43 in the Crimea, over the Black Sea, at Stalingrad and in the northern Caucasus.

However, I make no attempt to emulate his superb, forensic study. My objective, rather, is to simply tell the story of the airlift which came at the end of the long road that was Operation *Blau* – of its major personalities (the commanders), of the aircraft and their operations, of the ambitions, aims and objectives, of the adversities, of the boldness and madness, of the successes and failures, of the determination and courage shown by the aircrews and men on the ground. It is a story shaped by the dynamics of a crisis born of intransigent and ultimately doomed hubris (or what Adolf Hitler would have referred to as 'iron will'). It is a story which resonates strongly today, reaching down through successive generations who struggle to comprehend what happened – *how* it could happen.

There was a poignant instance as I was concluding work on this book. I contacted the Luftwaffe historian Georg Schlaug for his permission to quote a passage from one of his own works. In an e-mail from Germany, he happened to tell me;

> My wife's father, Josef Berning, was a member of the *Bäckerei-Kompanie* (Bakery Company) of the 16.*Panzerdivision*. He was very badly wounded on 14 December 1942 (totally, permanently blinded), and his comrades pulled him on a sledge ten kilometres from the Division's main first aid station to Pitomnik. According to his account, his comrades threw this wounded man onto an aircraft like a 'sack of potatoes' and he was flown out. After the war he tried to find his comrades. It was in vain. None of them returned. He died in 1962.

As someone who has, for many years, studied and researched the Luftwaffe and written, edited and published my own and other authors' books about its aircraft, units and campaigns, I can honestly say that when I began to read the diaries of the Luftwaffe commanders, and the reports of those who were charged with making the airlift at Stalingrad happen, I discovered one of the most compelling, fascinating and shocking aspects of its history.

Robert Forsyth
February 2022

Author's note

Readers should note that the time periods covered in each of the Chapters Nine to Seventeen correspond to the periods contained within the 'Karlsruhe Overview' (*Luftversorgung unter dem Kommando der Luftflotte 4*) as reproduced in Appendix 2: that is to say commencement of supply operations; the taking over of operations by VIII.*Fliegerkorps*; the *Wintergewitter* relief attempt; the period up to *Uranus*; the period to the loss of Pitomnik; and the loss of Gumrak, the use of Stalingradskaya and air-dropping to the ceasing of supply operations.

Acknowledgements

My interest in the Stalingrad airlift started many years ago. The principal cornerstones of my research then were provided by the diaries of the Luftwaffe commanders who organised and oversaw the operation, as well as key reports and papers issued at the time and in the early post-war years by those who were there. These, and many other sources, did not just magically appear on my desk, but came to my attention through the knowledge, helpful suggestions and recommendations of a small number of friends, fellow researchers and correspondents, some of whom have probably long since forgotten their kindness.

First and foremost, I must thank Dr. James H. Kitchens III, formerly of the USAF Historical Research Agency, who, in the early days, introduced me to translations of the Fiebig and Pickert diaries, and in so doing, was among those who sowed the seeds of the book you now hold.

Some years later, I was fortunate enough to meet the late Götz *Freiherr* von Richthofen, who gave me copies of his late father's diaries, shared many of his papers and was always willing to help with details of the Generalfeldmarschall's life and campaigns. I owe *Freiherr* von Richthofen considerable gratitude for his generosity and support.

My fellow Luftwaffe researchers Nick Beale, Christer Bergström, Steven Coates, Eddie Creek, Robert Forczyk, Chris Goss, Marcel van Heijkop, Ingo Möbius, Mikael Olrog, Martin Pegg and Georg Schlaug have been kind enough to share their knowledge, files, information and images.

As ever, I am especially grateful to Edwin 'Ted' Oliver for his assistance with translation, as well as for his opinions and advice on technical matters, particularly with regard to the design, manufacture and use of air-drop containers.

Sebastian Remus came to my aid at a difficult time and was able to locate key documents at the *Bundesarchiv-Militärarchiv* in Freiburg. My thanks also to Dr. Reinhold Busch, Professor Patrick G. Eriksson and Georg Schlaug for allowing me to quote from their own authoritative works. Also to the Orion Publishing Group for permission to quote from Joachim Wieder's and Heinrich *Graf* von Einsiedel's *Stalingrad – Memories and Reassessments* (Arms & Armour Press, London, 1993).

ACKNOWLEDGEMENTS

I am also very grateful to Javier Ruiz for enrichening this story by kindly contributing letters and photographs of his grandfather, Adolf Spohr, who flew one of the relatively few He 177s during the airlift. Also to Javier's mother and Adolf Spohr's daughter, Barbara Spohr.

Once again I have been very fortunate to work with the team at Osprey Publishing, and my thanks go to my publisher, Marcus Cowper, to my commissioning editor, Tony Holmes, and to my desk editor, Cleo Favaretto, in Oxford for all their support, patience and faith in me and for giving me the opportunity to turn what was an idea into a book.

Most importantly, my greatest thanks go to Sally who, despite sadnesses and pressures from elsewhere at the time, supported my efforts to write this book, as she has done with all the others. Thank you so much.

Robert Forsyth
February 2022

List of Illustrations and Maps

IMAGES

1 A Ju 52/3m makes its approach during a supply flight on the Eastern Front in early 1942. (Author's Collection)

2 German troops quickly haul away a sled laden with supplies from a Ju 52/3m possibly at Demyansk. (EN Archive)

3 Oberst Fritz Morzik, the Luftwaffe's foremost transport commander. This highly experienced airman oversaw the air supply and airlift operations at Demyansk, Kholm and Stalingrad. (EN Archive)

4 Mid-February 1943: Hitler and his generals pore over maps of Russia and Ukraine at Zaporozhye, shortly after the loss of Stalingrad. At far left is von Manstein, while to the right of Hitler is Zeitzler. Watching with a surreptitious air from the background (second from right) is Generaloberst Wolfram von Richthofen. (ullstein bild via Getty Images)

5 General Friedrich Paulus, commander of 6.*Armee*, directs his staff from a forward position during the advance on Stalingrad in late 1942. (ullstein bild via Getty Images)

6 The Stalingrad skyline seen from the east bank of the Volga in September 1942 during the German advance. (Forczyk Collection)

7 German infantry move forward to the outskirts of Stalingrad in September 1942 during Operation *Blau*. Smoke plumes from the city in the distance as a result of Luftwaffe bombing. (Heinrich Hoffmann/Mondadori via Getty Images)

8 A Ju 87 Stuka banks over Stalingrad towards the west and away from the Volga River. (EN Archive)

9 General der Flieger Hans Jeschonnek (right) accompanies Reichsmarschall Herman Göring for a ride on the latter's country estate in East Prussia in July 1941. Jeschonnek's assurance to Hitler that the Luftwaffe could sustain 6.*Armee* at Stalingrad by air was rash and ill-reasoned. (ullstein bild via Getty Images)

10 The ambitious, abrupt, abrasive, self-confident and industrious Generaloberst Wolfram *Freiherr* von Richthofen was commander of *Luftflotte* 4. He was a vocal opponent of the airlift. (Von Richthofen Collection – kindly donated to the Author)

27 German troops assisted by what appears to be a Luftwaffe airman in the right foreground, haul a cart of supplies away from a Ju 52/3m. (EN Archive)

28 Major Erich Zähr was the commander of I./KG.z.b.V.172 during the Stalingrad airlift. He was the first pilot of his *Gruppe* to land at Pitomnik airfield in November 1942. By the time he received the Knight's Cross on 23 December 1942, he had carried out 20 flights to Stalingrad. (Möbius Collection)

29 Wounded troops lie on canvas stretchers aboard a Ju 52/3m. Almost 25,000 wounded personnel were airlifted out of the Stalingrad 'fortress' by the Luftwaffe. (Author's Collection)

30 When horses were no longer available to pull the sleds, it was down to manpower. (EN Archive)

31 While this He 111 takes on fuel from a bowser, a mechanic uses a brush to sweep snow and ice away from the aircraft's control surfaces at an airfield west of the Don in the winter of 1942–43. (Author's Collection)

32 This Fw 200 is believed to have been assigned to KGr.z.b.V.200 from KG 40 for use at Stalingrad. It is possible that it was captured by the Russians, and that it is being inspected by Soviet troops in this photograph. (Goss Collection)

33 Groundcrew pull a protective tarpaulin across the left wing of a He 111H-20 during the Russian winter. This was intended to prevent flaps and ailerons from freezing up. During the Stalingrad airlift, such tarpaulins were in short supply, and it was usually left to mechanics to de-ice control surfaces in drastically sub-zero temperatures. (EN Archive)

34 Against a grey winter sky, a pair of Ju 86s from either KGr.z.b.V.21 or KGr.z.b.V.22 taxi out across the snow at the beginning of another mission to Stalingrad. Despite the valour of their crews, the contribution these aircraft made to the airlift was negligible. (Goss Collection)

35 A smiling Hauptmann Hans-Jürgen Willers (left) at Bordeaux-Mérignac in 1942. As a Major, Willers would take command of KGr.z.b.V.200, overseeing operations of the Condor during the Stalingrad airlift, as well as of the very limited use of the Ju 290. (Goss Collection)

36 The fuselage of Fw 200C-3 F8+FW of 1./KGr.z.b.V.200 broke when the aircraft landed at Zaporozhye, having been overloaded at Sslawenskaya on 12 February 1943. (Goss Collection)

37 Ju 290A-1 SB+QB at Stalino in January 1943, with its hydraulic, rear *Trapoklappe* loading ramp lowered. The aircraft managed only one flight to Pitomnik, during which it was attacked and damaged by Soviet fighters. It survived, but the damage was so extensive it had to be returned to Germany. (EN Archive)

38 and 39 The impressive sight of one of the two Ju 290s to reach Stalino for the airlift operation. In the top photograph can also be seen five Fw 200s of KGr.z.b.V.200. The Ju 290 could carry ten tons of supplies or 80 wounded men – by far the greatest load capacity of the six types used in the airlift. (EN Archive)

40 Major Kurt Schede, seen centre, saluting, was appointed to command I./FKG 50, leading the operations of the *Gruppe's* He 177s to Stalingrad from Zaporozhye. He was killed when his Heinkel crashed while returning from a supply flight to the pocket on 16 January 1943. (Goss Collection)

41 The snow has been cleared from this He 177A-1 of I./FKG 50 in Russia in early 1943. Both engine nacelles housed a pair of coupled 1,085hp DB 601 engines, one mounted either side of the gearing system, which together became the DB 606. In service this arrangement proved highly unsatisfactory. (EN Archive)

42 Heinrich Schlosser was awarded the Knight's Cross on 18 September 1941 in recognition of his sinking of 55,000 tons of merchant shipping while flying the Fw 200 with KG 40. He was transferred to I./FKG 50 in the summer of 1942, flying the troublesome He 177. Following the death of Major Kurt Schede, Major Schlosser took command of the *Gruppe*. (Goss Collection)

43 Oberleutnant Adolf Spohr of I./FKG 50 was a highly qualified instructor pilot who, earlier in the war, had instructed at training and blind-flying schools in France and Germany. Following training as a bomber pilot, he was among the early cadre to join I./FKG 50 and flew at least two missions to Stalingrad. He was posted missing following a flight over the city on 23 January 1943. (Ruiz Collection)

44 Go 242 gliders are visible just beyond the nose of a Ju 290 at Stalino. Milch championed the use of gliders to Stalingrad, but in this he was opposed by von Richthofen, Fiebig, Schulz and Morzik, who considered their deployment to be impractical. They were never used. (EN Archive)

45 The bleak scene at Zaporozhye-Süd in the winter of 1942–43 as two He 177s of I./FKG 50 are prepared for another mission. A generator cart has been attached to the aircraft in the foreground. (EN Archive)

46 Mechanics remove a protective tarpaulin from the starboard engine of a He 177A-1 belonging to I./FKG 50. In Russia, most maintenance work on the *Gruppe's* Heinkels had to be undertaken in the open, exposed to the elements. (EN Archive)

47 Groundcrew battle the elements to prepare a He 111 for the supply run to Stalingrad. (Author's Collection)

48 Intent on pleasing Hitler, Reichsmarschall Hermann Göring (left) gave his fateful assurance that 6. *Armee* could be supplied at Stalingrad by the Luftwaffe's transport squadrons. When Hitler became aware that Göring had badly misjudged the situation, he turned to the hard-headed and tireless Generalfeldmarschall Erhard Milch (right), who was sent to Russia in an attempt to invigorate the airlift effort. He failed. (EN Archive)

49 With its fuselage door open, and what appears to be a crewman and sack in the doorframe, possibly ready for an air-drop, grimy Ju 52/3m, 1Z+KY of 14./KG.z.b.V.1 passes low overhead. (EN Archive)

50 A Ju 52/3m makes a low-level air-drop. The problem arising from such flights was that often the supplies dropped were damaged in the process. (EN Archive)

51 A large supply crate intended for air-dropping awaits fixing to the external centreline mounts of a He 111. At one end of the crate is a parachute, while at the other is a shock absorbing coil to counter ground impact. (Author collection)

52 A soldier uses all his strength to pull a heavy air-drop container from deep snow using one of its parachute lines. In the Stalingrad pocket, which was covered in thick snow for much of the time, the poor physical condition of the men, few pack animals and vehicles in limited supply made the recovery of containers a difficult task. (Author collection)

53 A Ju 52/3m apparently photographed after having been attacked by Soviet fighters during the supply operation at Stalingrad. (EN Archive)

54 Three He 111s of KG 27 taxi out in a flurry of snow. Visibility at such moments would have been poor. From their initial base at Millerovo, these bombers performed estimable service as 'emergency' transports to Stalingrad. (Author's Collection)

55 A He 111 is guided in over packed snow. (Goss Collection)

56 Following an attack by the VVS, a wrecked He 111 and other debris litter the frozen expanse of one of the supply airfields. (Goss Collection)

57 Forlorn soldiers from 6.Armee march away from the ruins into Soviet captivity following the battle of Stalingrad. It is believed around 91,000 German personnel surrendered or were captured. (ullstein bild via Getty Images)

ARTWORK

58 Junkers Ju 52/3m 1Z+FZ of 15./KGr.z.b.V.1
59 Heinkel He 111H-6 1B+CK of 2./KG 27
60 Junkers Ju 86E VB+FN of *Luftflottennachrichtenschule* 3
61 Focke-Wulf Fw 200C-3 Wk-Nr.0049 F8+FW of 1./KGr.z.b.V.200
62 Heinkel He 177A-1 E8+HK of I./FKG 50
63 Junkers Ju 290A-1 Wk-Nr.0152 SB+QB
64 The *Mischlastabwurfbehälter* 1,000kg (mixed load air-drop container). This container could accommodate a payload of up to 720-800 kg depending on parachute weight (50-70 kg).

MAPS

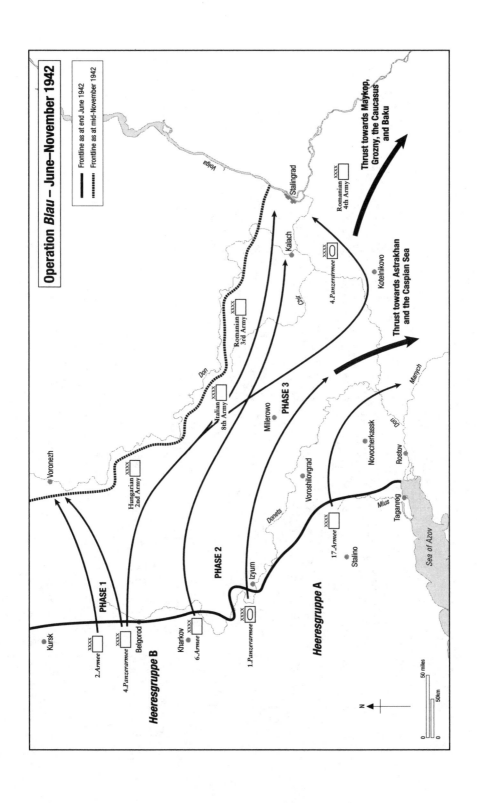

Operation *Blau* – June–November 1942

Frontline as at end June 1942
Frontline as at mid-November 1942

PHASE 1

PHASE 2

PHASE 3

Kursk

2.Armee

4.Panzerarmee

Belgorod

Heeresgruppe B

Kharkov

6.Armee

Izyum

1.Panzerarmee

Voronezh

Hungarian
2nd Army

Italian
8th Army

Romanian
3rd Army

Millerowo

Don

Stalino

Voroshilovgrad

Donets

Novocherkassk

17.Armee

Heeresgruppe A

Mius

Taganrog

Rostov

Don

Manych

Sea of Azov

Kalach

Chir

Stalingrad

Volga

4.Panzerarmee

Kotelnikovo

Romanian
4th Army

Thrust towards Maykop,
Grozny, the Caucasus
and Baku

Thrust towards Astrakhan
and the Caspian Sea

N

0   50km
0   50 miles

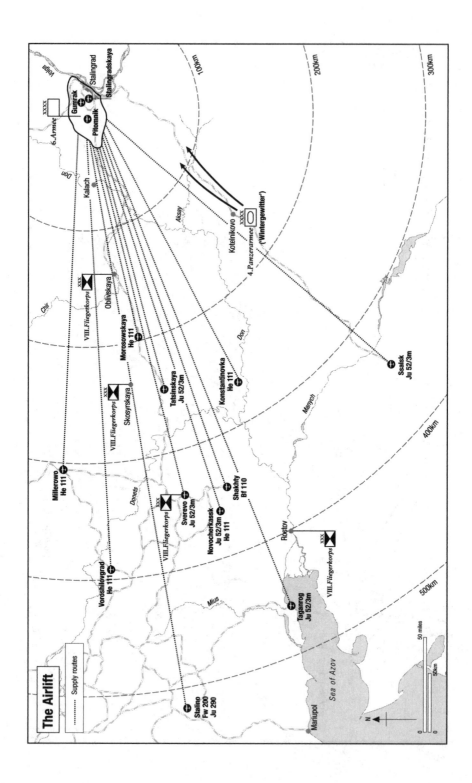

The Airlift

Supply routes

Volga
Stalingrad
Gumrak
Stalingradskaya
Pitomnik
XXXX 6.Armee
Don
Kalach
Aksay
Kotelnikovo
XXXX 4.Panzerarmee ('Wintergewitter')
Chir
XXX VIII.Fliegerkorps
Oblivskaya
Morosowskaya
He 111
Don
XXX VIII.Fliegerkorps
Skosyrskaya
Tatsinskaya
Ju 52/3m
Konstantinovka
He 111
Manych
Ssalsk
Ju 52/3m
Millerowo
He 111
Donets
Shakhty
Bf 110
Sverevo
Ju 52/3m
XXX VIII.Fliegerkorps
Novocherkassk
He 111
Rostov
XXX VIII.Fliegerkorps
Voroshilovgrad
He 111
Mius
Taganrog
Ju 52/3m
Stalino
Fw 200
Ju 290
Sea of Azov
Mariupol
N
100km
200km
300km
400km
500km
50 miles
50km

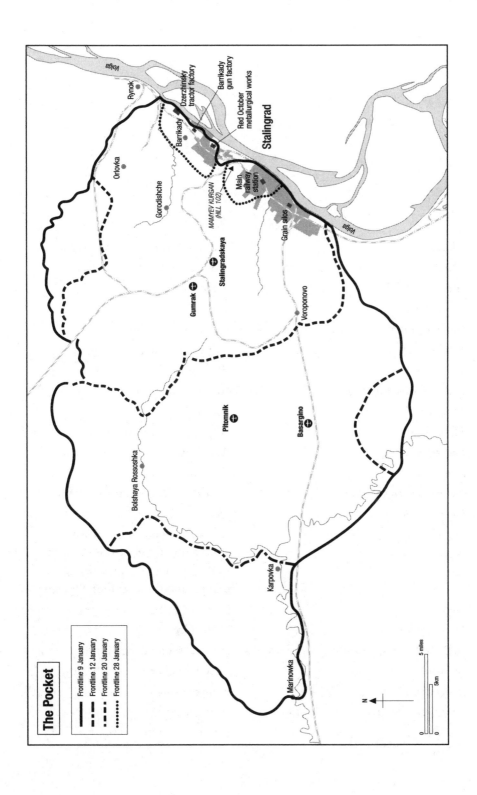

The Pocket

Frontline 9 January
Frontline 12 January
Frontline 20 January
Frontline 28 January

Volga

Rynok

Dzerzhinsky
tractor factory

Barrikady
gun factory

Barrikady

Red October
metallurgical works

Stalingrad

Orlovka

Gorodishche

MAMYEV KURGAN
(HILL 102)

Main
railway
station

Grain silos

Volga

Stalingradskaya

Gumrak

Voroponovo

Pitomnik

Basargino

Bolshaya Rossoshka

Karpovka

Marinowka

N

5 miles

5km

Glossary

Abteilung	Section, Detachment or Battalion
ADD (*Aviatsiya dal' nego deystviya*)	(Soviet) Long-Range Aviation
Armee	Army
Armeekorps	Army Corps
Blindflugschule	Blind Flying School
Feldbetriebskompanie	Airfield Servicing Company
Festung	Fortress
Flak (Flugabwehrkanone)	Anti-aircraft
Fliegerdivision	Air Division
Fliegerführer	Regional air commander
Fliegerkorps	Air Corps
Führungsstab	Command Staff
Generalluftzeugmeister	Inspector General of the Luftwaffe
Gefechtsverband	Combat Group
Geschwader	Luftwaffe flying 'wing' (usually comprising three or four *Gruppen*)
Gruppe	Luftwaffe flying 'group' (usually comprising three or four *Staffeln*)
Heer	German Army
Heeresgruppe	Army Group
IAP (*Istrebitel'nyy Aviatsionnaya Diviziya*)	(Soviet) Fighter Aviation Division
Igelstellung	'Hedgehog' defensive position
Jagdgeschwader	Fighter Wing
Kampfgeschwader	Bomber Wing
Kampfgruppe	Bomber Group

22

Kampfgruppe zur besonderen Verwendung (KGr.z.b.V.)	Bomber Group for Special Deployment
Kessel	Pocket
Kesselklar	lit. 'Pocket Clear' – an aircraft deemed serviceable to fly to Stalingrad
Kette	Flying formation of three aircraft
Kommandeur	Commander of Luftwaffe *Gruppe*
Kommodore	Commander of Luftwaffe *Geschwader*
Kriegswissenschaftlich	Military science
Luftflotte	Air Fleet
Luftgaukommando	Regional air administration command
Luftkriegsakademie	Air War Academy
Lufttransportführer (LTF)	Air Transport Commander
Luftversorgungsführer	Air Supply Commander
Panzerarmee	Panzer (Armoured) Army
Panzerkorps	Panzer (Armoured) Corps
Reichsluftministerium	Reich Air Ministry
Sanitätsflugbereitschaft	Airborne Ambulance Unit
Stab	Staff
Staffel	Luftwaffe 'squadron' (nominally, usually around 12 aircraft)
Staffelkapitän	Commander of a *Staffel*
Stavka	Soviet High Command
Stützpunkt	Fortified position
Transportflieger	Transport aircrews
VA (*Vozdushnaya armiya*)	(Soviet) Air Army
Vernichtungsstrategie	Strategy of annihilation
VVS (*Voyenno-Vozdushnyye Sily*)	(Soviet) Air Force
Wintergewitter	Winter Thunderstorm – name of German relief operation
Zerstörer	'Destroyer' (heavy fighter aircraft)

Table of Ranks

The table below lists the wartime Luftwaffe ranks, together with their equivalent in the Royal Air Force (RAF) and the US Army Air Force (USAAF):

Luftwaffe	Royal Air Force	USAAF
Generalfeldmarschall	Marshal of the RAF	Five-star General
Generaloberst	Air Chief Marshal	Four-star General
General der Flieger	Air Marshal	Lieutenant General
Generalleutnant	Air-Vice Marshal	Major General
Generalmajor	Air Commodore	Brigadier General
Oberst	Group Captain	Colonel
Oberstleutnant	Wing Commander	Lieutenant Colonel
Major	Squadron Leader	Major
Hauptmann	Flight Lieutenant	Captain
Oberleutnant	Flying Officer	First Lieutenant
Leutnant	Pilot Officer	Second Lieutenant
Oberfähnrich	Acting Pilot Officer	Flight Cadet
Fähnrich	Officer Cadet	–
Stabsfeldwebel	Warrant Officer	Warrant Officer
Oberfeldwebel	Flight Sergeant	Master Sergeant
Feldwebel	Sergeant	Technical Sergeant
Unterfeldwebel	–	–
Unteroffizier	Corporal	Staff Sergeant
Hauptgefreiter	–	Sergeant
Obergefreiter	Leading Aircraftman	Corporal
Gefreiter	Aircraftman First Class	Private First Class
Flieger	Aircraftman	Private

PART I

Conquest

We have been standing guard for Germany,
Keeping the eternal watch.
Now at last the sun is rising in the East,
Calling millions into battle.

'The Song of the Eastern Campaign', unattributed, 1942
(QUOTED IN ARVID FREDBORG, BEHIND THE
STEEL WALL, 1944)

The streets were shaking with explosions,
The terrible roar of engines filled the sky,
But our regiments stood fast like granite
To defend the Volga, or to die.

'To the Hero City', N. Panov, 1942
(QUOTED IN MARSHAL VASILI IVANOVICH CHUIKOV,
THE BEGINNING OF THE ROAD, 1959)

1

The Man for the Moment

In the cold, early morning darkness of 7 January 1942, forward units of the Red Army's North-Western Front under Col Gen Pavel A. Kurochkin slipped out from their forested readiness positions around the Valdai Hills in northern Russia and advanced through heavy snow towards the enemy. In this sector of the Eastern Front, the enemy – the Wehrmacht – held a line spanning some 230 km from Lake Ilmen to Ostashkov on the southern shore of Lake Seliger.

First came the silent, ghost-like figures of ski troops in their white winter smocks, swishing across the frozen surface of Lake Ilmen. They would be followed by tanks and infantry, the latter moving both on foot and on armoured, motorised sleds, while later, others would be towed off in gliders to be dropped into key locations in territory still held by the Germans. It was the start of a great Soviet winter counter-offensive – a riposte to the German attacks of the previous summer, little more than three weeks in the planning and intended to break through the line held by Generaloberst Ernst Busch's 16.*Armee*. The *Stavka* (Soviet High Command) had taken the initiative to form 'Shock Armies' in December, intended to smash through the German *Stützpunkte* (fortified positions) – something at which the units of 16.*Armee* had become adept at creating during their three-month defensive stance. In reality, the Shock Armies were not particularly fit for purpose, being inadequately equipped, with little in the way of artillery and tanks or the necessary engineering units to cut through the German minefields and wire, or to tackle anti-tank defences. Nevertheless, if such materiel resources were lacking, the Soviets had plenty of will.

With German defeats at Tikhvin and Kalinin in December, Stalin was convinced that the Wehrmacht was in a state of imminent collapse over most of its front. To exploit this, on 18 December, he had directed that the six division-sized shock groups of the North-Western Front attack the boundary between the right flank of the German *Heeresgruppe Nord* (Army Group North) and the left flank of *Heeresgruppe Mitte* (Centre) with the aim of tying down enemy forces around the towns of Staraya Russa, Kholm and Velikie Luki. These towns blocked the Red Army's route to the west, and the German forces there could be deployed strategically elsewhere against other Russian forces of the counter-offensive if they were not contested.[1]

Yet willpower alone does not win campaigns. Kurochkin's challenge was to advance his 170,000 troops and 186 tanks across a terrain with few roads in drastically sub-zero temperatures with little numerical advantage against a well-disciplined and fortified enemy. General-Major Nikolai E. Bezarin's 34th Army attacked from the Valdai Hills towards Demyansk, while adjacent to it, Col Gen Maksim A. Purkaev's 3rd Shock Army pushed west from the neighbouring Kalinin Front. After heavy fighting in very adverse conditions for both sides, the two Soviet thrusts enveloped the German II.*Armeekorps* under General der Infanterie Walter *Graf* von Brockdorff-Ahlefeldt and elements of X.*Armeekorps* around Demyansk. By late January Kurochkin's forces had almost completed the job, with just a narrow corridor through Ramushevo still open to the encircled Germans connecting them to 16.*Armee* at Staraya Russa, whose front was, effectively, in disarray. For the Russians, the way to the west was open, aside from a few stubbornly held German *Stützpunkte*.[2]

Busch's immediate superior, Generalfeldmarschall Wilhelm Ritter von Leeb, commander of *Heeresgruppe Nord*, felt increasingly uneasy about the situation that had developed along the northern front. He proposed pulling all German forces south of Lake Ilmen back behind the Lovat River, which ran south of the lake. In a series of long, wearisome telephone calls with Adolf Hitler's Eastern Front forest headquarters – the *Wolfschanze* ('Wolf's Lair') – at Rastenburg, in East Prussia, von Leeb endeavoured to force, directly or indirectly, military logic upon the *Führer*. He failed.

As far as Hitler was concerned 'every inch of ground' was to be defended.[3] He believed resolutely that an encirclement compelled an enemy to commit greater forces to a siege which could otherwise be deployed elsewhere, and he enforced this belief when, on 8 December 1941, he and the *Oberkommando des Heeres* (OKH – Upper Command of the Army) ordered that *Stützpunkte* and other fortified positions in the area of the *Heeresgruppe* should be supplied by air as a priority.[4] Leeb neither shared the *Führer's* opinion nor wished to be held responsible for what he believed would be the disastrous outcome of such intransigence. Certainly, in the air-supply operations that ensued over Demyansk and Kholm, more German assets were used to counter a relatively weak Russian force; and the determination to hold on to 'pockets' consumed significant numbers of support personnel, aircraft and aircrew, as well as fuel.[5]

On 12 January the Field Marshal was summoned to the *Wolfschanze* for a conference to thrash things out. The meeting did not go well. As Generaloberst Franz Halder, Chief of Staff of the OKH, noted, it was 'a particularly difficult day. The conference of Field Marshal von Leeb with the *Führer* produced no agreement. The *Führer* insisted on compliance with his order that the front of the Valdai Hills must be held.'[6]

Von Leeb complained about the lack of reinforcements, but his protests fell on stony ground. He requested to be relieved of the command of *Heeresgruppe*

Nord, the first army group commander to do so. Meanwhile, commencing on the 14th, von Brockdorff-Ahlefeldt began demanding reinforcements (that did not exist) as well as more supplies. On the 18th, the commander of II.*Armeekorps* warned that the exhausted and hungry condition of his troops, together with a lack of supplies and fuel, meant that he could hold out only for a few more days.[7] It was also very difficult to maintain sufficient supplies by means of a single, dirt road running from the railway at Staraya Russa.[8]

The situation was exacerbated when all attempts west of Demyansk to halt the Soviet forces approaching from north and south of the *Stützpunkt* failed.[9] When the pincers finally closed around Demyansk near Zeluch'ye and Ramushevo on 8 February, II.*Armeekorps* and some remnants of X.*Armeekorps* which had not made it across the Lovat became contained in a *Kessel* ('pocket') of about 56 km in diameter and an area of some 3,000 sq km. This force amounted to around 95,000 men comprising various elements of 16.*Armee* and a *Waffen*-SS unit – some six divisions in all.[10] They had enough supplies to last them until 13 February.[11] A similar encirclement by 3rd Shock Army, completed on 21 January, had trapped other German forces – assembled as *Kampfgruppe Scherer* – at the strongpoint of Kholm, some 130 km further to the south-west.

Demyansk itself was an inconsequential settlement of semi-dirt streets lined by typical Russian stuccoed dwellings, with humble wooden *izbas* on its outskirts. It had never figured greatly in Soviet offensive plans; in 1926 it had numbered just 2,500 souls. On its northern edge the German pocket encased the railway from Bologoe to Staraya Russa, Dno and Pskov, while its eastern edge faced the railway running to the south-west.[12]

Unlike the Russians, the OKW at the *Wolfschanze* saw Demyansk as being a crucial element in the strategic position of the Wehrmacht on the Eastern Front: although it did not lie on the main east–west railway line, the area surrounding the place was potentially important, and any resistance there and at Kholm would hopefully tie up Soviet forces for more than a year.[13] Busch relied on nothing but willpower when he told his unit commanders that he had no reserves and, in conformity with the *Führer*'s policy, ordered them to stand firm where they were.[14] At one point, however, II.*Armeekorps* radioed 16.*Armee*, 'When there is a chance to withdraw to the Lovat, we will withdraw immediately.'

Back came the response from the OKH:

Demyansk is to be defended until the last man![15]

This was easier said than done when the snow was chest-deep. What the OKH overlooked was the Red Army's advantage in its capability to better withstand the winter conditions on its home soil, however frozen, than the Wehrmacht. Fifteen fresh, well-equipped Russian infantry divisions supported by tanks and ski troops eventually gathered to surround the pocket that had formed at Demyansk.

By comparison, less than two months earlier, during the drive on Moscow in November 1941, the commander of XXXIX.*Panzerkorps* wrote to Generalleutnant Friedrich Paulus, a senior quartermaster officer in the OKH, to protest that many of his men were walking around with their feet swathed in paper, without gloves and suffering from frostbite. They were forced to steal clothes and boots from prisoners of war.[16] It should have been a warning. Indeed, in a prescient observation in January 1942, the same month the Russians launched their offensive against *Heeresgruppe Nord*, the newly promoted General der Panzertruppe Paulus, recently appointed as commander of 6.*Armee* in southern Russia, commented to his adjutant, Oberst Wilhelm Adam, 'We must not overlook the fact that the Russians are significantly better equipped for the winter than we are, and that they can resume unexpectedly ...'[17]

On 11 January the Soviet 11th Army had effectively severed the main supply route to Demyansk and on the 20th all overland communication between II.*Armeekorps* and 16.*Armee* was lost, but over the coming weeks the pocket held out.[18] From the *Korps* headquarters on 18 February, von Brockdorff-Ahlefeldt attempted to generate hope when he signalled his first order of the day:

> There are 96,000 of us. The German soldier is superior to the Russian: this has been proven! So, let the difficult times come; we are ready![19]

This was the moment the Luftwaffe was called upon to perform what was to be, in reality, more of a humanitarian relief effort for German forces remaining east of the Lovat rather than a military supply operation. In truth, pure air supply would be a new role for the Luftwaffe, for rather than backing up the Wehrmacht's operations of conquest, it would be supporting a defensive operation.[20] Yet aircraft offered the only reliable means with which to reduce supply delivery time to the pockets and with which to cope with the vast distances involved. Furthermore, aircraft were not dependent on the poor Russian road infrastructure. Indeed, in the winter of 1941, it had been judicious deployment of air transport by Oberst Fritz Morzik, the newly appointed *Lufttransportführer* (LTF – Air Transport Commander) headquartered in Smolensk, who had the job of coordinating air transport operations for General der Flieger Wolfram *Freiherr* von Richthofen's VIII.*Fliegerkorps*, that had helped to bolster defensive operations in the area of *Heeresgruppe Mitte* on the central sector of the front.

In the area of *Heeresgruppe Nord* in January 1942, however, the Luftwaffe 'air fleet' supporting the Army Group, Generaloberst Alfred Keller's *Luftflotte* 1 headquartered at Ostrov, had just one transport *Gruppe, Kampfgruppe zur besonderen Verwendung* (KGr.z.b.V.) 172, based at Riga and equipped with the standard Junkers Ju 52/3m tri-motor 'workhorse'. This unit alone was woefully insufficient for the task required of it. Thus, in early February, Oberst Morzik was ordered to transfer elements of KGr.z.b.V.9 from Vitebsk, in the area of VIII.*Fliegerkorps*, to Pskov-South to reinforce KGr.z.b.V.172. But even this move resulted in the availability of no more than 30 Ju 52/3ms.[21]

On 17 February Hitler emphasised that he wanted II.*Armeekorps* to hold out, and promised to give *Heeresgruppe Nord* more forces. To ensure that his requirement would be adhered to, 337 transport aircraft would be made available from Luftwaffe units elsewhere in the East and from within the Reich itself to supply the *Armeekorps* by air. From this point, much of Hitler's faith now rested upon the Luftwaffe's transport force.[22] On the 22nd he declared Demyansk a *Festung* (fortress).[23]

★　★　★

Fifty-one-year-old Friedrich-Wilhelm Morzik (known as 'Fritz') was the man for the moment. An extremely experienced airman of Prussian blood, Morzik was born the son of a mill worker on 10 December 1891 in the small town of Passenheim on the shores of the Grosser Calben See in the lakelands of Masuria. He had joined the still nascent Imperial German Flying Corps as an observer in 1914, but soon qualified as a pilot and saw service flying biplanes on the Eastern Front, Palestine and the Western Front during World War I. He ended the conflict with the rank of Leutnant, decorated with the Royal Prussian Army Pilot's Badge and the Iron Cross First Class and was the recipient of the Honour Goblet for a Victor in Air Combat, which indicates he was involved in the shooting down of at least one enemy aircraft.

An early post-war career saw him in the embryonic German airline sector and also working for the Junkers firm at Dessau in the 1920s, including time spent at the company's secret factory in Russia, as well as assignments to Portugal, Spain and Persia. An athletic figure of rugged features and some dash, Morzik went on to personify the inter-war German sporting aviator. Photographs taken in the 1930s show him in flying overalls, clutching a garland of flowers while standing in the cockpit of a sportsplane, assured, smiling and victorious. He won several European endurance competitions flying single-engined Klemm, Messerschmitt and Heinkel sports monoplanes.

The Nazis came to power in January 1933, and from April the following year, Fritz Morzik became involved in creating the new Luftwaffe. He was one of several experienced airmen recruited from the commercial sector to head up Germany's expanded network of flying schools and early covert military air units.

On 1 April 1938, Morzik was appointed simultaneously *Kommandeur* of *Kampfgruppe zur besonderen Verwendung* 1 (Bomber Group for Special Purposes) and *Kommandant* of Fürstenwalde airfield, where the *Gruppe* was based. KGr.z.b.V.1's designation was misleading for what was viewed officially as being a transport unit equipped primarily with Ju 52/3ms. Throughout the first three years of the war that followed, Morzik commanded his unit, by then expanded to a *Geschwader*, with distinction in airborne operations during the German attack on Scandinavia in April 1940 and in the West the following month.

Morzik was promoted to Oberst on 1 June 1940. Five months later, in November, in what was a prototype operation, III./KGr.z.b.V.1 transported specialist Italian winter warfare troops as well as winter clothing, weapons, ammunition and support equipment across the Adriatic to the Albanian capital of Tirana in order to support Italian operations against Greek forces. Return flights would see the Ju 52/3ms bringing back wounded troops and unserviceable weapons and equipment.

After the successful conclusion of the operations during the German campaign in the Balkans in the spring of 1941, Morzik's next role, from 1 May 1941, was to set up a specialist unit to assess the enormous Messerschmitt Me 321 freight glider known as the Gigant which had originally been developed and built at the end of 1940 in preparation for the planned invasion of Britain. Morzik is known to have considered the craft a 'beast'.

On 1 October 1941, he was appointed *Lufttransportführer* for the *Generalquartiermeister der Luftwaffe*, giving him full control over, and responsibility for, the support and organisation of the air transport units in terms of personnel and materiel, as well as the development of mission organisation and planning. Simultaneous to this appointment, and as a reflection of his expertise, Morzik was also commander of the Luftwaffe's blind-flying schools.

But when Kurochkin's offensive struck at Demyansk in January 1942, it would be the greatest test of his capabilities.[24]

2

Dangerous Precedents

On 18 February, at a meeting at *Luftflotte* 1's headquarters at Ostrov, the air fleet commander, Generaloberst Alfred Keller, asked Morzik and his operations officer, Hauptmann Metscher, if, in their opinion, transport aircraft could sustain a force of 90,000–100,000 men with full supplies in temperatures as low as -40°C in appalling weather and in skies frequented by enemy fighters for a period of weeks, if not months. He was talking about Demyansk. Neither Keller nor the *Luftflotte* staff had an understanding of what it took to mount a major air-supply operation.[1] Morzik considered the question carefully before responding. He could expect a maximum of some 220 aircraft to be brought up from the central and southern sectors of the front, but he knew that many of these would be in need of repair as a result of demanding missions on behalf of *Heeresgruppe Mitte*, with some already in Luftwaffe depots undergoing maintenance. Given the prevailing conditions, Morzik believed that only around one-third of the total would be serviceable.

Morzik told Keller that in order to supply Demyansk with a requirement estimated to be 300 tons per day, he would need 500 aircraft to ensure at least 150 serviceable transports, so the numbers available would have to be doubled, with aircraft being pulled in from other theatres of war and from the Reich itself. In addition, in order to perform efficiently in winter, he would need mobile workshops, repair centres and a guaranteed supply of tools, spare parts, engine-warming equipment and auxiliary starters. Furthermore, Morzik stated that he expected to be given authority to issue orders and requisition requests directly to the local *Luftgaukommando* (Regional air administration command) and other supply organisations, thus bypassing established lines of command protocol, but keeping all concerned headquarters advised. Keller agreed to Morzik's wish list on the basis he 'got on with the job'.[2]

Thus, Morzik and his small staff of eight officers and three typists relocated immediately from Smolensk, north to Pskov-South in the area of *Luftflotte* 1, where they were to assume full control of all air supply needs for II.*Armeekorps* at Demyansk. This meant the supply of assigned personnel, weapons, ammunition, equipment, clothing and provisions at the agreed rate of 300 tons per day. In addition, wounded soldiers were to be carried out of the pocket.

Morzik found operating conditions at Pskov–South, a pre-war Soviet military airfield located 270 km south-west of Leningrad with its two frozen grass runways, which had been in continuous use since 1927, to be rudimentary; his staff had the use of just one field telephone.[3] The airfield was also crowded. The Heinkel He 111 bombers of *Kampfgeschwader* (KG) 4 were already based there conducting offensive operations in support of *Heeresgruppe Nord*. Sometime later, in order to improve response and understanding, the LTF staff would provide a liaison officer to the staffs of the Senior Quartermaster of *Heeresgruppe Nord* and *Luftflotte* 1, while an officer from *Luftgaukommando* I Riga was assigned to the LTF.[4]

Keller kept his word. In addition to the Ju 52/3ms of KGr.z.b.V.172 and KGr.z.b.V.9 already arrived in the zone of operations, on 19 February, under LTF control, significant reinforcements flew in in the form of more Junkers from IV./KG.z.b.V.1 from Smolensk, which moved to Ostrov-Süd, as well as KGr.z.b.V.600 and KGr.z.b.V.800 from Orscha and Vitebsk, respectively, to Korov'ye-Selo, a large but primitive pre-war *Voyenno-Vozdushnyye Sily* (VVS – Soviet Air Force) field 20 km south-west of Pskov. KGr.z.b.V.700 and KGr.z.b.V.900 came from Orscha and Vitebsk, respectively, to Pskov-West, an emergency landing ground with little or no support infrastructure.

These latter four Ju 52/3m-equipped *Gruppen* had been formed hurriedly at bases in East Prussia in December 1941 using personnel drawn from Luftwaffe flying schools. They were commanded by experienced unit leaders such as Major Peter Ingenhoven, a veteran of World War I, who led KGr.z.b.V.900 and who had latterly flown operations over Poland, Norway, the West and North Africa, and who had been awarded the Knight's Cross on 11 May 1940 while deputy *Kommandeur* of KGr.z.b.V.103. Then there was Major Markus Zeidler, the former *Kommandeur* of *Blindflugschule* 2 who was appointed to take over KGr.z.b.V.600. Having survived being shot down by ground fire in Poland, he subsequently flew with distinction in Scandinavia and the West.[5]

However, by virtue of the speed with which these units were formed, their personnel 'skill sets' could be viewed as very uneven, with highly experienced senior officers such as Ingenhoven and Zeidler and their colleagues placed alongside crews fresh from flying schools. Ultimately, however, this proved more of an advantage than a disadvantage, for the 'old foxes' helped to encourage the less experienced crews, kept an eye on them, offered advice and generally aided unit cohesion.[6]

On 20 February, just 24 hours after the new units had arrived, operations to Demyansk commenced when the first 40 Ju 52/3ms flew to the pocket and landed at the primitive 800 m x 50 m, snow-covered, rolled grass airstrip built originally by the Russians and located three kilometres north-east of the town. The airstrip had small areas for taxiing and unloading and could handle 20 to 30 transports at one time, but only during daylight, as there were no navigation aids or lighting for night operations.[7]

This was utterly inadequate. And, because of the lack of infrastructure at Demyansk, Morzik flew in the necessary signals and direction-finding equipment, radio beacons, tools and spares. He also ordered his engineers to build a second landing ground within the pocket as a back-up to the original in case of enemy attack or worsening weather, or in case it became blocked by damaged aircraft. The site chosen was at Pieski, about 8.5 km south-east of the main strip. Here, the snow was flattened and rolled out and a crude 600 m x 30 m strip created, allowing just three or four Ju 52/3ms to operate at any one time. Only the most experienced pilots were able to use it, however, and loads were limited to one-and-a-half tons in case the snow gave way, but it was the best that could be done.[8]

The flight distance from Pskov-South to Demyansk was some 240 km – a flight time of around 90 minutes, with most of it being over enemy-held territory. Initially Morzik despatched the Ju 52/3ms singly or in groups of two to three, at low-level, but as time wore on the Russians firstly increased their anti-aircraft presence and then their fighters began to show up. The latter would hawk around over Demyansk until the Junkers arrived and then attack as the transports made their descents to land. Morzik duly switched to sending out tighter formations of Ju 52/3ms, flying at 1,800 m, with fighter escort provided by Messerschmitt Bf 109s from III./JG 3 and I./JG 51.[9]

During the initial phase of the air-supply operations, the German fighter units held air superiority in the local sector. Indeed, the pilots of Hauptmann Josef Fözö's I./JG 51 experienced a noticeable absence of Soviet fighters to the point where Fözö ordered his pilots to undertake fighter-bomber missions over enemy lines instead. Likewise, Oberleutnant Hans-Ekkehard Bob, the *Staffelkapitän* of 9./JG 54 which had been assigned to the Demyansk area to bolster the efforts of I./JG 51, flew 23 sorties over the pocket between mid-January and mid-February, encountering Russian fighters only once, and even on that occasion the four MiG-3s he ran into made a quick getaway from his small formation of Bf 109s.[10]

At night Morzik arranged for his LTF staff to brief the various transport *Kommandeure* and *Staffelkapitäne* on the latest situation on the ground around and within the pocket, the condition of the landing strips and the best approach and return routes. Those aircraft that were not fully serviceable, but which could still fly, were used to ferry ground personnel and equipment from the rear to the operational bases.

Despite these initiatives, on occasion Morzik and the LTF staff would find themselves compromised by their higher commands. When losses in Ju 52/3ms began to increase as a result of the Soviet anti-aircraft guns set up around the encirclement, Morzik asked for intelligence on the most favoured route to Demyansk. He was advised to simply 'select the route which offers the best chance of avoiding losses'. On another occasion the *Luftflotte* staff omitted to advise the LTF of an enemy paratroop landing in the pocket. This, in itself, was not the problem, but rather the damage caused to valuable Ju 52/3ms as a result of friendly fire from wary German anti-aircraft gunners in the pocket mistaking the Junkers for Russian aircraft.[11] Even at the take-off bases, Morzik and his staff had to battle with the inflexibility and lack of understanding displayed by individual supply units. For example, fuel was a priority, and yet when columns of trucks and tankers arrived at the airfields for unloading, it was often the vehicles carrying general goods that were unloaded first and not the tankers – 'without which', Morzik recalled, 'none of the missions could get off the ground'.[12]

In his post-war writings, Morzik breaks down the Demyansk airlift into three distinct phases: a first initial phase during which his crews mastered the Russian weather in what he saw as a 'valuable training period':

> Their eagerness, their courage and their increasing mastery of flight techniques all helped to overcome the difficulties connected with each mission. Because so many aircraft were not fully operable during this phase, some of the crews flew two or three missions a day.[13]

As flights increased, so did use of the 'satellite' strip at Pieski. Its hardened, packed snow held firm for quite some time, although, as mentioned, it was only usually the more skilled pilots who used the strip.

Morzik offers a damning opinion of the early stages of the supply operation:

> Gradually it was becoming obvious to all concerned that the decision to keep an encircled army corps supplied exclusively by air had been based on a completely erroneous, or at least over optimistic, estimation of the Russian winter, of the resources available to meet the technical requirements, and of the insurmountable difficulties inherent in covering the tremendous distances involved. Moreover, no one had realised that measures which would have been timely and effective under normal conditions either took a very long time to become effective or proved totally inadequate under Russian winter conditions, with the temperature at 40 degrees below zero.[14]

Spring brought a thaw – and mud. This was the difficult second phase in which organisation was affected badly by complications in taxiing and unloading in the pocket. Use of Pieski fell away, not just because of the soft ground, but because the local topography did not allow clearance of further unloading areas or roads. *Luftflotte* 1 reported that the sortie rate fell by 40 per cent between March and April.[15]

As Morzik mentions:

> It was futile to try to schedule the units in any kind of sequence or to assign them to specific landing times, for it was impossible for them to adhere to a definite schedule. There was no way to compensate accurately for potential delays in the take-off from the various bases, for the considerably longer approach routes from the Riga and Daugavpils areas, and for the sharply reduced freedom of action at Demyansk itself.

By this stage Morzik had revised his tactics so that the Ju 52/3ms would take off simultaneously in groups of two or six, sometimes more, as soon as they had been loaded. They would fly at between 1,850–2,500 m to remain above anti-aircraft range.[16] There would then be a time lag in the air between groups as a result of the different distances from the home bases to the pocket, or because of orders issued by the flight leader. This time lag helped to avoid congestion on the landing grounds at Demyansk, and although Morzik recognised that this situation did risk a greater margin for logistical problems, he viewed it, pragmatically, as 'a necessary evil.'[17]

To counter the mud problem to some extent, Morzik also set up the *Abwurfplatz Demjansk* ('Supply Drop Area Demyansk') – in reality nothing more than a marked area in open ground over which supplies could be air-dropped.[18] Nevertheless, the area was very clearly marked so that more experienced pilots would have no problem in recognising it and dropping supplies accurately at low speed from what Morzik described as 'hedge-hopping altitude'. For such flights, it was usually softer supplies that were dropped such as bales of straw, clothing and blankets and, on occasions, extremely well crated and protected, but weighty, boxes of ammunition which, in addition to some absorption by the snow, would be able to withstand violent impact with the harder ground beneath. It was found that the dropping of sacks of flour or potatoes, or fuel canisters, all of which were wrapped in straw to protect them, resulted in such items bursting open.

Furthermore, the process of recovery for the ground troops in freezing temperatures, high winds and deep snow (and dropped items were often unavoidably scattered) was both demanding and dangerous. As Morzik has written, 'The supply-drop operations can be viewed only as an emergency measure and the actual success they attained was in no way proportional to the amount of difficulty involved.'[19]

For return flights over the dangerous front areas, the Ju 52/3ms were assembled into ad hoc defensive formations regardless of their units or whether they were empty or laden with wounded. Once they reached the 'safety' of the Dno area, they would split up and return to their respective bases.

The third, and final, phase of the airlift was boosted by better weather and operating conditions, as well as improved signals and technology. These factors in turn led to improved scheduling, and Morzik instructed that a senior officer from each *Gruppe* was rotated to remain on the landing ground within the pocket to supervise air traffic control until the completion of the day's missions. He would be assisted by officers from the *Luftgaukommando* and the supply officer from II.*Armeekorps*. Losses were kept down to eight machines in April, while *Luftflotte* 1 claimed 260 enemy aircraft shot down.[20]

In order to increase the volume of supplies being delivered to the Demyansk pocket, and to avoid the need to expand the existing landing grounds, air-drop missions commenced using He 111 bombers of I./KG 4 from Pskov-South.

By 17 February the western, outer Soviet encirclement line at Demyansk ran from Lake Ilmen, east of Staraya Russa and south to Belebelka. From there, to the other German pocket at Kholm, was a 40-km gap monitored by bands of Soviet partisans and Red Army sled and ski patrols. Some 30 km from the outer line lay the inner Russian encirclement ring, but German resistance was stubborn. This resistance troubled Stalin, and he blamed it on a lack of unified command and coordination between the Kalinin and North-Western Fronts. He ordered

Kurochkin to apply further pressure and to 'liquidate the pocket' at Demyansk within the next four to five days.[21]

At the commencement of operations it was impossible for Morzik to project the duration of the air-supply mission, as such an operation was influenced entirely by the German defence effort on the ground and the impact and weight of the continuing Soviet offensive. Strangely, however – and fortunately for the Germans – it took until mid-February for VVS units in the area of the North-Western Front to react with any degree of intent to the air-supply operation. Thus, when 9./JG 54 was transferred to the north of Lake Ilmen, it was replaced by the Bf 109s of III./JG 3, which experienced regular encounters with Soviet fighter and ground-attack aircraft in strength – although by 19 February there were only 32 Russian fighters in the sector.[22]

During February more transport *Gruppen* arrived to bolster the air-supply effort. *Luftflotte* 4 in the southern sector of the Eastern Front gave up II./KG.z.b.V.1, which arrived at Ostrov from Dnjepropetrovsk, while KGr.z.b.V.500 flew to Pskov-West, the KGr.z.b.V. Posen to Ostrov-South and the KGr.z.b.V. Öls to Pskov-South. KGr.z.b.V.500, under the command of Major Ludwig 'Lutz' Beckmann (another 'old Eagle' from World War I, during which he had scored eight victories over the Western Front as a *Jasta* pilot), came from the Mediterranean. The personnel of Beckmann's *Gruppe* had had to make a quick transition. Having been formed as recently as 10 December 1941, the unit had been sent south to Brindisi, in Italy, from where it ferried supplies to North Africa. Its crews had had only a month to grow accustomed to the Mediterranean climate when they were ordered to head back to the chillier climes of East Prussia, and from there on to Russia.

By 19 February, the situation in Kholm had become critical, and the local commander made an urgent request for immediate personnel replacements and paratroop reinforcements, without which the pocket could not be held for much longer.[23] On 28 February, Halder recorded that at Demyansk, 'Situation in II.*Armeekorps* is difficult and unchanged. Airborne supply barely sufficient.'[24]

Halder perhaps failed to grasp that keeping a transport unit operational in such punishing weather was not easy. In some units aircrews were required to service their own aircraft because of a lack of groundcrews, and in the bitterly cold temperatures tyre rubber would go flat, turn brittle and split. Fuel and oil lines froze, as did hydraulic pumps and flying instruments, while radios and electrics also failed. Engines had to be started using the 'cold start' method in which oil viscosity was increased by adding fuel to engine oil in amounts of up to 2.5 per cent. But even then it was impossible to replace an engine with a new unit in the open air at temperatures 40 degrees below zero. Inevitably – and as Morzik had predicted – serviceability plummeted to around 25 per cent of total aircraft assigned.[25]

Indeed, the weather proved a relentless, brutal enemy, and yet Hitler seemed irrationally obstinate in his disregard of winter clothing for the troops he required to stand fast. It was the club-footed Nazi Minister for Public Enlightenment and Propaganda, Joseph Goebbels, who eventually initiated an appeal to the German population. Stirring newsreels screened in cinemas showed children, housewives and film stars donating woollen garments and fur coats, while winter sportsmen gave up their skis. At the *Wolfschanze*, Hitler proclaimed, 'The German people have heard my call'. When the donated items eventually arrived within the pockets, to the filthy, freezing, bemused soldiers shivering in their vermin-infested trenches, the clean, fresh clothing seemed as if it came from 'another planet'.[26]

Some troops fared better than others. The 'elite' soldiers of the SS-*Totenkopf* (Death's Head) Division were supplied with ample clothing drawn from an SS stockpile of confiscated goods in Riga. The SS men took delivery of fur-lined parkas, boots and gloves, woollen socks and long underwear. Despite complaints that the garments restricted movement and visibility, and that the gloves hampered efficient handling of light weapons and also absorbed moisture, the SS were better clothed than the soldiers of army units.[27]

By the end of February, conditions at the western edge of the pocket were grim. Here, the scattered units of *Totenkopf* under SS-*Gruppenführer* Theodor Eicke had fought tenaciously to keep the Russians at bay, but in the end the enemy breakthroughs had become so numerous and widespread that it was no longer possible to send badly wounded and sick to the SS hospital in Demyansk. Thus, their comrades simply made them as comfortable as they could in their dugouts while those with lighter wounds manned weapons and waited for the inevitable end. On 28 February, Eicke radioed that *Totenkopf* had lost contact with its neighbouring units and the situation appeared 'hopeless'.[28]

As a further measure of commitment to the air-supply of Demyansk and Kholm, three more *Gruppen* of transports arrived: KGr.z.b.V.4 flew into Riga, KGr.z.b.V.5 with Ju 52/3ms and He 111s also arrived at Riga via Daugavpils in south-eastern Latvia, and KGr.z.b.V.8 via Neukuhren to Daugavpils. A small number of elderly Junkers Ju 86s were 'press-ganged' from KGr.z.b.V.7 and transferred to other *Gruppen*, as well as some civilian Junkers Ju 90 and Focke-Wulf Fw 200 civilian airliners.[29] The danger to the crews was always present: the first two Ju 52/3ms to reach Demyansk on 20 February were shot down, four more fell prey to Russian fighters on the 23rd and another six and one He 111 on the 25th.[30]

The air supply mission for Kholm was, to all intents and purposes, a subordinate operation of the Demyansk mission. Here, 3,500 men of *Kampfgruppe Scherer*, cut off from their comrades at Demyansk, had been trapped in a pocket just two kilometres in diameter – an area too small in which to lay out even a rudimentary landing strip. Thus, the Ju 52/3ms bravely landed on a snow-covered field, after which crewmen pushed the supplies out of their fuselage doors while continuing to taxi, as the pilots turned, applied throttle and took off again before Soviet artillery, which was moving ever closer to the perimeter of the pocket, could range in. But during the mission of 25 February, which had come about because of pressure from the OKL in Berlin, of seven Ju 52/3ms from Oberstleutnant Johannes Janzen's KGr.z.b.V.9 operating from Pskov-South that were despatched to land in the pocket, four were destroyed.[31] Not surprisingly, this hazardous practice was soon abandoned, and the He 111s of KG 4 were brought in to conduct air-drops. The Heinkels also towed Gotha Go 244 cargo gliders, while Ju 52/3ms were used to air-tow smaller DFS 230s.

Gliders would land in front of the German lines or even on the landing field within the pocket. Eventually, as Russian infantry probed the pocket, even that became too dangerous, and so they took to landing on a main street in Kholm, where German troops would rush out from their positions to claim the supplies – if the Russians did not get there first. On such flights, the gliders were given some protection by the Heinkels, which would use their machine guns and cannon to cover their flights and landings.

But the lack of purpose-built transport aircraft required to keep the pocket supplied meant, in the opinion of one senior Luftwaffe staff officer, that the He 111s pressed into emergency service resulted in an 'unsound change in the relationship between transport and bombardment aircraft'.[32] In their almost daily missions to Kholm, the Heinkel crews would regularly have to fly in bad weather, often in snowstorms and low cloud or through dense fog. When the Russians managed to penetrate the southern districts of Kholm on 24 February, supply flights became extremely crucial and the He 111s managed to drop containers of bread and ammunition. But these missions took their toll; on the 25th the *Staffelkapitän* of 2./KG 4, Hauptmann Erich *Freiherr* von Werthern, was fatally wounded in the head and legs when his aircraft was hit by anti-aircraft fire. His heavily wounded pilot, Leutnant Heisig, managed to return their damaged aircraft to Pskov.[33]

At Demyansk, German commanders resorted to using transport aircraft as replacements for lost ground-based communication channels, and the very 'success' of the transport units in the operation would result, as we shall see, in misjudged handling and expectations of air transport capability.

Despite the heroic efforts of Morzik, the LTF Staff, the transport units, the groundcrews and the handlers in the pockets, and despite 100–150 aircraft being committed to the airlift, the supply situation deteriorated: the troops in the pocket began to suffer from malnutrition, and ammunition, particularly artillery shells, had to be carefully conserved.[34] The gun batteries fired between 80–100 tons of ammunition per day; indeed, a 15 cm battery could expend a ton in less than two minutes.[35] In reality, the stated supply figure of 300 tons per day represented the absolute *minimum* necessary to keep the encircled divisions sustained; this meant only two-thirds of the required food rations, half of what would be considered a satisfactory supply of ammunition and only a quarter of the oatmeal necessary to feed the 20,000 horses in the pocket. Horses, like men, suffered from hunger and cold.[36]

At a conference with the commanders of *Heeresgruppe Nord* on 2 March, Hitler stated again – and unequivocally so – that Demyansk must be defended 'like a fortress'.[37] That day he also approved a ground operation, to be known as *Brückenschlag* ('Bridge Blow'), to relieve the 'fortress', but on the 6th, Soviet airborne forces began to infiltrate the pocket and on the 19th Russian paratroops carried out a raid on the landing grounds. They were repulsed.[38] By late March, the pockets at both Demyansk and Kholm continued to hold out under the Soviet attacks, but the trapped soldiers received a boost in the knowledge that German forces had commenced *Brückenschlag* on the 21st.

Meanwhile, the German siege of Leningrad proved an incentive for the VVS to increase its activity against the two pockets. Twenty-three Ju 52/3ms were shot down between 16 and 25 March according to German reports, and it was little better for the He 111s of I./KG 4, which, on the 25th, reported just nine of its crews left alive from those assigned to the *Gruppe* in January.[39]

Then, at dawn on the 27th, a German artillery barrage fell on the Soviet lines between the 11th and 1st Shock Armies, intended to blast a way through to the defenders at Demyansk for the *Korpsgruppe Seydlitz*.[40]

From the beginning of April, as Soviet air activity continued and intensified, Morzik ensured his formations only flew in larger formations with fighter escort.[41]

On 21 April, elements of the *Korpsgruppe Seydlitz* finally linked up with the SS-*Totenkopf* Division near Ramushevo, and the next day the first supplies arrived through the land corridor.[42] On 18 May, the forces in the Demyansk pocket were finally relieved, having held out for 91 days, but still they were to remain in position.[43] Between May and September Kurochkin's forces attempted three more assaults to eliminate the pocket. It was hard-going. The German High Command simply asked for increased air transport to sustain the position.[44]

One source states that a total of 24,303 tons of supplies reached Demyansk during the period of encirclement, plus 3,146,376 litres of fuel and 15,446 personnel, while 22,093 wounded soldiers were flown out. After the pocket was opened, relieved and connected to the main German front, supplies continued to be flown in. From January 1942 until the German departure from the Demyansk pocket in early 1943, in the course of 33,086 sorties, 64,844 tons of materiel, equipment, ammunition, spares, fuel, clothing, food, medical supplies, mail and other items were airlifted into the pocket. According to Morzik, in the period 19 February–18 May 1942, the Luftwaffe's transport units delivered an average of 302 tons per day to the pocket – two tons *over* the *minimum* requirement.[45] On one occasion the daily figure achieved was 544 tons.[46] As late as mid-May 1942, two-thirds of II.*Armeekorp*'s daily supplies were being delivered by air, whereas only 50–100 tons came via the Ramushevo corridor.[47]

The transports even delivered 147 captured Russian light machine guns and ten 45 mm anti-tank guns to II.*Armeekorps*.[48] A total of 30,500 troops were flown in as relief forces and replacements, while 35,400 wounded and sick were flown out. These flights consumed 42,155 tons of fuel and 3,242 tons of oil.[49]

Because of support from the Luftwaffe, the Kholm *Stützpunkt* held out for 103 days under very heavy enemy attacks before being relieved. On 4 May, the survivors of *Kampfgruppe Scherer* radioed the He 111 crews of KG 4 to express their thanks and best wishes for maintaining their daily supply sorties, despite the adverse weather and enemy presence.[50]

It was not until 31 January 1943 that Hitler authorised the complete evacuation of Demyansk, an operation which began 17 days later and concluded on 28 February.[51]

★ ★ ★

Demyansk was the first battle of encirclement on the Eastern Front, and it became the longest.[52] It was also immensely costly in terms of materiel and had a wider impact on pilot training. Over nine months, the supply flights consumed the equivalent of 160 train-loads of fuel. *Luftflotte* 1 reported that 265 Ju 52/3ms were lost and 300 machines were taken from the pilot training programme for some four months.[53]

Morzik felt that Demyansk and Kholm, as 'stopgap' operations, had set 'a dangerous illustration of the potential usefulness of air transport', and that senior German leaders – in other words, Hitler, Reichsmarschall Hermann Göring and certain members of the OKL and the OKH – 'were inclined to be indiscriminately enthusiastic regarding its employment'.[54] While the Luftwaffe's transport force was successful in accomplishing its mission, that in itself was not a justification for ordering it in the first place.

Morzik identified fundamental weaknesses in Luftwaffe and Wehrmacht cooperation and methodology during the Demyansk and Kholm operations that were to have far-reaching effects:

> The lack of any definite instructions and the newness of the mission were responsible for the initial difficulties with the Army supply agencies. These agencies were completely unfamiliar with the technical requirements of an air-supply mission, they were unaware of the limitations inherent in the air transport forces, and they were incapable of estimating the demands which an air-supply mission must necessarily make on their own supply system. All of these factors, which naturally could not be overcome from one day to the next, acted to hinder operations in the beginning. As later events were to show, the lessons which might have been learned from these early phases of the operation were not applied systematically to future instances where the problem of air supply for encircled forces arose.[55]

And, as Morzik points out, 'freedom of action lay on the side of the enemy', meaning that the decision to supply II. *Armeekorps* was not a decision taken rationally and independently by the German command, but rather as a kneejerk initiative in response to an urgent situation. Furthermore, there had been no 'careful and critical evaluation' made before the Russians ensnared Demyansk and Kholm. For example, there had been no assessment as to whether the available lifting capacity was sufficient for the task that lay ahead.

When it came to Kholm, 27 Ju 52/3ms were lost before the pocket was relieved in May.[56] Morzik lamented that lessons on 'basic potentialities' should have been learned regarding the employment of air transport:

> The primary lesson, namely that air supply is never satisfactory as a stopgap solution within the framework of defensive operations on the part of encircled forces, was unfortunately never seriously considered, even though the Kholm operation provided such a clear illustration of the limitations in such a situation.[57]

Overlooking some realities, a Luftwaffe report of March 1944 noted, 'The possibility of supplying large encircled units *had been proved* [author emphasis] ... at Demyansk.'[58]

In a post-war article Generalmajor Wolfgang Pickert, who would play an important role in the Stalingrad airlift, commented that, 'This operation served as a dangerous precedent to the German Army High Command when it made the decision to attempt the aerial supply of the encircled German forces at Stalingrad.'[59] In this, he was correct.

3

The Führer Directive

For assessing German intentions and objectives for the summer of 1942, Directive No. 41 is, in more than one sense, a document of central importance.

PROF. DR. BERND WEGNER, *GERMANY AND THE SECOND WORLD WAR, VOLUME VI*, 2001

On 15 March 1942, as Morzik's transports continued to fly supplies to the beleaguered men still holding out in the mud-caked pockets at Demyansk and Kholm, Adolf Hitler travelled from his East Prussian headquarters to address the annual *Heldengedenktag* (Heroes' Commemoration Day) in the Baroque splendour of the *Zeughaus* on the Unter den Linden in Berlin. Oberst Nicolaus von Below, Hitler's Luftwaffe adjutant, recorded how 'It was becoming vitally important for him again to influence opinion with his speeches.'[1] Indeed, the heavy losses suffered over the winter in Russia had compelled him to make the trip.[2]

Just before midday, clad in a familiar long black leather greatcoat and formal military cap, the *Führer* stepped up to the small podium and leant forward, grasping each edge of the lectern. He was flanked by a helmeted honour guard of soldiers from all three armed services, ramrod backs, gleaming boots, the flags they held serving to bring a splash of colour against the stone backdrop of the *Zeughaus*'s elegant steps. Behind him, set beneath an ornate arch, was a huge Iron Cross. Hitler's rolling, rasping voice accentuated the sombreness of the occasion.

Before him in the courtyard stood a few hundred uniformed men – some of them 'heroes', wounded for the Fatherland. In the front row were their illustrious military bosses – Generalfeldmarschall Wilhelm Keitel, Chief of the OKW; Generalfeldmarschall Erhard Milch, Secretary of State for Aviation and Generalluftzeugmeister of the Luftwaffe; Großadmiral Erich Raeder, Commander-in-Chief of the Navy; and Reichsführer-SS Heinrich Himmler.

The greatcoat and cap may have hidden a somewhat frailer frame than that recognisable from the physically confident *Führer* of previous years. Hitler's quackish doctor had been prescribing him an ever wider range of medicines and pills, and recent visitors to the *Wolfschanze* had found the dictator to be grey and haggard, his moods more volatile.[3]

The speech was short of a rant, but he nevertheless rambled on about the threat from what he perceived as an international Jewish-capitalist conspiracy and how it had been responsible for the present war. *He* had wanted peace. He also viewed the fighting of recent months as a struggle against a winter of a severity that had not been experienced for almost 150 years – although, in fact, the winter of 1940–41 in the East had been even colder. At one point he looked out at his audience and declared, 'But one thing we know today. The Bolshevik hordes, which were unable to defeat the German soldiers and their allies this winter, will be beaten by us into annihilation this coming summer.'[4]

Evidently, however, behind the conviction, this preyed on his mind. Four days after the *Heldengedenktag*, Hitler confessed to Goebbels how close things had come to a 'Napoleonic winter'. He blamed Generalfeldmarschall Walther von Brauchitsch, the hapless former Commander-in-Chief of the Army, pouring scorn on what he saw as the man's vanity, cowardliness and mishandling of *Barbarossa*.[5]

Irrespective of decisions taken at high level, however, or of any failure in doctrine or strategy, as fighting men, the Wehrmacht's soldiers were professional and hardy, and had soaked up all Russia could throw at them. With the arrival of spring in 1942, memories of the dreadful winter that had just passed dissipated as thoughts turned to the prospect of the coming summer and the hoped for arrival of replacements for depleted ranks, as well as new weapons and equipment.[6]

Equally, the 'annihilation' of the 'Bolshevik hordes' to which Hitler alluded at the *Zeughaus* was founded on his aspiration of further military conquest in the East during the summer. This aspiration would manifest itself in the audacious operation which had germinated within the General Staff at the end of 1941. After some false starts and lengthy discussions, at a secret conference on 28 March 1942, Halder presented Hitler and a small number of selected senior staff from the OKW, the Wehrmacht and the Luftwaffe, with the outline draft of an operational plan for a summer offensive in Russia. Hitler approved it in principle and advised the Chief of Staff of the OKH of his own strategic goals. The then Generalmajor Walter Warlimont, the Deputy Chief of the *Führungsstabes* (Command Staff) at the OKW, recorded that:

Once more he proposed that the decisive areas should be the outermost flanks of this widespread front. There was only one difference; he had grasped the fact that the Army was no longer at full strength and that losses could not be made good; he had therefore been compelled to go for his two objectives successively rather than simultaneously, beginning in the south with the Caucasus.[7]

While the situation in North Africa remained uncertain, mainly because of logistics, and Hitler was concerned over the possibility of Allied landings in Norway or France, he believed firmly that the outcome of the war would rest in the East. That being said, his goal was to take the Caucasus and hold a line along the Don River in the winter of 1942–43 – objectives that were to be obtained not through deep advances, but rather through setting up smaller encirclements of enemy forces and destroying them.[8] Halder noted this during the conference *Time: Beginning of September: North Caucasus*.[9] Halder and his staff went to work to incorporate the *Führer's* requirements into a revised draft directive that he then re-presented for consideration. After General Alfred Jodl, Chief of Operations Staff at the OKW, had also had a go at it, he presented the draft to Hitler on 4 April. The *Führer* said he would study it and work over it himself. This was the moment, according to Warlimont, that Hitler 'seized upon the opportunity of showing how he interpreted his role as Commander-in-Chief of the Army.'[10]

Hitler made a number of substantial revisions and additions to a plan originally codenamed *Siegfried*, assigning it the new, less pretentious codename of *Blau* ('Blue'), apparently because he felt uncomfortable with references in the same grand vein of *Barbarossa*. He also 'entirely redrafted' the main part of it.[11] In its final form, as *Weisung* (Directive) 41, Hitler signed it off at the *Wolfschanze* on Easter Sunday, 5 April.

His somewhat tortuously worded summary was that the past winter battles had represented 'a defensive success of the greatest scale for German arms'. But the future was to be all about destruction – and the need for oil.

Generalmajor Herhudt von Rohden, former head of the Luftwaffe's *Kriegswissenschaftlich Abteilung* (military science branch), opined that the summer campaign of 1942 was based, despite noticeably increasing Allied pressure on the Reich at sea, in the air and in North Africa, solely on offensive operations – a 'ceaseless *Vernichtungsstrategie*' (annihilation strategy) which followed the German concept of war as developed by Clausewitz and continued by his 'spiritual successors', Helmuth von Moltke the Elder and Alfred Graf von Schlieffen. And this, according to von Rohden, was set against an 'increasingly senseless lack of understanding of the enemy's overall situation.'[12]

One of the Directive's stated principle aims was to 'finally wipe out the remaining Soviet military potential, and, as far as possible, deprive them of their most important military-economic sources of strength.'[13] But the stark reality was that in order for Germany to 'wipe out' any aspect of 'Soviet military potential', there was a need for oil, and by early 1942 Germany's existing sources of supply were insufficient to produce the quantity needed for grand offensive operations in the East. Only some 20 per cent of German crude oil was extracted domestically, and while synthetic fuel production had almost doubled to 4,116,000 tons in 1941 from the 1939 figure, this was offset by the decline in supply from Romania, which had slid by 3,124,000 tons between 1937 and 1941.[14]

Thus, essentially, Hitler wanted to hold the central sector of the front firm in the zone of *Heeresgruppe Mitte* but to take Leningrad in the north, and to link up with the Finns, while in the south, where he saw the 'main operation', he would force a breakthrough along the Black Sea coast to the Maikop and Grosny oilfields of the Caucasus which he craved. After an appalling Russian winter, a difficult spring campaign and high losses suffered in 1941, Hitler wanted a more limited offensive, but one which could offer rich benefits. Considerable forces were to be assembled that would, as the Directive envisaged it, 'decisively smash and destroy' Russian forces located in the Voronezh area to the south, west or north of the Don.

As Hitler had told Halder on 28 March, he wanted to snare Russian forces wherever possible by following up breakthroughs with close pincer movements: 'We *must avoid* [emphasis in original] closing the pincers too late, thus giving the enemy the possibility of escaping destruction.'[15]

The operation was to progress in three phases: this may have led to a complex procedure, but one historian argues that this was a deliberate measure intended to allow the Luftwaffe to apply its stretched resources carefully and with effect on successive, localised operations.[16]

Blau I would see an initial armoured and infantry thrust from east of Kursk towards the Don and the railway and industrial city of Voronezh, lying some eight kilometres beyond the river. This would be accompanied by an enveloping thrust from the Belgorod area. Once Voronezh had been taken, the second phase, *Blau II*, was to commence from the right flank of the southern pincer directed at Voronezh. It would thrust south between the Donets and the west bank of the Don towards Millerovo, rolling up the enemy as it went and connecting with another thrust advancing east from around 100 km south of Kharkov and moving over Izyum. This thrust would also destroy Red Army forces west of the Don.

In the third phase, *Blau III*, the aim was for these now combined thrusts to push further east into the Don bend towards Stalingrad, the industrial city on the Volga, and to link up with more forces advancing from the area north of Taganrog between the lower course of the Don and Voroshilovgrad, across the Donets.[17] This would catch any large Soviet formations in the vast bend of the river. The Directive stated:

> These forces are to link up finally with the Panzer army advancing on Stalingrad. The attempt must be made to *reach* [author emphasis] Stalingrad itself, or at least subject this city to the bombardment of our heavy weapons to such an extent that it is eliminated as an armament and transportation centre in the future.[18]

Whilst, in itself, the capture of Stalingrad could not play any foreseen part in the destruction of the Red Army west of the Don, of note here is the fact that of a total Soviet oil output of around 38,000,000 tons in 1941, the Germans estimated that some 9,000,000 tons was transported by river tanker and barge up the Volga via Stalingrad each year.[19]

The reference to 'reaching' Stalingrad was vague and held no hint of strategic intent as regards to the city in terms of whether it was to be encircled, bombed or penetrated and held.[20] No start dates for the offensive were suggested, nor were any details given for the intended fourth phase which would cover the drive into the Caucasus – an objective of far more immediate significance to Hitler than Stalingrad. In his view, Warlimont considered that the Directive was 'long and repetitive; it jumbled up operational instructions and universally known strategic principles; in general it was unclear and in detail it was complicated'.[21] Notwithstanding the opinions of Warlimont, this was a *Führer* Directive and so the German war machine would have to abide by it.

In the key southern sector, German forces were marshalled under *Heeresgruppe Süd* commanded since January by Generalfeldmarschall Fedor von Bock. This was a powerful force numbering more than a million German troops plus 300,000 more from countries allied to the Axis – Italy, Hungary and Romania. Together, on the eve of the offensive, the German manpower comprised 45 infantry divisions, 11 Panzer divisions, four light infantry divisions and five motorised divisions, plus a further 25 divisions drawn from an Italian, a Hungarian and two Romanian armies. This was, in itself, a sign that Germany was struggling with the manpower demands of a front of more than 2,700 km in length.[22] The Army Group could field 1,495 serviceable tanks, including the newer Panzer III and IV models armed with long-barrelled 50 mm and 75 mm guns, respectively, both capable of penetrating the armour of the Red Army's ubiquitous T-34.

In accordance with Hitler's orders, the Army Group would receive strong air support from Generaloberst Alexander Löhr's *Luftflotte* 4, comprising General der Flieger Kurt Pflugbeil's IV.*Fliegerkorps* along with *Fliegerführer Süd*, a Crimea-based tactical reconnaissance and anti-shipping command; *Gefechtsverband Nord*, a regional tactical command set up to oversee air operations over Voronezh; and the I.*Flakkorps*. Löhr's air fleet was further strengthened by the presence of Generaloberst Dr.-Ing. Wolfram *Freiherr* von Richthofen's VIII.*Fliegerkorps*, a powerful command specialising with impressive success in both dive-bombing and horizontal bombing operations.[23] The *Korps* had recently excelled itself in an intense horizontal bombing campaign in support of Generalfeldmarschall Erich von Manstein's 11.*Armee* against the port fortress of Sevastopol on the Black Sea.

Luftflotte 4 mustered 1,700 combat aircraft at the start of the offensive, of which 1,200 were operationally ready, including 350 bombers, 211 fighters, 161 *Zerstörer*, more than 150 Junkers Ju 87 Stukas, 91 fighter-bombers and 51 strategic reconnaissance aircraft.[24] Indeed, by June 1942, 61 per cent of Luftwaffe strength in the East had been sent to the southern sector of the front.[25] These aircraft would have their work cut out providing cover for *Heeresgruppe Süd*'s staging areas, conducting attacks in the enemy rear, especially the bridges over the Don, and establishing air superiority over the battle area.[26]

The first phase of *Blau* commenced in the early hours of 28 June. In the area of *Heeresgruppe Süd*, 4.*Panzerarmee* under Generaloberst Hermann Hoth, with 2.*Armee* on its right flank, advanced from Kursk towards Voronezh. Two days later, after heavy thunderstorms had forced Bock to delay its start, 6.*Armee*, under General der Panzertruppe Friedrich Paulus, moved off from its positions nearly 200 km further south under heavy artillery and air support from Ju 87s and horizontal bombers. This army made for Voronezh so that, in conjunction with Hoth and the Hungarian Second Army, three Soviet armies could be encircled. The role of 6.*Armee* was then to screen the northern flank of the Panzer armies, link up with 4.*Panzerarmee* at Millerovo and strike towards the Volga to take (or to 'reach') Stalingrad in cooperation with the *Panzerarmee* as *Blau* II.[27] 6.*Armee* progressed 35 km towards Voronezh on 30 June, while in the skies above, Luftwaffe bombers struck at the railway yards in the city, as well as those at Michurinsk, Svoboda and Valuyki.[28]

6.*Armee* had come into being in October 1939, commanded upon its formation by Generalfeldmarschall Walther von Reichenau. It had taken part in operations in France and Belgium in the spring and summer of 1940 and then acted as the spearhead for *Heeresgruppe Süd* during Operation *Barbarossa* in June 1941. When Reichenau died on 17 January 1942 following the crash of the aircraft in which he was travelling in order to receive treatment for a heart attack he had suffered a few days before, he was succeeded by his Chief of Staff, Friedrich Paulus. Paulus, a tall, thin and scrupulous man from an unremarkable background, had recently won acclaim for his command of a counter-attack at Kharkov in May in which, together with Generalleutnant Ewald von Kleist's 1.*Panzerarmee*, he had encircled a major Soviet force in the Izyum salient. As a result of this action, the Wehrmacht took nearly 240,000 prisoners as well as 2,000 guns and a large number of Russian tanks. Paulus became lauded by the Nazi propaganda machine and Hitler awarded him the Knight's Cross, praising the success of 6.*Armee* against overwhelming odds.[29] For Operation *Blau*, the *Armee* numbered 20 divisions in five *Korps*, including three Panzer divisions and three motorised infantry divisions, as well as several artillery and mortar regiments. It was also assigned the Luftwaffe's 9.*Flak-Division*.

Meanwhile, the rains had cleared and the ground had dried out. As 6.*Armee*'s divisions pressed eastwards in the first scorching days of July 1942, across huge fields of sunflower and corn, marching 30–40 km per day, with the Second Hungarian Army to their left and 1.*Panzerarmee* to their right, supported by the aircraft of IV.*Fliegerkorps*, there was a sense of renaissance and ebullience among the soldiers on the ground – a sense of vindication for holding out over the long, cold months of the winter. A German war correspondent noted how, 'As far as the eye can see, armoured vehicles and half-tracks are rolling forward over the steppe.'[30] That may have been how Goebbels' propaganda ministry wanted to portray things, but a British radio intercept from 3 July picked up a communication from *Luftflotte* 4 stating that 6.*Armee* had made 'only little progress' due to 'difficult local terrain'.[31] There was also some enemy resistance, mainly from dug-in and camouflaged T-34s, not easily seen by the Panzer crews or the Stukas above them. But the Panzers and dive-bombers dealt with them, with Red Army tank crews often forced to escape on foot.[32] In two days, 6.*Armee* had smashed into the Soviet Southwestern Front's 21st Army and pushed back the 28th Army.[33] And in doing so, Paulus recognised the value of his air support; he signalled Pflugbeil thanking him for the Luftwaffe's 'frictionless cooperation and never-failing support'.[34]

Far to the south in the Crimea, Sevastopol had finally fallen to von Manstein's 11.*Armee* on 4 July. Two days after that, most of Voronezh had been taken, but German forces in the area had been dragged into engaging Soviet rearguard units which fought back determinedly, and the battles for the bridgeheads continued for weeks as *Blau* progressed elsewhere.[35] As the first week passed, 6.*Armee*'s staff officers became aware of an unsettling phenomenon, as Oberst Wilhelm Adam, adjutant to Paulus, recorded:

> In the first few days we came to realise that we had been fighting against numerically weak but well-armed rearguards, their determined defence leading to high losses among our forces. Most of the Soviet troops were able to escape from the threatening destruction.[36]

Indeed, on one refreshingly cool evening, Adam accompanied Paulus for a walk. The army commander commented to his aide that Hitler's goal of destroying the enemy had not been achieved: 'Our attack was just a thrust into empty space.'[37]

Paulus was aware that 4.*Panzerarmee* was still tied up in clearing Voronezh and had not reached the Don bend to cooperate with 6.*Armee*'s own XXXX.*Panzerkorps*. And Russia was vast . . . so vast . . .

Adam wrote of this time:

> Before us lay the extensive Don Steppe. The July sun burned mercilessly out of an azure blue sky on the dust-covered marching columns. There were no proper roads here, no trees or bushes to give shade, no springs to quench the burning thirst. Wherever the eye looked, one saw only steppe grass and wormwood with legions of ground squirrels in between. This area was very scantily settled. Villages were almost only to be found in a few stream valleys running from north to south, visible from a distance along low depressions in the ground. They were just about empty. The population had gone off with their herds of cattle as the troops of the Red Army withdrew.[38]

At midday on 7 July Bock telexed Halder advising him that the Russians were in full retreat along 6.*Armee*'s entire front and:

> . . . that as presently deployed by the Army Command the double-sided envelopment will probably hit nothing, that in my opinion 'Blue 2' is dead

and the Army Command must consider with what intent and to where the Panzer forces of my left wing should now be sent.[39]

By mid-July, for all the territory the Wehrmacht had taken, a strange sense of equilibrium hung over *Heeresgruppe Süd*. While *Blau I* had concluded with some success, the Russian stance around Voronezh and other places had irked Hitler, and he had become irritated with his senior commanders who seemed, with superior forces, unable to execute his plan and to only frustrate the drive to the oilfields of the Caucasus.[40] Adolf Hitler was not in the mood for excuses or argumentative Field Marshals: on the 13th, Bock, who he deemed to have delayed the rapid drive south by unnecessarily engaging the Russians at Voronezh, was relieved of his command and 'placed at the disposal of the *Führer*'.[41]

4

The Decisive Factor?

The Luftwaffe Air Transport Force, summer 1942

*Military history indicates that the availability of logistical capability is
strongly correlated with the potential for victory or defeat.*
CAPT. JAMES H. DONOHO, *AN ANALYSIS OF*
TACTICAL MILITARY AIRLIFT, 1997

In the early summer of 1942, the armed forces of the Third Reich committed
more than eight million military personnel to their ambitions of conquest,
occupation and expansion. Concurrent to this, there were two massive principle
theatres of war: firstly, in the Mediterranean and North Africa, and secondly in
Russia, where German forces held a 1,900-km front stretching from Leningrad
in the north to the Sea of Azov in the south. In addition, manpower was assigned
to the occupations of France, the Low Countries, Denmark and Norway, as
well as to the defence of the newly created 'Atlantic Wall', while at sea, despite
appalling gales, German U-boats were at their operational zenith far out in the
Atlantic. At home, more men were needed to man the increasing numbers of
Flak guns necessary to defend against RAF Bomber Command's night raids
on German cities, factories and railway yards. It was a colossal war machine
to sustain: in 1942, the factories of the Reich turned out 15,409 aircraft,
37,000 aero engines, 9,300 tanks, 317,000 automatic weapons and more than a
million tons of ammunition. Industrial output included 32 million tons of steel,
264 million tons of coal, nearly five million tons of synthetic oil, 98,000 tons of
synthetic rubber and almost 264,000 tons of aluminium.[1]

One of the key challenges in servicing and handling this scale of political and
military control was supply. On a practical level, large quantities of vehicles, guns,
ammunition, food and fuel had to be moved by ship, but an inherent demand of
fighting such a massive, mechanised war was speed. Speed was not only required
to get fuel to far-flung armies and air units but, during the early years of rapid
conquest, it was an important element in delivering troops into key battle zones
and later, in the years of crisis, it was important in getting them out.

One of the greatest consumers of industrial output, manpower, fuel and oil was the Luftwaffe, which was tasked with supporting the German army and navy, as well as with providing the aerial defence of the Reich. This meant, in terms of combat operations beyond the Reich's borders, its aircraft were deployed in fighter, fighter-bomber, dive-bombing, horizontal bombing, anti-shipping and reconnaissance roles across the main battlefronts, as well as over the Atlantic and Arctic Oceans and the North and Mediterranean Seas. On 27 November 1941, the Luftwaffe had 5,712 operational aircraft on strength, of which 4,928 were engaged on the battlefronts. Of these, 2,478, or 50 per cent, were based in the East.[2] However, in the period 8 November–27 December 1941, the quantity of transport aircraft based in the East fell from 57 per cent to 41 per cent, representing the largest decrease in all aircraft types and reflecting the transfer of units to the Mediterranean to support the initiatives of the *Deutsches Afrikakorps*.[3]

In mid-1942, the Luftwaffe fielded five *Luftflotten* across the West, Russia, Scandinavia and the Mediterranean, with a similar command organisation dedicated to the air defence of the Reich. Each *Luftflotte* comprised between 500 to 1,000 bombers, fighters and reconnaissance aircraft, depending on the theatre of operations, and thus its tasks. There were around 260 combat aircraft under *Luftflotte* 2 in North Africa, for example, at the opening of Generaloberst Erwin Rommel's offensive against the Gazala Line (on 26 May 1942), with another 325 based in Greece, Crete and Sicily, whereas in Russia, under *Luftflotten* 1 and 4, there were 2,750 aircraft of all types.[4]

The fleets were usually assigned two or three *Fliegerkorps* or *Fliegerdivision* of between 250 and 500 aircraft that would cover air operations in any one area for a certain period of time. However, fleet and corps commanders would often work with smaller, tactical commands such as *Fliegerführer*, who would control around 100–250 aircraft in a small area of airspace that were intended to focus exclusively on providing air support for a specific army formation or for a defined area.[5] This enabled Luftwaffe commanders to execute a quick response informed by local tactical knowledge.

Strangely, however, air transport was excluded from the fleet structure, and yet it had no autonomous, self-governing command either. Indeed, it seems that despite the significant resources committed to the battlefronts in 1942, and the inherent need for supplies of men and material, air transport had become, to all intents and purposes, a blind spot in Luftwaffe operational thinking. The Luftwaffe failed to grasp how important it was to fully integrate a transport force into its functional and operational infrastructure; how transport needed to be viewed as much of a priority as fighter, bomber or ground-attack aviation, especially when set against the ambition of German strategic and offensive objectives. As late as 1939 no mention was made of air transport in the Luftwaffe's General Staff handbook.[6]

During the 1930s, planners at the *Reichsluftministerium* (RLM – Reich Air Ministry) had considered the main purpose of air transport to be the movement and immediate support of *Fallschirmjäger* units (i.e., 'air-landing').

A secondary purpose was to increase the mobility of Luftwaffe units by using air transport to a more limited degree. It was also recognised that airborne operations would occur only occasionally, and that the demand for appropriate aircraft would fluctuate according to the presentation of suitable opportunities. Consequently, only a relatively small force of transport aircraft was set aside for this particular purpose, and it was to be supplemented by aircraft drawn from training units immediately prior to specific airborne operations. A small number of transport aircraft were also allocated to the various *Luftflotten* and units within these commands for the movement of flying units.

During the last years of peace a scheme was devised for the universal use of the Ju 52/3m for both air transport and for the training of bomber pilots in order to optimise usage. However, the transport side of the system was designed for fast, highly mobile campaigns of brief duration, and it worked well in such short campaigns as the annexation of Czechoslovakia and the invasions of Poland, France, Denmark and Norway. But under the strain of ever increasing military reversals and the drawing out of the war from late 1941, it gradually began to break down, and the need for airborne operations was superseded by the urgency of air *supply* both to the Luftwaffe and to the Wehrmacht. The small allocation of Ju 52/3ms to the *Luftflotten* was insufficient for the unprecedented commitments that began to arise. From late 1941 onwards, therefore, there were frequent organisational changes in the management of air transport – all directed to further its efficient employment and to concentrate control so that aircraft could be switched to the most vital focal points. This mentality and method of operation became deeply embedded in the way the *Transportflieger* approached and accepted their tasks.[7]

To meet the aforementioned tasks it saw lying ahead, on 7 November 1938, in its *Konzentriertes Flugzeugmuster-Programm*, the Luftwaffe General Staff issued a target that the Luftwaffe should include four *Transportgeschwader* equipped with some 500 aircraft in total.[8] The Germans had observed Italian fortunes in Ethiopia, where unit mobility had been crucial, and during the course of 1939, most frontline Luftwaffe units were assigned two Ju 52/3ms for transport and/or deployment as radio or direction–finding aircraft.[9] At the end of August of that year, the Chiefs of Staff set a new target of 552 Ju 52/3m transports as an acceptable number with which the Luftwaffe could function.[10]

Longer term, as far as military aircraft were concerned, in its *Flugzeugbeschaffungs-Programm* Nr.11 of 1 April 1939, the RLM projected a requirement of 2,260 Ju 52/3ms running to 1 April 1942, but just three months later, on 5 August, Göring decreed that production was to be cut back in favour of the development of new combat aircraft such as the He 177, Ju 88, Me 210 and Bf 109. Thus a revised total of 1,400 Ju 52/3ms was to be built up to April 1942, with production capped at just 15 per month thereafter.[11] Unbeknown to Göring, this was to be at just the point when demand would be at its greatest, and yet there was an uncomfortable inconsistency between demand and the supply of fuel to maintain service. On 29 May 1942, the operations department of *Luftflotte* 4 on the southern sector of the Russian Front issued the following instruction to its Quartermaster General staff:

> The Chief of the Air Staff [Generaloberst Hans Jeschonnek] has pointed out the necessity of restoring or increasing the operational readiness of all air transport formations and the necessity of economising in aviation fuel. All air transports are to be limited to what is absolutely necessary. Air transports for the *Heer* are called for only when elements of the Army cannot be supplied by other means or when special arms and ammunition have to be despatched in the shortest possible time to a battle front. These transports are to be carried out only at the orders of *Luftflotte* 4. Within the Luftwaffe, the employment of transport aircraft is to be sanctioned only if moves of flying units have to be made so rapidly that moves by road or by rail would take too much time. The supplying by air and the collecting of replacement engines, spare parts etc., by air to maintain the operational readiness of flying units is necessary in the course of major operations, but may not be extended, without authorisation, to quiet fronts. The necessity of using transport aircraft is to be checked in every case.[12]

Within these contexts of scale, war demands and production, for much of the war, in terms of air transport, the Luftwaffe would use its Ju 52/3ms primarily as transporters to move supplies in bulk by air to support strategic initiatives such as in Operation *Marita* (the campaign in the Balkans in April 1941), or in the East in Operation *Barbarossa* later that year, or to sustain fuel and supplies for Rommel's forces in North Africa between February 1941 and the end of 1942. In Russia, even in the early phases of the campaign, the enormous expanse of territory meant that the Ju 52/3m units were always stretched: in October 1941 in the southern sector, owing to a shortage of aircraft fuel at forward airfields, 'all available' Ju 52/3ms were used for the transport of fuel.[13] At one point in December 1941, such was *Luftflotte* 2's need for Ju 52/3ms in its support for operations by *Heeresgruppe Mitte* that five *Gruppen* were sent from the Reich to Smolensk in the area of VIII.*Fliegerkorps* alone.[14]

As a paper on air transport prepared in March 1944 by the Luftwaffe's branch for *Kriegswissenschaftlich*, the 8.*Abteilung*, under Generalmajor Herhudt von Rohden, noted with the benefit of considerable and depressing hindsight:

> In certain situations transport aircraft constitute the *only* means by which a *definite operational objective may be attained*. The transport formations are part of the operational air force, and must be directed and employed according to corresponding principles. Therefore, when operational, they must be given the same facilities which are a matter of course in the case of battle formations.

And from this emerges a paradox, for just a few years earlier, between 29 July and 5 August 1936, 20 Ju 52/3ms, which had been donated by Hitler to General Francisco Franco and the Nationalist rebels in Spain, arrived in Spanish Morocco and were put to immediate use ferrying badly needed troops and ammunition from the *Ejército de Africa* over the Straits of Gibraltar to the mainland. Their presence greatly accelerated what became known as the *puente aéreo*, the first large-scale 'airbridge' or airlift in history. Each Ju 52/3m was capable of making four trips per day between Tetuán and Seville, carrying 22-30 men and equipment on each flight. In total, these aircraft flew 1,500 men, including six assault battalions, from Morocco to Seville, and in all 10,500 men were transferred to Spain from North Africa in July and August, followed by 9,700 in September. By its conclusion on 11 October, the airlift had transported just under 14,000 troops and some 500 tons of materiel, including 36 artillery pieces. Historians have taken the view that, in truth, the airlift saved the Nationalist cause in the summer of 1936 and enabled Franco to consolidate his position quickly; indeed, in 1942, Hitler declared that 'Franco ought to erect a monument to the glory of the Junkers 52.'

Yet this action in itself failed to generate much interest or initiative within the Luftwaffe General Staff to further and significantly develop an air transport arm. It is also somewhat mystifying why Hitler and his air chiefs did not recognise, as a result of experience gained in Spain, what benefits could be achieved militarily with a large, state-of-the-art airlift force. It is true that the German campaigns in the West in 1940 (particularly the action at Eben Emael) and the invasions of Denmark and Norway exploited air transport to tactical and strategic advantage in successful paratroop and air-landing operations, and illustrated how effective they could be, but air transport was still viewed as a subordinate support branch to Luftwaffe assault commands.

Despite the success in Spain, where the Ju 52/3m, which had already proved itself as a world-class civilian airliner both in Germany and abroad in the 1930s, was also used as a bomber, there was no effort made to increase production of the aircraft. To the contrary, for when, in 1937, there was a reduction in steel and aluminium allocations, output of the Ju 52/3m was curbed heavily.[15] Furthermore, any chance of increasing the strength of the transport *Gruppen* in the late 1930s and early 1940s was stymied by the need to use the Ju 52/3m as a main type within the Luftwaffe's training schools.

The post of *Lufttransportchef Land* (Chief of Air Transport [Landing]) had been created on 12 March 1940 and was filled by a reserve officer, former wartime pilot and Lufthansa executive, Oberstleutnant Carl-August *Freiherr* von Gablenz. In May 1940, the post was assigned the more general title of *Lufttransportführer*. But to exacerbate the sense of 'second line status', from 1 October 1941 to April 1942 the post of Chief of the Luftwaffe's *Blindflugschulen* (Blind-Flying/Instrument Schools) was doubled up with the post of the LTF, which served simply to split resources and introduce internal competition for them.[16] The man chosen to take over from Gablenz and to 'sip from the poison chalice' was Fritz Morzik. As he has written:

> Inasmuch as the *Lufttransportführer* was at the same time the *Kommandeur* of the *Blindflugschulen*, his position was one of dual subordination. As

Lufttransportführer, he belonged to the staff of the Quartermaster General, and as commanding officer of the instrument flight schools, to that of the Chief of Training. Inevitably, a certain amount of friction resulted, which also made its effects felt among the flying units and in the schools. Requests and pleas for a clarification of the situation were without avail, and a tug-of-war within the command headquarters ensued. The functions of the air transport officer and those of the commanding officer of the instrument flight schools were united in one man, who had two operational command staffs under him, one for each of his functions. This unfortunate solution to the problem of the command of two important activities was bound to result in the unintentional neglect of one of them.[17]

Even if we place the 1936 operation in Spain aside, there is evidence from the previously mentioned 8.*Abteilung* report to suggest that in *March 1944* recognition of the military and logistical value of air transport was only just being truly appreciated:

The compression of time and space brought about by the railway, the steamer and the motor engine had decisive consequences on the character of the war. The ever-increasing intensification of this development is based on the new influence of the Luftwaffe. Through its speedy and far-reaching action in attack and reconnaissance, the Luftwaffe is capable of determining and changing the course of the war. In air transport a new means of operation has come into being of great importance for the Luftwaffe, *in whose hands its performance* and safety lie, and through which the Luftwaffe title 'bearer of the Army's commands' is once again confirmed. A new means of decisive cooperation on the part of the Luftwaffe in the operations of the army is available in the shape of air transport.[18]

The reality was that since 1939 – a period of nearly five years – this 'new means' had, in a subordinate way, undertaken seven fundamental transport missions: 1) the transport of supplies and equipment for Luftwaffe units; 2) the transfer of operational units to new bases; 3) the transport of supplies for the Army; 4) the reinforcement and evacuation of Army personnel when other means of transport were difficult or when ground forces had been isolated, surrounded and cut off and/or when the Army's own efforts to supply had failed; 5) the air-evacuation of wounded; 6) parachute drops and air-landing operations; 7) miscellaneous missions such as courier flights and mail etc.[19]

Had an independent air transport organisation or *Flotte* been established in 1939 or in early 1940, that organisation would have had its own fleet commander – a position of senior rank, power and influence – as well as its own dedicated staff made up of officers with appropriate experience who would plan and oversee operations and administration with clarity and decisiveness.

If such a staff had been in place in the winter of 1941–42, then the supply operations at Demyansk and Kholm may have been handled with more finesse, and thus success over less time.[20] In fact the opposite happened, as Professor Richard Suchenwirth has described:

> Unfortunately, even the highest-ranking air transport officers were nothing more than recipients of orders from above; because of their comparatively lower rank, they were not even consulted as to the feasibility of the large-scale transport operations ordered by the Luftwaffe top-level command.[21]

Yet the 8.*Abteilung* report states confidently that 'The possibility of supplying large encircled units *had been proved* [author emphasis] . . . at Demyansk.'[22]

Finally, however, in April 1942, the position of LTF was made independent from the *Kommandeur der Blindflugschulen*; and yet Morzik still had no permanent operations staff, and so for each new undertaking a new staff had to be organised.

In the Mediterranean in December 1941, transport flights comprised mainly deliveries of fuel to German forces in North Africa. These were difficult missions: on 12 December a freshly delivered consignment of fuel to Derna, in Libya, was destroyed as it was feared the British were imminently about to attack the airfield. However, the fear proved groundless, and so the transports had to fly in a replacement load the following night. Deliveries of fuel to airfields surrounding the Gulf of Sidra, to the west of Derna, and thus further from Crete, were self-defeating – on the 14th Ju 52/3ms used up half the delivered fuel in order to return to the island.

But the transport situation worsened dramatically when the shadow of Demyansk fell across the Mediterranean. On 15 January 1942, KGr.z.b.V.500 was transferred from Brindisi to Russia to support the existing air supply operations there. Two units were left in place in the Mediterranean, III./KG.z.b.V.1 and KGr.z.b.V.400, but the latter continued to suffer losses in aircraft and crews. 'The young and inexperienced crews were simply not capable of meeting the demands made upon them', noted Morzik.[23] Yet, paradoxically, the haze and turbulent sea experienced at this time of year lay in the favour of the *Transportflieger* since there was less likelihood of encountering British fighters operating from Malta as the transports made crossings to and from North Africa.

An analysis of aircraft strength figures within the tactical commands of *Luftflotte* 2 in the Mediterranean for 4 April 1942, reveals the following – with bracketed number denoting serviceable aircraft:[24]

	Total Aircraft	**Transports**	As Percentage of Total
II.*Fliegerkorps*	390 (268)	**44 (30)**	11.28 per cent (11.19 per cent)
X.*Fliegerkorps*	95 (46)	**6 (4)**	6.3 per cent (8.69 per cent)
Fliegerführer Afrika	117 (83)	–	–
Total	602 (397)	**50 (34)**	8.3 per cent (8.56 per cent)

These figures show that while preparations were being undertaken for Rommel's offensive, which would require manpower and supplies, and the air offensive against Malta was in progress, the Luftwaffe's transport force was functioning at under nine per cent of the total force in the Mediterranean.

In the early summer of 1942, as forces prepared for Operation *Blau* on the Eastern Front, in the Mediterranean on 20 May, of 711 (438) aircraft assigned to *Luftflotte* 2, 75 (47) were transports, and by 20 June, of 656 (380) aircraft, transports numbered 77 (45).[25]

At the end of June 1942, there were around 150 Ju 52/3ms available to the Luftwaffe in the Mediterranean, as well as ten of the big six-engined Blohm & Voss BV 222 flying boat transporters of *Lufttransportstaffel See* 222, which made use of the harbour at Tobruk following the town's recent capture.[26] But even this number of Junkers had been reached only by calling on aircraft assigned to the signals *Staffel* of X.*Fliegerkorps*, ambulance units and the *Transport Staffel* of II.*Fliegerkorps*.[27] Operational readiness went into decline: one *Gruppe* had only 18 to 20 serviceable machines available per day, another just 12. Those aircraft remaining serviceable flew up to three missions per day, but still the requirement of the *Afrika Korps* could not be fulfilled. When IV./KG.z.b.V.1, KGr.z.b.V.600 and KGr.z.b.V.800 arrived in the Mediterranean as much needed reinforcements in July, the transports were finally able to deliver the 1,000 troops and 25 tons of equipment needed in North Africa.[28]

In Russia in 1941 and through to the summer of 1942, the transport units were used mainly to reinforce or to replace motor transport as the means of covering the leg between railheads and forward airfields. This was particularly important where the conditions of the Russian road network were poor and/or speed was of the essence.[29] Nevertheless, for the Luftwaffe's small LTF staff, dealing with the Army could be, at best, a one-way process and at worst a demoralising struggle. The air operation at Demyansk had shown that the Army's supply organisation had little, if any, understanding of what it took to coordinate and effect a major air transport operation. This was attributable to the lack of any cooperation at theoretical or practical level between the Army and the staff of the LTF, although Morzik acknowledges that both sides may have been 'at fault' in this respect.

Unlike the quick, victorious *Blitzkrieg* campaigns in the West, Scandinavia and the Balkans, in Russia the Army became the Luftwaffe air transport force's 'chief customer' for air-supply services. But Morzik remained unforgiving:

> Certain difficulties and failures in coordination were inevitable at first and had to be accepted as such; there was little excuse, however, for the complete lack of understanding displayed by some Army representatives in the beginning. If the Army supply people had been as willing to improvise as were the air transport personnel, there would have been considerably fewer difficulties for the latter to overcome.[30]

As the 8.*Abteilung* report noted in hindsight in March 1944, after the airlifts at Demyansk, Kholm, Stalingrad, the Kuban and Cherkassy/Korsun, 'Air transport is *a decisive factor* [author italics] in cases where encircled troops must be supplied . . .'[31]

This, in principle, was true, but only if certain operational criteria and conditions were applied – and only if there was cooperation and understanding between the forces on the ground and the air forces attempting to render them assistance. Which begs the question, did the Luftwaffe and military *high command* learn and understand this from the events at Demyansk and Kholm and, therefore, appreciate its importance and potential influence in late 1942?

This was the prevailing situation that existed between the Luftwaffe transport arm and the agencies of the *Heer* when German forces launched Operation *Blau* in June 1942.

5

'The Great Day'

'In the OKH, and in the OKW Operations Staff, we were still waiting
for a real great victory; it seemed to us that the enemy had still nowhere
been brought to a battle, as the small number of prisoners and the small
amount of captured equipment proved.'

WALTER WARLIMONT, *INSIDE HITLER'S*
HEADQUARTERS, 1964

*The Russian army is a wall which, however far it may retreat, you will
always find in front of you.*

ANTOINE HENRI JOMINI, 1854

In the mid-morning of 20 July 1942, a group of officers clad in the blue-grey
uniform of the Luftwaffe gathered expectantly at the edge of an airfield near
Mariupol on the Sea of Azov in south-eastern Ukraine. As was usual over
the Steppe by this time of day, the temperature had started to climb into the
mid-twenties – uncomfortable for tight-fitting uniforms, caps, fastened collars,
medals, belts, sidearm holsters and polished leather boots, let alone the gleaming
instruments held by the helmeted soldiers of the military band lined up a short
distance behind the officers. At one point, the men's murmured conversation
was interrupted by a noise; distant, like that of a buzzing bee. Collectively, they
cast their eyes up into the cloudless azure sky, searching, squinting and shielding
their vision from the glare of the sun. And like a bee, a small dot appeared over
the horizon, approaching from the west.[1]

A few minutes later, a lone, single-engined Messerschmitt Bf 108 touched
down and taxied to a stop, trailing a small cloud of dust. As the aircraft's Argus
engine and two-bladed propeller coughed to a stop, a junior staff officer hurried
forward and assisted the two occupants of the aircraft with unfastening the
machine's canopy. As it yawned forward and open, one of the occupants, also
wearing a Luftwaffe uniform, stood up, briskly climbed out of the cockpit and
jumped expertly from the wing down to the ground. The staff officer came to

attention and saluted as the brass band struck up a fanfare to commemorate the arrival of the new commander of *Luftflotte* 4.

Generaloberst Dr.-Ing. Wolfram Freiherr von Richthofen was a muscular, bull-necked man with a craggy, weathered face tanned to the shade of shoe leather and a skull crowned with reddish-grey cropped bristle that made him appear older than his 47 years. He tugged on his cap and strode over to shake hands with Generalmajor Günther Korten, the Chief of Staff of *Luftflotte* 4, who then introduced him to the other staff officers waiting in line to meet their new commander. If there was any sense of anxiety among the assembled officers as they shook von Richthofen's gloved hand and looked into his slate grey eyes, it was understandable. The Generaloberst had a formidable reputation, something that was accentuated by the Knight's Cross with Oak Leaves that dangled from his shirt collar.

Von Richthofen's appointment as successor to the Austrian Generaloberst Alexander Löhr as fleet commander may have caused little surprise but probably considerable trepidation among the fleet's staff. Although he bore the same illustrious family name of Manfred von Richthofen, the famed 'Red Baron', to whom he was a cousin, there was no doubt that Wolfram had ambitiously and, it is fair to say, ruthlessly carved his own successful career.

Born on a family estate in Silesia on 10 October 1895, von Richthofen had served as a cavalry officer on the Western and Eastern Fronts during World War I before learning to fly and joining his cousin Manfred's famed *Jagdgeschwader* I in France in April 1918, with which he flew the Fokker Dr I Triplane. He was credited with eight aerial victories over the Western Front. With an avid interest since boyhood in engines, mechanisation and aircraft construction during the inter-war years, von Richthofen graduated with a Doctorate in engineering in February 1929 while simultaneously serving with the Reichswehr. Two months later the Reichswehr sent him on a semi-covert assignment to Fascist Italy for three years, where he studied advances in Italian aviation and learned to speak the language fluently while reporting diligently to Berlin on what he had observed and learned in Rome and elsewhere.

Returning to Germany, von Richthofen joined the Technical Office of the embryonic RLM and worked on a number of projects including engine and rocket development, the early development of the aircraft and rocket testing centre at Peenemünde, and the pros and cons of dive-bombing and dive-bomber aircraft.

Von Richthofen developed a dichotomous personality. Outwardly, he possessed the easy and confident charm of his social class, as well as a sense of humour, and he delighted in the music of Beethoven, was an avid diarist and reader, spoke at least four languages, was a crack shot, a competent sporting pilot and a fast driver. He was also, in modern parlance, a workaholic. Yet he could be abrasive, lacking in sentiment, blunt, outspoken, quick-tempered and sharp-tongued to those who irritated him; and although a man who took regular and rigorous exercise, he was a chain smoker and suffered from lung problems even at a relatively young age.

By April 1936, as a result of a combination of intelligence, diligence and ambition, he had attained the rank of Oberstleutnant within the RLM, but his abrasiveness led him to clash with the new head of the Technical Office – and thus his immediate superior – the eminent and renowned former World War I fighter ace, Oberst Ernst Udet. Von Richthofen disliked Udet's flamboyance, and he was initially vehemently opposed to his views on dive-bombing.

German involvement in the Spanish Civil War provided von Richthofen with a convenient exit from the ministry corridors and led, in early November 1936, to him being appointed as commander of the development and testing *Kommando* of the *Legion Condor*, the air arm deployed to Spain by the Luftwaffe to support Nationalist forces. He learned much in Spain and would end the war as the *Legion's* commander. He also became a firm convert to dive-bombing and, in particular, the capability of the Ju 87.

The war in Spain marked the beginning of a singularly destructive military track record which saw von Richthofen, to put it crudely, bombing his way around Europe. However, he was not crude in his application of bombing in its various guises, whether it be high-level, low-level, dive-bombing or battlefield close-support, and he demonstrated tactical success time and again in Spain, Poland, Belgium, France, the Balkans and in Russia through an understanding of its principles and limitations. His post-war reputation is marred, however, as a result of his involvement with the infamous raids on Guernica, Warsaw and Rotterdam – but to von Richthofen, he was simply doing his job, and doing it as effectively as possible.

In July 1939 he was appointed the *Fliegerführer z.b.V.*. This was a specialist dive-bombing and ground-attack tactical command formation made up primarily of Ju 87 Stuka units that saw action in Poland, mainly rendering battlefield support to German ground forces. After the campaign in Poland the *Fliegerführer z.b.V.* was redesignated and expanded as VIII.*Fliegerkorps*. It was as commander of this formation, again comprised mainly of Ju 87 units augmented by fighter, *Zerstörer* and bomber *Gruppen*, that von Richthofen developed a reputation as a first-class tactician in close-support. He deployed his aircraft to effect during the German invasion of the West in 1940, over Dunkirk, the Balkans, Crete and in the northern and central sectors of the Eastern Front in the first year of *Barbarossa*, his Stukas being relied upon by the Wehrmacht to strike at transport, troop assembly, road and rail targets, bridges and strongpoints just behind enemy lines. The Ju 87s were used to pave a safer path for the Panzers in their spearhead breakthroughs.

Von Richthofen's distinctive – even exceptional – style, which he developed in Spain, was to lead from the front by establishing forward command posts as close to a bomb line as possible so that he could personally observe the effect of his air units against enemy positions. He also placed emphasis on efficient communications with the commanders of the ground forces which he was supporting. More recently, during May–June 1942, von Richthofen had developed a very effective air-ground partnership with Generaloberst Erich von Manstein, commander of 11.*Armee*, resulting in VIII.*Fliegerkorps* being deployed over the Crimea in support of successful operations against the port city of Sevastopol. To many army commanders, the *Korps* became known informally as 'the fire brigade' because of its numerous transfers to hotspots, or as von Richthofen's 'battering ram' on account of its style of deployment.

But when the more considered Generaloberst Alexander Löhr was moved from *Luftflotte* 4 to take over – unusually for a Luftwaffe officer – the 12.*Armee* in the eastern Mediterranean, von Richthofen's arrival from VIII.*Fliegerkorps* and his forceful personality would be felt throughout the Staff and the Fleet's component units. One former senior Luftwaffe staff officer who served under von Richthofen recalled:

> He possessed considerable military and technical knowledge in matters concerning the deployment of the Luftwaffe in support of the army. He was impressively clear and objective in his views on tactics and operational concerns of army leaders. He was, certainly, the only Luftwaffe commander who had the necessary qualities to influence generals, army commands and the senior army leadership, and as a result, not insignificantly influenced army fighting doctrine in accordance with his beliefs. He believed his perception to be the only correct one. He did not deviate from this outlook. But he saw Luftwaffe tactical operational support for the army as a basis for strategy. His way of thinking and his determination were geared solely to what was purposeful, and he ruthlessly and indifferently took advantage of people and had them replaced when they did not fit into goals he set for himself.[2]

Upon arrival at Mariupol, von Richthofen wasted no time in heading to *Luftflotte* 4's headquarters, which was housed in a large school in what he described as 'an awful industrial area' some way from the coast. Once there, he was briefed by Korten and other key members of the staff, including the Fleet's operations officer, Oberstleutnant Karl-Heinrich Schulz, who would play a key role in the coming airlift to Stalingrad, and who von Richthofen described as 'a very good man' – from von Richthofen, that could be considered high praise. Evidently von Richthofen made an impression: 'I must have a very bad reputation; everyone here is afraid! Well, so what? They have all become so tired that I shall not be able to restrain my temper for too long'.[3] Writing of von Richthofen in a post-war study, for his part Schulz described him as 'a man of remarkable personality and very violent views which he forced into practical application'.[4]

The structure of *Luftflotte* 4 remained much the same as has been described in Chapter Three, with General der Flieger Pflugbeil's IV.*Fliegerkorps* still assigned, along with von Richthofen's former VIII.*Fliegerkorps*, now under the command of Generalleutnant Martin Fiebig – both officers with whom von Richthofen enjoyed good working relationships. These men had been clear on their objectives since the instructions issued in Hitler's Directive 41 – that if a Soviet concentration was detected, it was the job of the Luftwaffe to bring 'the principal roads and railways leading to the battle area under constant attack well into the rear area. To this end, the first priority will be to direct destructive attacks against the railway bridges across the Don'. Furthermore, 'At the commencement of the operation (*Blau*), the enemy Air Force and its ground organisation in the zone of battle are to be attacked and destroyed with the concentration of all available forces'.[5]

The challenge for von Richthofen was that since Hitler's planning for *Blau* in the spring and the subsequent opening of the offensive, as well as the air operations conducted against Sevastopol, *Luftflotte* 4's serviceable strength had declined considerably to 718 combat aircraft, as reported on the day he took command. This figure comprised 212 bombers, 136 fighters, 118 tactical reconnaissance aircraft, 86 *Zerstörer*, 86 Ju 87s, 44 strategic reconnaissance aircraft and 36 ground-attack machines. This represented a 45 per cent decrease when compared to the previous month.[6] Not only that, but the operational area to be covered by *Luftflotte* 4 was vast, stretching the entire length of the Caucasus to Batumi, on the Black Sea, east along the Russo-Turkish border towards the Caspian Sea and north as far as Saratov on the Volga.[7]

In terms of reconnaissance alone, *Luftflotte* 4 was expected to cover Transcaucasia, the Caspian coasts, the Ural River, Saratov, the Volga region to its estuary, the Don region, the Kalmyck steppes north of the Caucasus, and the Black Sea.[8] Furthermore, shortly after assuming command, von Richthofen had to oversee air support for the drive on Rostov, the city at the gateway to the Caucasus, as well as preventing the Russians from building a defensive line on the Don.[9] Such multiple tasks would require great mobility on the part of *Luftflotte* 4's air and support units in order to maintain maximum force strength in the battle areas, and this would need a commander of the calibre of von Richthofen.[10] But even before he could deploy his first aircraft against Rostov, decisions taken elsewhere in Ukraine would influence strategy and outcome.

★   ★   ★

Some 850 km north-west from Mariupol, in a humid pine forest eight kilometres north of Vinnytsia in central Ukraine, Adolf Hitler brooded at his new eastern field headquarters. Retaining the somewhat melodramatic lupine theme, this compound was codenamed *Werwolf* and comprised a collection of rustic wooden buildings and two low bunkers complemented by a 'swimming pool' (in reality a concrete cistern for storing water in case of fire, and apparently never used on account of the water's cold temperature despite the summer heat), a cinema, a sauna, a barber's facility and the obligatory teahouse.[11]

The *Führer* had arrived there, for the first time, with his entire staff in 16 aircraft early on the morning of 16 July, four days before von Richthofen had reached Mariupol. Hitler did not enjoy his stay at Vinnytsia and he was edgy. He struggled with the cloying summer heat which, according to Field Marshal Keitel, he 'could not stand', as well as the oppressive surroundings of the forest. This was nothing like the clear air and breathtaking mountain scenery of Berchtesgaden, his Alpine lair; he even longed for the *Wolfschanze*. The humidity made the wooden cabins damp, and at night the temperature plummeted and the air became icy. Hitler was plagued by headaches, and his frame of mind and temperament suffered accordingly. 'Medicaments were useless against it', wrote Keitel, 'and in the conference chamber only temporarily alleviated his discomfort'.[12] As men like Keitel and Jodl, who formed part of Hitler's close-knit circle of military 'advisers', knew all too well, the atmosphere in the conference chamber could be akin to an intense battle that could be fought but not won.

Throughout the summer, the fluid, fast-moving situation in southern Russia preyed on the dictator, gnawing at his thoughts. He remained uncertain about Stalingrad: he *wanted* to take the city after securing the land-bridge between the Don and the Volga, but if that was not possible he would accept an advance to the Volga south of the city, provided enemy shipping from the Caspian Sea could be blocked.[13] As Generalmajor Wolfgang Pickert, who would be the senior Luftwaffe officer in the Stalingrad *Kessel*, pointed out in a post-war article, 'one of the most important reasons for the German offensive towards Stalingrad' was to stop the 'all-important' Volga River traffic, especially grain and shipments of oil from Baku.[14]

For their part, the higher Soviet government and military authorities had also slowly come to understand the significance of Stalingrad as a centre of industry, as well as a vital transport hub, and thus the potential for a German strike there. The origins of Stalingrad stretched back 500 years before the war when a Tatar fortress and trading settlement were established on the banks of the Volga. The place had seen occupation by Cossacks and Tsars, and it was known originally, before the Revolution, as Tsaritsyn. It had been renamed Stalingrad on account of the fact that Josef Stalin had led Bolshevik forces there during the Civil War, when it was taken by both Reds and Whites. As a town, it was nothing particularly remarkable, acting as a regional administrative centre with a population of just under 500,000 people and stretching out for some 20 km along the river.[15]

But Soviet leaders had only to consider recent history: the logistical importance of the Volga was proven during World War I, when it was clear that the Russian railways had inadequate capacity to carry oil and grain, especially when the Caucasus railways became insufficient to carry just military traffic to support Russian forces fighting the Ottoman Empire. Additionally, coal from the Donbass mining region in southern Ukraine was a vital northbound commodity, and some was moved by barge from Sarepta to the south of Stalingrad. Later, in November 1941, when the Germans managed to cut the Caucasus oil pipeline, the Stalingrad–Tikhoretskaia rail route was the only one left functioning, and thus, once again, the Volga became vital for shipments of oil and grain during the navigation season. By the late summer of 1942, a priority for the Soviet regime was to maintain supplies of food for the Red Army and to keep the flow of oil from Baku moving.[16] The Volga was also a 'meteorological frontier', marking the meeting point of cold air from Siberia and the steppes of Asia with warmer, moister air from the Black and Caspian Seas.[17]

The Red Army duly reinforced the area around Stalingrad, and from 20 July a state of emergency was declared. If one official Soviet account of the city just prior to the German onslaught is to be believed, this development must have come as something of a shock:

> Stalingrad was leading a productive life, all too peaceful a life it seemed. Plants, enterprises and institutions were operating. All movie houses were open, children played in the squares and on the boulevards, and the loudspeakers blared music and at certain times summaries from the front. The city was brim full of citizens from various regions of the southern part of the country. Everyone had found housing and settled in. The public food supply was good. None of Stalingrad's residents had any idea at that time that a terrible threat was already hanging over the city.[18]

And yet a concerted effort had been made by the regional military committee and the population to prepare for its defence. Some 200,000 men and women between the ages of 16 and 65 were mobilised into 'workers columns' by local Communist Party authorities. Equipped with shovels, women and teenagers set about digging bunkers, anti-tank ditches and anti-aircraft gun emplacements, while children, supervised by their teachers, constructed protective earth walls around petrol storage tanks. Troops laid mines along the western edge of the city and the air defences were strengthened, while the evacuation of certain key industries, food supplies and livestock was intensified.[19]

This being said, as early as 16 July Halder envisaged that a 'battle of Stalingrad' might have to be fought simultaneously to operations at and around Rostov. In any case, Halder noted, 'we must expect that the enemy will use every available means to hold Stalingrad'.[20] Assigned – alone – the task of taking Stalingrad was Paulus' 6.*Armee*, which had been reinforced by XIV.*Panzerkorps* and LI.*Armeekorps*. This assignment may have seemed a practical proposition in the wooden buildings at the *Werwolf* compound, but the reality for 6.*Armee* was that it would have to fight its way into a city held by a determined defence, occupy it securely, then block the land-bridge between the Don and the Volga, as well as the Don itself, while the remainder of *Heeresgruppe* B, formed of German, Hungarian and Italian formations, would 'play a static role' to cover the *Armee's* lengthening flank as it moved eastwards.[21]

On the 21st, in his Directive 44, Hitler, outwardly at least, broadcast confidence over the 'unexpectedly rapid and favourable development of operations' which:

> . . . entitle us to assume that we may soon succeed in depriving Soviet Russia of the Caucasus with her most important source of oil, and of a valuable line of communications for the delivery of English supplies. This, coupled with the loss of the entire Donets industrial area, will strike a blow at the Soviet Union which could have immeasurable consequences.[22]

For the troops on the ground, the push across the endless, featureless Don steppe in late July was thankless and exhausting. A member of the 384. *Infanterie-Division* described how:

> On this steppe, which was only broken up by deep, narrow ravines (*Balkas*), there were no forests to give protection from aircraft and, above all, no water for the men and horses. After a couple of rainless days, what was called a road was covered by a thick layer of dust that was stirred up by each vehicle and lay over the marching infantry like a heavy impenetrable cloud. The lips chapped and the faces were covered with a dust as if the men had painted them grey. Every now and then, a little green would put off our miserable dust-grey existences. It's been a long time since we had shelter from the open. The last ones were, at best, a pair of mud huts.[23]

Supporting the ground troops as best they could were several Luftwaffe transport *Gruppen*, including KGr.z.b.V.5 under Hauptmann Fritz Uhl. Since its formation at Fassberg in 1938, this *Gruppe* had been equipped with both Ju 52/3m and He 111 transports, but in April 1942 it had given up its Junkers tri-motors in favour of the adapted Heinkel. The *Gruppe* had left the Reich in mid-July and had relocated to Kharkov-Rogan in support of *Blau*. Oberleutnant Rudolf Müller was the unit's Technical Officer:

> Kharkov was a medium-sized city with many modern high-rise buildings. We only saw them from the air while flying over them during take-off and landing. The high-rises were built around 'Red Square', although it was actually circular, and they looked spooky because they were empty, and some were burned out. Our airfield had few permanent structures and was in the east of the city, surrounded by corn and sunflower fields. Most of the time we lived in tents or in bunkers dug into the ground. There were an awful lot of mice. If you took off your uniform overnight, you had to shake it out vigorously the next morning. Quite a few mice would fall out. We wrapped ourselves up in sleeping bags and had mosquito nets over our faces so that we could sleep more or less free from these pests.
>
> Our task was to fly equipment and ammunition, mainly 25-kg bombs, to the combat units further ahead. Our aircraft were spread out wide around the airfield. In order to reach them quickly, I had a BMW 500 sidecar combination. It was my first motorcycle. With an inspector and a mechanic, I would drive to every machine that landed in order to make sure it was ready for immediate use. Since, from time to time, there were some distant, off-field landings on the vast Ukrainian steppe, the *Gruppe* also had a Fieseler Storch. Sometimes we had to search laboriously for an aircraft which had made an emergency landing. Most of the time, aircraft remained undamaged from such landings.[24]

Down on the 'vast steppe', one corps commander described the weather as being 'as hot as Africa' and his Chief of Staff noted the temperature reaching 53°C.[25] But when the heat of the day ebbed away, others found a beauty on the steppe, including Oberst Wilhelm Adam, a staff officer at Headquarters, 6.*Armee*:

> I have seldom experienced such beautiful sunsets as we did here. The whole steppe seemed to glow. The air was filled with aromatic scents. There was life in the tall grass; crickets chirped, mice whistled, birds sang their evening songs. Then the night covered everything in deep silence.[26]

Rostov was on the point of being taken by *Heeresgruppe* A on 23 July – the day that, based on the erroneous assumption that his objectives in southern Russia had 'largely been achieved', Hitler took what is considered to be the monumentally catastrophic and strategically flawed decision to split the offensive momentum into two divergent thrusts. This would have the effect of extending the length of the front from 800 km at the beginning of the summer to 4,100 km at the eventual completion of operations.

Under the codename *Edelweiss*, *Heeresgruppe* A would be given the main task of destroying enemy forces south of the Don and then to advance along the eastern coastline of the Black Sea supported by what forces could be mustered from von Manstein's tired 11.*Armee*. Under the codename *Fischreiher* ('Heron'), *Heeresgruppe* B meanwhile, led by Generaloberst Maximilian von Weichs from 13 July, would establish a defensive line along the Don to cover *Heeresgruppe* A, to eliminate any enemy forces grouping at Stalingrad (which proved Halder's predictions to be correct), to take the city and to prohibit enemy land communication between the Don and the Volga. The problem with this was that in order for *Heeresgruppe* A to be successful in its objectives, *Heeresgruppe* B would have to be weakened. Furthermore, such measures meant that the reinforcement cupboard would be empty for 6.*Armee* in its drive to Stalingrad.[27] Already, *Heeresgruppe* A had most of the available mobile forces, which meant that *Heeresgruppe* B was disadvantaged.[28] Indeed, as Oberst Adam of 6.*Armee* noted, 'our already recorded losses had in no way been sufficiently replaced to meet such an extensive task'.[29]

Halder worried that this mish-mash of aims, along with the dissipation of any main thrust, was simply too much for German forces in southern Russia, spread, as they were, across such a vast tract of territory, along with the logistics challenges that would ensue. Generalfeldmarschall Wilhelm List, the commander of *Heeresgruppe* A, had already warned him that as a result of diverting forces from his army group to reinforce Paulus' advance to Stalingrad, it would be a 'great gamble' to send a weaker force deep into the Caucasus.[30]

Generalmajor Hans-Detlef Herhudt von Rohden of the Luftwaffe's Military Science Branch has summarised that:

> The aims of both offensives were fundamentally different. That of Stalingrad was directed, in the sense of a *Vernichtungsstrategie*, against the military might of the enemy, to continue to contain and destroy the Russians. Whether

this could be achieved, following the capture of Stalingrad, in a massive operation between the Volga-Don area and Moscow is questionable.

Also that:

The underlying notion of this operation extended, in its presumptuous vehemence, far beyond the gaining of oil at Maikop, Grozny and Baku. It overestimated considerably the existing capabilities of the Luftwaffe and the motorised and Panzer forces of the *Heer* for later making an effective advance to the Near East. The principal goal, most certainly, with the *Anschluss* that would take place of Persia and Turkey to the Axis was to turn this into an annihilating thrust through Iraq to Cairo. It will remain unfathomable how it had become possible that a military leadership paid no heed to proven concepts from past German military history, carrying out plans which, criminally, took no account of actual conditions.[31]

Halder appealed to Hitler to delay the move into the Caucasus until Stalingrad had been taken and the rear of the advance could be secured. In this he failed, no thanks to Keitel and Jodl who gave little support. Indeed, the tense atmosphere at *Werwolf* became further strained, and Hitler, unhappy at having his grasp of strategy questioned, lost his composure at Halder, who, concerned over the bottleneck of armour around Rostov with 'nothing to do', recounted on 23 July:

. . . he explodes in a fit of insane rage and hurls the gravest reproaches at the General Staff. This chronic tendency to underrate enemy capabilities is gradually assuming grotesque proportions and develops into a positive danger. The situation is getting more and more intolerable.[32]

Halder's concerns over Rostov do not seem to have been shared by von Richthofen. The same day that the Chief of Staff of the OKH was being berated by Hitler, in an example of his strategic awareness, and as a priority, von Richthofen met with Oberst Morzik at Mariupol to discuss the latest air transport situation. Despite their differing social backgrounds, von Richthofen and Morzik shared common ground – both men had flown in the last war and both were competitive inter-war sports fliers with a keen interest in the development of aeronautics. Both were also frank in their opinions. As such, one can only assume the conversation was of a concerned nature.

It had now become apparent that *Luftflotte* 4 would, effectively, be carrying out three separate campaigns; firstly IV. *Fliegerkorps* would strike at Soviet forces opposing *Heeresgruppe* A while, secondly, VIII. *Fliegerkorps* supported 6.*Armee* and 4.*Panzerarmee* in their respective drives on Stalingrad, and thirdly, to the north, *Gefechtsverband Nord*, which had been formed in June, would provide support to 2.*Armee* around Voronezh.[33] Resources would be stretched. Undaunted – at least outwardly – von Richthofen also attended to paperwork, but he was buoyed by reports on the accomplishments of his bomber units in the assault on Rostov. He noted in his diary:

> IV. *Fliegerkorps* hammers away continuously at the most concentrated enemy forces. Our spearheads are approaching the city from the north-east. The *Grossdeutschland* is already advancing eastwards to the Don. The 3. *Panzer*, against expectations and without orders, advances to the south; they meet with hardly any resistance and advance 30 km to the Don and establish a bridgehead over the nearest river. That's <u>very</u> good.[34]

The same day, in the area of VIII. *Fliegerkorps*, elements of *Stukageschwader* (St.G) 2, commanded by veteran Stuka pilot Major Paul-Werner Hozzel, flew into Tatsinskaya from Akhtyrka, where the unit's Ju 87s had been flying close-support sorties around Voronezh. Hozzel recorded of this heady period:

> We had been flying sorties again and again, day after day, from morning to night, ahead of our armoured divisions which were advancing rapidly to the south, keeping in constant contact with them by radio. The turrets of our own tanks were covered in black, white and red cloth so that we could, at any time, easily spot our spearhead units. The German divisions advanced so rapidly in pursuit of the enemy retreating into the depths of his vast space that the *Geschwader* had to transfer by jumps as far as 300 km or more from one airfield to another. We had to keep on the heels of the Soviet forces. After flying across fields of grain, covering hundreds of kilometres of fertile Ukrainian soil, we soon reached the Rostov area with the mouth of the Don river flowing into the Sea of Azov. Our targets were transport columns, freight trains, railway junctions, bridges and any movement detected in the enemy rear. It was our aim to give the enemy no rest by day and at night. We had fine, mid-summer weather, hot and dry.[35]

Following *Luftflotte* 4's successful operations around Rostov, von Richthofen's units were next to ensure 'the early destruction of the city of Stalingrad', and also to undertake attacks on Astrakhan and shipping on the Volga.

However, as early as the 26th, 6. *Armee* began to feel the inadequacy of supplies as a result of the decision to make a split/dual attack towards the Volga and the Caucasus. The *Armee* had been getting low on fuel and ammunition for two days, and there was no assurance from the Army Group of any deliveries for several days to come, so Paulus was compelled to pull back his spearheads from the Kalach area since half his daily supply tonnage was going to *Heeresgruppe* A.[36] The relentless advance also made care for sick and wounded men difficult, especially since virtually all available Ju 52/3m transports had been diverted to fly fuel for the Panzer units which had run dry.[37]

Indeed, the demand for transport space was almost unquenchable; at the end of July, the Ju 87s of St.G 2 had transferred from Tatsinskaya to Oblivskaya, on the Chir River, 170 km west of Stalingrad. The airfield at Oblivskaya offered wooden and earth revetments for the aircraft, bunkers for aircrew and ground personnel, a field repair hangar capable of replacing engines and other parts quickly and a signals communications unit, while the operational battle headquarters for the *Geschwader* and its *Gruppen* were housed in an assortment of converted buses and tents, the latter pitched behind splinter-proof walls. From here, St.G 2 prepared itself for operations against Soviet forces around Kalach, between the Don and the Volga and over Stalingrad. The *Geschwaderkommodore*, Major Hozzel, placed considerable importance on supplies and logistics in order to keep his unit operationally ready:

> Spare parts for engines and airframes reached us by Ju 52 transport units. Heavily damaged aircraft were dismantled on the spot, loaded into Ju 52s and flown home for repair. Ammunition of all calibres, including incendiary bombs and aviation fuel, were transported as far as possible by rail, then taken from the terminal by trucks and in road tankers to the airfield. Before the 6.*Armee* was encircled, there were no logistics problems at all. We had all we needed, although some of the supply lines were disrupted by partisan groups operating in our rear. The whole logistics organisation was an admirable feat of the quartermaster generals of the army groups, of the field armies and of the Luftwaffe.
>
> I personally think it necessary that no general staff officer should become a chief of staff of any high headquarters unless he has become familiar, at least for a certain period, with the duties of a quartermaster. By following such advice, headquarters would be saved from the catastrophic misjudgements over logistics and of existing possibilities as we would experience at Stalingrad later.[38]

As von Richthofen directed his air units from his headquarters at Mariupol, in the forested compound at Vinnytsia, Jodl announced solemnly at a situation conference on the 30th that the outcome of operations in the Caucasus would be decided at Stalingrad. As such, it would be necessary for *Heeresgruppe* A to now surrender some of its strength to 6.*Armee*. 'This is a dressed-up version of my own proposal', Halder penned in his diary, 'which I submitted to the *Führer* six days ago when 4.*Panzerarmee* struck across the Don. At that time, though, no one in the illustrious company of the OKW seemed to be able to grasp its significance'.[39]

On 31 July, Hitler intervened yet again, his focus now directed at Stalingrad. He remained convinced that while the enemy's railway link between the city and the Caucasus had been cut, thus hampering his overland supplies of oil, the Russians would bolster their defences in the area of Stalingrad in order to keep the Volga route open. Therefore, he ordered that the bulk of Generaloberst Hermann Hoth's 4.*Panzerarmee* – headquarters and three corps – be moved north towards Stalingrad. The remainder, one corps, would stay with *Heeresgruppe* A and go south with 1.*Panzerarmee*.[40] Halder considered this the 'rankest nonsense' in view of the fact that 'the enemy is running for dear life and will be in the northern foothills of the Caucasus a good piece ahead of our armour'.[41]

Despite the disagreements, by the end of July, the German advances had been almost as rapid as those of the 1941 offensives. Three main thrusts continued their momentum: eastwards towards the middle Don and Stalingrad, south-eastwards across the Don towards the Stalingrad-Tikhoretsk railway and south-westwards over the same river around Rostov.[42]

In the sky above the battlefields, Luftwaffe fighters bounced Soviet aircraft attacking German ground targets, attracting cheers and grateful waves from Wehrmacht troops below.[43] On the 27th, the OKL issued an appraisal based on von Richthofen's optimism on the state of the *Voyenno-Vozdushnyye Sily* (VVS) in the area of 6.*Armee*:

> The enemy appears in large numbers. Our fighters are able to score substantially. The commander of *Luftflotte* 4 reports a considerable drop in the quality of the Russian airmen. According to this report, our fighter pilots encounter no serious opposition in air combat. It is only a matter of catching the enemy, and when this is done, our fighter pilots are able to shoot down large numbers of Russian aircraft. Obviously, the enemy still has large quantities of materiel at his disposal, but is hampered by the low training qualities of the personnel.[44]

The day the report was issued, *Luftflotte* 4 claimed 29 enemy aircraft destroyed, but listed 19 of its own machines shot down or damaged badly in combat, while the regional Soviet air army listed just 11 aircraft lost in action.[45]

The last Soviet forces inside Rostov withdrew by nightfall on the 26th. Yet while there may have been speed and momentum to German operations, there was a sense of unease among German commanders; even as XIV.*Panzerkorps* attached to 6.*Armee* reached the Don bend near Sirotinskaya, Oberst Wilhelm Adam on the Army's staff noted how, 'yet again this was a blow into empty space. The enemy had escaped over the Don'.[46]

Oberst Wolfgang Pickert, who had only arrived in Russia a month earlier to take command of the Luftwaffe's 9.*Flak-Division* attached to 6.*Armee*, noted on 25 July, 'Rostov has fallen. Nevertheless, the sum total of operations to date does not seem adequate to me. The enemy succeeded in escaping with strong forces'.[47] And as historian Robert M. Citino points out, after the first month of the summer offensive, 'The Soviets had fled rather than face destruction, and 6th Army hadn't even gotten over the Don yet, let alone reached the Volga'.[48] Still, Stalin had already become uncomfortably aware that those Soviet forces pulling back towards and across the Don risked being destroyed, and that if the Germans were allowed to continue to the Volga, the Soviet Union could, effectively, be severed. His reaction led to his notorious slogan '*Ni Shagu Nazad!*' ('Not One Step Backwards!') as contained in Defence Order 227 which was to be distributed immediately throughout the entire Red Army. He was serious: 'panic-mongers and cowards' were to be 'destroyed' and the retreat mentality brought to a stop.[49]

The month of August would see the forces of *Heeresgruppe* B continue to advance doggedly towards Stalingrad supported by Fiebig's VIII.*Fliegerkorps*.

It was not all plain sailing. 6.*Armee*'s drive towards the city faltered due to an inadequate numbers of troops and an insufficient supply of replacement materiel. Russian resistance was also stiffening, and in places the enemy was even launching counter-attacks.[50] The tactically astute Lt Gen Vasili Chuikov, commander of the Soviet 64th Army, had recognised that German commanders and their Axis allies prepared for each attack carefully so that they took place when they could be assured of air support from *Luftflotte* 4's units. Chuikov thus attempted to use his artillery against German positions just before an attack, or to withdraw his own forces just before a German move so as to avoid the anticipated air strikes. As he recounted, 'Believing their tactics and methods to be infallible, the Germans followed exactly the same pattern here as when they had crossed the Don: air attack, then artillery, then infantry, then tanks. They did not know any other order in which to attack'. Chuikov was reasonably successful in this ruse, and it was one he would later deploy during the defence of Stalingrad.[51]

Von Richthofen was becoming increasingly conscious of the difficulties in supplies and frustrated at the splitting of his strike capability, as he expressed on the 2nd:

> 6.*Armee* is pitted against Stalingrad, but because of the strength of the enemy and especially due to the supply situation, it has ground to a halt. Unfortunately it is necessary to split up the air forces. VIII.*Fliegerkorps* has to help out 6.*Armee* at Stalingrad. They continually make attacks on roads and shipping on the Volga. IV.*Fliegerkorps* helps out Kleist and on the roads north of the Caucasus. We undertake supplies by air to 6.*Armee*.[52]

Over the coming days bombers from VIII.*Fliegerkorps* continued to focus their attacks on railways, river traffic on the Volga and enemy supply columns, while Ju 52/3ms under the control of the *Korps* flew in supplies to 6.*Armee*, although von Richthofen noted that, 'due to bad management there were serious anxieties over fuel; these will be remedied'. Nevertheless, when he flew in a Storch to visit Paulus he found him to be 'confident'.[53] Even the usually unfeeling von Richthofen noted on the 8th, 'There's terrific dust and heat; the poor infantry'.

On the 10th General Hans Jeschonnek, the Luftwaffe's Chief of General Staff, flew to Mariupol to meet with his friend von Richthofen. Over breakfast, Jeschonnek left von Richthofen in no doubt where the priority now lay. 'The absolute *Schwerpunkt* [the main point of the action] is Stalingrad and right now'.

When Paulus moved forward he did not head directly east from Kalach because of the terrain of deep gullies that would hamper progress, and which would provide the enemy with ideal defensive opportunities. Rather, he elected to drive for the north-eastern edge of the Don bend from where his army would launch his main attack from established bridgeheads. Within a week XIV. and XXIV.*Panzerkorps* had cleared the bend of enemy resistance and VIII.*Armeekorps* had secured two bridgeheads at the river bend's easternmost extent.[54]

One of von Richthofen's absolute priorities remained supply and transport for 6.*Armee*. He had managed to assemble '3,000 tonnes of transport space' by 10 August, and noted that 'supplies at Stalingrad amounting to around 10,000 tonnes are secured. They are working overtime in the depots. Premiums are being paid for transport and depot work!'[55] To this end, von Richthofen even issued orders that his bombers be brought in as emergency transports for 6.*Armee*. However, the only effective way to move supplies to the bomber bases was via the rail line through Stalino, and this could not now be used because of enemy air activity. 'It's a really difficult problem', von Richthofen admitted, because until recently it was the *only* way to keep the bombers supplied.

Five days later he flew from Mariupol to Rostov to meet with General der Flieger Albert Vierling, the commander of the Rostov administrative air region, in order to assess how the transport situation was developing. It was a tetchy affair, as von Richthofen revealed in his diary:

> The order that everything, but everything, for this big transport operation was to be brought up was clear and precise. We need, urgently, to fly almost 2,000 tonnes, but because, even by harnessing all our manpower, we <u>are able daily to send over only 1,000 tonnes or less</u>, everything must keep moving! But what did I find? In the available transport area, only about 30 per cent [of capacity] was, in fact, being utilised! Within one hour, instead of 2,000 tonnes, 5,000 tonnes of column space was set underway, the routes shortened and the ferrying speed doubled.[56]

On the 19th, orders for the main assault on Stalingrad went out from 6.*Armee* headquarters to all the Army's component command staffs. During a visit to one headquarters that day, Oberst Wilhelm Adam noticed some aerial reconnaissance photographs pinned to a wall. He was struck by how large the city was, compared with the familiar, small symbols which represented it on the large-scale maps at which he usually looked:

> It extended for more than 60 km in a four- to seven-kilometre wide strip along the western bank of the Volga. I had not realised how big it was until now. The question immediately arose: 'Will we be able to take this vast city in the first attempt off the move?'[57]

Von Richthofen wrote in his diary on the 19th, 'Stalingrad! The enemy is getting ever stronger there and determined to do battle'.[58] As a measure of the intensity of the air war over the Don at this time, that day flying their new Bf 109Gs, pilots of I./JG 53 lodged claims for 22 enemy aircraft shot down over the river bridges, with Unteroffizier Wilhelm Crinius of 3.*Staffel* claiming four. The next day, as 13 unescorted Soviet Pe-2 twin-engined bombers were shot down by Bf 109s of III./JG 3 and I./JG 53 over the crossing at Dubovyy Ovrag, near Kalach, von Richthofen flew in the Storch once again to see Paulus.[59] The two commanders agreed that the final move on Stalingrad would not take place before the 23rd.

In the early morning of 21 August, German infantry and engineers, under support from several hundred dive-bomber, ground-attack and fighter aircraft of VIII.*Fliegerkorps*, crossed the Don at Vertyachiy, north of Kalach.[60] An anxious Paulus remained hunched over his map table, smoking cigarettes, his face twitching.[61] For his preparation, von Richthofen spent much of the 21st visiting the commanders of LI., XIV. and VIII.*Armeekorps* and also the command posts of 384. and 389.*Infanterie Divisions*. He was generally unimpressed by what he saw, but felt that the Russians were much 'weaker' than he expected, and that the army 'constantly overestimated' the enemy's capabilities.

Von Richthofen also worked to set up an efficient supply infrastructure: in this regard supplies were transported by rail from the rear to hub airfields east of Rostov at Taganrog, Mariupol, Stalino and Makeyevka. VIII.*Fliegerkorps* then set up forward airfields on the steppe, behind the frontline, that allowed the air transport units to bring in supplies directly in support of the advance.[62] No fewer than nine *Gruppen* of Ju 52/3ms and an He 111 *Gruppe* that towed cargo gliders were deployed to airlift supplies to air and ground forces on the Don. Morzik states that the air transport units delivered 33,397 tons of supplies for the Luftwaffe comprising 9,492.6 tons of bombs and aircraft ammunition, 20,173 tons of aviation fuel and 3,731.8 tons of spare parts and equipment, while the army received 9,233.4 tons, including 1,787.8 tons of ammunition, 4,615.6 tons of fuel and 2,830 tons of equipment, as well as 27,055 troops. Another 51,018 wounded men were evacuated.[63]

Von Richthofen also called in more Ju 87s from I./St.G 77 based to the south to assist in paving the way for 6.*Armee*. This *Gruppe* flew into Oblivskaya from Kerch, where, for a brief period, it joined St.G 2. Hauptmann Herbert Pabst was assigned temporarily to the *Gruppe* at this time as its *Kommandeur*.

> I have been put in temporary charge of a *Gruppe*. When I land here I find some old friends who will be easy to work with. Our tents are close to the aircraft among bare, low sand dunes. Mine stands a little apart. Furnishings: a lean-looking kitbag, a briefcase, my accordion, a telephone. The telephone is the worst; it often wakes me during the night. Our usual time for being woken is between two o'clock and half past in the morning.
>
> The terrain we're flying over is unutterably desolate, with flat, limitless sand, steep, plunging gorges and dry river beds right as far as the Volga, which can be seen meandering uncertainly between white, sandy banks. I'm tired from today's sorties and am going to blow the candle out. 2200 hrs.[64]

By late on 22 August, elements of 6.*Armee* were in bridgehead positions east of the Don and resisting strong Soviet counter-attacks against VIII.*Armeekorps* east of Akatov.[65]

Then, on the 23rd, amidst all the progress, the dust and the euphoria of the generals, there was a portentous hitch. The three divisions of General Gustav von Wietersheim's XIV.*Panzerkorps* had advanced 60 km during the course of the day in the territory between the Don and the Volga, where, at that point, the two rivers lay only 58 km apart. Elements from the *Korps* reached the northern outskirts of Stalingrad, but almost inadvertently they became surrounded and isolated by a Soviet counter-attack. 16.*Panzer-Division* together with a regiment from 9.*Flak-Division* had by this time consumed most of their fuel and supplies as they pressed forward to gain ground. Thus they adopted a series of *Igelstellung* ('hedgehog' defensive circles) and promptly turned to the Luftwaffe to air-drop supplies, which was duly arranged. During the night of 24–25 August, after urgent requests from 16.*Panzer*'s one-armed commander, Generalleutnant Hans-Valentin Hube, supplies were dropped, but the parachuted crates fell beyond the German lines. Hube acted quickly and addressed his regimental and staff officers:

> The shortage of ammo and fuel is such that our only chance is to break through to the west. I absolutely refuse to fight a pointless battle that must end in the annihilation of my troops, and I therefore order a breakout to the west. I shall personally take responsibility for this order, and will know how to justify it in the proper quarters. I absolve you, gentlemen, from your oath of loyalty, and I leave you the choice of either leading your men in this action or of handing over your commands to other officers who are prepared to do so. It is impossible to hold our positions without ammunition. I am acting contrary to the *Führer*'s orders.

Fortunately, any fears Hube and his fellow officers may have harboured were allayed when they were relieved by a German battle group with tanks and motorised support. Nevertheless, this incident served to illustrate how quickly an advanced spearhead could become surrounded and cut off, as well as the unreliability of air-drops even in good, clear weather.[66]

Meanwhile, as the tanks and vehicles of Hoth's 4.*Panzerarmee* only managed to stutter forward to the south because of a shortage of fuel and ammunition, 6.*Armee*'s great push on Stalingrad from the Akatov and Vertiachii bridgeheads commenced – 120 Panzers and more than 200 other armoured vehicles raced across the dry grasslands of the steppe, trailing great clouds of dust.[67] In support, from dawn, *Luftflotte* 4 launched massive strikes on the city, led by Fiebig's VIII.*Fliegerkorps*, which, in the words of one historian, had become, to all intents and purposes 'Sixth Army's air support command'.[68] Fiebig's units flew 1,600 sorties and dropped 1,000 tons of bombs, including many incendiaries, which represented a scale of effort greater than that deployed in support of operations against Sevastopol, which had been regarded by von Richthofen as a 'tough nut to crack'. He described the 23rd in his diary as 'The Great Day', and he rose early to be in the Don area, from where he watched the first stage of the advance. Von Richthofen then flew to the forward command post of 16.*Panzer-Division* to watch proceedings with the divisional commander, General Hube. Typically, he 'urged' Hube to 'accelerate' his advance. Indeed, German vehicles and men moved forward just metres behind the Luftwaffe bombardment, feeling the effects of showers of shrapnel and blast.[69] Von Richthofen committed virtually his entire *Luftflotte* to supporting 6.*Armee*'s drive on the Volga, which had been reached by 1600 hrs.

Hauptmann Herbert Pabst of I./St.G 77 flew several sorties that day:

> Again and again, since early this morning, we have been out over the spearhead of tanks to help them forwards with bombs and machine gun attacks. Land . . . refuel . . . sling bombs . . . refill ammunition belts . . . take off. There has been plenty of action and the advance is going well. As we flew up, we met other aircraft coming away.
>
> On one occasion I was caught by a gaggle of Russian fighters. I had already emptied my guns against ground targets and Woletz's rear gun had jammed. They fell on us – three against one. One of them stuck to my tail – I could see the flashes from the barrel of his machine gun as he fired. An instinct for self-preservation made me throw the aircraft into a tight turn and I got away without a single hit.
>
> I flew back low along the road marking our line of advance. The cornfields and steppe on either side were burning for some kilometres and column after column of troops and armour were rolling eastwards enveloped in huge clouds of dust, while bunches of prisoners without any guard were trotting towards the west. It was an unforgettable picture of war.[70]

At around 1600 hrs, soldiers from 16.*Panzer-Division* reached Rynok, just to the north of Stalingrad. Directly in front of them flowed the great river. Many of them blinked in weary disbelief. One soldier recalled:

> We were on the Volga. The first tank stood on the dominant west bank of the Volga. Quietly and majestically, the wide black stream flowed below, barges drifted downstream, the Asiatic steppes extended endlessly, proud and open, and a look of amazement covered the faces of the men.[71]

As evening fell, in the sky above the burning city, a formation of Bf 109F fighters from II./JG 3 based at Tusow headed out to escort bombers undertaking another attack on central Stalingrad. It was to be their last mission before returning to the Reich the next day, where the *Gruppe* was to begin conversion to the improved Bf 109G variant. Participating in the mission was 22-year-old Unteroffizier Kurt Ebener, a member of 4.*Staffel*, who had been credited with 14 aerial victories. At one point Ebener and his wingman banked their Messerschmitts low over the Volga just to the north of the city, and as they turned back to the west they saw below them waves of advancing German tanks and infantry:

> Now the objective, towards which our operations have been aimed for months, is within our grasp. We already know that our II.*Gruppe* will be relocated back to Germany the next day for re-equipping with new machines. Therefore, on our last flight on the evening of 23 August, we are

pleased to be able to pass over the armoured spearhead, and in low-level flight over the burning steppe, we see the first ground troops have finally penetrated the northern districts of Stalingrad. The exuberant joy and gratitude of our comrades below us are what inspire us to carry out victory rolls over the advancing divisions on the flight back to Tusow.[72]

A soldier from 389.*Infanterie-Division* wrote in a letter home, 'What a feeling of security we get when our pilots are above us, because you never see any Russian aircraft.'[73]

The next day, the ground and air assault on the city continued. Von Richthofen sent in wave after wave of Stukas and close-support aircraft. He observed 'huge fires'. On the 25th, von Richthofen's aircraft kept up the pressure. Hauptmann Herbert Pabst was flying once more with the Stukas of St.G 77:

I am awake by 0500 hrs, the sun shining onto the tent and it is so warm and comfortable after the cold of the night. There is no wind at all. The great cloud of dust thrown up by the aircraft as they take off hangs tenaciously over the area and covers everything with a pall of grey. You have to climb to about 2,000 m to reach clearer air.

Over the battle area, the cloud of smoke and dust from the moving tanks and troop columns and from fires and explosions is so thick that it's extremely difficult to find your way or to locate the target. You see tanks crawling over the steppe; are they ours or theirs? It is so difficult.

We had a strange landmark today. In an otherwise cloudless sky, there stood above Stalingrad a single, giant, snow white cumulus cloud, towering high out of a base of thick black smoke and visible for kilometres. It was caused by the hot air from the burning city cooling and condensing as it rose.[74]

On a visit to 76.*Infanterie Division* von Richthofen met both Paulus and the Demyansk veteran and commander of LI.*Armeekorps*, General Walther von Seydlitz-Kurzbach. He found Paulus, whose nervous facial tic had become more noticeable, in a tense mood:

The Russians had just begun to assault with tanks through a gap, but they were shattered by our *Schlacht* units. The infantry are stuck fast to the left and right and at present cannot provide help to the Panzers that have broken through. At 1300 hrs the first incendiaries were dropped, at 1400 hrs the first clouds of destruction began to rise and at 1430 hrs a second incendiary cloud rose to over 3,500 m. The air units were unable to see anything anymore; they reported (naturally very exaggeratedly) that the town was destroyed and that there were no longer any worthwhile targets! I calmed Paulus down, who was very nervous.[75]

'*Luftflotte* 4 has been bombing the city ceaselessly since 23 August', recollected Oberst Wilhelm Adam, who was also present:

Stalingrad was just a single sheet of flames. The thick black smoke showed that the oil tanks had been hit. The whole landscape was bathed in sunlight on this beautiful late summer day. But from the west, flanked by fighters, came the squadrons of bombers to drop their loads on the city with ear-deafening noise and prominent mushrooms of smoke. 'That's how it goes all day long', commented an officer of the engineer staff.[76]

Indeed, as one example, between 23 and 31 August, the He 111s of Major Werner Hoffmann's I./KG 100 operating from Morosowskaya carried out multiple operations on four days, with as many as four missions in one day, attacking railways, buildings and transport targets in and around the city. On the 30th, the *Staffelkapitän* of 1./KG 100, Hauptmann Hansgeorg Bätcher, reported destroying or damaging 17 trucks during the course of four missions against Soviet motorised columns in the Karpovka River valley to the west of Stalingrad.[77]

Yet on the ground, one general remarked to Oberst Wilhelm Adam that day that the heavy losses suffered by 6.*Armee* in its advance to Stalingrad were having a dampening effect on the troops' morale; many had not reckoned on such tough resistance and had begun to doubt whether they would ever reach the city itself. Another general stated that the closer the German attack edged towards Stalingrad, the smaller became the gains. But as far as von Richthofen was concerned, with more fighting spirit the city could be taken in two days.[78]

It was this lingering dissatisfaction with the performance of 6.*Armee* in its assault on Stalingrad – something that he had experienced time and again in Russia with the *Heer* – that compelled von Richthofen to despatch his trusted operations officer, Oberstleutnant Karl-Heinrich Schulz, on the 27th on a mission to relay to Reichsmarschall Göring and Jeschonnek his opinions on what he perceived to be the 'nervousness and weaknesses' of army commanders. When Schulz returned the next day, evidently his mission had been successful. Von Richthofen preened in his diary, 'The Reichsmarschall is gracious; the situation report turned out to be successful. The *Führer* and the Reichsmarschall request me (emphatically) to continue to act as a "morale enforcer" with the army!'[79]

A few days later, von Richthofen appointed Schulz as his senior Quartermaster. An experienced, conscientious and dependable officer, Karl-Heinrich Schulz was born in the Baltic port city of Wilhelmshaven on 6 May 1906. After finishing school, at the age of 18 he joined the German Navy and in April 1926 was assigned to the torpedo and naval signals school at Mürwik. Schulz later undertook voyages to Iceland and Greenland on survey and fishery protection work. After being commissioned, Schulz progressed steadily on a career at naval training schools and bases on the Baltic coast. Then in April 1935 he transferred to the new Luftwaffe and qualified as a pilot.

With his naval background, Schulz was soon assigned to maritime aviation, and after a period as an instructor, he was appointed *Staffelkapitän* of the newly formed 1./*Küstenfliegergruppe* 706 at Nest equipped with He 60 reconnaissance biplanes. He also attended the *Luftkriegsakademie* at Berlin-Gatow for a senior staff course. Subsequently, Schulz embarked on a series of staff positions within the RLM, focusing on administration and training. With the outbreak of war, Schulz returned to squadron service, and on 3 June 1940 he was appointed as *Kommandeur* of He 111-equipped *Kampfgruppe* 126 at Marx. Just a month later, however, on 2 July 1940, he was shot down over France while on a bombing mission and was hospitalised. After recovery, Schulz returned to staff duties when he joined *Luftflotte* 4 in October 1940, with whom he remained until late April 1945. Von Richthofen would need men like Schulz over the coming months.[80]

Von Richthofen spent 30 August flying all over the front. He met with Paulus in the morning and persuaded the army commander to accept three light Flak batteries from VIII.*Fliegerkorps* – which would be delivered in Ju 52/3m transports – to secure one of 6.*Armee's* extended flanks. Also present with Paulus was General Gustav von Wietersheim, commander of XIV.*Panzerkorps* which had spearheaded the attack on Stalingrad. 'He's completely done for', von Richthofen observed. 'He's lost every ability to think and is incapable of any action'.

Returning to his headquarters after visiting He 111-equipped KG 55, meeting with other Luftwaffe commanders, dealing with paperwork, making various telephone calls and snatching an hour's sleep, von Richthofen summed things up in his diary:

At 6.*Armee*, all is quiet. 4.*Panzer* has advanced well against a fleeing and dissolving enemy; they have erected bridgeheads over the Krapovka. All is going well.[81]

6

Rubble and Fire

Stalingrad lay ahead on the near horizon to the east, stretching for some 40 km along the higher west bank of the Volga, from the Rynok and Spartanovka settlements in the north to Krasnoarmeyskiy Rayon in the south. Yet its lengthwise sprawl, bisected by the Tsaritsa River, was countered by its depth – never more than four kilometres at its widest, and down to just over a kilometre in places.[1] From the west the landscape was flat, but it gave way at the perimeter of the city to a series of hills and ridges, through which wound the deep Tsaritsa Gorge. It was a good landscape for defence.

Late on 2 September, this view greeted soldiers from 71.*Infanterie-Division* of 6.*Armee*'s LI.*Armeekorps* as they linked up with troops from the Romanian 20th Infantry Division attached to Generaloberst Hoth's 4.*Panzerarmee* pushing in to the western edge of the city.[2]

The bomb-shattered outlines of the great tractor and ordnance factory buildings in the north, the power station to the south and the modern, white-walled apartment blocks and administration centres shimmered through a permanent haze of dust and smoke. To the low-flying aircrews of VIII.*Fliegerkorps*, the rooftops, the public gardens and parks and the snaking course of the Volga drifted in and out of view below them, their visibility similarly marred by palls of smoke and the overlying cloud of thick dust – the results of their own work. And hundreds of kilometres away in Moscow and Vinnytsia, respectively, the military situation in southern Russia was fast becoming an exasperating obsession in the minds of the two dictators.

In Moscow on 3 September Josef Stalin lost his reserve, unable to understand why his generals did not seem to understand that the loss of Stalingrad would have grave implications: potentially, the south of the Soviet Union would be cut off, and thus the country's main water transport route, and possibly its supply of oil, would suffer a similar fate. He ordered Gen Georgi Zhukov, hero of the defences of Leningrad and Moscow, to make an immediate limited counter-attack.

Four days later in Vinnytsia, Jodl had just returned from Stalino, where he had met with Generalfeldmarschall List at the latter's request. List had explained that the advance of *Heeresgruppe* A into the Caucasus had been slowed because of a lack of troops and the extreme terrain: the progress of the 4th Mountain Division had taken it along a 100 km mountain path with supplies being carried by no fewer than 2,000 mules. This failed to convince Hitler, who flew into a rage and yelled at Jodl that he was lying. Jodl attempted to remind Hitler that List was acting under the *Führer's* orders. Hitler strode from the conference room, refusing to shake hands with either Jodl or Keitel – a slight he kept up until January 1943.[3]

Fiebig sent his aircraft to bomb Stalingrad remorselessly on the 3rd and the 5th; Ju 88s and He 111s attacked by day and night, releasing their bombs from between 1,000 to 4,000 m. Other strikes were made against Soviet airfields east of the Volga and against railways and river traffic.[4] Von Richthofen ensured that there was an efficient air-ground communications system between VIII. *Fliegerkorps'* air liaison officers attached to the advancing ground forces and the commanders in the air – something that he had first introduced in Poland in 1939, having recognised a need for it in Spain. At Stalingrad, VIII. *Fliegerkorps* set up an advanced command post in the city immediately adjacent to an army observation post that enjoyed views as far as the Volga. From there, the most up-to-date targeting information could be relayed to units in the air using a small-scale grid superimposed onto aerial photographs.[5] As the Knight's Cross-holder and *Geschwaderkommodore* of St.G 2, Oberstleutnant Paul-Werner Hozzel, remembered:

> In order to support the army in its struggle for the final occupation of the city, reconnaissance aircraft had prepared an aerial mosaic which each pilot had in front of him in his cockpit when flying sorties against targets in Stalingrad. Likewise, each air liaison officer in the spearheads of the divisions had that aerial mosaic map with him. A system of coordinates plotted on the mosaic enabled the air liaison officer to indicate to the commander of an approaching Stuka unit by radiophone exactly every target, and to direct him to it. Throughout the battle for the city, this kind of cooperation was excellent.
>
> A distance of only 40 km separated us from Stalingrad. This meant that we needed for each sortie a chock-to-chock time of not more than 45 minutes, which included taxiing to the start, take-off, approach flight, the climb to altitude of 4,000 m, target pick-up, dive-bombing attack, low-level departure flight, landing, taxiing to the apron. Each turn-around – i.e., new loading and a short technical check-up – took us another 15 minutes. We were consequently able to fly with each aircraft about eight sorties from sunrise to sunset, which on days of large-scale fighting we actually did. On some days we managed to fly a total of about 800 sorties. This was a great feat by our crews. Every minute of the day we kept the enemy on the go with Stuka, *Schlacht* and fighter attacks.[6]

The fighting raged in the outer districts of the city over the next five days, often at close quarters in the streets and ruins. Things were not made easy for the Stuka crews as a result of Col Gen Aleksandr Rodimstev, commander of the 13th Guards Rifle Division, implementing a policy that the Soviet frontline was to be no further than 45 m from the German line, thus making targeting from the air extremely difficult – and that was on top of the 'mask' of dust and smoke.[7]

For Hauptmann Herbert Pabst and his fellow Stuka pilots of St.G 77, life had developed into a grim routine, as he described on 9 September:

> The days all follow the same pattern. In raid after raid with bombs and machine gun fire, we play our part in the advance. The Russians are fighting with incredible determination, hanging on desperately at every village, every height, every railway embankment. They dig themselves in in a thousand holes with an amazing instinct.[8]

The He 111 transport crews of Hauptmann Fritz Uhl's KGr.z.b.V.5, flying now from Makeyevka in eastern Ukraine, were given a different kind of 'ordnance' to drop – leaflets, tons of them. These implored Soviet troops to surrender, promising them good treatment if they lay down their weapons, but it proved a futile initiative and was abandoned after eight days.[9]

On the 10th, tanks from Hoth's 4.*Panzerarmee* were able to push in between the Soviet 62nd and 64th Armies, and in doing so isolate 62nd Army.[10] Von Richthofen, who had returned to the Stalingrad front after a whistle-stop visit to Berlin and the northern sector of the Eastern Front, during which he complained about the lack of army leadership to Göring, Jeschonnek, Milch and probably anyone else in authority who would listen, met with Fiebig at a forward fighter airfield 15 km from the city in the early morning of the 13th. The two men discussed operations, but they bickered and von Richthofen felt dissatisfied once more at general progress: 'Only mediocre successes at Stalingrad. I request of Luftwaffe High Command to strive for a more cooperative leadership from the army facing Stalingrad'.[11]

At 0730 hrs on 14 September, 6.*Armee* launched a major assault on the central and southern districts of the city. Over the next few days, it was able to fight its way deeper into Stalingrad, engaging in the fiercest close-quarter combat with Russian forces; for example at *Stalingrad 1-i* (the Central Railway Station), located just west of what the Germans knew as Red Square (Square of the Fallen Fighters) and the ferry stage. According to the 62nd Army's war diary, at 0800 hrs on the 14th, the station was held by the Germans. Forty minutes later it had been retaken. An hour after that, the Germans recaptured it, but by 1320 hrs it was held once more by the defenders.[12] The station changed hands a further five times on the 15th, and no fewer than 15 times over five days.[13] There were also bitter clashes on Height 102 (the ancient burial mound known as the Mamayev-Kurgan that divided Stalingrad, and from the top of which there were views across the city as far as the sprawling factories to the north), the *Krasnyi Oktiabr* (Red October) iron and metal works, the *Barrikady* (Red Barricade) ordnance factory and the Dzerzhinsky Tractor Factory.

It was not just on the ground that Soviet resistance was stiffening, for the VVS was growing in numbers and in confidence. Once the *Stavka* had given the Stalingrad and South-eastern Fronts the missions of defending the city and attacking the enemy beyond it, as well as on the Don, the VVS was assigned the task of providing air support to the 62nd and 64th Armies fighting inside Stalingrad. 8th VA (Air Army) under Maj Gen Timofei Khryukin, a veteran of combat in Spain and China, together with units of the ADD (Long-Range Aviation) attacked German formations approaching the city with their Pe-2 bombers and Il-2 fighter-bombers covered by Yak-1 or La-5 fighters, while more bombers struck troop concentrations, artillery locations and facilities in the German rear, just two to three kilometres from the frontline. Some ground-attack pilots would fly up to three sorties per day at this time, while on occasion Soviet fighter pilots would resort to airborne ramming as a drastic, last ditch tactic to bring down German aircraft. On 14 September, flying a Yak-1 in cloudy conditions, Sgt Ilya Chumbarev of 237th IAP (Fighter Air Regiment) rammed a twin-engined Focke-Wulf Fw 189 reconnaissance aircraft from behind and below at 1,000 m over his unit's airfield under radio-assisted direction from the ground. Despite suffering a head injury, Chumbarev remained in control and landed in a field close to Soviet troops.[14] The Fw 189 was destroyed.

In mid-September there was a marked change in the weather, which, in addition to the presence of the VVS, introduced a further new factor that German soldiers and airmen would now have to contend with, as Ju 87 pilot Hauptmann Herbert Pabst noted in his diary on the 16th:

It was bitterly cold yesterday morning when I slunk out of my tent. It was 0345 hrs, the first pale shimmer in the east, low cloud, a biting wind from the north-west. The wind drove grey eddies of dust and sand before it. The sand lashed the skin with a thousand needles.

I strapped myself, shivering, into my aircraft. Above the Don the clouds thinned and we flew into the cold light of the early morning, blinded by the sun rising red before us. At first, the heat of the engine warmed the cockpit slightly, but at 3,000 m above the target the cold was penetrating and we were frozen stiff when we arrived. All day long we had wind and showers, it remained bitterly cold and everyone was chilled to the bone. Five times over Stalingrad – seven hours in the aircraft; that's quite enough for any man.

Today, the same again: four times. On one mission we dived out of a clear blue sky – a perfect gift to the furious and uncomfortably accurate enemy Flak. Another time we crept up slyly above the clouds, then turned, found the target and dived suddenly from among the towering clouds; that way the twisting and turning amidst the pursuing Flak is much briefer. Once today, a formation of 20-30 Russian fighters caught me as I approached and I had to turn back. There was a moment of wild dodging and speeding through the clouds. At one moment Woletz was firing behind us, at another I had one of them in the sight of my forward machine guns. A little way back from the target area I assembled my 'flock'. Three of the crews radioed that they would have to return home because their machines had taken direct hits, but the others were soon back in formation. We climbed back into the protection of the clouds, and this time managed to reach the target area. We unleashed our loads. The fighters returned, but they were too late; we had vanished before they got there. It's no good; we're just better at it. Of my three damaged crews, I found two back at base, but the third had to make an emergency landing because they had lost fuel.

Three hours later, we had reloaded bombs and were back over the same target. Eating between raids is a very short, hasty business; reports are written, the telephone rings, charts and aerial photographs are studied.[15]

Oberstleutnant Paul-Werner Hozzel, commander of St.G 2, also experienced the hazards of the notorious Russian anti-aircraft batteries:

For the protection of his troops in Stalingrad, the enemy had, of course, built massive anti-aircraft emplacements on both banks of the Volga, also in the areas of the city occupied by him. They fired at us with all the calibres at their disposal, inflicting heavy casualties on us. Most dangerous were their medium 4 cm and light 2 cm guns, which caught us at times in dive recoveries at altitudes between 800 and 500 m. Even their heavy anti-aircraft guns fired quite accurately up to altitudes of 4,000-5,000 m. I remember a sortie I flew east of the Volga when my left wing was hit the moment I started diving. The wing had been pierced by a heavy, unexploded shell. The hole torn into it was so large that I had to break off the sortie, realising that the wing would never have withstood the nose dive. It is a fact that in its sorties on the Eastern Front, and particularly over Stalingrad, the *Geschwader* suffered its most severe losses by anti-aircraft fire and very few by Soviet fighters.[16]

Von Richthofen agreed with Pabst on the weather; the same day he noted in his diary that it was 'bitterly cold'. From daybreak the Luftwaffe commander was out again touring the Stalingrad front, but he remained like a bear with a sore head. In his opinion he found the 'combing through' of Stalingrad by 6.*Armee* was moving ahead too slowly against what he perceived to be a 'weak enemy', while 'our own people are lethargic'. He did not stop there: when he visited LI.*Armeekorps* he found:

The same picture. The people there, without the necessary encouragement, make very slow progress. As they see it, they have plenty of time, since they think they are supposed to remain here over the winter and have no other plans. The incentive from higher up is all theoretical, and hence is ineffective. The Generals only issue orders but do not lead by example or through any kind of encouraging performance of their own. General Paulus is upright, but is not forceful enough.

Von Richthofen then went on to berate the hard-working and conscientious Fiebig again:

> I took him to task seriously about his methods of operations. He's not active and adaptable enough; he doesn't try to eliminate the ongoing supply problems or other issues off his own back. He applies himself in a dreary way and without any panache.

And as for Oberst i.G. Klaus Uebe, Fiebig's Chief of Staff at VIII.*Fliegerkorps*, von Richthofen felt the man did not really work hard enough with either the *Luftflotte* staff or the Army; in other words, effective air-ground coordination was lacking.[17]

Von Richthofen did have a point about the supply situation. The reality was that *Luftflotte* 4's sortie rate had decreased noticeably: between 5 and 12 September the air fleet carried out 7,507 sorties, or an average of 938 per day, whereas at the start of *Blau* in June a total of 10,750 was flown in the same number of days, equating to a daily average of 1,343. The decline was attributable to a high consumption of parts, lack of replacements and other supplies to operational bases and an increase in attrition from combat operations. Aircraft strength had reduced from 1,150 at the commencement of *Blau* to just 550 following a period of nearly three months' continuous operations. The bomber units had been the hardest hit: in June the fleet listed 480 machines on strength, but by 20 September it had only 232, of which just 129 were operational – and again, the increasing size of the zone of operations should not be overlooked.[18]

18 September was a day which exemplified the strain under which *Luftflotte* 4 was working: in response to a Russian attack on the north flank of 6.*Armee*, von Richthofen was forced to use just about everything he had against the enemy breakthrough. 'It looked very ominous', he noted. 'Everything was concentrated there'. In addition to VIII.*Fliegerkorps*, von Richthofen deployed what small forces remained from IV.*Fliegerkorps* in the area. By evening, the enemy incursion had been dealt with and the original frontline restored.

Beneath the bombing, conditions in and around the city were appalling for both sides. In mid-September, Oberst Wilhelm Adam made a journey to Gumrak, where, in the company of an officer on a fact-finding visit from the OKH's Personnel Office, he visited the main dressing station that had been established there. He arrived as enemy artillery shells were landing dangerously close by. Adam wrote how:

> Wounded were constantly being brought in by ambulances, trucks and horse-drawn carts. Not all were lying on stretchers. For many, there was only a woollen blanket beneath them, while others were simply laid out on the bare floor of the truck. The surgeons and their assistants were working in a big room on two operating tables. Amputees were dealt with first, then windpipe injuries, then came the stomach and lung cases. Apparently one had to give preference to stomach injuries, but these operations lasted two or three hours here, so that the chances of survival were low.

Having unintentionally witnessed treatment being administered to the horrific injuries suffered by amputees, Adam and his companion left the room. 'We had seen enough'. But in another room, he stopped to offer a cigarette to an infantryman who had had a leg amputated following a grenade wound suffered in the street-fighting now taking place further into the city. 'All hell is let loose out there', the soldier told Adam. 'I have never experienced anything like it in this war. And I have been in it since the beginning. These Ivans won't go back a step. The way into their positions goes only over corpses. But many of us bite the dust before that. Every ruin, every stone is defended. Death is waiting everywhere. We have to learn close-quarter fighting all over again'.[19]

Indeed, one example of this had been the close combat in the *Stalingrad 1-i* main railway station, where Soviet riflemen fought German infantry in the outbuildings, along the platforms and from within the wreckage of burned-out rolling stock. Another case was a giant grain elevator building which both sides contested for several days and nights. The diarist of a Soviet marine brigade recorded how:

> In the elevator the grain was on fire, the water in the machine guns evaporated, the wounded were thirsty, but there was no water nearby. This was how we defended ourselves 24 hours a day for three days. Heat, smoke, thirst – our lips were cracked.[20]

On the 17th, having fought their way tenaciously forward, elements of LI.*Armeekorps* and XXXXVIII.*Panzerkorps* met on the Tsaritsa.[21] That day, Hauptmann Pabst of St.G 77 once again recorded in his diary how the weather conditions had changed:

> It is so cold at night that our vehicles freeze. Yet only a few days ago the steppe was gasping in the searing heat; this is a land that does nothing by halves.
>
> For days now, fighting has been taking place in Stalingrad itself. The Russians are sitting tight in the burning ruins and refuse to budge. There is hardly a house left standing; it's a stupendous chaos of rubble and fire into which we still hurl bomb after bomb. Behind lies the broad ribbon of the Volga over which there is no bridge – but the Russians refuse to yield.
>
> We have no idea how long it will last. We arrived in August from the heat of the Crimea. I can't hold out much longer in this cold; the tents are too thin and my men lack clothing. I must see to it that I get hold of some blankets, greatcoats, gloves, etc. We shall have to build bunkers; it's warmer under the ground.[22]

At Oblivskaya, the base of St.G 77, on the 19th Pabst noted:

> It was blazing hot again yesterday. Today we had showers, storms and a biting cold wind. Today I flew my 228th sortie. That means I have flown as many raids in the last three months as previously over Poland, France, England, Yugoslavia and Russia together.[23]

Following Hitler's outburst at Jodl at his *Werwolf* headquarters on 7 September, the atmosphere around the *Führer* and his closest military advisers had worsened. He felt he could trust or depend on no one in the army, least of all Generaloberst Franz Halder, the Chief of Staff of OKH, who, in reality, was dedicated, dependable and insightful. His warnings over the risk of leaving 6.*Armee*'s extended northern flank exposed along the upper Don between Stalingrad and Voronezh had gone unheeded. Rather, Hitler's bile had manifested itself in making jokes about Halder's conservatism behind his back and mocking his suggestions publicly.[24] From his point of view, Halder felt that Hitler demonstrated only a 'pathological reaction to impressions of the moment, and a total lack of understanding of the command machinery and its function'.[25] On 24 September Halder was dismissed; he noted in his diary, 'My nerves are worn out; also his nerves are no longer fresh. He is determined to enforce his will onto the army'.[26]

That night at Oblivskaya, 148 km west of Stalingrad, Herbert Pabst sat freezing in his draughty tent, despite a thick blanket, as he wrote home:

> Three raids today, none of them child's play. I was over Stalingrad on one occasion, then far out over the Kalmyck Steppe towards the south-east to attack shipping on the Volga. In the evening, we were again deep inside enemy territory to the north-east. Over the Volga, I got a fat tanker in my sights. The bomb landed exactly on the ship's side and a gigantic column of flame shot skywards; as I withdrew I could see the fire and the steep, black column of smoke for a long while. One aircraft had to make an emergency landing in enemy territory, but the crew was rescued by a colleague who landed immediately alongside.
>
> In the evening we blew up two transport trains about 80 km behind the front. But as I was gathering my comrades back together again after the dive, some enemy fighters came roaring up and harassed us mercilessly with repeated attacks from all sides. There was a wild mêlée of banking and firing until we at last reached the front, when they turned back. I reached our airfield as darkness was falling, with all my 'lambs' safe and sound. Now I'm tired. A great yellow moon – the effect of dust over the plain – is making it eerily light outside. All I want to do is sleep.[27]

To make conditions even more grim for the troops in the trenches, dugouts and ruins in and around the city, the *rasputitsa* had arrived, bringing rain. The water level rose to ankle height and the rats came out to feed off corpses.[28]

The second German assault on Stalingrad commenced on the 27th at 0600 hrs with a ferocious Stuka attack followed by wave after wave of infantry supported by tanks, a force of 11 divisions in all. On this occasion Russian counter-attacks stifled progress, but the top of the Mamayev Kurgan was re-secured by the Germans. Lt Gen Vasili Chuikov was shaken by the assault, reflecting, 'One more battle like it and we'll be in the Volga'.[29] Two days later, on the 29th, he admitted that his army was taking 'heavy losses'. One of his divisions lost three regimental and three battalion commanders on that day alone, and his armoured force was left with just 17 tanks; it had 'virtually ceased to have any real fighting power'. The few remaining crews were turned over to the infantry.[30] 'Five sorties, seven hours in the cockpit, stifling heat', wrote Hauptmann Pabst at the end of the day:

Stalingrad is burning under a hail of bombs and shells. We bank and dive through the thick black smoke which literally blots out the sun up to 3,000 m. As we fly towards the area, the divisional transmitter below gives us the target [a 'large group of houses – strong enemy resistance there']. It's extremely difficult to make out these awkward targets and hit them in the thick smoke. And the aim must be accurate, for our own troops are usually poised just in front. The Russians are hanging on to the blazing northern quarter and just will not move.

A sharp wind is blowing across the steppe and whipping the dust up everywhere into giant eddies. Visibility is remarkably poor in the thick dust haze. The final flight back into the low sun was very difficult; we were completely blinded, rushing at great speed into dazzling nothingness. Compass and watch were the only guide as to when we were back near our airfield. If we looked down behind us (that is, looking with the sun), we could make out the ground through the swirling grey dust. There is just featureless steppe, without any landmark, until we reach the light, sandy banks of the almost dry River Chir.[31]

On 30 September Hitler was back in Berlin, where he addressed a hand-picked audience at the *Sportpalast* to mark the opening of the annual winter relief campaign. His address was aggravated in tone, lacking sparkle, indignant over what he perceived as the British knack of dressing up defeats and retreats, such as Dunkirk, as 'victories' and glossing over recent ill-fated ventures such as the joint British-Canadian raid at Dieppe, when, by comparison, the German soldier had accomplished so much more:

If we advance to the Don, finally reach the Volga, overrun Stalingrad and capture it – and of that they can be certain – in their eyes that is nothing!

He assured his audience that no man would shift German soldiers from Stalingrad. He also promised that with the trials of the previous winter behind them, it would not be long before the economic benefits which the occupied territories could offer would start to be felt.[32] But according to Wilhelm Adam, 'By the beginning of October it was obvious to us at 6.*Armee* headquarters that we would not be able to take Stalingrad with our badly hit divisions before winter set in'.[33] The *Armee* advised the headquarters of *Heeresgruppe* B that, 'in spite of the most intensive efforts by all forces, the low combat strengths of the infantry will prolong the taking of Stalingrad indefinitely if reinforcements cannot be supplied'.[34]

For the time being, however, battle-strained 6.*Armee* continued to defend its northern flank against attacks from Lt Gen Konstantin Rokossovsky's Don Front and to fight for Stalingrad street-by-street, house-by-house, ruin-by-ruin, sewer-by-sewer. This form of claustrophobic urban warfare, where snipers could lurk around every corner and could fire from every rooftop, where danger hid in the shell-blasted shadows and cellars, was alien to the German tactical principles of quick manoeuvre with infantry and tanks. The soldiers christened it *Rattenkrieg* ('Rats' War').

For the benefit of 'higher authorities', the *Armeewirtschaftsführer* (the German Army's Economic Officer) issued a report on 3 October based on the latest combat accounts received from Stalingrad. It made grim reading:

> The districts to the east of the railway line (mostly stone buildings) are totally destroyed. In the districts to the west of the railway (mostly wooden houses), the destruction amounts to 85 per cent. Factories, especially armaments plants, are, with few exceptions, totally destroyed. Refineries and storage tanks still in enemy hands are on fire. The population is living in cellars and caves in the ground. The great majority of the population is female. There are very many children.[35]

For the next few days, a calm of sorts settled over Stalingrad as Paulus allowed his troops a brief respite after weeks of fighting. The Russians too seized the opportunity; the frontline of Chuikov's 62nd Army ran for 20 km, with parts to a depth of 2,500 m while at other points it was down to just 250 m; movement in such a constricted area could only be undertaken at night.[36] Then, on the 8th, *Heeresgruppe* B issued – not unexpectedly – orders for a further mass assault aimed at the city's northern industrial district to take place no later than the 14th.[37]

Thus, at 0600 hrs on 14 October, the Germans launched their third assault against Stalingrad. Paulus deployed three infantry divisions and 200 tanks from two Panzer divisions against a four-kilometre front in the factory area to the north of the city, but the momentum and shock of the earlier German attacks had been lost. Nevertheless, Chuikov described what followed as 'fighting of unprecedented ferocity'.[38] The Soviets did not yield and counter-attacked wherever they were able.

Von Richthofen deployed every single available Ju 87 and the Luftwaffe dropped more than 600 tons of bombs on the city.[39] According to Chuikov:

> We recorded some 3,000 sorties by enemy aircraft on that day! German aeroplanes bombed and machine-gunned our troops without stop. The enemy's artillery and mortars bombarded the whole battlefield from morning to night. It was a sunny day, but the smoke and dust cut visibility down to 100 yards. Our dug-outs shook and caved in like houses of cards.[40]

Down on the ground, amidst the ruins, the noise of massed engines overhead was deafening, to which was then added the firing of Russian anti-aircraft guns, the howl of diving Stukas, the blast of bombs, and the explosions of crashing aircraft. One Soviet commissar wrote to another in Moscow, 'Those of us who have seen the dark sky of Stalingrad in these days will never forget it'.[41] Metre by metre, the German infantry and tanks moved forward. Generalmajor Hans Doerr, who was then serving as the liaison officer to the Romanian 4th Army, has left an evocative account of the push towards the Dzerzhinski Tractor Factory:

On October 14 began the greatest operation to date: an attack by several divisions against the Dzerzhinski Tractor Factory. From all sectors of the front, even from the army's flanks on the Don and the Kalmyk steppe, engineer and anti-tank units were brought up as reinforcements, although they were needed just as much where they had come from. The Luftwaffe flew five engineer battalions in from the Reich. The attack was supported by the entire VIII. *Fliegerkorps*.

The troops advanced two kilometres, but could not overcome the resistance of the three Russian divisions defending the factory and occupying the sheer bank of the Volga. During the day our soldiers did succeed at some points in reaching the bank, but at night they were forced to retreat, as the Russians in the gullies were cutting them off from the rear.[42]

Oberstleutnant Hozzel led a formation of some 120 Ju 87s of St.G 2 against the factory. It was an extremely difficult mission, as he describes:

The plant extended from east to west, over a length of about 1,000 m and a width of 50 m. In the north, west and the south it was closed in by our infantry, but it was open to the east – i.e., enemy territory. Generaloberst von Richthofen made us understand that our *Geschwader* had to execute precision bombing so as to avoid any danger to our own troops, being entrenched close to the target area. He wanted to watch our sorties jointly with General Paulus from his command post at the western outskirts of the city. This was, indeed, a very delicate order.

We could not risk making a dive-bombing attack from 4,000 m altitude because of the wide zone of dispersion. We had to fly a shallow dive attack, releasing bombs directly above the roofs. We had, in fact, to push the bombs into the target like 'loaves of bread into an oven', from one aircraft succeeding the other.

We loaded one 500-kg bomb each with tank-busting warheads and delayed action fuses for piercing the cellar vaults, and two 250-kg high-explosive bombs loaded under the wings, so each aircraft had to carry a load of 1,000 kg. Each pilot was fully briefed in accordance with the aerial mosaic and informed about the sequence of attacks to be flown. It was planned to drop the bombs in rapid succession so as to wear down the enemy by endless detonations. The order of the attacking *Staffeln* was carefully planned. The *Geschwader* assembled at altitudes between 1,000 and 2,000 m in a holding area west of Stalingrad, outside anti-aircraft range, without fighter escort. From there, the individual *Staffeln* started their shallow dive approach in the sequence ordered.

The *Stabskette*, having signalled the attack, started first and dived on its target, dropping its bombs from a very low altitude. Then, pulling our aircraft around, we left the range of anti-aircraft fire in low-level flight, gaining altitude west of the city so as to observe the attacks of the aircraft following us. As on a string of pearls, one aircraft succeeded the other within intervals of a few seconds, throwing the bombs on the oblong target area divided up among us. Not one single bomb missed its target. This brought our crews high praise from the infantrymen in the target area.[43]

By midnight the tractor plant was surrounded on three sides. The approaches to the industrial colossus was littered with bodies and wounded; wounded Soviet soldiers were still crawling towards the Volga when the Panzers smashed through the walls of the factory and lumbered through the wrecked workshops with their mangled steelwork.[44]

Von Richthofen seemed satisfied with operations:

There is good progress in Stalingrad. The dreaded tractor factory has been captured, the Russians having been taken rather by surprise. The Volga has been reached along a width of three kilometres. VIII. *Fliegerkorps* release the *Dickster Zauber* ['greatest magic' – heaviest firepower].[45]

While there was little doubt about the ferocity of VIII. *Fliegerkorps'* attack, the air commander may have been a little hasty in his assessment, for as Paul-Werner Hozzel reflected on St.G 2's raid on the factory:

What was the result of the whole operation? It was next to nothing! When the division resumed its attacks in order to test the effects of the bombing raid, it unexpectedly met with fierce counter-attacks as though nothing had happened – as if the *Geschwader* had dropped toy torpedoes instead of bombs. I reported on this at great length to make clear that Russian soldiers, particularly those of Asiatic strain, can take a lot of punishment.[46]

This was a factor that was felt by other Luftwaffe pilots. A maudlin Herbert Pabst reflected one night while squatting on a crate in his tent to take a shave in his tiny mirror:

The Ivans are different. They sleep in holes in the ground. They don't notice the dust in their hair, in their clothes and between their toes. When 50 of them are blown to pieces in the fire and filth, 100 more take their place and continue the resistance. But in this brutal war, the only things that count are violence, fire, unbridled cunning and slaughter by every possible means.[47]

By the 16th, Pabst's Stuka *Gruppe* had moved to an airfield at Marinovka, some 50 km from the centre of Stalingrad. The *Gruppenkommandeur*, Major Kurt Huhn, his staff, as well as all pilots and groundcrew, slept on straw on the floor of an old stable. 'It isn't far to Stalingrad from here', wrote Pabst:

Yesterday I made eight sorties. Bomb after bomb crashes down into the shattered ruins of the last areas of the city where the Ivans are hanging on grimly. I just cannot understand how men can continue to live in such an inferno, yet the Russians refuse to be shifted from the ruins, sitting tight in the *Balkas*, cellars and the twisted steel skeletons of the last factories. Early this morning I completed my 300th mission. On the 301st, I was involved in a violent dogfight with Red fighters – a 'ballet' among lines of tracer and puffs of Flak over the burning city. An Ivan bore down on me from dead ahead, guns blazing. I fired as well, and there we were, heading towards each other at a terrifying speed. The one who can fly the longest towards the other, firing all the time, has the advantage. At the last moment, I had to give way. The Russian was more stubborn after all and would have rammed me. So we tore past with five metres between us. My aircraft was undamaged.

Active in and around the German occupied areas of the city during September and October was the recently promoted Generalmajor Wolfgang Pickert, commander of 9.*Flak-Division*. His 88 mm guns had been in action on the 14th, and for much of the Stalingrad campaign, against Soviet tanks and heavy weapons: as he noted on the 15th, 'We are playing a big role'.[48]

Pickert was born in Posen on 3 February 1897 and had served as an artilleryman during World War I. From October 1934 he had progressed through the Luftwaffe Flak arm, serving variously as an instructor at the Flak Artillery School at Döberitz and other locations, as an advisor to the RLM's Inspectorate of Flak Artillery, and as a battalion commander in a Flak regiment. Pickert was appointed Chief of Staff of I.*Flakkorps* in September 1940 and then made commander of 9.*Flak-Division* on 25 June 1942. He was regarded as a hard-working, conscientious officer.

During the advance on Stalingrad, Pickert's Flak batteries had provided fire support for the units of both 6.*Armee* and 4.*Panzerarmee* as they moved into the city, as well as targeting shipping on the Volga and the river crossings. This last role was important because it hampered Soviet supply and reinforcements crossing from the eastern bank. In combination with VIII.*Fliegerkorps'* airborne attacks, the Flak batteries forced the local Volga Flotilla to reduce its daylight river crossings significantly. Admittedly, when the Russians attempted night crossings, it meant that the *Korps'* aircraft could not attack with great accuracy, but Fiebig made sure that daylight attacks against the landing stages were kept up.[49]

Like von Richthofen, Pickert 'hopped' around the battlefront in a Storch, visiting his units as well as coordinating with army commanders. Flights over the steppe 'seemed endless', he wrote. 'One feels like a grain of sand in these enormous, empty spaces'. But he took a dim view of Stalingrad itself: 'A horrible dump,' he noted on 7 October, 'now badly destroyed, but it has always been a miserable dump. A lot of poor buildings. Some good streets, but a great deal of bad pavement. Great misery among the population. The Party buildings are completely destroyed – they must have been the city's paltry showpieces'.[50]

On the 17th, Pickert journeyed by car to Kalach to inspect his units there. He passed columns of refugees, and his observations were testimony to the recent report by the Army's Economic Officer:

Nearly all these people travel on foot, carrying their belongings on their backs. One seldom sees a pushcart or a vehicle. There are many children. Often the mothers carry children and have no baggage at all.

The fighting in Stalingrad continues and a successful conclusion seems to be in the offing. There will be nothing left of the city. We are using all ways and means to get out wood for fuel and for construction of emplacements. Nearly all substantial buildings have been destroyed.[51]

Forty-eight hours later, Pickert noted that it rained for most of the day, turning into sleet for a while during the morning. 'The roads will be in a hopeless condition', he complained, 'hampering all motor vehicle movements and especially ammunition supplies. Not good! It hurts us more than it does the enemy'.[52] Nevertheless, 6.*Armee* had fought its way through several hurdles of resistance and taken more ruined ground, their guns now aimed at the bread factory and the *Krasnyi Oktiabr* metal works. But this did little to satisfy von Richthofen, who recorded in his diary:

Total confusion in Stalingrad. In the town, it appears that divisions have been over-optimistic in their reports! No one knows what's going on. Every division, every *Korps*, reports something different. Fiebig is despondent because the infantry do not take advantage of his assaults. What is one supposed to do?[53]

As temperatures fell, daylight hours lessened and the grip of winter set in, many in the German command began to worry about the issue of supply over the months that lay ahead. 'How would it be when winter came', wondered Oberst Adam, 'if additional warm clothing, heating material and fodder for horses had to be delivered, if there were also deep snowdrifts and black ice?'[54]

At Vinnytsia, Hitler's Luftwaffe adjutant, Oberst Nicolaus von Below, had observed a characteristic of the *Führer's* behaviour as the fighting at Stalingrad intensified:

Frequently reports would come in describing bitter fighting for a block of flats. Hitler insisted that at Stalingrad every house had to be fought for. Only in this way could the Russians be forced out of the city. I believed that we had arrived at the crossroads of events. Hitler often seemed unduly pensive and far away – almost as if he no longer had confidence in the strategy. The extent of the fronts had become enormous, the supply of weapons and munitions problematical. But Hitler made increased demands.[55]

By the time he left *Werwolf* on 1 November, there was evidence that Hitler was losing some grasp on the reality of the situation. As much as he had mocked the

British for snatching victory from the jaws of defeat in his September address at the *Sportpalast*, he now talked of a 'highly active defence' somehow alongside 'victory' at Stalingrad. Orders were issued from the *Führer*'s headquarters to move some of 6.*Armee*'s 150,000-plus draught animals – mostly horses, but also oxen and a number of camels – which were herded between the Don and the Volga, back to the rear so as to save supply train capacity in moving fodder in the direction of the front. In any case, steppe grass held very low nutritional value, and the prospect of a mass slaughter of exhausted horses as had taken place the previous winter was generally abhorred (although a number of divisions did commit to a premature slaughter programme so as to boost food rations).[56] Some motor transport and other support units were also pulled back – not an ideal state of affairs should a crisis arise. As a positive, new reversible winter clothing started to arrive, but this did not detract from the fact that by the end of October, physical exhaustion and a lack of ammunition had brought the final assault against the city to a standstill.[57]

7

Uranus

*The Red Army is defeated, it has no more worthwhile reserves, so is in
no condition to engage in large attacks.*

ATTRIBUTED TO GENERAL KURT ZEITZLER, CHIEF OF THE
ARMY GENERAL STAFF, IN A TELEPHONE CONVERSATION
WITH GENERAL FRIEDRICH PAULUS, EARLY NOVEMBER 1942[1]

On 3 November 1942, Gen Georgi Zhukov, the Soviet Deputy Supreme
Commander-in-Chief and First Deputy People's Commissar of Defence,
and Gen Aleksandr Vasilevsky, Chief of the Soviet Army's General Staff and a
Deputy People's Commissar of Defence, accompanied by several senior Red
Army 'experts in their fields', visited Lt Gen Nikolai Vatutin, commander of
the recently formed Southwestern Front and his senior staff officers. They also
met with corps and divisional commanders of the Front's 5th Tank Army under
Maj Gen Prokofii Romanenko. The objective of their visit was to hold detailed,
final talks prior to the opening of an imminent and surreptitiously prepared
counter-offensive to be directed at the extended flanks of Paulus' 6.*Armee* with
the aim, ultimately, of sealing the Army off from *Heeresgruppe* B by means of a
classic pincer movement – thus encircling it. According to the Eastern Front
historians David Glantz and Jonathan House, the effective architect of what
would become known as Operation *Uran* (*Uranus*) is believed to have been
Lt Gen Andrei Eremenko, commander of the Stalingrad Front.[2]

The *Stavka* was aware of just how much careful and secret preparation
was required for an operation of such scale, involving three Fronts, while
simultaneously fighting a battle as intense as that being fought at Stalingrad.
In an account written during the 1960s, Zhukov described how:

We were also concerned with our artillery preparations – the barrage
density that would be needed, the likelihood of destroying enemy targets,
and coordination between artillery and ground forces during the offensive.
We also worked on coordinating air support and artillery, assigning them
targets, and coordinating them, in turn, with tank forces both during and

1 A Ju 52/3m makes its approach during a supply flight on the Eastern Front in early 1942. (Author's Collection)

2 German troops quickly haul away a sled laden with supplies from a Ju 52/3m, possibly at Demyansk. (EN Archive)

3 Oberst Fritz Morzik, the Luftwaffe's foremost transport commander. (EN Archive)

4 Hitler and his generals pore over maps of southern Russia and Ukraine at Zaporozhye, shortly after the loss of Stalingrad in February 1943. (ullstein bild via Getty Images)

5 General Friedrich Paulus, commander of 6.*Armee*, directs his staff from a forward position during the advance on Stalingrad in late 1942. (ullstein bild via Getty Images)

6 The Stalingrad skyline seen from the east bank of the Volga in September 1942 during the German advance. (Forczyk Collection)

7 German infantry move forward to the outskirts of Stalingrad in September 1942 during Operation *Blau*. (Heinrich Hoffmann/Mondadori via Getty Images)

8 A Ju 87 Stuka banks over Stalingrad towards the west and away from the Volga River. (EN Archive)

9 The future Chief of the Luftwaffe General Staff, General der Flieger Hans Jeschonnek (right) accompanies Reichsmarschall Herman Göring for a ride on the latter's country estate in East Prussia in July 1941.
(ullstein bild via Getty Images)

10 Generaloberst Wolfram *Freiherr* von Richthofen, the commander of *Luftflotte* 4. (Von Richthofen Collection – kindly donated to the Author)

11 Von Richthofen relied considerably on Oberst Karl-Heinrich Schulz, the dependable Senior Quartermaster of *Luftflotte* 4. (Author's Collection)

12 Generalleutnant Martin Fiebig, the earnest, intelligent, dedicated, yet somewhat sensitive commander of VIII.*Fliegerkorps*, was in immediate command of the supply operation to Stalingrad. (Author's Collection)

13 A Ju 52/3m climbs into a grey Russian sky for another supply sortie.
(Author's Collection)

14 Ju 52/3m 1Z+FZ of 15./KG.z.b.V.1 flies low over a frozen river and close to another
aircraft in Russia in the winter of 1942–43. (EN Archive)

15 Oberst Otto-Lutz Förster, at far left, *Kommodore* of KG.z.b.V.1, discusses operations with three of his transport pilots during the Stalingrad airlift while the engine runs on a Ju 52/3m immediately behind them. (Möbius Collection)

16 Aircrew in fleece-lined winter flying suits and ground-support officers chat in front of a Ju 52/3m. (Author's Collection)

17 Supplies for Stalingrad stockpiled at Tatsinskaya. (Author's Collection)

18 An aircrew Feldwebel (centre, with cloth sleeve rank insignia) secures the lower platform of the fuselage loading hatch of a Ju 52/3m as soldiers unload supplies of matting and crates of ammunition. (EN Archive)

19 Fuel drums lie in the snow close to a Ju 52/3m. (Author's Collection)

20 This Ju 86E, coded VB+FN and fitted with BMW 132E radial engines, was assigned to *Luftnachrichtenschule* 3 but was commandeered for the Stalingrad airlift. (Author's Collection)

21 Oberst Dr. Ernst Kühl, the *Kommodore* of KG 55 and the *Lufttransportführer Morosowskaya* in immediate control of the He 111 transport and bomber units involved in the Stalingrad airlift. (Author's Collection)

Top and Above 22 and 23 Groundcrew load *Versorgungsbomben* (supply bombs for air-dropping) into a He 111H-20, apparently of KG 27. (EN Archive)

24 A He 111 from an unidentified unit airborne during a Russian winter. (EN Archive)

25 The senior Luftwaffe officer to remain in the Stalingrad pocket for any length of time was Generalmajor Wolfgang Pickert, commander of 9.*Flak-Division*. (Author's Collection)

26 Veteran transport pilot Oberstleutnant Ludwig Beckmann is seen here after the award of the Knight's Cross on 14 March 1943. (Möbius Collection)

27 German troops assisted by what appears to be a Luftwaffe airman in the left foreground haul a cart of supplies away from a Ju 52/3m which bears an owl emblem, possibly that of *Flugzeugführerschule* (C) 16. (EN Archive)

28 Major Erich Zähr was the commander of I./KG.z.b.V.172 during the Stalingrad airlift. (Möbius Collection)

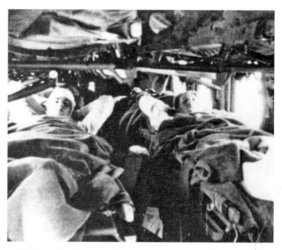

29 Wounded troops lie on canvas stretchers aboard a Ju 52/3m. Just under 25,000 wounded personnel were airlifted out of the Stalingrad 'fortress' by the Luftwaffe. (Author's Collection)

30 When horses were no longer available to pull the sleds, it was down to manpower. (EN Archive)

31 While this He 111 takes on fuel from a bowser, a mechanic uses a brush to sweep snow and ice away from the aircraft's control surfaces at an airfield west of the Don in the winter of 1942–43. (Author's Collection)

Opposite Below 32 This Fw 200 adorned with the 'World in a Ring' emblem as used by KG 40 over the Atlantic is believed to have been assigned to KGr.z.b.V.200 for use at Stalingrad. (Goss Collection)

33 Groundcrew pull a protective tarpaulin across the left wing of a He 111H-20 during the Russian winter. (EN Archive)

34 Photographed here against a grey winter sky, a pair of Ju 86s (an E-model to left and a G-model to right) from either KGr.z.b.V.21 or KGr.z.b.V.22 taxi out across the snow at the beginning of another mission to Stalingrad. (Goss Collection)

35 Hauptmann Hans-Jürgen Willers (left), an experienced bomber pilot, photographed here while with KG 40, would go on to take command of KGr.z.b.V.200 at Stalingrad. (Goss Collection)

after the breakthrough. Operations between neighbouring armies also had to be coordinated, especially in the case of mobile forces advancing deep into the enemy's defences.[3]

The next day Zhukov and Vasilevsky held similar meetings with officers of the 21st Army of the Southwestern Front and the 65th Army of the Don Front.[4] Vasilevsky also went on to visit the 51st, 57th and 64th Armies of the Stalingrad Front which would contribute the southern pincer push. According to Zhukov, the meetings 'demonstrated that commanders and political commissars had carried out the complex planning work with a high degree of responsibility and initiative'.[5]

Following these talks they drafted a plan for the *Stavka* that included particulars of combat readiness accompanied by detailed operational maps. Divisional strength varied on the three Fronts involved directly in the offensive: on the Southwestern Front, average strength was 8,800 men per division; on the Don Front 5,580 men; and on the Stalingrad Front, 4,000–5,000 men.[6] When they delivered their findings verbally to the *Stavka*, Zhukov and Vasilevsky advised that while the strengths of the opposing sides were generally equal, the Red Army held the advantage in key areas as a result of the influx of *Stavka* reserves. Furthermore, they were able to report that no sizeable enemy reinforcements had been detected moving to Stalingrad, nor had there been any significant shifting of formations within German-held territory, although there was a degree of uncertainty as to whether 6.*Armee* would hold out, and how long for.[7]

According to Zhukov, he returned to Moscow with Vasilevsky to brief Stalin on progress on the morning of 13 November, although this was quite probably 6 November. In any case, in one of his written accounts, Zhukov recorded such a meeting with the General Secretary of the Central Committee of the Communist Party of the Soviet Union, and found him to be in 'a good mood'.[8] In their report, Zhukov and Vasilevsky attributed some of the success in assembling the vast numbers of forces and supplies to the Fronts to the 'titanic work' undertaken by the workers of the rail and river transport services who had overcome autumn rains and mud to maintain logistical efficiency.

One of the most crucial items in the encirclement plan was the location of the link-up between the Southwestern and Stalingrad Fronts – the closing of the pincers. On this point, the intention was that, 'The junction of the tank and mechanised forces of the Southwestern and Stalingrad Fronts is to take place on the eastern bank of the River Don in the area of Kalach–Sovietskii, timed for the evening of the third or fourth day of operations'.[9] An outer ring to the closed pincers would be provided by the 4th Mechanised Corps of the Stalingrad Front.[10] The report concluded by stating that 'There is now every reason for the offensive to be opened by the troops of the Southwestern and Don Fronts on the 19th, and by the troops of the Stalingrad Front on the 20th'.[11]

On the eve of *Uranus*, Soviet forces assigned on what was termed the 'Stalingrad axis' totalled just over a million men, 13,541 guns (excluding anti-aircraft batteries and mortars), 894 tanks and 1,115 aircraft.[12] They had been brought into position by means of carefully orchestrated and scheduled movements, accompanied by considerable camouflage and stringent security measures (orders were not written down), as well as deception, such as the diversionary tactic of overtly increasing what appeared to be troop activity around Moscow, the construction of false bridges over the Don and the crossing of 160,000 men, more than 15,000 vehicles, guns and tanks and more than 10,000 horses over the Volga under the cover of darkness.[13]

Although somewhat abstruse in its origins, the military 'science' of the plan was simple[14]: two pincers – one main 'jab' from the north (Southwestern Front) in a south-easterly direction from the 65 km-wide Serafimovich bridgehead south of the Don, accompanied by a shorter, inner thrust by the Don Front from Kletskaya, and one from the south (Stalingrad Front) – would thrust towards each other and meet at Kalach, close to the Don, having cut through the enemy's flanks. In doing so they would envelop and isolate the German 6.*Armee* and, as much as possible, 4.*Panzerarmee*. The attack would exploit the weak line held by the Romanian 3rd Army, positioned between 6.*Armee* and the Italian Eighth Army, by smashing through from the north with infantry shock troops backed up by mobile forces. Eremenko's push from the south would also break through a Romanian army, this time the 4th.[15]

The *Stavka* was aware of the diminishing strength of *Heeresgruppe* B, and particularly 6.*Armee*, as they pushed eastwards with lengthening flanks, extended lines of supply and mounting casualties. On 19 November 1942, in terms of combat troops and tanks the Soviets outnumbered the Axis forces by a ratio of at least three-to-one (782,548 Soviet troops versus 234,252 Axis; 1,550 tanks versus 508; 22,019 guns and mortars versus under 10,000). In the air, the Red Air Force could draw upon 1,277 serviceable aircraft against 402 Luftwaffe machines, a ratio of 3.2-to-1.[16]

★ ★ ★

On the German side, it did not take a supreme amount of insight to recognise that the Russians might well take advantage of 6.*Armee*'s vulnerable left flank along the Don. All the divisions along the Axis northern front had reported movements and concentrations of enemy forces. Remarkably, Oberst Wilhelm Adam of the 6.*Armee* staff even went as far as recording that, 'At army headquarters and among the commanding generals *there was no doubt about the enemy's intention to surround the 6.Armee and 4.Panzer-Armee*.'[17] [Author's emphasis]. Neither was von Richthofen left in any doubt about the situation that was developing:

In front of the Romanians on the Don the Russians continue, very determinedly, to make their assault preparations. I deploy elements of the VIII.*Fliegerkorps* and other forces from the Fleet and Romanian air forces continuously against them. We gather our ground reserves together. When will the Russians go into action? At present they supposedly have a lack of ammunition. But artillery positions are now beginning to be stocked up. Hopefully the Russians will not be able to make serious inroads![18]

Also of significance is the post-war comment of Generalmajor Wolfgang Pickert, who commanded Luftwaffe forces in what became the Stalingrad 'pocket':

> The Russian offensive did *not* [original emphasis] come as a surprise. Enemy preparations for the offensive, particularly north of the Sixth Army in the area of Serafimovich and Kletskaya, had been known for a long time; the Russians had already successfully established bridgeheads across the Don River in these areas. For this reason, the Romanian forces which were stationed there were not surprised by the Russian attack.[19]

Indeed, from October 1942, Luftwaffe reconnaissance flights provided proof that the Soviet rail route from the north via Frolovo to Stalingrad was busy, with large numbers of troops assembling around Frolovo which then moved towards the Don, mostly at night in an attempt to conceal their progress. Night reconnaissance aircraft also picked up armoured columns driving with headlights switched on.[20] Von Richthofen noted that:

> The Russians are moving their forces to readiness positions on the Don in greater strength, supposedly because we are attacking their rear area assemblies from the air. I believe, however, that their moving forward is for the purpose of mounting an attack.[21]

But when such suspicions and evidence were relayed to the *Wolfschanze*, they were disregarded, as Wilhelm Adam recalled. 'The High Command simply did not take 6.*Armee*'s reports seriously, doubting that the Red Army could even think of another counter-offensive'. General Kurt Zeitzler, Chief of the Army General Staff, even went as far as to tell Paulus via telephone, in patronising tones, that the Red Army had been defeated and no longer had any meaningful reserves. The effect of such misinformed hubris greatly affected Paulus, and he seemed no longer able or willing to take an independent viewpoint. Adam succinctly encapsulated the moment when he stated 'Military obedience won over reason'.[22]

Meanwhile, in the shattered city, it had even become difficult to determine exactly where the 'frontline' was. In mid-November, Wilhelm Adam journeyed as far as the bank of the Volga with a pre-war acquaintance who had gone on to be the commander of an infantry regiment. Adam found the landscape desolate:

> Ruins, nothing but ruins. In the cellars among them huddled soldiers. Bomb craters and heaps of rubble made the once smooth street virtually

impassable. Glass splinters, window casements, bits of machines, wrecked cars, bedding, remains of furniture, cooking utensils, stoves, electricity cables, tram cables – an inconceivable jumble of destroyed and damaged objects of all kinds. Roske and I moved forward only with difficulty. No one could say exactly where the frontline ran in this rubble. Enemy troops could appear behind our soldiers at any time. Death lay behind every ruin and at every crossroads.[23]

Yet when Major Gerhard Engel, Hitler's army adjutant, made a visit to Stalingrad at around the same time, he was surprised at Paulus' degree of optimism over the future, and the fact that the army commander still believed the remaining Soviet-occupied parts of Stalingrad could be taken 'slowly but surely'.

From Bavaria, Hitler had signalled Paulus on the 16th that he appreciated the difficulties of fighting in Stalingrad and that the army's strength was greatly reduced, but, equally, the Russians would be contending with ice drifting down the Volga. Therefore, this was the time to exploit hampered enemy movement. Hitler thus wanted Paulus and his troops to summon their last reserves of energy and to fight through to the Volga, or at least take the metal works and ordnance factory.[24] However, Paulus complained to Engel about supply, and asked for greater aerial support, as well as more reserves to place behind the Italian and Romanian units west of the Don bend. He also told Engel that if any enemy development took place on his army's flanks, then 'it would be crazy to hold on to Stalingrad'.

Two days after Engel had returned to Rastenburg, on the 16th, he found Hitler to be in a 'grim, dark mood'. The dictator was apparently feeling the effects of his age and exhaustion.[25] The first snow fell over Stalingrad the same day, and there was still a very inadequate amount of winter clothing reaching the front.[26]

One historian has expressed surprise that at this time the commanders of 6.*Armee* had not organised a mechanised strike force ahead of the Russian offensive, and that even after it had commenced, Paulus did nothing in this regard – although it has to be said that so deep had his army gone into the city by this stage and so difficult was the urban battle environment there that creating such a force would have been a challenge. The vehicles and armour of 16. and 24.*Panzer-Divisions* were simply left stuck in Stalingrad.[27]

★ ★ ★

Uranus literally blasted into action on the morning of 19 November: for more than an hour the 3,500 guns and mortars of Vatutin's Southwestern Front and Rokossovsky's Don Front laid down a tremendous blanket of fire which tore up the frozen ground around the positions of the Romanian Third Army. Then, following the barrage, at 0850 hrs, columns of Soviet infantry and armour from the 1st Guards Army and the 5th Tank Army moved forward from the Serafimovich bridgehead through a chill mist, guided in places by members of the local population. The temperature fell to -6°C. Deep, drifting snow overnight had reduced visibility to near zero and had turned the terrain into a flat, white, featureless, plateau, relieved only by the tips of the tallest frozen steppe grass. The snow concealed roads, gullies and ditches.

Undaunted, the second Soviet thrust launched by the 21st Army commenced from the Kletskaya bridgehead. Both thrusts were heading for the bridge at Kalach on the Don, between 80 and 160 km from the Soviet starting line and about 80 km west of Stalingrad.[28] Within a short time, men from advanced rifle battalions together with combat engineers supported by a small number of light tanks came to within 200–300 m of the German and Romanian forward line, where they began to cut through barbed wire and remove mines wherever they discovered them. The main battle tanks and infantry arrived shortly afterwards.[29]

Romanian resistance to the attack was varied; in places it simply crumbled, while elsewhere there was patchy defence. The problem was that the Romanians lacked effective anti-tank weapons, most being of antiquated 37 mm and 47 mm calibre, with very few of the better German 75 mm guns. Furthermore, due to a lack of material to build field fortifications, the Romanian infantry and gunners were left largely exposed.[30] The net result was that the Red Army's armour punched through. By nightfall, forward units of the 5th Tank Army had advanced around 50 km through a gap in the line of the Romanian II. Army Corps at Blinov.[31]

It was not long before the staff of *Heeresgruppe* B realised that the isolating of 6.*Armee* was the objective of the Soviet attack. At 2200 hrs that evening, its commanding officer, Generaloberst Maximilian von Weichs, signalled Paulus warning him that the situation in the area of the Romanian Third Army meant that in order to secure the flank of 6.*Armee*, all offensive operations within Stalingrad should cease immediately. Weichs told the army commander to pull out three Panzer divisions and an infantry division and to relocate them to meet the Russian attack to the west.[32]

Meanwhile, at the headquarters of *Luftflotte* 4 at Mariupol on the evening of the 19th, von Richthofen recorded:

> This morning, the Russians started their expected great assault on the Don and broke through on a wide front. The Romanian *Korps* was torn apart and Russian tanks rolled into the hinterland. Our reserves held themselves in readiness for a counter-attack. By stopping the assault on Stalingrad, forces from there were also drawn into the battle. However, the effects will become apparent over the next few days. The situation is unclear at the moment. But the Russians are now deep within our forces. The weather is bad, with icy fog, snow and freezing rain. No sorties whatsoever are possible. Hence we can get no clarification on the situation from the air. Hopefully, the Russians will not get as far as the large supply railway – a possibility which is certainly to be reckoned with. I begin the process of relocating all forces of IV.*Fliegerkorps* to the breakthrough front so that

in the Caucasus, aside from two *Jagdgruppen* and the reconnaissance units, nothing more remains there. In practice, however, this does not work because of the weather. As soon as good weather appears and we are able to deploy all our forces, the Russian phantom will blow away, assuming he does not first of all catch us on our airfields.[33]

Generalmajor Wolfgang Pickert conceded in his diary that, 'The situation is becoming very grave'.[34]

To the south of Stalingrad on the 20th, where Eremenko's Stalingrad Front had been delayed for several hours because of fog, the 51st Army commenced its attack between Lakes Sarpa and Tsata, running into the Romanian VI. Army Corps. As Stalingrad Front thrust forward, the Romanian resistance collapsed and broke at Tundutovo too. Around 12,600 Romanian troops had no option other than to retreat into the ruins of Stalingrad.[35] 4. *Panzerarmee* commander Generaloberst Hermann Hoth remarked contemptuously that the 'work of weeks had been ruined in a day'.[36]

In the early morning of the 21st, tanks from Romanenko's 5th Tank Army continued to press on towards Kalach. Near Mayarov, it ran into elements of 24. *Panzer-Division* that had managed to extricate themselves from Stalingrad. Although the Panzer crews fought a determined battle lasting five days, with the benefit of massed armour and infantry, the Soviets eventually outflanked the German force and advanced towards the Liska River, which was reached on the 22nd, only some 40 km from Kalach. By nightfall, the bridge over the Don was captured by 26th Tank Corps and the surviving elements of Generalleutnant Hans-Valentin Hube's XIV. *Panzerkorps* retreated eastwards back across that river.[37]

Meanwhile, on the 21st, Paulus had moved his headquarters from Golubinskaya on the Don to Gumrak, closer to the 'front' at Stalingrad. In the interim, however, together with his Chief of Staff, he flew to Nizhne-Chirskaya at the junction of the Don and the Chir, where it was planned to build a winter headquarters for 6. *Armee*, and where already direct communications had been set up with *Heeresgruppe* B, OKH and the *Wolfschanze*. Paulus wanted to acquaint himself with the quarters and to take advantage of the communications there to more fully understand the overall situation around the Don and Stalingrad. But hardly had he arrived than Hitler, who had misinterpreted Paulus' intentions, gruffly signalled him to return to Stalingrad. He further ordered 6. *Armee* to remain where it was, regardless of any 'temporary encirclement'.[38]

Some cracks did appear in the Soviet arrangements: those formations pushing from south of Stalingrad were committed without adequate supplies because they had not been able to be ferried in time across the now almost icebound Volga. Food stocks quickly ran low.

Nevertheless, in overall terms, *Uranus* had been well planned and well executed; it exploited the fact that 6. *Armee* had become embroiled in deep urban warfare where lack of movement or slow movement at best, difficulties in supply, worsening weather and the exhaustion of its troops had adversely affected its ability to defend itself against a strong assault from its rear. Within four days, the Romanian Third Army in the north had suffered the loss of 75,000 men, 34,000 horses and the equipment of five divisions.[39] Furthermore, 6.*Armee*'s parent command, *Heeresgruppe* B, had become committed to too many objectives to render the necessary support, but in any case, it did not have the resources.[40]

Meanwhile during the evening of 22 November, infantry-laden tanks from the Soviet 20th Tank Regiment under Maj N. A. Doroshkevich, representing the spearhead of Col M. I. Rodionov's 36th Mechanised Brigade, arrived in the little town of Sovietskii, which they then cleared of enemy forces. Doroshkevich duly reported to Rodionov on his position, and the latter informed his immediate superior, Gen Vasily Volsky, commander of 4th Mechanised Corps. Later that evening, Stalin telephoned Eremenko to seek confirmation of the capture of Sovietskii. When the Front commander replied in the affirmative, a delighted Stalin responded, 'Tomorrow you can link up with the Southwestern Front whose troops have taken Kalach'.

And so finally at 1600 hrs on 23 November, the advanced elements of the Soviet pincers linked up in the area of Sovietskii-Marinovka, 20 km east of Kalach, when five T-34 tanks of Col Pyotr Zhidkov's 45th Tank Brigade from 21st Army's 4th Tank Corps, Southwestern Front, met forward tank crews from Rodionov's brigade. As the jubilant brigade commanders met, in the traditional Russian way, they kissed three times.[41]

Stalin, Eremenko, Zhukov and Vaslievsky had more than achieved their objective. As the Red Army pincers closed up east of Kalach four days after *Uranus* had commenced, the German 6.*Armee*, together with elements of 4.*Panzerarmee* and what was left of two Romanian divisions, in all amounting to more than 250,000 Axis troops from 23 divisions and their support units, plus some 100 tanks, around 2,000 guns and more than 10,000 vehicles, as well as 12,000 Luftwaffe personnel comprising 9.*Flak-Division* and various signals and support units, became – if not entirely encircled – then trapped. They were effectively cut off and isolated from *Heeresgruppe* B in a 'pocket' – or *Kessel* – spanning just 50 km from west to east and 40 km from north to south.[42] The reality for the Germans was that this was much, much more than a mere *Stützpunkt*, while for the Russians it was the first time their forces had sealed off an entire German army.[43]

8

'Impossible'

Objective comparison of the conditions at Demyansk with those at Stalingrad should have warned German planners that the air supply of the Sixth Army was a military impossibility.

GENERALMAJOR FRITZ MORZIK, *GERMAN AIR FORCE AIRLIFT OPERATIONS*, 1961

Adolf Hitler was exhausted. He needed some rest and decided to head for his mountain-top retreat, the Berghof, in the Bavarian Alps. But it was not to be the most relaxing or restorative of 'holidays'.

In the afternoon of 7 November, he departed the *Wolfschanze* in his command train to journey south, firstly to Munich, where he would commemorate the 19th anniversary of the Beer Hall *Putsch* by speaking to an audience of 'old fighters' at the *Löwenbraukeller*. His restless sleep was disturbed in the early hours of the following morning when his train was halted by a signal at a small, rural railway station deep in Thuringia. An official clambered aboard the train with an urgent message from the Foreign Ministry in Berlin. Reports were coming in that the bad situation in North Africa had worsened as British and American troops poured onto the beaches of Morocco and Algeria to mark the beginning of the Allied landings there under the codename *Torch* – the largest amphibious invasion in history. Nevertheless, determined to enjoy some rest and recuperation, after delivering his distracted speech to the old comrades in the beer hall, and accompanied by his personal adjutants and members of his inner circle, Hitler departed for his retreat in Berchtesgaden.[1]

High in the clear air, amidst the snow-capped mountains, the battles in North Africa and Russia seemed a world away. But on the morning of 19 November, the *Führer* received a telephone call from the *Wolfschanze* which shattered any sense of relaxation he may have been enjoying. At the other end of the line was General der Infanterie Kurt Zeitzler, Halder's younger replacement as Chief of Staff at the OKH.

The 47-year-old Zeitzler had taken up his new position on 24 September. He was very different in character to the conservative Halder, being known by the moniker *Kugelblitz* (Ball Lightning) on account of his energy and confidence. Not a particularly widely known figure and of relatively junior rank until the spring of 1942, Zeitzler had been plucked by Hitler from his position as Chief of Staff to Generalfeldmarschall Gerd von Rundstedt in the West, where he had played a part in the defeat of the British-Canadian raid at Dieppe in August. But if Zeitzler was something of a mystery, he was at least known to those close to Hitler – men like Jodl and Generalmajor Rudolf Schmundt, Hitler's personal adjutant. Zeitzler indicated his style at his first staff meeting at the *Wolfschanze* when he welcomed his fellow officers with a resounding 'Heil Hitler!'[2] This picture of him has to be set against the much more 'mellow' tone he adopted in his post-war account of how he found the atmosphere at Hitler's headquarters at this period:

> I took up my duties and immediately became aware of the most peculiar atmosphere which prevailed at Supreme Headquarters as a result of the breakdown of the offensive in the East. To an officer coming from an operational staff in the field, this atmosphere was not only weird but positively incredible. It was compounded by mistrust and anger. Nobody had any faith in his colleagues. Hitler distrusted everyone.

Many officers, believing they were in disgrace, appeared utterly disheartened. Hitler's fury was directed against the eastern armies as a whole, and particularly against the army and army group commanders there. He now lead an entirely retired life, brooding upon his suspicions. He would shake hands with no general.[3]

For the moment, Zeitzler had Hitler's favour. On this occasion, however, for all his bravado, Zeitzler did not relish what he had to impart to the *Führer* as he informed him that massed Soviet armour had broken through the Romanian line on the Don. Further worrying updates followed during the afternoon, and resulted in what Engel has described as a 'bad evening situation conference'.[4]

When the second Soviet strike of *Uranus* commenced the following day from south of Stalingrad, Hitler realised that both 6.*Armee* and 4.*Panzerarmee* were threatened with being surrounded. He immediately contacted Generalfeldmarschall von Manstein in northern Russia and told him he was to take charge of the newly formed *Heeresgruppe Don* – in reality a composite formation made up of the battered Romanian Third Army, what had not been spliced away of 4.*Panzerarmee* into the Soviet encirclement and the trapped 6.*Armee*.

Generaloberst Hans Jeschonnek, the Chief of the Luftwaffe General Staff, was called by Hitler to the Berghof on the 20th. He had arrived from East Prussia in the absence of Reichsmarschall Göring, the portly Commander-in-Chief of the Luftwaffe, who was chairing (conveniently) a conference at Carinhall – his plush country residence in the Schorfheide Forest north-east of Berlin – on problems associated with getting oil out of the Maikop wells.[5]

At 42 years of age, Jeschonnek was an upright Prussian officer who had seen flying service in the final months of World War I. He was young to hold such a senior and highly demanding office in the Luftwaffe – he had performed this role since February 1939. Jeschonnek was also something of a mercurial character – cool, sober, intelligent and perceptive, yet often evasive and not the strongest personality; popular with the lower ranks, yet he could be waspish with his colleagues. In fairness to Jeschonnek, he had weathered a difficult post and had absorbed much unjustified tongue-lashing from Göring, operating under the stress and tension that working with such a personality brought. Hitler and von Richthofen, however, liked him, which meant the megalomaniac Göring distrusted him. Jeschonnek's other problem was that his outward strength and bearing masked a lack of confidence and a dislike of confrontation.

Almost as soon as Jeschonnek arrived at the Berghof, Hitler raised the plight of 6.*Armee* with him. It seems that the unwary and unprepared Chief of Staff was convinced by Hitler that the *Armee's* predicament would be temporary, and that the 'newly raised' army group to be led by von Manstein would shortly be launching a relief effort towards Stalingrad. In this context, when the *Führer* raised the prospect of supplying 6.*Armee* by air for a period, Jeschonnek may well have had the precedents of the fundamentally successful Demyansk and Kholm air supply operations of the previous winter in mind when considering his response.

If that was the case, it was an error. However, it is believed that Jeschonnek advised Hitler at this point that provided both dedicated transport aircraft and bombers brought in as emergency transports were deployed, and as long as satisfactory airfields both inside and outside the *Kessel* were available and maintained to the required operational standard, then an air supply operation was possible.

This was not realistic. At Demyansk, amidst harsh winter conditions but without much threat from the VVS, the Luftwaffe needed to deploy 500 Ju 52/3m transports – almost the entire transport force – in order to maintain 150 serviceable aircraft that could carry II.*Armeekorps'* daily required supplies of 300 tons for its 100,000 men. Yet Jeschonnek overlooked, or avoided, or forgot, that fighters were available for escorting the transports to and from Demyansk, that the approach and return routes were reasonably short and that the airfields used remained constant throughout the operation. Furthermore, the men in the pockets at Demyansk and Kholm were at least able to look forward to spring, whereas at Stalingrad, winter would be setting in. Nevertheless, human and materiel losses sustained at Demyansk and Kholm were high.[6]

The situation developing at Stalingrad was much more magnified: if the 250,000 men became trapped there they would, logically, require 750 tons per day. 6.*Armee* had indicated that it could continue to function on 500 tons per day, and that for basic *survival* it would need 300 tons per day – a figure that excluded the materials and equipment needed to actually fight. To fulfil 750 tons per day, the Luftwaffe would need 1,250 Ju 52/3ms to ensure 375 serviceable aircraft – way beyond its capability, even if it brought in bombers as emergency carriers. Furthermore, the weather was turning, and around Stalingrad the VVS presence was not just increasing but becoming more hostile. Losses could be expected from both of these threats.[7]

Nevertheless, Jeschonnek's response was what Hitler wanted to hear. He – and Jeschonnek – assumed that until von Manstein launched his relief effort, Paulus would stand firm for perhaps a week, possibly ten days, and the Luftwaffe could do the rest. On the afternoon of the 21st Hitler sent his signal to Paulus warning him to stay put despite 'temporary encirclement' [see Chapter Seven], adding, *'Über Luftversorgung folgt Befehl'* ('Regarding an airlift, orders to follow').[8]

Jeschonnek must assume some responsibility for the path of subsequent events, for although von Richthofen's diary entry for 17 November indicates that he was expecting a visit from the Chief of Staff, it appears that Jeschonnek's travel arrangements to southern Russia were delayed due to the prevailing bad weather. But in any case, the summons from Berchtesgaden would have taken priority over a visit to von Richthofen. Whatever the case, however, there is no evidence to date to indicate that he attempted to discuss 6.*Armee's* situation with either von Richthofen or Fiebig *before* he saw Hitler, and thus obtain the latest views from the regional air commanders. Furthermore, when discussing the notion of keeping the army supplied by air, he did not ask Hitler for some time while he contacted and consulted the senior Luftwaffe *Lufttransportführer*, Oberst Morzik. This may have been as a result of an instilled ignorance or lack of understanding about airlifts, simply because there were no specialist airlift or transport officers with first-hand experience (and Morzik was a mere colonel) to advise Göring and/or Jeschonnek on risks and potential pitfalls based on earlier operations.[9] Metaphorically, the writing was on the wall (although it was not read).

Conditions in southern Russia were changing rapidly – and not for the better. As a typical example, at Tatsinskaya, an airfield that would play a major part in the coming airlift, the air- and groundcrews of the Ju 88-equipped bomber *Gruppe* I./KG 51, under Major Fritz-Herbert Dierich, were finding it increasingly difficult to operate in support of German ground forces. The *Gruppe* had returned to Tatsinskaya after almost a month based at Sarabus, a relatively peaceful airfield in the Crimea where their aircraft were overhauled and the men rested and took walks in the fresh air of the vine-clad hills. On 3 November they transferred north as the Russian winter started to bite and the temperature dropped from zero to -34°C. Life was spent in earthen dugouts as fierce, icy gales blew across the steppe. Groundcrews would have to leave whatever shelter they had in the middle of the night to shovel snow away from the Ju 88s and start their engines. In checking engines, bomb-release gear and radio equipment with gloveless hands, technicians frequently suffered frostbite. Guns and oil froze.[10]

At the new forward headquarters of VIII.*Fliegerkorps* at Oblivskaya, as the weather worsened in the early evening of the 21st, the *Korps* commander,

Generalleutnant Martin Fiebig, was becoming increasingly concerned over the position of 6.*Armee*; after all, it was the prime mission of his units to render air support to Paulus and all other army operations in the Stalingrad area.

The 51-year-old Fiebig, a Silesian like von Richthofen, was a competent, conscientious and experienced air commander who bore a stern expression beneath his thin-rimmed spectacles. He had served as a battalion adjutant in an infantry regiment in World War I, seeing action at the battle of Tannenburg and the Masurian Lakes before joining the Imperial Air Service, in which he qualified as a pilot in 1915. He was promoted to Oberleutnant in September of that year. After serving as an aerial observer in a *Feldflieger-Abteilung*, Fiebig was appointed *Staffelführer* of *Kampfstaffel* 13, a part of *Kagohl* 3, with whom he carried out operations in Gotha G.IV heavy bombers over the Western Front from Sint-Denijs-Westrem, in Belgium. On 10 May 1917, he survived when his Gotha made an emergency landing in a ploughed field and ended up on its nose. Fiebig flew several missions over England, including one on 7 July 1917 when he took a series of photographs of central London in daylight from 4,300 m. Fiebig was also a recipient of the *Ehrenbecher für den Sieger im Luftkampfe* for shooting down a French Voisin bomber. He was promoted to Hauptmann and given command of *Bogohl* 9 in the final months of the war.

After working as a flight despatcher for Deutsche Lufthansa in the 1920s, Fiebig joined the still covert new German Air Force in 1934, where he met and worked with von Richthofen and other young officers who would go on to become Luftwaffe generals. In July 1938 he was appointed to command KG 253, a bomber wing based at Gotha, which was redesignated KG 4 'General Wever' in May 1939. As *Geschwaderkommodore*, Fiebig led the He 111–equipped wing in missions over Poland in 1939, but he was later shot down and captured over the Netherlands on 10 May 1940. After a spell in the RLM as head of flight safety, he took command of IV.*Fliegerkorps* on 2 April 1941 during the campaign in the Balkans, then in June Fiebig was appointed to lead II.*Fliegerkorps* in central Russia. As commander of both these formations, he specialised in close-support work, at which he was very successful. Fiebig was a natural candidate to take charge of von Richthofen's old command, VIII.*Fliegerkorps*, on 1 July 1942.[11]

Although Fiebig was not a man given to unnecessary alarm, since the start of *Uranus* – and in view of its impetus – he feared that the men at Stalingrad may not be fully appraised of the quickly developing situation on the ground. He therefore telephoned the *Armee*'s Chief of Staff, Generalmajor Arthur Schmidt, to inform him that strong Soviet armoured forces had reached the Don highway north-west of Kalach, and were thus threatening the bridge, and also that more Russian tanks had reached Sety, indicating another enemy thrust to the north-west. Schmidt responded that a 'sufficiently strong unit' armed with anti-tank guns was committed to defending the bridge at Kalach, and thus he saw no immediate danger.

Fiebig then asked Schmidt, given this situation, what the immediate intentions of 6.*Armee* were. Down the line some 70 km away, Schmidt replied that Paulus was considering an 'all-round' defence of Stalingrad – or as Fiebig later termed it, an *Igel* (an all-around perimeter defence known as a 'hedgehog' or *Igelstellung*), but a final decision on that would be made early the following day at a meeting with Generaloberst Hoth, the commander of 4.*Panzerarmee*, at Nizhne-Chirskaya. Fiebig recalled of the subsequent conversation into which General Paulus listened from time to time from a second telephone:

> Going further into the possibility of an *Igelung* defence, I asked how they were thinking of supplying 6.*Armee* since the supply line from the rear might be cut very soon. Generalmajor Schmidt answered that the supplies would then have to be carried by air. I explained that I thought it impossible to supply a whole army by air, particularly at a time when our transport aircraft were being used in great numbers for the campaign in North Africa.[12]

Fiebig duly reported his conversation to von Richthofen, who summarised things in his diary that night:

> The weather is bad everywhere. Nowhere is it possible to fly. The Russians advance from the Don further to the south and capture the bridge at Kalach, which, strangely enough, was not defended at all. The left wing of 6.*Armee* bends ever more backwards. 6.*Armee* sways in its decision-making back and forth, and arrives increasingly at the conclusion that they 'hedgehog' themselves between Stalingrad and the Don. They believe they are unable to hold Kalach [the town].
>
> 6.*Armee* believes that in their *Igel* position, they can receive provisions and supplies through the *Flotte*. An attempt will be made by all available means to prove to them that this cannot be done, as the necessary means for transporting the required quantities are not available. This has also been notified to the Ob.d.L. [*Oberbefehlshaber der Luftwaffe* – Commander-in-Chief of the Luftwaffe], the OKH, and the *Heeresgruppe*.

Late into the night over a 'dreadful number' of telephone calls, a frantic von Richthofen endeavoured to contact, either successfully or unsuccessfully, in order to spell out to Göring in Berlin, Jeschonnek at Berchtesgaden (when it was too late), Zeitzler at the *Wolfschanze* (again too late), Weichs at *Heeresgruppe* B, and even to his old Chief of Staff at VIII.*Fliegerkorps*, Generalmajor Rudolf Meister, who was assigned to the *Luftwaffenführungsstab*, that an airlift was not a viable option to sustain 6.*Armee* while it waited for von Manstein.[13] It got him nowhere, and his attempts to speak to Hitler were also refused.

Evidently now vexed, Fiebig rose early next morning and went straight to the telephone. He wanted to speak to Schmidt again urgently ahead of the planned meeting he was due to have with Paulus and Hoth that day:

> At 0700 I called up Schmidt again, telling him that I thought we were relying too much on our air supply. I explained again that, after long

deliberations, based on my experiences and with my knowledge of the available resources, I thought it impossible to supply 6.*Armee* by air. Also, weather conditions and the enemy situation were completely incalculable factors; I wanted to tell him this before his conference with General Hoth, but General Schmidt then mentioned that Hoth had just come through the door. Our conversation ended.[14]

This conversation serves to illustrate the breakdown in communication at senior level within the German forces' command and the lack of comprehension over the practicalities of mounting and sustaining a major airlift at a time of worsening military predicament – and weather. What took place between Fiebig and Schmidt would, over the coming weeks, be replicated and amplified in terms of miscalculation, stubbornness and downright ignorance at the very highest levels, resulting in extremes of desperation and horror.

More firm evidence of the efforts to which *Luftflotte* 4 went to try to convince the *Luftwaffenführungsstab* of the fallacy of an airlift can be seen in the radio signal intercept decrypts of German wireless traffic as produced by the British Government Code and Cypher School at Bletchley Park, in Buckinghamshire. One signal of 22 November from Oberst Karl-Heinrich Schulz, the Senior Quartermaster with *Luftflotte* 4, to the *Luftwaffenführungsstab*, noted:

> Any appreciable supply by air to 6th Army (daily need roughly estimated by Army Group B at 1,000 to 1,100 tons 'O' fuel ['Otto' – Diesel]) is not possible on grounds of transport available (80 Ju 52s), fuel and weather situation.[15]

If the army commanders needed another viewpoint from the Luftwaffe, they received it from Generalmajor Pickert, whose Flak units remained stationed in the Stalingrad area. He met with them after Schmidt had talked with Fiebig:

> At about 0800 hrs I met with Paulus, Schmidt and Hoth at the AOK [*Armeeoberkommando* – Army Higher Command]. Schmidt briefly described the situation to me, and asked for my decision. I said, 'We must break out to the south-west at once'. Schmidt felt this couldn't be done due to the shortage of motor fuel, and that such a move would result in disaster such as suffered by Napoleon.

Pickert offered 160 of his 2 cm Flak guns and ammunition to support a breakout. Even without motor fuel to haul them, the Luftwaffe general said that his gun crews could man-haul their guns across the steppe if necessary:

> But the decision to go into an *Igel* and not to break out for the present remains unchanged because the orders to remain at Stalingrad are binding. This was decisive: Schmidt said we would enter an *Igel* and get our supplies by airlift. I immediately countered that I did not believe it was possible to supply an entire army by an airlift, particularly since the weather was bound to present great difficulties in winter. Schmidt [replied], 'It will just have to work; in the meantime, I guess we can eat up all these horses inside the pocket'.[16]

Thus, a situation had been reached where, in Paulus' opinion, the *Führer's* order had to be obeyed, while members of his staff thought that the best course of action was to form a 'hedgehog' defence and rely on air supply until relieved by *Heeresgruppe Don.* This decision was vehemently opposed by the Luftwaffe generals von Richthofen, Fiebig and Pickert. They were not without support from the army – although some of it was unknown to them.

One source states that on the 22nd, the commander of LI.*Armeekorps,* General der Artillerie Walther von Seydlitz-Kurzbach, who viewed the prospect of an *Igel* defence, and thus the ceasing of movement, as 'unthinkable'. He duly arranged a meeting of his fellow corps commanders of IV. (Generaloberst Erwin Jaenicke), VIII. (Generaloberst Walter Heitz), XI. (General der Infanterie Karl Strecker) and XIV.*Panzerkorps* (Generaloberst Hans-Valentin Hube) at Gumrak, inside the pocket. Collectively, the generals agreed to attempt a staged breakout on the 25th.[17] Curiously, von Seydlitz-Kurzbach's unilateral initiative was given approval by *Heeresgruppe* B, but without Paulus' knowledge.[18] Indeed, Generaloberst Weichs, to whom von Richthofen had spoken on the 21st, felt the only practical option was for a breakout, despite the inevitable heavy losses, and he was sufficiently concerned to send a signal to Zeitzler via his operations officer at 1845 hrs on the evening of the 23rd, the text of which is reproduced in Manfred Kehrig's seminal study of the Stalingrad battle:

Despite the extraordinary gravity of the decision to be made, the implications of which I am fully aware of, I have to report that I consider the withdrawal of 6.*Armee*, as suggested by Paulus, to be necessary.

It is not possible to supply an army of 20 divisions by air. With the available air transport space – assuming the appropriate weather conditions – only 1/10th of the actual daily requirement can be flown into the pocket each day.[19]

The fly in the breakout ointment was the rear perimeter (previously the front) – in essence, the Volga. The ability to carry out an immediate breakout in a lightning fashion, redolent of that which 6.*Armee* had performed so well at Kharkov in May 1942, was impossible because the Army's rear was open to enemy attack and so had to be secured, thus requiring precious forces and depleting attacking strength.[20]

More than 2,500 km away from Stalingrad, in Berlin, with the oil conference concluded, and a whole day *after* Jeschonnek had spoken with Hitler, on the evening of the 21st, Hermann Göring had hauled himself onto his plushly fitted personal train, *Asien* (Asia), and set off for the Berghof to report to the *Führer*. The Reichsmarschall had been summoned by a telephone call from Hitler earlier in the day, during which he spoke about the mounting crisis at Stalingrad. Göring did his best to allay Hitler's apprehension; he told the *Führer* that the Luftwaffe could be counted on to do what was necessary. At this point, once the telephone call was over, the Reichsmarschall set about instructing General der Flieger Hans-Georg von Seidel, the Luftwaffe's Quartermaster General, and Generalleutnant Otto Langemeyer, the Chief of *Abteilung* 4 (Quartiermeister) of the Luftwaffe General Staff, to make ready every available transport aircraft – including those assigned to his own courier flight – for a major air supply operation.[21] Curiously, Morzik, as the *Lufttransportführer* on von Seidel's staff, was not present, nor was he consulted.[22]

Göring knew what lay ahead at Berchtesgaden, but that did not deter him from his plans to move on as soon as possible to Paris, where he wanted to tour the art galleries for some acquisitions to add to his private collections of paintings, tapestries, statues and antiques. He travelled with his valet, nurse and a heart specialist, as well as a small fleet of luxury Mercedes loaded on flat cars coupled to various baggage wagons.[23] It was bad timing: *Asien* pulled into Berchtesgaden late on the evening of the 22nd as Hitler was preparing to return on his train to the *Wolfschanze*. Perhaps with some relief for Göring, the meeting with Hitler was, necessarily, to be brief. As Göring strode into the Berghof, Hitler once more asked him about Stalingrad. Explanations of Göring's subsequent response survive in the recollections of two of his close associates, and each explanation offers a different angle: firstly, the notion that Hitler applied a form of blackmail over the airlift as recounted by General der Flieger Bruno Loerzer, who quoted Göring as saying with some degree of feebleness:

> Hitler told me, 'Now listen, Göring, if the Luftwaffe can't do it then 6.*Armee* is lost!' So he had me by the sword-knot and I had no choice but to agree, otherwise I and the Luftwaffe would have been guilty of the loss of 6.*Armee*. So I had to say, 'My *Führer*, we can do it!'[24]

Göring may have been worrying a little needlessly over this point, since as Hitler's chosen successor, it is unlikely that Hitler would have wanted to burden and tarnish Göring's reputation with the responsibility of a failed airlift.[25]

Secondly, the Reichsmarschall later told Oberstleutnant Paul Körner, the Secretary of State for the Prussian State ministry and the Four Year Plan, that in his absence Jeschonnek had already presented a plan to Hitler for an air supply operation. According to Körner, Göring admitted:

> Before I had a chance to see the plan, Hitler had already seen it! All I could say was, 'My *Führer*, you have the numbers. If they are correct, then I shall be available'. I myself would give the men in Stalingrad a free hand to decide what to do for themselves. But if the *Führer* has made a decision, I have to go with it despite any concerns I may have.[26]

This, crucially, was despite the fact that while still at the Berghof, Göring took a call from Jeschonnek, who had realised he had made a critical error in his calculations (aside from an overestimation of aircraft resources). When it came to the externally-loaded 250-kg and 1,000-kg air-drop containers to be carried by bombers, he had based his tonnage figures on the kilogram description used for the respective container – thus, for example, '1,000 kg' for the *Mischlastabwurfbehälter* 1000 (mixed load) unit. This denoted the *gross weight* of the device, whereas the actual *internal payload* was only around 720-800 kg.[27] Being the honest, responsible officer he was, Jeschonnek immediately advised Göring, but the Reichsmarschall ordered his Chief of Staff not to advise Hitler of this miscalculation.[28] Fatefully, Jeschonnek did not have the strength of character (unlike von Richthofen, Zeitzler or von Manstein) to object to Göring, for as one senior Luftwaffe General Staff officer has commented:

> He made no clear-cut contradiction of the idea of carrying out a vast airlift operation. This could be explained by the fact that Jeschonnek always considered it to be his sole duty to execute to the letter, without criticism, the desires of his *Führer*.[29]

And with that, during the evening of the 22nd, Göring departed for his shopping trip to Paris in *Asien*, while at 2200 hrs, Hitler's train also rolled out of Berchtesgaden, the *Führer* cutting his 'holiday' short to return to East Prussia, where he would deal with the pressing military situations in Russia and North Africa, about which Zeitzler kept sending alarming updates.

Paulus, meanwhile, had been floundering in indecision throughout the 22nd and much of the 23rd over the question of whether to 'remain on the Volga', as the favoured term among Hitler's close staff at Berchtesgaden went, or to attempt to fight out of encirclement towards the south-west. He finally summoned the courage to signal Hitler at 2345 hrs on the 23rd, requesting 'freedom of action'. In fairness, the army commander was as blunt as he could be, and in so doing Paulus echoed Napoleon's maxim as referred to in the Introduction to this book:

> My *Führer*, since the arrival of your signal of the evening of 22.11 there has been a rapid aggravation of the situation. It has not been possible to seal off the pocket in the south-west and west. Enemy breakthroughs are clearly imminent there. Ammunition and fuel are nearly used up. Numerous batteries and anti-tank weapons have run out of ammunition. *Timely and adequate supplies are out of the question* [Author emphasis]. The Army is facing annihilation in the immediate future. This demands the immediate withdrawal of all divisions from Stalingrad, and of strong forces from the northern front. The inescapable consequence must then be a breakthrough towards the south-west. Admittedly, a great deal of material will be lost, but the bulk of valuable fighting men will be saved. I accept full responsibility for this appraisal, although I wish to record that Generals Heitz, von Seydlitz, Strecker, Hube and Jaenicke share my assessment. In view of the circumstances, I once more request freedom of action.[30]

The signal reveals succinctly what was, at best, the dramatic reverse of fortune facing the *Heer* on the Volga, and at worst – and more realistically – the prospect of impending military catastrophe.

Meanwhile, that evening, von Seydlitz-Kurzbach had begun to make preparations to move his units from the northern Stalingrad front to prepare for a breakout; he issued instructions for his troops to burn their stores, such as overcoats, uniforms, boots, documents, maps, typewriters and food, and to destroy their positions. But the resulting fires attracted the Russians, and the 94th Infantry Division suffered nearly 1,000 casualties as it made its move. Hitler was furious and blamed Paulus. The *Führer*'s solution was to split command of Stalingrad in two, appointing none other than von Seydlitz-Kurzbach to lead the northern sector. It was Paulus who handed an embarrassed von Seydlitz-Kurzbach the signal from *Heeresgruppe Don*, but von Manstein managed to get the order amended.[31]

Hitler's tedious train journey from Bavaria back to East Prussia over 22–23 November was not helped by the frequent stops, as his Luftwaffe adjutant Nicolaus von Below described:

> The journey took 20 hours. Every three to four hours we made a long stop for a telephone conversation with Zeitzler. He was making urgent demands for permission to extricate 6.*Armee* before the net closed. Hitler would not allow a single step back.[32]

Hitler remained out of contact from all the key players in Russia: from *Heeresgruppe* B, from 6.*Armee*, from von Richthofen and Fiebig.[33] These were crucial hours – when consultation with those with direct knowledge of resources and the prevailing military predicament would have been paramount. When he finally arrived back at the *Wolfschanze* around midnight on the 23rd, Zeitzler was waiting for him in the cold outside air. Hitler was outwardly calm and smiling; he shook the general's hand and told him that he had done all he could. Zeitzler's expression was grave. Hitler told him not to be upset, to show strength of character at such times and to remember Frederick the Great.[34]

Bizarrely, at 0200 hrs on the 24th, Zeitzler advised Weichs that he had succeeded in convincing Hitler that a breakout was the only way to save 6.*Armee*.[35] But Hitler was intransigent: at 0140 hrs he signalled Paulus ordering 6.*Armee* to stand firm: 'Hold the current Volga Front and the current Northern Front (LI.*Armeekorps*) under all circumstances'. He added, following Göring's and Jeschonnek's assurances, that, 'Air supply through a further 100 Junkers is starting up'.[36]

During the course of the day, von Richthofen called Zeitzler from Mariupol and urged him 'emphatically' to again authorise 6.*Armee* to immediately fight its way out of Stalingrad towards the Don and Bokovskaya. The air commander also called Weichs and spoke with the crestfallen Jeschonnek three times. Evidently irritated by what he perceived as inaction and unable to speak with Hitler personally, he wrote in his diary:

Weichs and Zeitzler are of the same view as me, whereas Jeschonnek has no opinion at all. The *Führer* wants to keep 6.*Armee* firmly on the Volga, and believes that it will remain capable of surviving and be able to hold out. I request Zeitzler and Jeschonnek to bring to the *Führer's* attention my contrary point of view.[37]

Later, at the *Wolfschanze*, when Zeitzler expressed support for von Richthofen's view, and stated that he believed that unless 6.*Armee* fought its way westwards it would be doomed, Hitler retorted angrily, 'I won't leave the Volga!'[38] The dictator chided the army Chief of Staff for paying too much heed to 'defeatist' commanders.[39] Hitler probably felt he had good reason to level the 'defeatist' tag at the Luftwaffe generals, for he had been encouraged by a message from von Manstein to OKH that day in which the lauded Field Marshal and hero of Sevastopol had concluded that a relief effort by *Heeresgruppe Don* could probably commence as soon as early December *if* the promised reinforcements arrived, although von Manstein stopped short of a guarantee.[40]

By this stage, based on Hitler's promise to Paulus of 100 more Ju 52/3ms, the process of commencing an airlift to maintain 6.*Armee* at Stalingrad while it awaited the arrival of forces from *Heeresgruppe Don* had started, and the first aircraft had already taken off for the pocket. The aircrews making the first supply flights must have found the view from their aircraft depressing. In the area beyond Stalingrad, towards the Don, following the closure of the Soviet pincers, the steppe resembled some kind of apocalyptic, hellish landscape. For kilometre after kilometre thousands of German and Romanian soldiers wearing very little winter clothing wandered through the snow in search of food, the Romanians cursing their German allies, while around them were littered endless human corpses and thousands of dead and starving horses. In Kalach, according to one journalist, only one house was left standing.[41]

Ironically, it was the prospect of a German attempt at a relief operation at Stalingrad that resolved the *Stavka* to 'finish the job' around the city. The three Soviet Fronts on the Volga continued to press into the beleaguered German army at Stalingrad on the 25th, akin to tightening a noose. Simultaneously, forces from the Southwestern Front attacked towards Oblivskaya – once the location of an airfield for the Stukas of St.G 77 during the attack on Stalingrad in the early autumn – and Surovikino, while the Stalingrad Front attacked towards Kotelnikovo.[42]

At the headquarters of *Luftflotte* 4, von Richthofen, who had finally – somehow – managed to get his feelings through to Hitler (possibly through Zeitzler), was hovering somewhere between frustration and despondency. He noted bitterly in his diary on the 25th:

My report for the *Führer* got through. The *Führer* listened to it all and decided against it, because he does not believe that we could then get to Stalingrad again and that the *Armee* would be able to hold it. I remain by my opposite assessment. However, orders are orders, and everything will be done to carry them out. It's tragic that there are no responsible leaders, even when they supposedly possess trust, to be able to exercise any kind of influence. The way things are now, one is, from an operational perspective, merely a highly paid Unteroffizier.[43]

Somewhat surprisingly, the OKW war diary made a relatively realistic appraisal of the situation as it was on the 25th, recognising the need for far more transports than were immediately available:

The trapped 6.*Armee* has held all its fronts, but its supply situation is critical, and because of the unfavourable winter weather and the enemy's fighter superiority, it is very doubtful whether the 700 tons of food, ammunition and fuel, etc. demanded by the army for daily supplies can be carried into the pocket by air. There are only 298 transport aircraft in *Luftflotte* 4; around 500 are needed. Generaloberst von Richthofen therefore suggested to the *Führer* that 6.*Armee* should first move west in order to attack again later, but the *Führer* has refused this from the outset.[44]

There was nothing more to be done. The survival of 6.*Armee* would now rest with the Luftwaffe and its transport force.

But as Fiebig noted cynically on the 26th as the Red Army fought to contain limited German counter-attacks as well as continuing its offensive operations:

Well, everything must be done to carry out the *Führer's* orders. New operations have been started to relieve 6.*Armee*. But will they be able to hold out until we can send them sufficient supplies by air? Won't the Russians squash Paulus with their tanks in the meantime?

PART II

Crisis

'Army completely encircled . . . ammunition situation critical; food supplies on hand for six days; the Army intends to hold the territory between Stalingrad and the Don River and has made the necessary preparations. Success depends upon closing the gap on the southern front and on whether or not adequate food supplies can be delivered by air . . .'

RADIO MESSAGE FROM GENERALOBERST FRIEDRICH
PAULUS, COMMANDER 6.ARMEE, 22 NOVEMBER 1942

It was obvious that the Sixth Army could hold out only if supported by an air logistical operation of sufficient size, the duration of which could not be determined in advance, but which would certainly have to be maintained for several weeks. The decision for the army to hold its positions was thus intimately linked with the question of the possibility of carrying out an airlift operation.

GENERALLEUTNANT HERMANN PLOCHER,
*THE GERMAN AIR FORCE VERSUS
RUSSIA, 1942*

9

The Stalwarts of Stalingrad

Junkers Ju 52/3m

The Ju 52/3m (the '3m' designated tri-motor) was a civilian airliner designed by Ernst Zindel in 1931. Of a distinctive all-metal, corrugated construction, it saw impressive service during the 1930s as both a civilian and military transport throughout South America, Australia, Western and Eastern Europe, China, India, the Near East, Mozambique and South Africa, while Deutsche Lufthansa had become one of the world's premier airlines largely due to the success of the aircraft. The Ju 52/3m went on to become the 'workhorse' transport aircraft of the Luftwaffe, operating on every battlefront and gaining a truly multi-role reputation as a transporter, bomber, paratroop-carrier, ambulance, float-equipped seaplane, mine-hunter, courier and trainer. After its invaluable service in ferrying Nationalist forces to Spain from North Africa at the commencement of the Spanish Civil War, Hitler is reputed to have famously voiced the opinion that Franco should have erected a monument to the aircraft, while to the Wehrmacht it was known fondly as *Tante Ju* ('Aunt Ju'). It is entirely correct to view the Ju 52/3m as one of the most important aircraft in the Luftwaffe's inventory.

Ju 52/3m (military transport)
Wingspan: 29.25 m
Length: 18.90 m
Height: 6.10 m
Wing area: 110.5 m^2
Empty weight: 5,900 kg
Total freight: 4,100 kg
Flying weight: 10,000 kg
Wing loading: 90.5 kg/m^2
Power loading: 5.06 kg/hp
Power/wing area loading: 17.9 hp/m^2
Max speed: 300 km/h

Max cruising at 2,500 m: 283 km/h
Economical cruising at 2,500 m: 270 km/h
Landing speed: 104 km/h
Range at cruising speed: 1,500 km
Climb to 1,000 m: 4.1 min
Climb to 3,000 m: 14.5 min
Ceiling: 6,600 m

Heinkel He 111

With its glazed nose and wide elliptical wings, the twin-engined He 111 medium bomber is an enduring and unmistakeable symbol of Luftwaffe offensive intent. Under the direction of shrewd aircraft designer and manufacturer Ernst Heinkel, the He 111, like the Ju 52/3m, first entered service with Deutsche Lufthansa as an airliner for its domestic routes during the 1930s following a design created by the brothers Siegfried and Walter Günter. Early military variants of the He 111 made their debut in the Spanish Civil War, and successive versions went on to serve on every battlefront on which the Luftwaffe fought. From Dunkirk to Stalingrad and from Narvik to Tunis, it became the mainstay bomber, as well as an effective torpedo-bomber. It was also widely used by the Luftwaffe against the British Isles, where He 111 units undertook anti-shipping and bombing missions both by day and night. In the second half of 1940 and the first half of 1941, the He 111 became synonymous with the 'Blitz' night-bombing campaign against London, Coventry, Bristol and other British cities. Although largely overlooked as a multi-task aeroplane, the He 111 carried passengers, dropped bombs, released torpedoes, launched flying bombs, flew in supplies, evacuated the wounded from isolated pockets, carried secret agents, dropped leaflets, cut barrage balloons, checked the weather, dropped paratroops, towed gliders and ferried generals throughout the war. It remained in service as a military transport until the end of hostilities.

He 111H-16 (medium bomber and combat aircraft)
Crew: 5
Engines: two Junkers Jumo 211F-2s
Combat performance at 5,300 m at 2,400 rpm: 2 x 1,060 hp
Combat performance at sea level at 2,400 rpm: 2 x 1,140 hp
Take-off rating at 2,600 rpm: 2 x 1,350 hp
Propellers: three-blade Junkers VS 19 propellers of 3.50 m diameter
Wingspan: 22.6 m
Length: 16.40 m
Height: 4.00 m

Wing area: 86.5 m^2
Wing loading at 14 t gross weight: 162 kg/m^2
Power loading at 14 t gross weight: 5.22 kg/hp
Gross weight: 8,680 kg
Crew: 500 kg
Fuel (max. 2,550 kg): 2,425 kg
Oil: 190 kg
Bombs: 8 x SC 250 in ESAC cells, totalling 2,000 kg
Ammunition: 205 kg
Take-off weight: 14,000 kg

Maximum speed at:
2 x 1,120 hp at 0 m fully loaded – 350 km/h without bombs and half fuel
    load (365 km/h)
2 x 1,220 hp at 2,000 m fully loaded – 380 km/h without bombs and half
    fuel load (400 km/h)
2 x 1,030 hp at 4,000 m fully loaded – 390 km/h without bombs and half
    fuel load (410 km/h)
2 x 1,050 hp at 6,000 m fully loaded – 405 km/h without bombs and half
    fuel load (435 km/h)

Average range and performance at maximum endurance:
2 x 910 hp at 0 m – 1,950 km/330 km/h
2 x 1,025 hp at 2,000 m – 1,930 km/370 km/h
2 x 900 hp at 5,000 m – 2,060 km/385 km/h

Average cruising performance:
2 x 700 hp at 0 m – 2,200 km/285 km/h
2 x 800 hp at 2,000 m – 2,250 km/330 km/h
2 x 750 hp at 5,000 m – 2,170 km/365 km/h

Climbing time fully loaded:
to 2,000 m – 8.5 min
to 4,000 m – 23.5 min
to 6,000 m – 42 min

Service ceiling: 6,700 m
Service ceiling (without bombs and half fuel load): 8,500 m
Service ceiling (with one engine at weight of 12,000 kg): 2,000 m

Runway/take-off distance requirement to 20 m: 700/1,150 m
Best climbing speed at take-off: 4.4 m per second
Ground speed: 195 km/h

Climbing performance with gear retracted, flaps neutral: 3.6 m per second
Ground speed: 225 km/h
Landing speed with gross load of 11,000 kg: 130 km/h

Weapons
A-Stand: 1 MG FF with 180 rounds
B-Stand: 1 MG 131 with 1,000 rounds
C-Stand: 1 MG 81Z with 2 x 1,000 rounds
Beam: 2 MG 81Z with 2 x 500 rounds

Offensive load:
1,000 kg on ETC rack
1,000 kg in ESAC
2,500 kg on ETC
750 kg in ESAC

	kg	kg	kg
Structural weight	8,815	8,815	8,815
Crew	500	500	500
Fuel	3,175	3,175	1,040
Oil	300	300	190
Bombs	1,000	1,000	3,250
Ammunition	205	205	205
Take-off weight	13,995	13,995	14,000
Range at 5,000 m*	13,995	13,995	14,000

*Based on outward flight with full bomb load and return flight at cruising speed.

Junkers Ju 86

By late 1942 the Ju 86 was an obsolete aircraft, and its deployment at Stalingrad was a reflection of the dire measures to which Göring, Jeschonnek and the RLM went to accelerate and inflate the number of machines for the airlift, irrespective of their true capability. Certainly, the internal 'freight' load capacity of the Ju 86 as a transport aircraft was negligible. That is not to say that the Ju 86 was a 'bad' aeroplane; it was not – as is proved by its impressive export record. Like the He 111, the origins of the Ju 86 lay in an RLM and Lufthansa requirement from the early 1930s for a design that could be employed as both a high-speed airliner and as a medium bomber, and the man behind the aircraft, Ernst Zindel, also designed the Ju 52/3m.

Roughly concurrent with the development of the He 111, the intention had been to power the aircraft with a pair of 600 hp Jumo 205 six-cylinder heavy oil (diesel) engines, but these were not available in time and so were substituted by two 550 hp Siemens SAM 22 nine-cylinder radials. The aircraft took the form of a twin-engined, low-wing, all-metal monoplane with a semi-monocoque fuselage and twin fins and rudders, and it served as a pre-war airliner with Lufthansa, Swissair, Lloyd Aero Boliviano, Línea Aérea Nacional de Chile and South African Airways, while machines also went to Manchuria, Japan and Spain.

The diesel engines on the first military examples proved troublesome and the aircraft became known to its crews by the unhappy moniker of 'The Flying Coffee Grinder'. In German hands, as with the Ju 52/3m and He 111, it first saw military operational deployment in Spain in April 1937. Ultimately, however, even with redesigns and engine changes, the Ju 86 enjoyed only a limited military career with the Luftwaffe as a bomber-trainer and, on a few occasions, as a high-altitude reconnaissance aircraft and bomber over England, the Mediterranean and North Africa.

Ju 86E
Initial year of production: 1937
Engines: two BMW 132Fs (E-1) or Ns (E-2)
Length: 17.86 m
Wingspan: 22.50 m
Wing area: 82.00 m^2
Net weight: 5,200 kg
Payload: 3,000 kg
Crew: 2–4
Maximum speed at sea level: 365 km/h
Range: 2,000 km

10

'The Cost in Blood will be High'

24–29 November 1942

Diligent and proactive as ever, as early as 22 November, von Richthofen, Fiebig and their staffs had drawn up plans for the supply by air of a surrounded army. Oberst Karl-Heinrich Schulz, the Senior Quartermaster with *Luftflotte* 4, wrote that, 'The command and the units were very aware of the heavy responsibility they bore, and despite all the doubts concerning the execution of the airlift, they determined to carry out the task at all costs'.[1]

The initial plan was to base a senior Luftwaffe officer of General rank in the Stalingrad pocket as the *Luftversorgungsführer* [Air Supply Commander] *Stalingrad*, and he would be assisted by a general staff officer acting as his operations officer. They would be augmented by an intelligence officer, a meteorological officer, a signals officer, a transport officer and a radio specialist. This staff would manage the airfields and technical facilities within the pocket, direct air traffic, install and maintain direction-finding equipment and oversee aircraft maintenance activities. Alongside this staff would be a combined Luftwaffe–Army supply and administration section which would oversee and process supply matters and requests and supervise aircraft loading and unloading, as well as handling onward transport and distribution within the *Kessel* and procurement of the required personnel, vehicles and other ground services as and when they were needed.[2]

On 26 November, in something of an expedient move, von Richthofen notified his staff that 9.*Flak-Division* under Generalmajor Pickert, along with 'assigned Luftwaffe units', would be placed under the jurisdiction of 6.*Armee*. With his rank, this made Pickert the senior Luftwaffe officer in the pocket, and as such he was appointed the *Luftversorgungsführer Stalingrad*. Thus, as a Flak commander, despite having very little experience in the operations of flying units, Pickert became responsible for the preparation and coordination of transport aircraft in the pocket and ensuring that fighter protection was available to the air supply flights. Von Richthofen appointed Generalmajor Viktor Carganico, the serving *Kommandeur des Flughafenbereichs* [Airfield Command] *Tatsinskaya*, as the senior *Luftversorgungsführer* for the airlift. Based at Tatsinskaya (known to aircrews as 'Tazi'), Carganico would be directly subordinate to *Luftflotte* 4. According to von Richthofen:

His task is to maximise the air supply capability of *Luftflotte* 4 in order to supply 6.*Armee* to the point that it remains viable and capable of fighting.[3]

Fifty-five-year-old, bespectacled Viktor Carganico was a highly regarded 'old eagle' who had set a number of aeronautical records before World War I. After wartime service as a bomber pilot on the Eastern Front, Carganico had, according to one source, acted as an advisor to the Mexican Air Force during the inter-war years. He joined the nascent Luftwaffe in 1934 and went on to command a number of airfields and *Flughafen-Bereichs-Kommando* (FBK – air administration areas) prior to being given command of FBK 1/VI in October 1942.[4]

Luftflotte 4's Quartermaster, Schulz, was to establish a small staff for Carganico that was to operate with assistance from the *Luftgaukommando Rostov*, and a reliable radio link was to be set up between this staff and Oberst i.G. Robert Bader, the senior army Quartermaster outside the pocket.[5] In the same way that von Richthofen had liaised directly with army commanders during offensive operations in the West, the Balkans and Russia, he envisaged Carganico having similar direct contact with Paulus and Pickert in order to efficiently and swiftly coordinate supply requirements.

Simultaneously, von Richthofen instructed that Tatsinskaya, a complex of three grass airfields located 247 km west-south-west of Stalingrad that had been under German control since 21 July, was to become the 'main operational base' for all the available Ju 52/3m units which were to be deployed to the pocket. The main field, at Tatsinskaya South, had a 1,500 m runway, with its satellite fields known as West and North, although these were little used by the Luftwaffe. The facilities at Tatsinskaya had been expanded in October and boasted a *Schwere Funkfeuer* (heavy radio beacon) – longwave and shortwave radio ground stations (with another at Tsimlyanskiy, on the Don), backed up by an Elektra multi-beam guidance set and a short-wave radio landing beacon at Zaporozhye, which gave great assistance during night and bad-weather missions. There were four single and one double wooden-framed flight and repair hangars, and two small workshops. All other accommodation comprised basic wooden huts or tent encampments. It is believed that up to 96 Ju 52/3ms could be dispersed at the sides of the field.[6]

The Ju 52/3ms would be placed under the day-to-day control of an *Einsatzstab* (operational staff) to be known as the *Lufttransportführer im Luftflottenkommando 4*, formed from the *Geschwaderstab* of KG.z.b.V.1 under that unit's *Kommodore*, Oberst Otto-Lutz Förster. Bespectacled like Carganico, Förster was a highly experienced, veteran airman who had flown as a fighter pilot in World War I and in 1939–40 as a reconnaissance pilot in the campaigns in Poland and the West. He had subsequently led KGr.z.b.V.108 and I./KG.z.b.V.1 with distinction over Norway, Crete and Russia.[7]

Under von Richthofen's arrangement, all supplies to be carried to Stalingrad were to be forwarded to Tatsinskaya. In order to prevent overcrowding on the airfield, any aircraft that became non-operational were to be 'moved away in good time'. Furthermore, the Ju 88 bomber and reconnaissance units of VIII. *Fliegerkorps* based at Tatsinskaya were to be cleared and relocated to Rostov-West, while Romanian units based there were to be moved to Novocherkassk.

Luftflotte 4 had the following Ju 52/3m transport units under its command at Tatsinskaya in mid-November:

Stab KG.z.b.V.1	Oberst Otto-Lutz Förster (under VIII. *Fliegerkorps*)
KGr.z.b.V.50	Major Otto Baumann 48 Ju 52/3ms (under VIII. *Fliegerkorps*)
KGr.z.b.V.102	Hauptmann Walter Erdmann 53 Ju 52/3ms (under VIII. *Fliegerkorps*)
KGr.z.b.V.172	48 Ju 52/3ms (under *Luftgau Rostov*)
KGr.z.b.V.900	Oberst Alfred Wübben 50 Ju 52/3ms (directly under *Luftflotte* 4)

The grass airfields at Morosowskaya (known to aircrews as 'Moro'), 202 km north-east of Rostov, had been taken by the Germans in August and were somewhat better equipped for handling the He 111 than those at Tatsinskaya. Morosowskaya was to become the 'main operational base' for all the He 111 bomber and transport units that would take part in the Stalingrad mission.[8] The main airfield lay adjacent to major rail and road connections, and was noted by Allied intelligence as being sufficiently equipped with *Leichte Funkfeuer* (a light radio beacon station), direction-finder and heating equipment to keep aircraft engines warm during cold weather operations. Supplies intended for delivery by the units at Morosowskaya were to be directed there from Carganico's facility at Tatsinskaya, and the airfield was to benefit from 'the strongest protection possible' in terms of light and heavy Flak batteries.[9]

The Heinkel *Gruppen* at Morosowskaya were to be placed under the coordination of Oberst Dr. Ernst Kühl, the *Kommodore* of KG 55, who became the *Lufttransportführer Morosowskaya*.[10] Trained as a lawyer and civil servant, the 54-year-old Silesian from Breslau had served as an artilleryman during World War I, gaining his pilot's license at the age of 44 in 1932. Subsequently, he took part in several flying competitions, and when the Luftwaffe was formed in 1935, Kühl joined as a reservist in the bomber arm. On the outbreak of war Kühl was sent to KG 55, and with the rank of Major flew missions over Poland and England. On one occasion his Heinkel was shot down over the English Channel, but he survived, having spent several hours in a life raft. In March 1941 Kühl was appointed *Kommandeur* of II./KG 55, and he enjoyed considerable operational success on the central and southern sectors of the Russian Front. He also led night attacks on Moscow. Promoted to Oberstleutnant in April 1942, Kühl was made *Kommodore* of KG 55 on 27 August that year. He was awarded the Knight's Cross on 27 October 1942 following his 230th combat mission. Of his eventual 315 combat missions, 200 would be in the East.[11] Von Richthofen once observed, 'Kühl makes a calm, reliable impression and does his job well'.[12]

Von Richthofen gave Kühl a dual task: firstly, as a de facto transport commander he would oversee his Heinkels' supply flights to Stalingrad, and secondly, he would use them in the bomber role to attack the Russians and prevent them from taking either Tatsinskaya or Morosowskaya. Kühl was assisted by two staff officers in this task. The units available to him were:

At Morosowskaya

Stab KG 55	Oberst Dr. Ernst Kühl
I./KG 55	Major Rudolf Kiel
II./KG 55	Major Hans-Joachim Gabriel
	(KIA 20/11/42 – replaced by Major Heinz Höfer)
III./KG 55	Oberstleutnant Wolfgang Queisner (Morosowskaya from 30/12/42)
1./KG 100	Major Paul Claas (Morosowskaya from 25/11/42)

At Millerovo

Stab KG 27	Oberstleutnant Hans-Henning Frhr von Beust
II./KG 27	Major Reinhard Günzel
III./KG 27	Major Erich Thiel
III./KG 4	Major Werner Klosinski (Voroshilovgrad from 4/1/43)

In addition to these units, Major Fritz Uhl's KGr.z.b.V.5 was also assigned to Kühl. This *Gruppe* had originally been established at Fassberg in August 1938 and equipped with the Ju 52/3m, but it was disbanded only two months later. The unit was reformed at Radom in February 1942 and equipped with both the Ju 52/3m and the He 111 under Hauptmann Reinhard Zahn, but he was succeeded by Uhl the following July. Uhl and his *Staffelkapitäne* had flown supply missions over the Kholm pocket and other areas of enemy territory, but for the Stalingrad mission the unit was assigned to KG 55 and its crews were able to impart their experience and tactical methodology as transport pilots to their bomber crew comrades. Likewise, the bomber crews were able to help train up some of KGr.z.b.V.5's observers, who, having flown mainly drop missions for the *Fallschirmjäger*, needed instruction on navigation and homing, although as Uhl noted:

> Finding the target was not too difficult, even on moonless nights, with existing navigational aids and distinctive navigational features (such as the Volga, the Volga bend, Stalingrad city), and did not cause any particular difficulties.[13]

Each *Gruppe* was led by its own or an assigned staff from another of the *Gruppen* based at Tatsinskaya or Morosowskaya for day-to-day operations, irrespective of its original parent organisation. This was done to ensure a simple and defined chain of command, as well as to optimise aircraft servicing, which would be eased by each airfield group operating only one type of aircraft.[14]

Despite the initiatives and energy shown by von Richthofen and Fiebig, at the point the decision was taken to supply 6.*Armee* by air, the Luftwaffe was a far weaker force than it had been at any time, especially in Russia, while conversely, the VVS had grown in strength, if not quality. It was therefore logical to reason that in the winter of 1942–43, an airlift attempt would be more likely to suffer from enemy attack than operations such as those a year earlier at Demyansk and Kholm, both of which were smaller in scale than Stalingrad.[15]

Most of the aforementioned units had been flying continual operations throughout the summer, and as such average serviceability had dropped to around 40 per cent. A number of units and aircraft had been withdrawn progressively to the Reich for replenishment and refit.[16] Just before the commencement of the airlift, however, aircraft availability was still meagre: on 22 November there were only some 20 transports at Tatsinskaya.[17] Indeed, as a result of continuous deployment since the commencement of *Blau* in the early summer, by mid-November 1942 the operational readiness of *all* Luftwaffe units in southern Russia, including the transport units, in terms of aircraft, equipment and personnel was so depleted that *Luftflotte* 4 was forced to amalgamate some available aircraft and crews from one *Gruppe* into another to limit the demands on the servicing infrastructure. At this time serviceability in all units within the air fleet stood at around an average of 30 per cent, with the most battered being the close-support/ground-attack *Staffeln*.

Luftflotte 4, therefore, scoured all of its transport, bomber, liaison, support and ambulance *Staffeln* for every single suitable transport machine, in the process of which, according to Schulz, it ruthlessly 'disregarded their previous functions.' Schulz further recorded how, back in Germany, at the start of the airlift and in accordance with Göring's orders:

> The *Oberbefehlshaber der Luftwaffe* instituted extensive support for the *Luftflotte*, somehow bringing in every suitable superfluous aircraft from the *Transportgruppen*, the *Sonderstaffeln*, individual transport aircraft from the stocks of replacement and relief machines, courier aircraft, Lufthansa aircraft, special ministerial aircraft and, from training units, the best instructor aircrews.[18]

A British decrypt of German radio traffic revealed that an additional 60 transports had been sent to *Luftflotte* 4 by 26 November.[19]

In addition to some of its aircraft, Deutsche Lufthansa even contributed crews, but on the downside, the bringing-in of instructors from the Luftwaffe's advanced flight-training schools to boost pilot numbers obviously had a detrimental impact on pilot training in the Reich, and even resulted in the closure of some specialised schools.[20] Furthermore, the result was a wide variance in experience among the

Ju 52/3m crews assembling at Tatsinskaya; some were highly experienced men who were veterans of operations in Scandinavia or France, others were former Lufthansa pilots with thousands of kilometres of peacetime flying to their name, or they were highly qualified civil or military instructors. Many, however, were fresh from flight-training schools, with little or no operational experience.

Some of the Ju 52/3ms were in desperate need of servicing, while others were literally factory-fresh. Some aircraft had been used as courier machines and lacked vitally needed radio and D/F sets or armament.[21] But one of the most challenging problems was that many Ju 52/3ms arriving from Greece, Italy and North Africa via the staging bases at Kirovograd and Zaporozhye had not been configured for winter operations, so they had to be fitted out accordingly for cold weather starting procedures before being able to commence airlift operations. These aircraft simply became an additional burden as they cluttered the field at Tatsinskaya. To many working on the Junkers transports on the ground, it appeared as if they had been forwarded by personnel at the staging bases, as unprepared as they were, simply to boost the statistics for Berlin.[22]

As a counter-measure to overcrowding at Tatsinskaya and Morosowskaya, a situation which favoured attacks from the VVS, refitting or repairs as a result of accident or operations could only be authorised to an individual aircraft if they could be completed within two days. Aircraft requiring more intricate repair were to be moved to the rear areas for the completion of the required work, either via Zaporozhye for the Ju 52/3ms or via Kirovograd for the He 111s. These fields served as clearing points between the zone of operations and facilities in the rear, or even the Reich itself, where aircraft could be registered as arriving from operations or going back, having been repaired and checked. Aircraft that were deemed mechanically suitable to operate under the prevailing weather conditions to Stalingrad were classified as *Kesselklar* (literally, 'Pocket Clear'). Every aircraft that arrived from the Reich or from other locations had to transit through these bases in order to undergo maintenance and safety checks ahead of being assigned to operations. This took time and used up manpower.[23]

And yet, even by the height of the airlift in December, less than half of Germany's transport aircraft, including commandeered machines, were in Russia.[24] To a great extent this could be attributed to the airbridge operating across the Mediterranean to Tunisia. Following defeat at El Alamein and in the aftermath of *Torch*, German forces now depended on their hold of Tunisia. At the beginning of November 1942 no fewer than 150 Ju 52/3ms were sent to the Mediterranean to ferry troops, weapons and fuel to bolster Axis forces in North Africa, with another 170 arriving at the end of the month. This considerably reduced the numbers of transport aircraft able to be committed to Stalingrad, not to mention causing an impact on the blind-flying, bomber and multi-engined training schools. Even worse was the fact that the Luftwaffe lost 128 Ju 52/3ms throughout November and December.[25]

When it came to the ground support infrastructure in southern Russia at the time, according to Schulz:

Since the spring of 1942 the ground organisation in the newly-occupied territory was still in the process of expansion. Most favourable was the situation south of the Don, where the terrain was more suitable and numerous airfield installations, untouched by the enemy, could be taken over. In the region north of the Don, particularly eastwards of the Donets, as well as in the region between the Don and Stalingrad, the situation was much less favourable.

In terms of rail and road, this was largely untouched terrain, and there were few Russian airfields and great supply difficulties, and only a few airfields had been established near to the frontline along the Lichaya–Stalingrad railway line. All available construction resources and all available materiel was used to make these, as well as the airfields in the area of *Heeresgruppe* A, winter-protected, so that the erection of airfields in the rear area between the Mius and Donets had to be set aside. It was, initially, an insignificance which, however, during the course of events in the winter of 1942–43, turned out to be a disadvantage. The expansion of winter-protected auxiliary airfields was almost complete in November 1942.[26]

Indeed, it had been as a result of the rapid push into Russia during *Blau* that there had not been sufficient time or resources available to fully equip all the airfields along the lines of advance, especially east of the Donets. As autumn came, the more established airfields became crowded, and thus, despite falling temperatures, the ground became churned and soggy under the heavy usage. Often, there was a lack of wire communications between airfields, and so command had to be exercised by radio and liaison aircraft. It was common for the transport *Gruppen* to operate from improvised accommodation and bunkers, and in some cases crews were quartered in little more than mud huts – just as winter approached, although winter clothing and equipment were procured as early as possible.[27] But from his command post located just behind the main frontline at Oblivskaya, Fiebig rose to the challenge, sending out his *Korps'* bombers to carry out repeated attacks along the Chir River where the Russians were massing. Such was the intensity of the flying that some Luftwaffe crews flew as many as ten to 14 sorties in one day.[28]

At the very beginning of the air-supply mission to Stalingrad, there was a belief within various strata of the German command that an airlift would be only an immediate, short-term operation, intended to provide 6.*Armee* with the means to effect a breakout from its entrapment. In other words, to supply it with, as a priority, fuel and ammunition, while the shortage of food could be alleviated by reduced rations for a time as the Army fought its way out. Yet, the truth was that the Army had been living a hand-to-mouth existence since early November. Food was a tricky issue: the assurance of sufficient stockpiles rested on knowing, accurately, how many troops were trapped in the first place, as well as where such stockpiles could be kept safely and healthily. Nevertheless, on 26 November, rations were cut for the first time, resulting in an allowance of 350 grammes of bread, 120 grammes of meat or horsemeat and 30 grammes of fat issued per man per day. On 1 December the bread allowance was lowered to 300 grammes.[29] And although it was reasoned that without fuel and ammunition, 6.*Armee's* ability to effect its breakout would be severely limited,[30] it was *fuel* which, as Wolfgang Pickert has described, was 'the crux of the supply problem from the beginning'.

Very soon the prospect of a quick operation faded, and all von Richthofen and Fiebig could argue for was that if the air-supply mission extended in time, then it would be on the proviso that the two main bases at Tatsinskaya and Morosowskaya were held at all costs.[31]

Recent writers have, rightly, questioned whether two airfields were enough to sustain an airlift of the scale required, even if it was to be a rapid operation, and they state that logistical theory demands at least one runway per 10,000 combat personnel being supplied. This being the case, *Luftflotte* 4 would have needed no fewer than 25 airfields to maintain supply with effect![32] Of the sites to be used inside the pocket, at least four were primitive strips, wholly unsuitable at the best of times for such an operation, let alone in the depths of a Russian winter, and this in itself would have served to slow down turnaround times.

Tatsinskaya was the principle hub for supplies for the airlift to Stalingrad, yet it was fed by only a single, narrow-gauge railway line from Rostov, while road access was stymied because of the poor quality of those roads that did exist, as well as limited numbers of lorries and fuel.[33]

The historiography presents very varied tonnage requirement figures supposedly put forward by the various parties responsible for sustaining 6.*Armee*. The pre-eminent German historian Manfred Kehrig places Göring at a conference at the Luftwaffe's command headquarters at Wildpark-Werder, on Berlin's western fringes, on the evening of the 23rd, so this being the case, he must have just returned from Paris. The Reichsmarschall told those in attendance that 500 tons of supplies per day – a figure also tabled by *Heeresgruppe* B – was required by 6.*Armee*, but this was later revised to a more workable 350 tons based on realistic available capacity. The senior *Oberquartiermeister* in the pocket, Major i.G. Werner von Kunowski, stated that a daily supply of 300 cubic metres (cbm) of fuel and, as soon as was possible, 200 tons of ammunition was required, with 150 tons of rations being added as required at a later point.[34]

According to von Manstein, around 24 November it was the assessment of the staff of the embryonic *Heeresgruppe Don* that 'an absolute prerequisite for accepting the risk of not making an immediate breakout from Stalingrad was that 6.*Armee* should daily receive 400 tons of supplies by air'. This figure was seen as the minimum requirement for motor fuel and ammunition. Once existing ration stocks had been consumed, this '*basic minimum*' [author emphasis] rose to 550 tons.[35] 6.*Armee* had stated that its daily supplies requirement amounted to 750 tons. In order to carry this tonnage successfully, without loss, into the pocket (i.e., aircraft actually landing and unloading), a fleet of 375 Ju 52/3ms, each with a payload of two tons, would be required. Allowing for a realistic operational readiness level of 35 per cent, the Luftwaffe would have needed 1,050 Junkers transports, but facilities at Tatsinskaya, as described, were not capable of handling such a number of aircraft. In any case, the Luftwaffe had only some 750 such aircraft in total at this time.

As *Luftversorgungsführer*, Generalmajor Carganico was to receive daily supply requests directly from the Quartermaster 6.*Armee*, who remained outside the pocket. Carganico was to execute these requests using, as a first step, the Ju 52/3m *Gruppen* in order to allow – in theory – Fiebig to use the free He 111 bomber units for offensive operations. If the available Ju 52/3ms were insufficient for the Army's requirements and/or the supplies to be delivered, Carganico was to request the necessary number of He 111 bomber aircraft from VIII.*Fliegerkorps*. Von Richthofen deemed it essential that Carganico's requests for additional aircraft be met under all circumstances. Fighter escort was also to be requested from VIII.*Fliegerkorps*.[36]

From 23 to 28 November the supply effort to Stalingrad was maintained exclusively by the Ju 52/3m-equipped units, and they managed to achieve a daily average delivery during this period of 40 cbm of fuel and nine tons of ammunition.[37] From Tatsinskaya, the Ju 52/3ms operated around 260 km from Pitomnik, which was well within their 1,100 km cruising range. With two tons of supplies on board and flying at speeds of around 215 km/h, a Ju 52/3m could cover the distance to the city in about 1 hr 15 min. Allowing three-and-a-half hours for handling and turnaround at Pitomnik, including refuelling, reloading and taxiing, one sortie with return to Tatsinskaya would take six hours, and thus, in theory, four sorties could be flown per aircraft in a 24-hour period to carry eight tons.

According to Morzik, by early December 1942 there were 320 Ju 52/3ms available to *Luftflotte* 4, although the serviceability rate was only 30 per cent. On this basis, applying the earlier logic, 96 Junkers could carry 768 tons in 384 sorties per day. This was a figure that would have pleased Göring, for it made 500 tons achievable while using less than half of the Luftwaffe's inventory of 750 Ju 52/3ms.[38] But this was the theory – and it was based on the assumption that aircraft could, and would, fly night and day, that the airfield infrastructures both in and outside the pocket would operate without problem, that aircraft could always be laden with their maximum payloads, regardless of any fuel or payload limitations, that there would be no enemy action, and that the weather would allow flying.

In the early stages of the airlift, in daylight, when the weather conditions were good and the cloud ceiling high, the transports flew as *Staffeln* or in small formations of five aircraft, with an escort of Bf 109s. In bad weather, with poor visibility and low cloud, only blind-flying-experienced crews could take to the air in groups; the remainder flew singly or, on occasion, in *Ketten* of three aircraft. At night, the transports always flew singly, with take-off schedules being carefully arranged by the *Lufttransportführer* at Tatsinskaya and Morosowskaya.[39]

On 24 November, some of the initial supply flights to the pocket were disrupted by VVS fighter attacks. Von Richthofen had reluctantly sanctioned leaving a small number of Bf 109Gs from I./JG 3 in the pocket; these were so few in number that they would not be able to fully provide cover for Pitomnik, and their pilots and groundcrews would mean more mouths to feed, along with more parts and fuel to supply.[40] Nevertheless, what was known as the *Platzschutzstaffel Pitomnik* (Airfield Defence Squadron) was formed from volunteers from this *Gruppe* and II./JG 3, who commenced operations over the pocket on a rotational basis from the 19th, with around six pilots at Pitomnik at any one time. The Messerschmitts were dispersed at one edge of the field, well away from the passage of transports as they took off and landed, and as long as weather allowed, a *Rotte* – a tactical unit of two fighters – would be kept at immediate readiness at all times in order to be scrambled against any VVS attacks. The presence of the Bf 109s would prove itself entirely justified over the coming weeks.

Feldwebel Hans Grünberg was a pilot with 5./JG 3, and by the end of November 1942 he had been credited with six victories, all claimed over southern Russia. Having quickly gained a reputation as an effective 'close-range' fighter pilot, he was among the small number of men assigned from II. *Gruppe* to the *Platzschutzstaffel*. Grünberg recalled the conditions he experienced:

> One day – it was at the beginning of December – I was ordered to lead four machines to Pitomnik for a week's flying. What I found there was bad. My bed was a medical stretcher. We slept and ate in a smoky earth bunker. Thank God I had taken a sleeping bag with me. I knew of course that no luxury hotel awaited me in Pitomnik, but I had never spent the night in such quarters. I obtained two old blankets from my comrades, to avoid freezing. The initially planned one week of operations in Pitomnik then became extended until this airfield was abandoned, as our relief never took place. We thus had to stay to the bitter end in the pocket. In Pitomnik we were 12 fighter pilots, from different *Staffeln* of *Jagdgeschwader Udet*. Our duties there were to protect the ground troops and the few German aircraft from enemy air attack, and to protect the landings and take-offs of the transport aircraft. Often, it was not possible with only one or two Me 109s to protect the airfield, as well as transport machines unloading supplies and loading in the wounded. We had to watch as Ju 52s and He 111s were shot down as they collected in the air for the return flights, and fell burning with the wounded on board, to their deaths on the ground.[41]

From his command train on the Don, von Richthofen noted on 25 November that:

> We fly supplies with all Ju's, but we have only 30 of them. Out of the 47 we had yesterday, 22 dropped out. From the 30 of today, nine dropped out. Today, we flew in 75 tonnes instead of the 300 tonnes ordered from above, which with the few Ju's we have would, normally, not be possible. I reported this formally to the Ob.d.L.[42]

This was not a terribly encouraging start: it meant that on the second day of the airlift, the Luftwaffe managed a serviceability rate of just 46.8 per cent, and 30 per cent on the third day – not to mention a shortfall of around 225 tons against 6.*Armee*'s daily subsistence needs.

Seven 'landing grounds' – and that term has to be applied with some elasticity and optimism – are believed to have existed within the Stalingrad pocket at various points: Pitomnik, which 6.*Armee* designated on 22 November as the initial and main field for landing supplies, as well as Basargino I and II (which were close to the front), Gumrak, Karpovka (also close to the front), Gorodishche and Stalingradskaya.

Realistically, only one – Pitomnik – was able to handle large-scale aircraft movement by day and night. Just under 23 km from the city to the east of the Dubovaya Gorge, this natural-surface airfield is believed to have at one time been a rudimentary training airfield and had a runway. Lying roughly in the centre of the pocket for most of the airlift, it could be reached by roads from Karpovka, Gonshara, Voroponovo and Gorodishche. It was thus well located for the delivery and distribution of supplies, although it was not connected directly to the railway. When 6.*Armee* arrived, the site gradually filled with tents and wood-walled bunkers and huts. Later, the *Luftgau-Kommando Rostov* installed *Leichte Funkfeuer* (light radio beacon) and direction-finding gear. But the flat, treeless, frozen landscape meant little could be done to provide shelters for aircraft. Despite this, Pitomnik became the main airfield in the pocket, and as such Pickert placed several of his Flak guns there for defence. Joachim Wieder, an intelligence officer with 6.*Armee* who was quartered in a makeshift bunker at the airfield, described the spot as being:

> . . . probably the saddest and most desolate place I had laid eyes on in the east. A bare, naked, dead steppe landscape with not a bush or tree, not a village for kilometres around. A single trunk without branches stuck up five kilometres away in the little hamlet of Pitomnik, where a few houses were still standing, and served as a signpost. Near the hamlet were a number of *balkas* – deeply eroded, steep-banked rain gullies – that gave some protection. Occasionally, an ice grey mist from the Volga drifted over this desolate piece of ground and the wind, which cut through everything with its biting edge, blew unmercifully over the boundless, snowy waste. The loneliness of the eastern expanses was depressing, and this eerie feeling was increased by the early fall of darkness.[43]

The field – and that was all it was – known as Basargino I lay 22 km west of Stalingrad, north of the railway line and 7.5 km south-east of Pitomnik. There was just a small station and one or two houses there. The other locations were little more than fields with grass landing strips which lacked accommodation, shelter, night-landing capability, servicing, radio and air traffic control facilities. But in any case, as mentioned, to properly support the airlift operation the Germans ideally needed 25 airfields.[44] At the commencement of the airlift the Luftwaffe did recommend that at least two more equipped airfields were prepared for day and night use. This did not happen, and as Generalleutnant Hermann Plocher of V.*Fliegerkorps'* General Staff commented, 'The Sixth Army is not blameless for this situation'.

The Luftwaffe also proposed further development of the field at Gumrak, but until shortly before the loss of Pitomnik, this was rejected on account of its proximity to the Army's headquarters. Despite the fact that officers of 6.*Armee* were of the opinion that all the airfields were useable as they were, additional better-equipped sites should have been developed which would have allowed a much greater volume of landings in the pocket.[45]

On the 26th, 27 Ju 52/3ms flew into the pocket, and on the 27th another 30.[46] That day, Oberst i.G. Bader, the senior Quartermaster outside the pocket, based with *Heeresgruppe* B, proffered to Carganico that if 150 Ju 52/3ms were made available, which could undertake two missions per day, then 600 tons per day could be flown in.[47]

Meanwhile, it soon became apparent that Carganico and his small staff at Tatsinskaya lacked the experience for such a demanding and specialist role and were unable to cope with the urgency and military enormity of the task.[48] On the 28th von Richthofen, who was more than aware of the urgency of the situation, arrived at a solution:

The *Versorgungsführer*, Carganico, is not functioning properly as yet, despite continual warnings. I'm wrestling in my mind about the organisation of airlift leadership and supplies. After some to-ing and fro-ing, I arrive at the following solution: VIII.*Fliegerkorps* to only take care of supplies for the Stalingrad battle; IV.*Fliegerkorps*, as previously ordered, to go south of the Don to the Kotelnikovo area; the Romanian *Fliegerkorps* to the Chir Front; and the *Gefechtsverband Rohden* to Bokovskaya. The main concentration is to provide supplies to Stalingrad.[49]

The next day, amidst 'miserable weather', von Richthofen flew to Tatsinskaya, where he had called a conference. He had summoned Generalmajor Carganico, representatives of IV. and VIII.*Fliegerkorps*, the Romanian Flying Corps *Luftgau-Kommando Rostov* and Oberst i.G. Steltzer, the Chief of Staff at *Luftwaffenkommando Kaukasus*. Also in attendance was Dr. Heinrich Potthoff, a former World War I artilleryman and aviator who was the Chief Medical Officer of *Luftflotte* 4. At von Richthofen's request, he had flown into Tatsinskaya from Essentuki in a Ju 88 with Steltzer the night before. The two officers arrived at dawn. Potthoff recalled:

The conference took place in the large room of a Russian *dacha*. On one wall was hung a large situation map, which enabled one to gain a good picture of the military situation in the Stalingrad *Kessel*, as well as outside of it. Detailed briefings on the enemy's position and on our own situation in the *Kessel* and outside of it were given, assessed, and decisions were made.

Transport of the sick and wounded out of the *Kessel* and that of supplies were addressed.

Thus began for me, and the Luftwaffe medical service, a heavy task. The human, moral, military and specialist burdens that had been assigned to me were enormous. Even greater were the tasks of *Luftflotte* 4, their commanders, the high command of the Luftwaffe and their units by reason of having to master such a despairing situation. VIII. *Fliegerkorps* became – very much to the detriment of *Luftflotte* 4 – a *Transportfliegerkorps*, which meant that He 111-equipped bomber units were to be pressed into service as supply aircraft for the *Kessel*.[50]

Von Richthofen announced that, in the interests of efficiency, he was revising his orders of a just few days previously. Fiebig was to be temporarily relieved of command of VIII. *Fliegerkorps* and appointed as *Luftversorgungsführer Stalingrad* (replicating Pickert's title), thus replacing Carganico.[51] For Fiebig, this was a swift and dramatic change in function and responsibility, but his staff had much more experience in the handling of large air formations than Carganico's ad hoc team, as well as liaison with fighter units for escort duties, and they also had a good communications net and meteorological personnel.[52] Thus, very quickly, VIII. *Fliegerkorps* was relieved of its combat operations in order to take over full responsibility for the airlift for 6. *Armee*.[53]

At the end of the meeting the officers trudged out into the snow. Von Richthofen spent some time chatting over things with Fiebig while the engines of their respective aircraft idled and warmed up close by. Potthoff joined them as the Storch assigned to him from a *Sanitätsflugbereitschaft* (Luftwaffe Ambulance Flight) was made ready for flight. He was already thinking about what arrangements would be necessary to prepare for the arrival of large numbers of wounded troops from the pocket. He took the opportunity to ask von Richthofen whether there was anything else that was required of him:

> He replied that it was down to me! It was a decisive reply, and with it came self-responsibility. I had freedom of action. I took this as a measure of trust and therefore determined to do everything in my power to make things work. Without any feelings of uneasiness, I went to work.[54]

In his diary, Fiebig recalled:

> VIII. *Fliegerkorps* is relieved of its combat mission and, from 30 November, will start to supply 6. *Armee* by air. An honourable, but difficult task. It must be accomplished, even if the Russians try their best to prevent it. Skill and finesse must be used day and night to prevent the Russians from carrying out their mission. The cost in blood will be high, of that I am certain.[55]

Fiebig was right. Von Richthofen noted in his diary that evening, 'The supplies situation is better today, but there's still no conclusions. We are continually suffering heavy Ju 52 losses; seven again today! Most of them lost their way'. And the He 111 units commenced operations on this day too, fitted with air-drop containers instead of bombs, but one *Staffel*, 2./KG 55, lost an aircraft when it had to make an emergency landing because of engine failure south-west of Kalach while on a flight to Pitomnik. One of the Heinkel's crew was injured and another posted missing.[56]

According to a set of 'Special Instructions' issued by the Quartermaster's Section of *Luftflotte* 4 on the 30th, the revised command structure for the airlift was as follows:[57]

Deployment of transport units – Operations Officer, VIII. *Fliegerkorps*.

Coordination of supplies for airlifting in consultation with Senior Quartermaster 6.*Armee* – Quartermaster, VIII. *Fliegerkorps*.

Supplies for the transport units and the escorting fighter and *Zerstörer* **units** – Oberstleutnant Lehmann at *Kdo.Flughafen-Berich* 4/XI.

For loading and unloading of supply flights and execution of flights, the respective *Lufttransportführer* – Oberst Kühl for He 111 units at Morosowskaya and Oberst Förster for Ju 52 and Ju 86 units at Tatsinskaya.

Organisation of Pitomnik airfield within the Stalingrad pocket – Hauptmann Finsterbusch, Quartermaster for the *Festung* at VIII. *Fliegerkorps*, liaising with Major von Kunowski, Quartermaster Staff, 6.*Armee* [Finsterbusch was assigned a small staff comprising an army liaison officer, a Luftwaffe transport officer and an officer from a Luftwaffe *Nahaufklärungsgruppe*].

The Quartermaster of 6.*Armee*, who, as mentioned, was based outside the pocket, was to work closely with the Senior Quartermaster of *Heeresgruppe Don*, who would organise supplies from stocks held by *Heeresgruppen Don*, A and B and arrange delivery to the airfields in conjunction with liaison officers at VIII.*Fliegerkorps*. The Quartermaster of 6.*Armee* was to advise his requirements between 1700 and 2400 hrs latest for flights to Stalingrad departing the next flyable day. Urgent or special requirements were to be made known by telephone and telex to VIII.*Fliegerkorps* no later than four hours before a planned take-off, subject to weather conditions. These requirements would be relayed in summarised form by the Quartermaster of VIII.*Fliegerkorps* by telephone and telex by 1700 hrs that night, or three hours before a planned flight for urgent supplies or special orders. Arrangements would be confirmed to the Quartermaster of 6.*Armee* by telex and to the pocket by radio.

The respective *Lufttransportführer* were to report, by 1600 hrs at the very latest, their aircraft availability figures for the next day, including the number of serviceable machines available within 24 hours and also beyond 24 hours; the number of non-serviceable machines with reasons for same; the number of operationally ready aircrews capable of full blind-flying; the number of remaining operationally ready aircrews; and the number of non-operationally ready aircrews, giving the reasons for same.

VIII.*Fliegerkorps* stressed that supplies were to arrive at Morosowskaya and Tatsinskaya in good time and in such a way 'that no delays whatsoever in loading of the transport aircraft will ensue'. However, in order to minimise the effect of any enemy action, supplies were to be spaced out as much as possible on the airfields, and splinter-proof shelters were also to be provided for storage. For the same reason, the transport aircraft were to be widely dispersed, fire-fighting teams were to be on readiness at all times and the possibility of nightfighter defence was to be explored.[58] Furthermore:

> Loading of items by the Army may only be undertaken with agreement of the Senior Quartermaster at 6.*Armee*. In the case of an aircraft being not fully loaded, the Quartermaster at 6.*Armee* is to have ready a *Zusatzbelading* [additional load plan]. The aircrews are to ensure that all free transport space is fully utilised. For the bringing-up of supplies, storage and guards on the airfields, and for loading and unloading, the Senior Quartermaster of 6.*Armee* is requested, under personal agreement with the *Lufttransportführern*, to make available sufficient army personnel and trucks.
>
> By making available a sufficient number of personnel and lorries, the Senior Quartermaster in the *Festung* is to ensure that unloading of the supplies on the airfields in the *Festung* Stalingrad takes place smoothly. In the event of unforeseen delays occurring in the loading and unloading of supplies items, the *Lufttransportführer* and Quartermaster/*Festung* are authorised to call upon immediate assistance from personnel and lorries from all flying units and supply services of the Luftwaffe (operations by flying units are not to be endangered thereby).

A similar system was to be actioned for flights returning from Stalingrad, with appropriate advanced notification of evacuated wounded personnel. The crews were under strict orders to return directly to their home bases and not to make any interim landings. It was further ordered that 'Delays to the transports must not occur which would cause dangers in the air'. Unloading of army equipment and wounded at Morosowskaya and Tatsinskaya was to be undertaken by the army, while any Luftwaffe equipment was to be handled by personnel acting under the *Lufttransportführer*.

On the 27th Fiebig described the weather at Tatsinskaya as 'the worst we've ever had. One snow flurry after another. A desolate situation'.[59] If the weather was cold at Tatsinskaya, the atmosphere was, as General der Infanterie Kurt Zeitzler has described it, 'chilly' later that night some 2,000 km away at the *Wolfschanze* in East Prussia. Unsuccessful attempts had been made to contact Göring during his art-shopping sojourn in Paris, but it seems by the 27th he was at Rastenburg, where he would be drawn into what has become something akin to Stalingrad 'folklore'. In 1956 Zeitzler included an account of his confrontation with the Reichsmarschall at Hitler's headquarters as part of the volume *The Fatal Decisions*.

Zeitzler had argued with Hitler the previous day over the German position on the Volga, and the undercurrent between the *Führer* and the OKH Chief of Staff was tetchy.[60] The situation report for the Eastern Front that evening stated that the enemy's distribution of forces at Stalingrad seemed 'very favourable to the intentions of 6.*Armee*', and that the supply situation was better than previously assumed. However, only 27 Ju 52/3ms were reported as having flown into Stalingrad the previous day, although there were 298 Ju 52/3ms that could 'carry around 600 tons to Stalingrad every day; for the time being 700 tons are needed daily, later 1,500 tons [will be required] after consumption of present food stocks'.[61]

Zeitzler told Hitler that he considered the prospect of supplying 6.*Armee* by air as 'not possible'. Hitler responded in an 'icy' manner that Göring had assured him that it was. Zeitzler held his ground and repeated his belief, at which point Hitler sent for Göring. Fresh from Paris, Göring entered the room a short while later and Hitler asked him directly whether 6.*Armee* could be kept supplied by air. Göring apparently shot up his right arm in the Nazi salute and declared, 'My *Führer*! I assure you that the Luftwaffe can keep the Sixth Army supplied'.

Hitler beamed at Zeitzler like a cat that had got the cream, but the latter simply replied coolly that he disagreed. The indignant Reichsmarschall duly told Zeitzler that he was not in a position to be able to give an opinion. Zeitzler then presented the facts as he had them from *Luftflotte* 4 and *Heeresgruppe Don*. 6.*Armee*'s existing supplies stocks, allowing for minimum needs and the allowance for non-flyable weather, meant that a daily amount of 500 tons needed to be flown into the pocket if an 'irreducible minimum average is to be maintained'. According to Zeitzler, 'Göring replied, "I can do that". I now lost my temper, and said "My *Führer*! That is a lie"'. The Reichsmarschall stood 'white with fury', while Hitler glanced at both men with 'perplexity and surprise'. Unshaken, Zeitzler asked one more question – whether he would be able to submit to Hitler the exact daily tonnage figures for each 24-hour period? Göring objected, but Hitler granted Zeitzler his request and the conference ended.[62]

There was also discord in the Stalingrad pocket, with von Seydlitz-Kurzbach trying to persuade Paulus to break out, as he believed it to be the only way of saving the trapped Army. The corps commander recommended disregarding Hitler's order to hold the city since it was clear that the *Führer* was not in possession of the most up-to-date information. Furthermore, 6.*Armee* had no idea what, if any, firm action was being taken to free it, and when it might happen. In his account of the battle first published in Germany in 1950, the former war correspondent Heinz Schröter describes a meeting at around this time between Paulus, Schmidt and their corps commanders. Hube maintained that the 'only hope is to fight our way out', while Heitz commented that he would 'sooner survive with five divisions than perish with 20'.[63] For his part, General Erwin Jaenicke, commander of IV.*Armeekorps*, constantly pushed Paulus to 'Break out as fast as possible and we shall go through the Russians like a hot knife through butter'. But Jaenicke also felt that:

> What was required at this juncture in the Stalingrad pocket was a forceful commander in harmony with his chief of staff. Unfortunately, this factor was lacking. In spite of his high intelligence, Generaloberst Paulus was far too pliable to cope with Hitler. I am convinced that this is the real and deeper cause of his failure.
>
> Generaloberst Paulus saw only Hitler's Sword of Damocles over him, and he knew that there had already been suggestions to have Seydlitz replace him. This, I am firmly convinced, together with the mentality of the Commanding General of 6.*Armee* as I knew it, is the deeper reason why the decision to break out was not taken.[64]

On 25 November von Seydlitz-Kurzbach sent a bluntly worded memo to Paulus. He advised his commander that at the Army's current rate of ammunition expenditure, if the Soviets were to make a major assault against the entire perimeter front then 6.*Armee* would 'shoot itself dry within one or two days'. Von Seydlitz-Kurzbach also made no secret of his (entirely accurate) scepticism about the feasibility of an airlift:

> It is clear that adequate supply by airlift of LI.*Armeekorps* alone is questionable, and therefore completely impossible for the whole army. What 30 Ju (on 23.11), or the further 100 Ju that have only been promised so far, can bring in is only a drop. To attach hopes to this means grasping at a straw. Where the large number of Ju required for the supply of the army is to come from is nowhere in evidence. If they exist at all, the aircraft will have to be flown in from all over Europe and North Africa. Because of the distances to be covered, their own fuel requirements would be so great that coverage is highly questionable given the fuel situation as experienced so far, not to mention the operational consequences for the whole conduct of the war. Even if 500 aircraft were to land daily, instead of the envisaged 130, they could only bring in 1,000 tons of supplies, which would not suffice to cover the needs of an army of approximately 200,000 men engaged in heavy combat and without stockpiles.[65]

Von Seydlitz-Kurzbach also raised the point that because of the lack of food, all the horses in the pocket would likely die within a few days, and therefore tactical mobility would suffer accordingly. Furthermore, enemy fighters could be expected to harass the landing fields within the pocket, and yet it was doubtful the Luftwaffe would be able to supply continuous and effective fighter cover for the transports. The corps commander concluded that an airlift would only 'delay the exhaustion of supplies by a few days'.

Towards the end of November, as the demand for airlift capability for Stalingrad grew, von Richthofen was forced to use almost all of his Fleet's bombers for air transport missions, leaving IV.*Fliegerkorps* unable to provide the tactical support for German forces in the Terek area, and for the drive on Tuapse, in the Caucasus. The net result was that *Luftflotte* 4's units struggled to provide support for the divergent Stalingrad and Caucasus operations.[66] The groundcrews worked flat out and as fast as they safely could to maintain and, if possible, increase the numbers of sorties.[67]

Throughout the last days of November, the transport units flew day and night to the pocket. While the Ju 52/3ms operated from Tatsinskaya, the He 111s of KG 55 at Morosowskaya were augmented by Heinkels of KG 27 under Major Hans-Henning *Freiherr* von Beust based at Millerovo. Commencing 28 November, the He 111s of KGr.z.b.V.5 at Morosowskaya were also fully committed, as the *Gruppenkommandeur*, Major Fritz Uhl, reported:

> At the beginning of the supply operation we flew day and night. This was disadvantageous in that there was practically no time to maintain our machines. When, because of the strengthened Russian fighter defences, we had to switch to night missions, our technical personnel had opportunity to properly maintain the aircraft during the day, which had a very positive effect on operational readiness. Most successful were night missions of two to three aircraft. Due to the significantly lower number of damaged aircraft as a result of enemy action, operational readiness and thus transport performance of the *Gruppe* increased noticeably.[68]

Whenever it was possible, these units would receive local escort during daylight from the small number of Bf 109Gs of Major Klaus Quaet-Faslem's I./JG 3 based in the pocket at Pitomnik, although the strength of the local fighter force had recently been depleted – if not halved – with the transfer of III./JG 3 from the pocket to Oblivskaya on the 21st. The latter *Gruppe*, led by Major Wolfgang Ewald, would continue to fly escort for the transports from its new base, but the range of the Bf 109G was insufficient to cover the round trip, and so the Messerschmitts would have to land at Pitomnik, where they would be replenished by drawing fuel from the wing tanks of the transports.[69] Nevertheless, in the early stages of the airlift, the presence of even a small number of Luftwaffe fighters served to keep the VVS at bay.[70]

Pickert had flown back into the pocket on the 28th. The next day he toured his light Flak platoons as they started to dig in. He noted in his diary:

> This is very difficult in the steppes due to there being practically no wood and the ground being frozen. But the men are very sensible and maintain excellent morale. In the worst kind of weather – 80 m low ceiling, 1–2 kilometres visibility – He 111 supply aircraft appeared on the scene; a splendid accomplishment. I praised them all profusely.[71]

According to his memoirs, also at some point in late November, von Manstein decided to fly into the pocket in order to meet with Paulus so as to gain a personal and accurate assessment of the Army's situation and its capabilities. In this he was dissuaded by his Chief of Staff, General Friedrich Schulz, and his senior Operations Officer, ostensibly on account of the weather, which would probably detain the field marshal in the pocket, and thus deny him contact with OKH at a very pivotal time. Von Manstein therefore despatched Schulz in his place. Schulz later returned with the impression that provided 'it were properly supplied from the air', 6.*Armee* 'did not judge its chances of holding out at all unfavourably'.[72] Indeed, according to *Heeresgruppe Don's* war diary, there was 'no immediate danger to Sixth Army, having overcome the first days of crisis. The constant supply flights and the successful air combat by our fighters over the pocket contribute to cement confidence and morale'.[73]

Fiebig had noted in his diary on the 26th that:

> The 6.*Armee* would not consider its tactical situation unfavourable if it could get 300 cubic metres of fuel and 30 tons of tank ammunition daily. Rations are sufficient for one month.[74]

An 'enemy' growing in magnitude even more than the Red Army was the harsh Russian weather. By late November, the conditions had well and truly started to change, heralding the beginning of the Asiatic winter, but between 25–29 November the Ju 52/3ms managed to deliver 269 tons to Stalingrad.[75] However, from these early flights, it became clear that even if they flew through snowstorms, sleet, rain and fog, the numbers of aircraft committed to the airlift were insufficient to deliver anything near the tonnages of food, fuel, ammunition and equipment required by 6.*Armee*.[76] In all, by the end of the first week of the airlift, the Luftwaffe had delivered 350 tons, included in which were just 14 tons of food – a figure way off the required daily tonnage of 30 tons needed to survive, although it should be remembered that at this early stage there was still an intention to consider a breakout; an effort which would need fuel and ammunition as a priority over food.[77]

11

'A hard and dangerous way for the men to earn their bread'

30 November–11 December 1942

From the end of November and through the first week of December, the Russians maintained the pressure against the German pocket at Stalingrad by attempting to seal it off from the air and by a concerted attempt to split 6.*Armee*. In the resultant ground fighting, 6.*Armee* lost almost half of its remaining tanks. Despite the resolution of the Wehrmacht's soldiers in the *Kessel*, who had been down to one-third rations since the 23rd, they were, in the words of Oberst Wilhelm Adam, to a man 'extraordinarily worn out physically, and emotionally very exhausted'.[1]

On 30 November, the innovative commander of the VVS, Gen Alexander Alexandrovich Novikov, instructed the commander of 16th VA, Gen Sergey Ignat'yevich Rudenko, to assign one fighter and one ground-attack air regiment specifically to combat the Luftwaffe transports supplying the trapped German Army. Novikov's plan was to destroy the transports at their hub airfields at Tatsinskaya and Morosowskaya, as well as in the air, and to blockade the key airfields in the pocket. He would soon refine his plan to make it even more effective.[2]

That day, 40 He 111s flew with the Ju 52/3ms for the first time, and their presence meant that around 130 tons of fuel were delivered in one day – also for the first time.[3] Von Richthofen remarked in his diary, 'It was a great day for the VIII.*Fliegerkorps*: 52 shoot-downs at Stalingrad, 131 tons of fuel and 30 tons of ammunition was flown in'.[4] There were losses though, including those witnessed personally at Pitomnik by Generalmajor Pickert:

> Twenty-six Ju's arrived in close formation. Two Ju's were shot down, loaded with motor fuel. They went up in flames. Incredible sight.[5]

As November ended, the beginning of December was marked by bitterly low temperatures and howling winds, bringing sleet, snow and ice that covered all the airfields being used for the airlift. 'Terrible how the Junkers and Heinkels have to grope around in the snow on their return from Stalingrad, but no mishaps yet', noted Fiebig on the 1st. He had prudently just moved the headquarters of VIII. *Fliegerkorps* from Oblivskaya back to Tatsinskaya, but he left a command post at the forward location.

Engine and pipe warming equipment was not available for the majority of the aircraft, which meant thawing out frozen machines took precious time, especially in the hours before dawn. With careful management and application by the groundcrews, the He 111 units were usually still able to operate. At Morosowskaya there was always a shortage of groundcrew, and this field, especially, suffered from a lack of hangars in which to protect the Heinkels from the elements. Due to a paucity of timber and metal parts, it was not possible to build protective shelters for spare engines, and although a small quantity of warming equipment was available, after a short period of regular use it began to break down. Astonishingly, the *Wiso-Truppe* (*Wintersonder-Truppen* – Special Winter Units) were not properly trained in how to use the equipment. Kühl and his staff endeavoured to rectify this by collecting all the most important equipment in a heated hangar, where it was kept running continuously to maintain warmth. He wrote of the problems they faced:

> Because aircraft had to undergo maintenance parked in the open, without protection from sub-zero temperatures, wind and snowstorms, there was an increased need for heating equipment, not just for the aircraft, but for the FBK [airfield servicing companies], which caused, in turn, an increase in the need for heating vehicles. At one point, the *Wiso-Truppen* were unavailable because they had not been assigned winter clothing.
>
> Due to the lack of replacement parts for the heating vehicles, repair was only possible by cannibalising vehicles that were not in a usable condition. The numbers of FBK and repair workshops was sufficient; the field repair platoons, under the leadership of a disciplined and highly qualified engineer from the *Luftflotte*, were combined and performed very well. It was only the more unusual items of repair work on the older variants of aircraft in the z.b.V. units [He 111F, P-2, P-4, H-3 and H-5] that the FBK and *Feldwerften* [field repair workshops] could not, for a time, undertake satisfactorily. The acceptance of replacement aircraft for the bomber units worked rapidly and with ease because, through *Luftflotte* 4, the *Lufttransportführer* for the He 111 units was able to call in and distribute operationally-ready aircraft and aircrews from the Heinkel base at Saki, in the Crimea, without any tiresome reporting, and assign them immediately according to the models and losses of individual units.[6]

In a similar manner, under approval from the *Luftflotte*, Kühl and his staff were able to pull in replacement parts from the stores at Zaporozhye. When older variants of aircraft were lost in action or gradually withdrawn, the supply stream for replacement parts for newer variants proved less efficient. Indeed, parts were only made available after vociferous demand via the established channels and supply stations, which resulted in considerable lost time. Kühl described how:

> Of great importance is that when collecting [replacement] equipment, a member of the unit (the Technical Officer or Technical Inspector) flies along

too so that the required replacement parts can be found independently, and in the case of an item that is unavailable, he is able to select an alternative, usable part. It is therefore necessary to allocate the units their own transport aircraft. A transport aircraft that is able to quickly bring replacement parts for several aircraft at one time within a short period in order to make them operationally ready achieves more than if it is employed on operations.[7]

At Tatsinskaya, attempts were made to shelter the Ju 52/3m air- and groundcrews from the extreme elements. For the mechanics, 'every engine change became a torture', but a lack of wood meant there were few fires to light. Indeed, as Pickert recalled:

> The cold caused unimaginable difficulties in starting aircraft engines, as well as engine maintenance, in spite of the well-known and already proven 'cold start' procedures. Without any protection against the cold and the snowstorms, ground support personnel worked unceasingly, to the point where their hands became frozen. Fog, icing and snowstorms caused increasing difficulties, which were compounded at night.[8]

The crews also had to be ready at a moment's notice, at all times, so that any period of good weather could be exploited to the full.[9]

The Luftwaffe stressed to the supply organisations the urgency of timely and coordinated delivery of goods to the Morosowskaya and Tatsinskaya hubs, with particular attention being paid to weight and efficient utilisation of space, as well as consideration of the ability of certain goods to withstand sub-zero temperatures. Standard bread, for example, which contained water, would freeze and had to be thawed out, which often left it unpleasant to consume. To overcome this, Kühl's staff suggested that flatbread, crackers or *Dauerbrot* (a canned bread which could be preserved for six months) replace normal bread. Likewise, fresh meat was not favoured as it contained too much water, and tinned vegetables were heavy. The most important thing was to provide food which gave energy (sugar and chocolate, for example) and nourishment. Provisions contained in sacks, such as flour, were not considered practical because sacks would often tear or burst open while being moved around within or outside an aircraft or upon impact with the ground.

When loading an aircraft internally with goods or when carrying wounded personnel, it was important to leave sufficient room for the crew to be able to move quickly to man the defensive armament in an emergency.

Motor vehicle fuel could be carried within the fuselage of a He 111 or in externally mounted containers, and in order to enable rapid emptying of drums, tanks and containers when on the ground, the staff at Morosowskaya recommended the fitting of fast-pumping equipment beneath the fuselage.[10] Generally, during the early stages of the airlift, the supply of fuels and air-drop containers was never too much of an issue.

At the end of November the Luftwaffe had, in total, in all theatres 878 Ju 52/3ms on strength, of which just 357 were operationally ready.[11] By early December, however, mountains must have been moved to shift the bulk of them to the East, as well as combing Lufthansa and government users, so that the airlift force had available around 200 serviceable Ju 52/3ms in nine *Gruppen*, 20 Ju 86s in two *Gruppen* and 100 He 111s.[12] The Ju 52/3m units were of varying strengths, and some had suffered attrition more than others – KGr.z.b.V.9 and KGr.z.b.V.500 had lost half their strength in the week 20–27 November.

Serviceable figures in brackets where known[13]:

Ju 52/3m units		
KGr.z.b.V.9	Oberst Adolf Jäckl	Moving from Konstantinovka to Taganrog-Süd – 43(15)
KGr.z.b.V.50	Major Otto Baumann	Moving from Oblivskaya to Tatsinskaya – 33(13)
KGr.z.b.V.102	Oberstleutnant Walter Erdmann	Tatsinskaya – circa 52
KGr.z.b.V.105	Major Rüdiger Jakobs	Tatsinskaya – circa 36
KGr.z.b.V.172	Major Erich Zähr	Tatsinskaya – circa 29(11)
KGr.z.b.V.500	Major Ludwig Beckmann	Tatsinskaya – 45(35)
KGr.z.b.V.700	Major Ferdinand Muggenthaler	Moving from Oblivskaya to Tatsinskaya – circa 53
I./KG.z.b.V.1	Major Ernst Maess	Tatsinskaya – circa 50
II./KG.z.b.V.1	Oberstleutnant Guido Neundlinger	Tatsinskaya – circa 53

From 29 November, the He 111 units at Morosowskaya comprised:

		Variants on strength
KGr.z.b.V.5	Major Fritz Uhl	P-2, P-4, H-2, H-3, H-6
KGr.z.b.V.20★	Major Hermann Schmidt (from 3 December)	D, F-2, P-4, H-3
Stab/KG 27	Oberst Hans-Henning Frhr. von Beust (*Kommodore*)	
I./KG 27	? (at Millerovo)	H-6
II./KG 27	Hauptmann Reinhard Günzel (at Millerovo)	H-6
III./KG 27	Major Erich Thiel (at Millerovo)	H-6, H-16
Stab/KG 55	Oberstleutnant Dr. Ernst Kühl	H-6, H-16
I./KG 55	Major Rudolf Kiel	H-6, H-16
II./KG 55	Major Heinz Höfer	H-6, H-11
III./KG 55	Oberstleutnant Wolfgang Queisner	H-6, H-11, H-16
I./KG 100	Major Paul Claas	H-6, H-14, H-16

★Not believed to have arrived until 16/12/42

The Ju 86 *Gruppen* comprised:

KGr.z.b.V.21	Hauptmann Ernst Hetzel
KGr.z.b.V.22	? (at Tatsinskaya)

Before departing the Reich for Russia, KGr.z.b.V.20, KGr.z.b.V.21 and KGr.z.b.V.22 were all instructed to take five extra men on each aircraft – presumably additional aircrew, mechanics and technicians that were vitally needed to reinforce the airlift effort.[14]

★ ★ ★

On the morning of 2 December, take-off of the Ju 52/3ms slated to fly to Stalingrad was delayed until 1130 hrs when their fighter escorts were eventually able to rendezvous with the transports.[15] As Fiebig noted starkly:

> After yesterday's snow, everything is frozen now. We can still get He 111s out, but Ju 52s only after 11.30, and in two formations. Lack of heating equipment. Not enough was supplied for the large number of aircraft. Transport aircraft have no business to be here. Thawing takes too much time and is too much work.[16]

Despite this, Ju 52/3ms of KGr.z.b.V.700 doggedly headed out towards Stalingrad, but they lost two of their number.[17] If that was not bad enough, marauding Soviet *Okhotniki* (patrolling fighters) took the opportunity to strafe airfields in the pocket, and in the process claimed to have destroyed no fewer than 17 transports, although in reality this figure far exceeded actual German losses.[18] To 2 December around 17 He 111s and 19 Ju 52/3ms had been lost, and not all down to VVS fighters or enemy anti-aircraft fire.[19]

He 111s of I./KG 100 also flew three supply missions, carrying ammunition into the pocket and flying wounded men out, some of the pilots having to evade the Russian fighters as they did so.[20] Oberstarzt Dr. Heinrich Potthoff, the Fleet Doctor for *Luftflotte* 4, saw at first-hand the arrivals of the wounded in Ju 52/3ms at Tatsinskaya at this time. He recalled:

> Immediately after an aircraft rolled to a stop, our ambulances with their medical personnel were at the spot ready to take the wounded off. One medical officer supervised the onward transportation to the army reception points for the sick and wounded. Our medical service tents on the airfield were only used when a temporary 'traffic jam' occurred as a result of the arrival of further transports. The unheated tents – they were former cavalry tents – were there for an emergency.
>
> During the night there was always hectic activity at the airfield. One aircraft after another landed, refuelled, loaded-up with all sorts of supplies, and was made ready for take-off again. But snow, snowdrifts, low temperatures and ice made operations and providing supplies more difficult. The sick and wounded suffered very much because of that. Those sick and wounded that had been flown out were bodily and psychically at a considerably low ebb. They suffered from exposure due to the cold. Especially endangered were the wounded following loss of blood, shock and collapse. The medical services in the pocket very much had their hands full.[21]

Commencing on the 2nd, the Soviet Don and Stalingrad Fronts resumed their attacks against the pocket. The fighting was ferocious, but somehow 6.*Armee* held its lines across all its fronts and even launched local counter-attacks. Lt Gen Pavel Ivanovich Batov, commander of the Don Front's 65th Army, related how, after two days of preparations, his forces:

> ... tried to penetrate through the western crest of the heights. We did not succeed in doing so. The fighting was fierce. As soon as our units advanced forward, and did not manage to dig in, the counter-attacks began.

But the final balance sheet told the real story. In repulsing two assaults by the Soviet 21st Army, 676.*Infanterie-Division* on the western edge of the pocket reported the killing of 25 enemy soldiers, with another 19 captured, as well as the destruction of seven tanks and the capture of five machine guns. However, the division later reported 44 men killed, 72 wounded and one missing.[22] Pickert, who spent much of the day visiting his Flak crews, found them to be of 'good faith and confidently bearing all the trials and tribulations'. The following day, he had his midday meal with one of his batteries – 'Food is scant: two slices of bread per day and thin soup'.[23]

Meanwhile, at VIII.*Fliegerkorps* headquarters, evidently the pressure on Fiebig was beginning to mount. On the 3rd he revealed his true feelings in a somewhat cryptic diary entry:

> No take-offs. No supplies. Hail, snow and fog. Am trying to fly to the *Luftflotte* commander in a Storch. Fog all around Kamesk. Von Richthofen does not have the courage to express his views intelligently. Terrible situation. Do I, a subordinate, have to bridge the gap? I am trying to call him, but am unsuccessful – he is not well.[24]

On the 4th, Kühl managed to get 17 He 111s and 50 Ju 52/3ms, including three Romanian machines of the *Escadrila* 105, out in 'the worst weather' to take around 140 tons of ammunition, fuel and supplies to Pitomnik.[25] As the *Lufttransportführer* noted:

> Maintaining operational readiness during the air supply period was made much more difficult because in flying continual day and night operations, every time a mission was planned, possible changing weather conditions had to be considered and, wherever possible, exploited.[26]

Meanwhile, the same day from Moscow, the commander of the VVS, Gen Novikov, instructed the commanders of 8th VA (Gen T. T. Khryukin) and 16th VA (Rudenko) to refine the existing modus operandi of action against the German transports and the air blockade around the Stalingrad pocket. This highly focused campaign had become regarded as one of the most important being undertaken by the VVS.[27] Novikov planned a series of four zones which wrapped around the pocket. Zone 1, the outer zone, ran from a point on the Don some 300 km north of Morosowskaya, around Stalingrad, extending east from the Volga by almost 300 km, and then to a point some 250 km south of the lower Don. The northern part of the zone would be covered by 17th VA, while the southern part would be patrolled by around 450 fighters, Il-2 *Shturmovik* ground-attack aircraft and bombers of 8th VA. The second, circular zone of some 100-150 km radius, was segmented into five sectors, the two northern sectors covered by 175 serviceable aircraft of 16th VA and the three southern sectors by 8th VA. A third zone comprised a circular, ten-kilometre-wide anti-aircraft belt enclosing the pocket, while the fourth, inner zone covered the airspace directly over the German-occupied pocket. Zones three and four were the most difficult to penetrate, and because of the gun belt, Luftwaffe crews were forced to deviate from their pre-set, radio beacon-assisted routes, resorting to visual navigation in bad weather.[28]

Novikov also wanted the airfields in the pocket regularly photographed in order to gain up-to-date intelligence on conditions and movements on the ground. Furthermore, such was the importance of operations over the blockade zones that, as an incentive to his airmen, Novikov ordered that any pilots who distinguished themselves in action over the pocket were to be immediately recommended for awards. He also demanded that the numbers of enemy transport aircraft shot down were to be immediately reported by telephone to the headquarters of the local VVS commander, with detailed summaries sent in by radio by 2200 hrs each evening. To this end, a network of radio beacons and guidance stations was established around the ring of encirclement.[29]

On the 5th, such was the adversity of the weather at daybreak that some of the 36 Ju 52/3ms that made the run to the pocket were forced to perform blind take-offs. When they reached Pitomnik, the ceiling was only 120 m and lowering, with visibility up to 670 m. The conditions deteriorated further, and yet the crews still landed in the pocket, with some having to make seven attempts in the process.[30] An optimistic von Richthofen commented:

No bombing sorties. In place of that, we made excellent supply sorties in the face of ground fog at the take-off and landing airfields. The *Transportverbände* are acting superbly and with great self-sacrifice. I praise them officially, and in writing, and from the depth of my heart. It's a hard and dangerous way for the men to earn their bread.[31]

That night at Pitomnik, Pickert was in a reflective mood, as he noted in his diary:

Every night I pray to God, not for myself, but for our people and the Fatherland, for the salvation of our 6.*Armee* and for victory. I feel deeply impelled to do this. But for myself and my own insignificant fate I can find no words.[32]

At Morosowskaya, Kühl, as the *Lufttransportführer*, understandably placed emphasis on the need for experienced personnel:

When a supply order is given, it is vital that no time is lost in making available personnel and transport to effect loading. It is also important that parachutes [for air-drops] are checked and correctly packed. Of decisive importance is the need for an experienced, senior officer of the Luftwaffe or the Army to be assigned to the *Lufttransportführer* who will:

a Issue loading orders according to instructions received from the Army Quartermaster and oversee the distribution and/or destination for the transport of motor vehicle fuel according to the condition of the flight-cleared aircraft.

b That any problems arising with loading as a result of changes to original orders, especially at night, are solved and dealt with immediately. It is also necessary to assign an officer or technical inspector to each *Gruppe* who will be responsible for the smooth distribution of supplies and the loading of *Gruppe* vehicles.[33]

It was to be an uphill struggle. There was little time to offer those crews arriving from Germany, the Mediterranean or the West any familiarisation on local conditions such as the terrain, the weather, or the conditions that they would witness in the pocket. Many of the younger, less experienced crews thus suffered trauma at what they would come to see and experience.[34] KGr.z.b.V.20, for example, had been formed hurriedly in Germany only in November under Major Hermann Schmidt with a strength of 54 He 111 transports. Within a very short time, on 3 December, it was sent prematurely with 12 freshly trained crews to Morosowskaya to bolster the airlift. But their preparation for what lay ahead had not been sufficient, and Kühl and other officers from KG 55 had to oversee their further training at Morosowskaya, which was not an ideal situation with the limited time and resources that they had. Inevitably, this *Gruppe* – and others – would go on to suffer high losses.

Another three seemingly semi-autonomous and possibly equally poorly prepared units, the so-called *Gaede*, *Glocke* and *Gratl Staffeln*, were incorporated into I./KG 55, I./KG 100 and KGr.z.b.V.5, respectively, where each received some basic operational training.[35] And when they arrived at Morosowskaya they would have been left in little doubt as to conditions there, for on the 3rd the field was bombed during the day by Soviet A-20 bombers, but only slight damage was reported.

Schulz describes the typical mission profile during the early stages of the airlift:

Aircraft made ready for missions during the morning were reported during the previous night to the *Heer*, who then loaded them. They stood ready for take-off from daybreak onwards. As soon as the weather picture at take-off, and on the flight route, as well as in the pocket, permitted flying, and if there was clear weather and fighter protection was available, the aircraft were ready to go. The units got into formation after take-off, gained altitude and flew on the ordered flight route. Fighter protection was picked up on the way. The formation dispersed over the pocket and landed as quickly as possible in succession.[36]

To place conditions in to context, in a thesis on the Stalingrad airlift from 2004, USAF officer Maj Willard B. Akins II described succinctly the often fragile mechanics of the airlift process:

> The most efficient way to run a sustained airlift operation is to have regularly scheduled missions, with enough time between landings so that organic ground personnel and offloading equipment can immediately begin and complete the offload prior to the arrival of the next aircraft. Of course, if there are sufficient groundcrews and equipment to support simultaneous offloading operations, the schedule can be adjusted to reflect this capability. However, in a hostile environment, planners need to stagger arrival times to maintain an element of unpredictability to decrease the enemy's ability to anticipate arriving aircraft. In either case, planners need to meticulously deconflict inbound aircraft. Otherwise, the offload site becomes saturated, forcing additional arrivals to wait short of the offload site, increasing aircraft ground time, which, in turn, increases exposure to enemy threats. If the aircraft arrive too rapidly, it is possible that there will not be room for additional aircraft to land. If the inbound supplies are not critical, those aircraft can return home, wasting only a sortie (or sorties, depending on the number of aircraft) and jeopardising an aircraft and crew over enemy territory for no reason. If, however, the supplies must be delivered, the aircraft are compelled to orbit, where they will be at risk to enemy aircraft, artillery and infantry, until there is sufficient room to land. It was this exact scenario that played out at Pitomnik.[37]

In the pocket, as soon as a Heinkel landed it was guided off the narrow runway and men would quickly gather around the aircraft to begin the unloading process. Crates of ammunition were passed through the bomb-bay doors, while quantities of fuel were siphoned from the wing tanks, some for the airfield's fighter defence unit and some for the pocket's fleet of motor transport. Then walking wounded would clamber aboard and the aircraft would turn around for its return flight. On occasions when the weather had cleared, the He 111s adopted the policy of 'safety in numbers' and would usually wait until a *Kette* could be formed, thus providing increased defensive firepower in the event that Soviet fighters appeared. Once back at Morosowskaya, the process would begin all over again, as Schulz recalled:[38]

> After landing and unloading, as soon as the aircraft were cleared and fighter protection was ready, they took off again, reformed, gained altitude and flew back. After landing at the home airfield, as long as the aircraft had suffered no damage, they were made flight-ready as soon as possible, loaded and redeployed. In poor but flight-capable weather, as well as at night, the aircraft were sent off individually at five-minute intervals. If the weather permitted flying, but no landing was possible in the pocket, following precise determination of the airfield location via radio beacon, the loads were air-dropped without the crew being able to see the drop area. Errors

in air-dropping were frequent in such cases. For dropping supplies by air, besides He 111s, Ju 52s were also used, but only after the goods to be dropped had been wrapped in blankets or straw. In air-drops, considerable quantities of supplies became lost due to the He 111 containers or bundles dropped from Ju 52s not being located in the snow or because of damage or lack of observation, they had been whisked away [by the enemy]. In any case, although air-drops were very uneconomical, when a landing was not possible, efforts were always made to provide supplies.[39]

The Ju 52/3m could carry two tons for unloading on the ground, but a crew could also discharge unpacked supplies from an open fuselage door in a kind of crude air-drop. The Ju 86 was only able to unload its 0.8-ton load on the ground.

The different variants and sub-variants of the He 111 resulted in variations in external and internal load configurations. For example, the He 111H-6, could carry supplies in four 250-kg *Abwurfbehälter* AB 250 air-drop containers. Also known as *Versorgungsabwurfbehältern* (VB – air-drop supply containers), these weighed 50 kg when empty and were 1,618 mm in length and 373 mm in diameter. Despite considerable manufacturing and transport difficulties, they remained in good supply throughout the airlift, but employing them presented difficulties. They were fitted with parachutes, which overcame the ground-impact problem. However, the parachutes introduced another alarmingly common occurrence – premature opening within the bomb-bay while the carrying aircraft was in flight. This became dangerous when the bomb-bay doors of a He 111 were opened during the drop approach. The only solution was for the crew to attempt the difficult process of manually cutting the parachute cords to release the containers.

If premature opening occurred, there was also a risk to the aircraft's ventral *Bola*, which could be battered, resulting in damage, and the parachutes and their cords could also become entangled around the tailplane, increasing the danger of a crash-landing. The parachutes even presented problems on the ground, and they had to be checked regularly because when stored in conditions of humidity and low temperatures they became unsuitable for air-dropping.

The Luftwaffe also used two types of large air-drop container in the '1000' class, both of which took the form of purpose-designed and built, wooden cylindrical air-drop containers intended for supplying ground forces with munitions, weapons, provisions, general supplies and unwieldy items in heavier load amounts. At each end of the cylinder were nose cones intended as shock absorbers.

The *Mischlastabwurfbehälter* 1000 (mixed load air-drop container) was an interim 'emergency' design built within the aluminium casing of an aerial mine (LMB – *Luftminenbombe*) capable of carrying an 800-kg load. It was to be dropped from a height of not less than 200 m. However, because of shortages of aluminium (which was needed for mines and bombs), this variant saw only limited use, and was superseded in favour of the similarly named, wooden-bodied *Mischlastbehälter* 1000. With its larger internal capacity, this container was well-suited for carrying food and ammunition on flights where an aircraft could be assured of landing. It was only possible to air-drop a 1,000-kg container loaded with food, since ammunition of all kinds could be dangerously compressed upon impact with the ground.[40]

The *Mischlastbehälter* 1000 was 660 mm in diameter and had a length of 3,174 mm. Unloaded, the container weighed 200 kg and had a useable capacity of 460 litres or a payload of 720 kg. The clear internal length of the stowage compartment was 1,690 mm, with a diameter of 600 mm. The wooden nose cones at each end of the cylindrical main body were fitted with *Stosskappen* or *-puffer* (shock absorbers or buffers) filled with foam rubber padding or coiled rubber tubing intended to reduce the impact of landing. If these shock absorbers were damaged or missing, then the nose cones could be filled with pine or birch tree branches, or a similar type of branch, in order to create an expedient buffer. The *Mischlastbehälter* 1000 could only be loaded and fitted by specially trained personnel. The containers were locked by two clips and opened on the ground by unfastening them and then turning screws using a screwdriver or coin to remove the clips.

Release from an aircraft could not take place at speeds above 350 km/h and from an altitude not less than 300 m and no higher, if possible, than 1,000 m. The deployment of the parachute was effected by means of a timed-release device with a seconds setting scale. Upon release from an aircraft, the maximum total weight suspended from a parachute (which weighed around 75 kg) was 925 kg. The *Mischlastbehälter* would fall at a speed of five–six metres per second. However, this type of container was only available in limited numbers.[41]

The He 111H-11 was especially well suited for accommodating three 1,000-kg *Mischlastabwurfbehältern* plus a fuselage load. The H-16 on the other hand, was less suitable for supply flights, since with eight 250-kg containers suspended in two rows in the bomb-bay, only a smaller further load could be accommodated internally.

One problem, in reality, was that the supply depots were often late in loading and delivering 1,000-kg containers, which meant that aircraft fitted with external suspension points for these larger units would fly to the pocket carrying only 250-kg containers.[42]

In order to locate containers in the snow once they had landed, Kühl's staff proposed the use of red parachutes or a similarly coloured smoke canister for daylight drops and coloured flares for use at night, but it is not clear if such measures were ever employed beyond the trial stage, if at all. However, Schulz wrote that, 'In order to make the air-drop containers more easy to find in snow, painstaking work was undertaken at the airfields to colour the parachutes red'.

In his paper on the Stalingrad airlift, Maj Willard B. Akins II wrote:

The problem with airdrop missions is that they are inherently less efficient than air-land missions. Airdrop loads require more time to pack, load and rig the cargo for the airdrop. An airdrop mission, no matter how expert the crew, will seldom drop the supplies exactly where the customer (the Sixth Army in this case) demands, whereas an air–land mission can put the cargo literally at the customer's feet. Airdrop missions result in more damaged cargo due to the impact velocity. It does not do the army any good to receive water they cannot drink, food they cannot eat and bullets they cannot shoot. Airdrop has no provision for backhaul; there is no way to evacuate the wounded and sick.[43]

It was clear to those in command of *Luftflotte* 4 what they faced, as Schulz recalled:

With regard to the number and condition of available airfields, as well as in terms of the supply operation, it was barely possible to attain the required number of sorties. And with the increasingly precarious situation east of the Donets, it was doubtful whether the supply bases would remain in our own hands for the duration of the required air supply. If a shift to the rear of the air supply bases were to become necessary, the capability thus diminished with the increase in distance, as far as it remained at all within the range of the Ju 52 at 350 km. With a lower number of possible sorties by each aircraft per day, this increased the total number of aircraft needed.

The enemy would conceivably attempt to utilise all means to prevent the air supply to 6.*Armee* through deployment of fighters and Flak against our transport aircraft, as well as through bombing raids on the supply bases and landing grounds in the pocket. The distance between the supply bases and the pocket already offered the enemy possibilities which, with increasing distance, had to grow in his favour. The few fighters we had in the area could hardly offer protection. But a shift of the supply bases further to the rear was out of the equation due to range considerations. With that, there were limits for the whole transport aircraft operation.[44]

According to Schulz, 500 tonnes of air supply represented the consumption of 500,000 litres of aviation fuel, and so Ob.d.L. allocated extra stocks of fuel for the airlift effort as well as replacement parts and tools, heating equipment, maintenance personnel and also civilians from industry who were brought in to assist in the aircraft repair workshops. The problem was that behind the *Luftflotte*'s zone of operations, a large number of trains began to back up because of the poor throughput and capacity of the Russian rail network, and so deliveries were slow; the *Luftflotte* had a daily allowance of just eight trains.[45]

Yet those at the front received little help from their superiors in the Reich who believed that enough had been done to ensure that the airlift would sustain 6.*Armee*. Among the offenders were Göring and Jeschonnek, who failed to appreciate the impact of the extreme weather on operations, despite the experiences in Russia of the previous winter. They also failed to recognise that the airfields inside the *Festung* would soon come into range of Soviet artillery, but few, aside from von Richthofen, dared to speak out for fear of accusations of defeatism.[46]

To 6 December, the end of the second week, the Luftwaffe delivered 512 tons; that was less than a quarter of the *minimum* requirement. According to Zeitzler, over the first days of the airlift, Göring remained unconcerned. Despite the Army Chief of Staff fulfilling his request to Hitler and presenting the disheartening daily delivered tonnage figures, Hitler continued to place his faith in the Reichsmarshall and his Luftwaffe. According to Zeitzler, Göring parroted Hitler daily with hollow assurances:

> Göring promised improvements. He alleged that the airlift was only beginning to function: within a few days all would be working smoothly and he would surely be able to fulfil the promises he had made. Hitler accepted these excuses and indeed repeated them to others. 'The Reichsmarschall has given me his word. The Reichsmarschall is preparing a better organisation. The Reichsmarschall is bringing up more aircraft'. But in fact the situation was deteriorating.[47]

On the 7th, a day of 'vile weather' according to Pickert, I./KG 100 was among the units that went to Stalingrad: the *Gruppe* flew three operations during the course of the day.[48] Despite the difficulties involved in loading and delivering cargo through bomb-bay doors, the Heinkel air- and groundcrews proved inventive and resourceful: often the He 111s would carry – as Schulz put it – 'just enough' fuel to reach the pocket and return to Morosowskaya. This gave the benefit of a gain in payload allowance, usually in the region of 2.4 tons. Another option was to isolate the wing tanks and fill them with motor vehicle fuel, although this did necessitate an increase in loading and unloading times.[49] Night operations were thwarted initially by dense fog, despite the fact that the groundcrews had somehow managed to thaw out engines.[50]

But this day saw an all-time high supply figure delivered. Fiebig, who had wanted to fly to the *Kessel* on the 7th but was frustrated in his attempt because of an unserviceable He 111, found some slim reason for cheer. 'Today was a good day for the transports. About 100 He 111s and 60 Ju 52s delivered about 380 tons'.

Nevertheless, VVS fighters from 8th VA had swarmed over the supply routes, claiming 27 unescorted enemy aircraft shot down. Kapitan Petr Naumov of 201st IAD claimed two kills and two shared, and he would be joined by at least two other Soviet pilots claiming 'doubles'. The Axis air forces reported the loss of eight Luftwaffe Ju 52/3ms and six He 111s, as well as one of three Romanian Ju 52/3ms that made the trip.[51]

One man who was successful in reaching the pocket was *Luftflotte* 4's senior medical officer, Oberstarzt Dr. Potthoff. He had left Tatsinskaya and flown to Morosowskaya 'over the wintry steppe at a height of around 50-80 m' in a Storch air ambulance belonging to a *Sanitätsflugbereitschaft*. Upon arrival, he was assigned to a Ju 52/3m for the onward flight to Stalingrad. Unfortunately, he experienced a common problem – the aircraft had suffered a wireless equipment failure. Potthoff recalled:

From the crew I learned that, having arrived from the Balkans, they wanted to make their first take-off into the *Kessel* but they had had no previous experience of the Russian winter. I tried to put them in the picture as to the operational conditions, but as I wanted to leave as soon as possible I looked around for other options.

Potthoff eventually 'hitched a ride' in a He 111:

> Whilst on the way, despite the fact that we could see rounds fired off by enemy Flak very close to us, we were neither hit nor did we see any Russian fighters. We were lucky. We were soon flying over the *Kessel* and were able to head for Pitomnik airfield, where we landed on the icy runway.

Potthoff made his way to the flight control hut, where he enquired of the exhausted personnel about the difficulties being faced. They informed him of the challenges in handling so many take-offs and landings in such primitive and adverse conditions, as well as the gathering of large numbers of wounded and sick at the assembly points who were scheduled to fly out, but for whom there was simply not enough transport space. Potthoff next went to one of the army field hospitals:

> I watched what was taking place. The surgeons, doctors and their assistants were flat out, but they went about their work with composure and with a great sense of duty. The rooms in which the teams of surgeons worked were indescribably simple, surrounded by debris and constantly subject to the danger of being destroyed by enemy action. These were apocalyptic conditions. The possibility of providing sufficient help from the outside was minimal.
>
> I had flown voluntarily into the *Kessel*. But before I made my way to the airfield for the journey back, I left behind all of my personal belongings for those who might need them. At Pitomnik, where it was growing dark, I selected a Ju 52 for the return flight. The aircraft was heavily overloaded with sick and wounded. On take-off, that was not a good situation. For flying out of the *Kessel*, a climb to a height of 2,500 m or more was the usual procedure. Our machine managed to climb to just over 2,000 m. We then flew under radio guidance for Tatsinskaya.

It was on this occasion that Potthoff also witnessed the extreme and desperate attempts made by some men for whom there was no further space on a departing aircraft for which they had queued – attempts which Potthoff viewed with disdain:

> When an overloaded aircraft was rolling on its take-off, they made the reckless and stupid attempt to cling to the undercarriage of a Ju 52 so as to be taken out 'externally'. I saw this on the aircraft in which I was flown out during the night of 8 December to fly back to my base.

Pothoff continues with the description of his flight:

> We observed fire from heavy Russian Flak. At times, I had the distinct impression that their rounds detonated pretty close to us! Once again luck was on our side, but at the same time the radio operator reported that our antenna had become unserviceable. That wasn't good news, but there was no sign of concern among the pilot, the co-pilot and the radio man. I later learned that the antenna had apparently become iced-up. We flew compass course West. I was sitting in the co-pilot's seat. After about 20 minutes' flying time we saw to the west, in the dark, individual lights in line astern, but they were dimmed. The lights grew nearer and we guessed that we were in the neighbourhood of Morozovskaya. Suddenly, the radioman came up, beaming all over his face, to announce that the antenna was functioning again. In the meantime we had descended to a height of 1,000 m. From the Russian Flak, we now saw only distant flashes. Radio contact with Morozovskaya was established, and with that, we were able to land there.
>
> Quickly, medical personnel came over to us with ambulances to transport the sick and wounded. We had been lucky. We had seen no sign of Russian nightfighters.
>
> After we landed, I went to the flight control in order to telephone the *Luftflotte*. Like the others, the medical orderlies gave me hot Russian tea, some dry bread and, in addition, about three or four cooked, but frozen potatoes. The food did me good. I had been hungry. The marching rations, and some alcohol that I had been given some days before, I had left untouched back in Stalingrad.[52]

On the 8th, despite thick fog shrouding the Stalingrad area, 70 Heinkels flew to the pocket with around 140 tons and the transports brought 750 men out, but few Ju 52/3ms were able to complete their missions because of Soviet fighter activity. The slower Junkers were now prey for the VVS, and on that day they managed to deliver just 60–70 tons, their formations having suffered losses and been scattered.[53] Four He 111s were destroyed on the ground in the pocket, while in total 12 Ju 52/3ms and eight He 111s were lost during the operation.[54] Inevitably, this reduced supply levels. That day, Hauptmann Winrich Behr, a highly decorated former *Afrika Korps* officer recently posted to 6.*Armee* headquarters, sent a blunt and cynical note out of the pocket:

> Condition of the men is unfortunately shit, living on 200 grams bread ration and for the most part sleeping in the open. Not short of cardboard though, so morale excellent.[55]

There were also constant air attacks on Morosowskaya and Tatsinskaya; the latter field was bombed by 18 A-20s/Boston IIIs of 57th *Bombardirovochnaya Aviatsionnaya Polk* (BAP – Bomber Regiment), which later claimed 17 aircraft destroyed on the ground, as well as strikes to fuel and ammunition stocks.[56] But German records reported the loss of only a single Ju 52/3m from a signals unit on the ground, along with 15 men killed, including the doctor in charge of coordinating the arrival of the wounded from the pocket.[57]

From the Reich, the Wehrmacht issued its daily bulletin on 8 December, and for the first time acknowledged the contribution of the *Transportflieger*:

> Luftwaffe transport units on the Eastern Front and in the Mediterranean have once again proved their worth in continual missions, often under strong enemy action, and have contributed decisively to combat operations.[58]

This did not particularly impress von Richthofen, who noted in his diary that day:

> At last, the transport units have been cited in the Army report. It had been quite a battle to accomplish this, but the way in which they have been mentioned is a disappointment![59]

At Morosowskaya, following his return from the pocket the night before, Oberstarzt Dr. Potthoff was trying to get back to Tatsinskaya. He eventually found a Storch ambulance. It was to be an eventful flight, as he recalled:

> Shortly before take-off a Panzer Hauptmann and an Unteroffizier, both with facial burns, came over. They had been assigned to fly with us at the last moment. In a Storch, four persons was an overload. Despite that, we all boarded the aircraft and, after a long take-off run, we rose unsteadily into the air. We flew on at a low height over the steppes.
>
> Just as we were approaching Tatsinskaya, we saw heavy bombs falling there. Fountains of earth shot upwards and told us what was happening. We turned around in a low-altitude flight towards the south, so as to gain time and not wind up in the middle of the Russian bombing raid on the airfield. Eventually, when we thought that the raid was over, we landed. Unfortunately, a lot of damage had been done. The good Oberarzt Winter and several medical staff were dead. Others were wounded. The medical tent near to the flight control, where I had stayed on the 6th, was badly damaged. My steel helmet and my gas mask were 'goners'. Just in front of the tent, a *Kübelwagen* and its driver had been hit. The surprise attack had resulted in many more wounded and losses in materiel. Oberarzt Winter had not been in his billet in the village, but instead he had continued, without relief, to take care of the sick and wounded upon his arrival.[60]

On 9 December 14 Bostons of 221 *Bombardirovochnaya Aviatsionnaya Diviziya* (BAD – Bomber Division) carried out an attack on Tatsinskaya, destroying four more Ju 52/3ms and setting ablaze 75 tons of fuel and 6,000 rounds of ammunition destined for 6.*Armee*. Two He 111s of Major Fritz Uhl's KGr.z.b.V.5 attempted to fly to Stalingrad, but they were shot down in the process.[61]

As of the 9th, 38 Ju 52/3ms had been reported as being lost since the start of the airlift, while 11 more needed repair as a result of enemy action. Fifteen

He 111s had also been lost, and in total 100 aircrew had been killed or were missing.[62]

I./KG 100 went back to the pocket and brought more men out, but it was also around this time that the decision was taken to start evacuating all the German nurses remaining there, even ahead of wounded men. The nurses could not be allowed to fall into Russian hands.[63]

That day (9th) at Stalingrad, Pickert attended a meeting at Paulus' headquarters 'concerning the future'. He found the mood to be 'confident. Provided we manage to hold out. The morale of the men continues to be excellent'.[64]

Of a mission flown on the 10th, Unteroffizier Fritz Linke, a gunner aboard a He 111 of 5./KG 55, recalled:

Today we made two flights into the cauldron. We are faced with the usual opposition: anti-aircraft fire, bomb-dropping, *Shturmoviks*, etc. During our second flight two Me 109s swept the skies and found a rich harvest. While our aircraft was hastily unloaded, between landing and take-off, we saw three Russian aircraft plunge earthwards.[65]

The Bf 109s were probably from Hauptmann Johannes Steinhoff's II./JG 52. This *Gruppe* had moved into Morosowskaya-West from Maikop on 26 November. It numbered some of the Luftwaffe's top-scoring fighter aces, including Knight's Cross-holders Steinhoff, Oberleutnant Gerhard Barkhorn (*Staffelkapitän* of 4./JG 52) and Leutnant Walter Krupinski. Between them, by the end of November, they had accounted for 269 enemy aircraft destroyed. Since arriving in the Stalingrad sector, the *Gruppe's* Messerschmitts had been in almost continual action flying fighter sweeps, transport escort missions to Pitomnik and Gumrak, and reconnaissance flights over the Don area and the Kalmyck Steppe. That morning the *Gruppe* made six claims, including one by Steinhoff for a LaGG-3 shot down west of Pitomnik as his 126th aerial victory, while Barkhorn claimed a P-40 during the afternoon for his 88th.[66]

With the fighters of JGs 3 and 52 severely stretched by their various tasks, VIII.*Fliegerkorps* called up the twin-engined Bf 110 *Zerstörer* of Major Günther Tonne's II./ZG 1 from Krasnodar, in the northern Caucasus, to Shakhty, 67 km north-east of Rostov. However, whilst the Bf 110s may have had the safe range to escort the transports to Stalingrad, they were unable to make much of an impact on the fighters of the VVS. Not only that, but they started to suffer from combat attrition themselves, and by the end of December the *Gruppe* had only a small number of aircraft left.[67]

Soviet pilots tended to be more cautious of the He 111's defensive armament, especially when manned by nervously alert and determined crews.[68] On the 11th, for example, in a comparison between Heinkel and Junkers operations, Fiebig noted, 'Supply with 80 He 111s is good, but bad with Ju 52s due to clear visibility. Six were shot down from one convoy'.[69] As time wore on, increasingly the Heinkel units were deployed to the pocket by day and night, in *Ketten* or

Staffel strength, but with aircraft flying singly, with or without escort in daylight hours and with sufficient cloud cover at take-off and during approach. This method ensured the highest number of sorties, allowing continuous operations, and because aircraft went out singly, it resulted in the least level of disruption to loading and unloading. It also meant that aircraft did not need to waste time assembling into formation or to wait for rendezvous with escort fighters, which was of particular significance with the onset of sub-zero temperatures.

However, with the cloudbase usually above 1,500 m, fighter protection over the pocket was necessary, as VVS fighters would try to attack aircraft emerging from cloud and preparing to descend. Aircraft making single flights to Stalingrad at night would often remain in the pocket overnight and then form up with other Heinkels into mutually protective *Ketten* or *Staffel*-sized groups for the return flight by day.

Because of the pocket's relatively small area, it was crucial that an aircraft exited cloud at the right spot in order to avoid friendly fire from the Flak defences on the airfield perimeter and, if necessary, a crew could orientate itself on the more prominent and safer western edge of the *Festung*. It was perhaps inevitable that in the early missions there were losses among the younger and less experienced Heinkel crews – particularly among the *Transportverbände* – either as a result of enemy action or accidents, but as time went on, crews became more familiar with the routes, the weather and the potential hazards. Kühl recalls that:

> For navigation just prior to breaking through cloud, *Eigenpeilung* [direction-finding from on board the aircraft] was found to be generally sufficient, and it was only with younger crews, mainly from the transport units, that *Fremdpeilung* (direction-finding by means of a ground station) was required. On occasion when it became necessary to make a landing – anywhere – in conditions of low cloud or with poor visibility because of fog or mist, in the majority of cases, the aircrews demonstrated outstanding flying ability.[70]

When it came to conditions of clear daylight weather, or when there was little cloud, initially, the He 111 units, especially many of the crews of Major Uhl's KGr.z.b.V.5 who had flown missions to the Kholm pocket the previous winter, favoured *Kette*-sized operations since this smaller formation was found to be adequate for defence against the usually half-hearted actions of VVS fighters. However, as Uhl described:

> When the [Russian] fighter defence around the *Festung* intensified, individual sorties were no longer possible in good weather. We had to fly in at least a *Kette* formation and, if possible, with fighter escort. In almost all instances, the presence of two of our own fighters was enough to keep the Russian fighters away.[71]

The strengthening of Russian fighter activity in the area between the Don and the Volga eventually made *Staffel*-sized formations necessary for self-defence, and yet in neither case was fighter escort always found to be necessary. The most dangerous moment was the breaking up of the *Kette* when approaching to land in the pocket, when the aircraft were briefly flying alone and vulnerable. One unit, KGr.z.b.V.20 under Major Hermann Schmidt, which was disadvantaged by a lack of experience in formation flying, suffered several losses as a result of aircraft flying singly in clearer weather. In any case, as temperatures fell, none of the Heinkel *Gruppen* were able to take off in *Staffeln* simultaneously because of the lack of warming equipment. This meant that continuous operations were not possible as aircraft had to wait upon each other at take-off, and thus sortie rates declined.[72]

At 0715 hrs on the morning of 11 December, Fiebig, accompanied by Major Kurt Stollberger, the Quartermaster for VIII.*Fliegerkorps*, flew out of Morosowskaya in a He 111 to Gumrak airfield in the pocket. They were airborne in the cold, clear air for about an hour. Reaching the pocket, Fiebig held what he described as 'sober' discussions with Paulus, Schmidt and Pickert. Indeed, the situation was grim. It became evident as the officers talked that the now 270,000 men in the pocket were about to run out of food, and that the reserves planned to be issued on the 16th would last no more than two days. But by then 6.*Armee* commanders were banking on being relieved. 'If that does not take place', wrote Fiebig later, 'then who knows what may happen'.

The army officers advised the Luftwaffe commander that the numbers of wounded were increasing at a rate of 1,000 per day. According to Fiebig, he was told, 'The Russians take walks in front of the line since we can't shoot at them anymore'. They further informed Fiebig that even if a land corridor to the pocket was opened, three or four divisions would need to be replaced, otherwise it would not be possible to hold the line at the Volga, as the enemy was already able to cross the river on the ice. On the issue of air supply, Fiebig was informed that the supply mission was not providing the required amount of fuel, light field gun ammunition or rations. A daily amount of 600 tons was needed, and had been promised. The daily average, so far, of just 120 tons was not enough for the Army to maintain combat readiness, and 'did not even suffice to keep it fit and alive'.

Fiebig reiterated his earlier position, as explained to Paulus and Schmidt on 21 and 22 November, on the impossibility of an airlift, even though more aircraft had since been made available. He also stressed that supply was greatly dependent on the weather, and his concern over the strong possibility that the Russians could soon be in a position to prevent aircraft from taking off and landing at Pitomnik. According to a later testimony from Stollberger, both Paulus and Schmidt acknowledged Fiebig's opinions to the 'fullest extent'. However, according to the Quartermaster:

> They were indifferent to the reasons that could slow down supply by air such as weather conditions, the enemy etc., and were interested only in tonnage.[73]

Between 30 November and 11 December a total of 1,167 tons had been flown into Stalingrad.[74] VIII.*Fliegerkorps* was also increasingly using those Heinkels from KGs 27 and 55 that it had assigned to combat operations for airlift work as well. It was a grim task: Hauptmann Hans Grah of I./KG 55 who had recently arrived to fly supply sorties noted that, 'The mood is one of complete dismay and shock'.[75]

Proof that Novikov's radio-assisted blockade was having an effect came on the morning of 11 December when, following an alert from a radio guidance beacon, 18 Yak-1 and La-5 fighters of 3rd and 9th *Gvardeyskii Istrebitelyenaya Aviatsionnaya Polk* (GvIAP – Guards Fighter Aviation Regiments) took off under the command of Col I. D. Podgornyy, commander of 235th *Istrebitelyenaya Aviatsionnaya Diviziya* (IAD – Fighter Aviation Division). In the vicinity of Bol'shiye Chepurniki, they engaged 18 Ju 52/3ms and He 111s flying towards Stalingrad escorted by four Bf 109s from Hauptmann Steinhoff's II./JG 52. In their first attack, the Russian fighters claimed to have downed ten of the transports, while eight turned for home, but in the space of seven minutes, Steinhoff accounted for two Yak-1s for his 127th and 128th aerial victories and Oberleutnant Barkhorn claimed three for his 89th–91st. Eight German airmen were captured and Steinhoff was later hit by Flak, but survived.[76]

Remarkably, as the remaining three Bf 109s turned back over the bleak steppe for Morosowskaya, some 200 km to the south-west, Generalfeldmarschall von Manstein had just about completed his frantic preparations for a last, bold, do-or-die gamble to relieve the trapped German forces at Stalingrad. It was a gamble built upon a dilemma, for von Manstein was alive to the distinct possibility of a second Soviet offensive launched towards Rostov which had the potential of isolating and destroying both *Heeresgruppe Don* and *Heeresgruppe* A. He therefore had to be very careful about depleting his own Army Group of significant forces to relieve 6.*Armee*. Any such initiative would, therefore, be, as he termed it, 'a race for life or death'.[77]

12

'The Führer was appalled'

12–21 December 1942

A month is a long time to an encircled army.
EARL F. ZIEMKE, *STALINGRAD TO BERLIN*, 1968

At dawn on 12 December, under the code name *Wintergewitter* (Winter Thunderstorm), the tanks and infantry of General der Panzertruppe Friedrich Kirchner's LVII.*Panzerkorps*, effectively the strike force of Hoth's 4.*Panzerarmee*, moved off from its start positions around Kotelnikovo, some 200 km south-west of Stalingrad, as the first step in the drive to reach and relieve the beleaguered 6.*Armee*.[1] For 12 days von Manstein had been preparing his meagre forces in *Heeresgruppe Don* as best he could, compromising and cutting back where necessary, waiting for reinforcements, tolerating delays, a poor supply chain, and dealing with existing threats from the Russians. He even disagreed with the very idea of retaining the now ruined city on the Volga. In his mind, it was better to regain operational mobility 'if disaster was to be avoided'.[2] And yet, in the true Machiavellian mindset of the German high command, the relief operation was seen as von Manstein's plan, for as the OKW diary noted on 2 December, 'Generalfeldmarschall von Manstein wishes to attack towards Stalingrad on 9 December'.[3]

While there is little doubting the intent, effort and urgency of *Wintergewitter*, given its limited resources and the military and meteorological adversities against which it was pitted, with the benefit of hindsight it is not unreasonable to conclude that its objective was over-ambitious. In fairness, von Manstein had originally envisaged a two-pronged attack, deploying 4.*Panzerarmee*'s other formation, XXXXVIII.*Panzerkorps* (comprising a single Panzer Division, an infantry division and a Luftwaffe field division) in conjunction with LVII.*Panzerkorps*, but these forces would not be available before the commencement of the operation. In any case, the involvement of XXXXVIII.*Panzerkorps* would be denied because of increasing pressure from the Red Army along the Chir.

Many commanders would have felt challenged and compromised, but not von Manstein. The mastermind of *Blitzkrieg* and operational elasticity, the conqueror of the Crimea, regarded by many as a military genius, he was carried by an innate, optimistic ambition, and pressure stimulated him. That was why Hitler liked him. But even von Manstein could not pull miracles out of thin, freezing, foggy air. He needed more tanks and more troops to make *Wintergewitter* count. He waited, depending on Hitler's authorisation, but it was in vain. Although down to one corps, the *Führer* would not release the additional Panzer Division which von Manstein needed to add weight to the operation. By the 9th – von Manstein's intended start date – his aim for a two-corps thrust had reduced to a two-division thrust.

Von Richthofen did his best to lend von Manstein air support, as he had done at Sevastopol the previous summer, but considering the multitude of conflicting demands on *Luftflotte* 4, its declining serviceability figures, loss rates and the conditions in which it was having to operate, this was no mean feat. On 9 December, the air commander issued a directive on the carrying out of operations along three main deployments. Firstly, the support of 4.*Panzerarmee* by Pflugbeil's hard-pressed IV.*Fliegerkorps* using St.Gs 2 and 77 and Schl.G 1, with fighter support from II./JG 52 and ZG 1. Secondly, the continuation of air supply, without any let-up, to 6.*Armee* at Stalingrad by VIII.*Fliegerkorps*, drawing additional support 'if needed' from elements of KG 51 (which was ultimately not used), KG 55, I./KG 100 and II./KG 27. And, thirdly, at the same time using all of these units to support combat operations against massing Soviet forces around the Chir bridgehead in the direction of Kalach.[4]

But hardly had von Richthofen's directive gone out to his units than von Manstein, unknown to von Richthofen, revised the start date of *Wintergewitter* to 12 December as freezing weather took hold after a period of thaw and rain had turned the ground into mud, unsuitable for vehicles. Despite this, a mood of optimism coursed through Hitler's headquarters. That day, the OKW war diarist noted:

> If weather conditions permit, Generalfeldmarschall von Manstein will commence the relief of 6.*Armee* on 11 or 12 December; he expects to complete it by the 17th. The *Führer* is very optimistic. He wants to regain our positions on the Don. In his opinion, the first phase of the great Russian winter offensive has been completed without any decisive success.[5]

At 0800 hrs on the 11th von Richthofen left his new headquarters at Novocherkassk to fly to a meeting with General Hoth. The commander of 4.*Panzerarmee* informed von Richthofen that his drive to Stalingrad would now commence the next day instead, admittedly with far less strength than he would have liked. But time was of the essence because from the 16th, the pocket would run out of food. Von Richthofen was furious at not being informed. It was now too late to bring back units the Ob.d.L. had chosen to deploy on the Don (St.G 77 and KG 27) so as to render Hoth support. 'I now have very serious concerns about 6.*Armee*', he noted in his diary, 'for if Hoth is not able to get through without problems, they'll be liquidated'.

With his units also supposed to be operating over the Chir, von Richthofen knew things would be very tight:

> Looked at logically, there is no way Hoth will get through without at least some difficulty. Since, for the foreseeable future, Hoth is the last arrow that can be shot before 6.*Armee* is destroyed, at the moment I see no good outcome. I protest officially to everyone by telephone and teleprint, for otherwise things would just take their course. Tomorrow I shall take things up with Manstein about the poor cooperation with his staff.[6]

It should not have been unexpected to the Germans at this point that on the Soviet side, preparations were being made to eradicate the Stalingrad pocket. The initial attempts to split up 6.*Armee*'s hold on Stalingrad had failed, and so Gen Vasilevsky, Chief of the Soviet Army's General Staff, requested significant reinforcement of forces in the area, to which Stalin agreed, as well as the provision of the powerful Second Guards Army from the Don Front to bolster the Stalingrad Front to the south from where Hoth was approaching. Vasilevsky then devised a new plan to smash the pocket codenamed *Koltso* (Ring) and submitted it to Stalin and the *Stavka*, who approved it on 11 December. It was agreed that in the first of two stages, *Koltso* would break into the pocket in the area of Basargino and Voroponovo to liquidate the western and southern German groupings by 23 December. In its second stage, a main assault by all armies of the Don and Stalingrad Fronts would finish the job and eliminate the enemy immediately to the west and north-west of Stalingrad.[7]

But no sooner had *Koltso* been agreed than it was confounded as *Wintergewitter* commenced in a mixture of faith, determination, excitement and apprehension. When, following a short artillery bombardment, Kirchner's units started off across the bleak landscape flanking the railway line that ran from Kotelnikovo to Stalingrad, only one, 6.*Panzer-Division*, was anywhere near full combat strength, with around 160 tanks and assault guns having only recently been refitted in France. By comparison, its companion 23.*Panzer-Division*, depleted after heavy fighting in the Caucasus, numbered just 20 tanks. As von Manstein wrote in his memoirs, 'Anyone could see that 4.*Panzerarmee* was not going to reach Stalingrad with only 6. and 23.*Panzer-Divisions*'.[8]

Initially, they made relatively good progress, however, pushing to the north-east across the flat steppe, one division either side of the railway. Aside from some scattered clashes with two Soviet rifle divisions and mobile units north of Kotelnikovo, the advance met little resistance, although progress eventually started to slow down. Yet *Wintergewitter* had reinforced Hitler's will. He reiterated to those assembled for a situation conference at Rastenburg on the 12th that 'under no circumstances' was he prepared to give up Stalingrad. He and Zeitzler (for once in agreement) concurred that, if nothing else, the loss in army artillery, mortars and equipment snared in the *Festung* could never be replaced.[9] According to Warlimont, Hitler warned, 'If we give it up, we in fact give up the whole object of this campaign'.[10] Thus, the city which had been on the periphery of the original thinking for *Blau* had now become pivotal.

Meanwhile, the Red Army was faced with the dilemma of continuing with *Koltso* in the hope that the assault on, and crushing of, 6.*Armee* could be completed before 4.*Panzerarmee* reached the pocket, or to postpone *Koltso* in order to tackle *Wintergewitter*. An irked Stalin agreed with Vasilevsky's request to do the latter, along with allocating Second Guards Army to the Stalingrad Front where it could push back Hoth's advance.[11]

However, even before *Koltso* came into being, Vasilevsky had been working on a much larger operation which he had presented to the *Stavka* on 26 November. Operation *Saturn* was intended as a major pincer manoeuvre launched by Vatutin's South-Western and Golikov's Voronezh Fronts from the Don to cut through Germany's allied Italian Eighth Army and the composite force *Armeeabteilung Hollidt* (formed on 23 November from XVII.*Armeekorps* to cover the northern flank of *Heeresgruppe Don*) on the left flank of *Heeresgruppe Don*. This would be followed by another thrust via Millerovo towards the northern Donets and Rostov, with the aim of isolating 4.*Panzerarmee* and *Heeresgruppe* A in the Caucasus. Although approved on 2 December, the operation was rescheduled from the 10th to the 16th mainly because of transport problems in the prevailing weather.[12] This, along with the fact that the Wehrmacht had proved capable of a surprise initiative with force in the area, prompted a re-examination of the entire concept. Acting quickly, the Russian command moved the emphasis from the destruction of enemy forces south of the Don to finally pinching out 6.*Armee* and ensuring its total isolation from *Heeresgruppe Don*.

Thus was born Operation *Malvyy Saturn* (Little Saturn). This smaller-scale envelopment plan was for the South-Western and Voronezh Fronts to advance in a south-eastwards route on Morosowskaya, destroying the Italian army, *Armeeabteilung Hollidt* and the remnants of the Romanian Third Army south of the Don and on the Chir, as well as severing von Manstein's lines of communication. Crucially, from the perspective of this book, it also aimed to capture the airlift supply fields at Morosowskaya and Tatsinskaya. This plan was approved in Moscow on the 13th.[13]

Meanwhile, as LVII.*Panzerkorps* pressed on towards Stalingrad, conditions in the pocket were fast becoming untenable. Cold and hunger were gnawing at the trapped soldiers, debilitating their stamina and reserves of willpower. Unwashed, unshaven men in filthy, field-grey greatcoats, thin scarves and balaclavas were no longer able to stand on their feet, and when they slept, they simply dropped into holes in the ground and covered themselves with tarpaulins. Mice and rats scurried over them freely, and in such conditions, sickness and infection spread, a common illness being dysentery. The easiest method was to squat in a hole over a shovel and then throw the waste as far as possible out into the snow, possibly towards the occupants of another hole. Most wretched of all were the lice, which spread epidemics. One *Panzer-Grenadier* officer wrote, 'Lice are like Russians. You kill one, and ten new ones appear in its place'.[14]

To support *Wintergewitter* the efforts of the airlift were thus intensified, for if Hoth and Kirchner were successful, then 6.*Armee* would need adequate fuel and ammunition with which to fight its way out.[15] Indeed, between 12–21 December, as 4.*Panzerarmee* attempted its relief operation, 1,377 tons of supplies, or the equivalent of 137 tons per day, were flown into the pocket.[16]

In this period the He 111 again proved its ruggedness, although not without cost: at Hitler's headquarters the record of the daily situation conference on the 12th noted:

> Yesterday 50 tons of ammunition, 15 cbm of fuel and eight tons of rations had been flown in to the Sixth Army. That was not very much. Losses had amounted to four He 111s. The *Führer* was appalled.[17]

On the 16th, a day when the temperature in the pocket dropped to -30°C, Fiebig noted that 70 He 111s and 20 Ju 52/3ms flew to Stalingrad. They delivered 180 tons of supplies. But this was not without cost – according to Fiebig, 'two Ju 52s nose-dived from the clouds, crashed, burned'. The Heinkels, which were from I./KG 100, lost one of their number when the crew of the H-6 of Unteroffizier Herbert Grosshans of 3.*Staffel* failed to return.[18]

This was also the day that the Russians opened the *Malvyy Saturn* offensive with a 90-minute heavy artillery barrage in the pre-dawn hours that pounded the Italian, Romanian and German lines and which preceded the advance of Kharitonov's Sixth Army and Kuznetsov's First Guards Army. At dawn the Russian formations rumbled forward through the thick fog that hung over the ice-covered Don and snow-blanketed steppe. But the going proved frustratingly arduous in the gloomy weather, not made easier when Russian tanks found themselves in a minefield which Red Army engineers had failed to clear. Yet it took several hours for the staff at *Heeresgruppe Don* to recognise that a Soviet offensive was underway. By nightfall, however, the Russians had broken through the Italian line and caused a complete breakdown in defence and an ensuing rout.[19] *Heeresgruppe Don* was now at risk.

Dawn on the 17th was clear, but the temperature never rose above -15°C. With the ground firm, the Red Army was able to continue to deploy its tanks and mobile forces against the pocket and around the Chir. As such, the Luftwaffe was now unable to provide adequate fighter protection for all the transports, and so only the He 111s could fly to the pocket. But with increasing Soviet air and anti-aircraft activity, fewer Heinkels got through. Despite this, Fiebig was forced to continue the supply flights rather than divert aircraft to tactical operations on the Chir because of the perilous supply situation at 6.*Armee*. 'It must succeed! The alternative is unthinkable', he wrote.[20]

Fog blanketed Tatsinskaya on the 18th, preventing the Ju 52/3ms and Ju 86s from flying, and only five He 111s reached the pocket from Morosowskaya to deliver ten tons. 'It is doubtful they will be able to fly during the night', noted a frustrated Fiebig. But he was wrong: once again the Heinkels went out, despite the weather, to deliver 70 tons during the night. Throughout the following day,

73 He 111s, 50 Ju 52/3ms and 13 Ju 86s delivered a total of 270 tons, with crews of I./KG 100 flying two or three missions to Pitomnik.[21]

By mid-December the situation at Pitomnik resembled something of an infernal wasteland as the number of sick and wounded men awaiting air evacuation climbed into the thousands. Oberleutnant Rudolf Müller, the Technical Officer of KGr.z.b.V.5 at Morosowskaya, remembered how, after a Heinkel had unloaded, there would be the harrowing sight of 'emaciated soldiers storming the aircraft. However, we were only allowed to fly out wounded. They lay close together in the fuselage of the He 111'.[22]

In order to be airlifted out of the pocket, a man had to be granted official, written medical authorisation, and once issued on paper or cardboard, this precious item would be pinned to clothing or clutched by a frozen hand inside a tunic or greatcoat pocket. Without a medical permit, no one could be flown out on medical grounds; those found abusing the system risked death by firing squad at the hands of military police. The medical teams would often give priority to the lightly wounded, who at least stood a chance of recovery and therefore could return to duty, rather than to those suffering from more serious wounds. But this in itself created an appalling paradox, for the removal of the lightly wounded weakened the fighting strength of the Army, while leaving only the seriously wounded would continue to place a drain on the medical teams.[23]

Pitomnik was some eight kilometres from the railway line, and the wounded would have to walk along a road covered in snowdrifts and ice that connected the two locations. War correspondent Heinz Schröter has left a graphic description of the route to the airfield:

> Down this road came the wounded, escaping from the stricken city. All sorts and conditions of men could be found on this highway: private soldiers and generals, the sick, the wounded, the crippled and the healthy, with and without orders. They wore furs, or skins, or charred uniforms or leather waistcoats. They had blood-stained bandages about their heads and across their stomachs. There were brave men and cowards among them. Some came in lorries, others crawled on hands and knees.[24]

Leutnant Joachim Wieder was an army intelligence officer who was based in a primitive, wood-lined bunker at Pitomnik with six comrades. He remembered:

> The Russians knew only too well that the heart of the Stalingrad army was beating at Pitomnik, which was the only really serviceable air base in the pocket, although an auxiliary base had been established at Gumrak. This was where the vital food and supplies for men, weapons and machines were being landed. Here were located important command posts and communications centres, air traffic control, the supply staff and the supply administration with its bunkers in which the treasures of bread, biscuits, meat, vegetables, drinks and canned goods flown in were stored until they could be distributed. Here, too, in the centre of the pocket, was a main dressing station, to which the sick and

wounded were brought from all sides in their thousands and, later on, in their tens of thousands.

Nearby was an assembly point for soldiers who had lost contact with their units, where frightened, confused and desperate human beings from shattered formations all over the front gathered together. Here at Pitomnik there was a constant coming and going, a feverish hurrying and bustling, an incessant grinding of engines, constantly recurring firing and explosions of bombs, a never-ending worrying, fearing, hoping and despairing. Small wonder the Russians saw this base as a particularly worthwhile target for air attack![25]

On one occasion, the engine of a Ju 52/3m flying low over the pocket was shot away by Russian fighters. Both the aircraft and its separated engine fell to the earth and both killed troops below. Indeed, Pitomnik resembled an aircraft graveyard. Writing of conditions there, Wieder recalled that:

> Occasionally a huge jet of flame erupted on the airfield with an ear-splitting bang. That meant a transport, its belly crammed with fuel, had been hit after landing. In the course of December the shot-down wrecks of every conceivable type of aircraft piled up on the airfield. Peacefully they lay there, from small Russian fighters to the lamed or destroyed big birds, many of which had crashed on take-off. There was even a Fieseler Storch that had frozen to the ground.[26]

Because of the sheer volume of men trying to reach Pitomnik from the railway, conditions became ever more grim. Many hundreds simply collapsed into the piled snow to the side of the road to perish overnight. Motorcycles, ambulances and lorries would endeavour to drive around the frozen corpses – if their snow-concealed mounds were seen in time. The more this happened, so the road became wider as drivers did their best to avoid the bodies. As Heinz Schröter has written:

> But before they died these men crawled, metre by metre, or their comrades dragged them on tarpaulins or boards or in ammunition cases. Then more snow would fall and in the darkness the lorries would jolt over things that splintered and broke beneath their wheels. Frozen bones crack like glass.[27]

In mid-December a landing ground of sorts was established at Karpovka, but generally this field was disliked and avoided by the transport crews as it was extremely difficult to locate amidst the monotonous terrain. At the same time, *Luftflotte* 4 requested that Gumrak, an old Soviet airfield of very poor quality 13.5 km west-north-west of the city, and therefore closer to it, be made operational again in order to have a landing ground in the event that Pitomnik or Karpovka were lost to the enemy. But this request was declined by 6.*Armee*; 'a regrettable decision', noted Schulz, 'which in the last days of the air supply was to have uncomfortable consequences'.[28]

Yet for all the endeavour of the aircrews, there was a bitter irony, for sometimes what they flew into the pocket was either useless or downright bizarre. On one occasion Wilhelm Adam recalled receiving advance notification of the imminent arrival of a consignment of medals in recognition of bravery in the face of the enemy. Aside from Knight's Crosses, German Crosses in Gold, Iron Crosses 1st and 2nd Classes, combat clasps and wound medals, the shipment would also include two cases of Croatian decorations, and yet there was only one Croatian unit – an artillery regiment – in the pocket. The next day, a transport landed in the pocket and unloaded the container of medals. It was so vast and heavy it needed four men to move it away from the aircraft and under cover. An NCO eventually used an axe to smash it open, only to discover it was filled to the brim with Croatian medals. When Adam later mentioned this episode to the senior Quartermaster of 6.*Armee*, he was advised acidly that among recent deliveries had been 12 cases of condoms, three tons of sweets, four tons of marjoram and pepper and 200,000 parcels of Wehrmacht propaganda material. Other items deemed by the supply agencies to be worthy of use in the pocket were out-of-date newspapers, neck ties, roofing felt and barbed wire. Yet, with the tonnages being flown in, there was a daily deficit in bread of ten tons. Units that still had horses were envied as they had access to meat.[29]

Meanwhile, east of the Don, Hoth's advance had slowed down, having encountered gradually stiffening enemy resistance in the Kumskii area, halfway between the Aksai and Myshkova Rivers, and yet spearhead elements of 4.*Panzerarmee* were within 48 km of Stalingrad. This was despite, at last, the arrival of 17.*Panzer-Division*.[30]

There were also indications that the Russians were about to withdraw some forces away from the ring surrounding 6.*Armee* in order to further strengthen the wall against the German thrust from the south. Other Soviet forces were attacking the Italian Eighth Army and Romanian Third Army of *Heeresgruppe* B on the left wing of the Chir line. This threatened the flank of *Armeeabteilung Hollidt*, which in turn threatened *Heeresgruppe Don*. It was what von Manstein had feared; it was now questionable whether 4.*Panzerarmee* would be able to maintain its momentum and progress as far as 6.*Armee*'s southern fronts. It was time to act, time for 6.*Armee* to break out. He needed to confer with Paulus because the prospect of a link-up between 4.*Panzerarmee* and 6.*Armee* rested with the latter.[31]

However, because, from his own account, he was now very concerned about such developments, von Manstein perhaps understandably chose to remain in command of his army group headquarters at Novocherkassk. Thus, on the 18th, in what is viewed as a controversial move, he despatched Major Hans Georg Eismann, *Heeresgruppe Don*'s Intelligence Officer, to the pocket to discuss plans for a fighting breakout by 6.*Armee* to the Donskaya Tsaritsa River under the codename *Donnerschlag* (Thunderclap). Eismann flew into Pitomnik and journeyed in one of the few remaining staff cars to Paulus' headquarters. Paulus and his Chief of Staff, Generalmajor Schmidt, were both puzzled and, it seems, somewhat affronted by von Manstein's decision to send a mere young Major from his intelligence staff as his representative to discuss such an important matter. Why not his Chief of Staff or his senior operations officer? Furthermore, 6.*Armee*'s leadership felt that *Heeresgruppe Don* had not kept the Army sufficiently advised as to its intentions or as to the progress of LVII.*Panzerkorps*.[32] As Paulus commented to Wilhelm Adam:

> Manstein knows the situation within and outside the *Kessel*. Apparently the commander-in-chief of *Heeresgruppe Don* is not ready to go against Hitler of his own accord. I have spoken much about the *Kessel* in my personal talks with Manstein. Now he must lay his cards on the table. Schmidt too cannot understand Manstein handling 6.*Armee* on the brink this way, sending us his youngest staff officer. Now we have to wait yet again.[33]

Notwithstanding this, evidently a main concern of Paulus was the lack of fuel and ammunition with which to effect a breakout. Eismann was informed by Schmidt that he thought such a proposal 'a catastrophic solution'. Infamously, the Army Chief of Staff further opined that '6.*Armee* will still be holding its position at Easter. All you people have to do is to supply it better'.[34]

The concluding view of Paulus was that a breakout would be in contravention of the *Führer*'s orders and would therefore not take place. It is unlikely that von Manstein would not already have recognised this as being the likely reaction from a man as scrupulous and conventional as Paulus. He also knew that Hitler was resolute about remaining on the Volga.

Pickert, the senior Luftwaffe officer in the pocket, seemed to have accepted the situation, for as he remarked in his diary:

> Reports of the approaching *Panzer Armee* sound favourable, although its approach is slow. The enemy is shifting heavy forces to the south, past our front. Too bad we cannot prevent this by a thrust from our *'Festung'*: but we can only afford one decisive thrust, when the *Panzer Armee* is at sufficiently close range.[35]

After Eismann had returned to *Heeresgruppe Don*, at 1730 hrs that evening Paulus and von Manstein communicated with each other by teletype. Paulus summarised the three options available to 6.*Armee*: 1) to breakout through Buzinovka to connect with 4.*Panzerarmee* – this was only possible with armour but that would leave the *Festung* vulnerable in the interim; 2) to breakout without connecting with 4.*Panzerarmee* – but only in an extreme emergency; and 3) to continue holding the present position, which would depend on flying in reinforcements and sufficient supplies which, to that point had, been 'completely inadequate'. However, in the current situation, holding out was 'no longer possible'.[36]

Meanwhile, von Richthofen had just about had enough of Hitler, Göring, Jeschonnek, the OKW and Zeitzler; he was not in the best of moods with von Manstein either. His diary entry for the 18th made his feelings clear:

> From 6.*Armee* comes a catastrophic signal regarding the food situation there. I passed it on to the Ob.d.L.. Apparently they can only maintain their reduced daily ration (200 grams of bread) if it is sent to them by air. They need 130 tons of food supplies per day. Of course we can deliver

250 tons on the best of days, but as a daily average only 70 tons, and because we have to deploy units in support of Hoth, the conclusion is therefore obvious! I no longer see any positive outcome.

Apparently there's a big meeting at the Ob.d.L. and at the OKW today. Despite my attempts, nobody can be reached. Since the 16th, I have not had any telephone contact with Jeschonnek because all the proposals one puts forward are rejected, or after verbal agreement, orders are issued to the contrary. In addition to that, I definitely have final proof that certain things which I have said have been passed on as quite the opposite. I will continue to send only telegrams from now on: today, a four-page one about the situation. In it, I requested orders for the conduct of the campaign, for in recent days nothing in terms of orders have been received, just bitching. Perhaps they have no ideas.

That evening von Richthofen retained his temper sufficiently to hold a lengthy meeting with von Manstein. They discussed the feasibility of a breakout by 6.*Armee*, since the two commanders knew that it was impossible to fly in the supplies that Paulus needed. They also lamented the 'listless' way in which operations were being overseen by the OKW. Von Richthofen noted in his diary:

> This evening the *Führer* is said to be discussing a breakout. Manstein acts as though it's already been decided upon. For this purpose, I need to have reinforcements. Manstein recommended I call Zeitzler. I do that. Zeitzler told me that from the very beginning I, in particular, was in favour of maintaining a firm hold on the Volga! What a cheek![37]

The next day (19 December), as the *Malvyy Saturn* offensive continued to gain ground, events took a worrying turn for the Germans when the Soviet Sixth and First Guards Armies ripped a 150-km breach in the Axis front held by the Italian Eighth Army.[38] Von Manstein, very conscious of three Soviet armies heading towards the rear of *Heeresgruppe Don*, communicated with Zeitzler. He asked the Chief of Staff to tell Hitler that with LVII.*Panzerkorps* unable, reliably, to gain further ground, despite having reached the Myshkova, *Donnerschlag* should be activated. Then 6.*Armee* should break out, giving up Stalingrad sector by sector, pulling back its northern front as it left; this would at least save some of the Army's equipment, including the artillery pieces Hitler and Zeitzler had been concerned about. He also instructed 6.*Armee* to at least link up with LVII.*Panzerkorps* on the Myshkova and form a corridor so as to allow truck convoys carrying 3,000 tons of supplies coming up behind the *Korps* to get through. Paulus resisted because the few tanks he could spare to force his way out of encirclement did not have the range of action. Crucially, however, Hitler refused to sanction von Manstein's request, or at least refused to take a decision one way or the other.[39]

In the air, 73 He 111s, 50 Ju 52/3ms and 13 Ju 86s flew 270 tons to the pocket. A nonplussed Fiebig confessed to his diary, 'I cannot make head or tail of what's going on. Generaloberst Paulus sent thanks for the amount of supplies flown in today, of which 220 tons were rations.'[40] It was needed, for according to Pickert, 'The air supply assumed major proportions today, but it was high time! The bread supply was about to give out, despite a 200-gram cut in rations. The daily requirements of bread alone are 40 tons!'[41]

And yet while German soldiers were starving at Stalingrad, that day Oberstarzt Dr. Potthoff, *Luftflotte* 4's senior doctor, happened to be in Rostov on his way to the Caucasus to inspect the Luftwaffe medical units there. As he waited at the city's main railway station, he spotted, in a siding, a railway carriage marked up as heading back to the Reich, and into which were being loaded all kinds of 'desirable' items. Potthoff decided to investigate, and as a result he confiscated the carriage. Potthoff recalled:

> It was supposed to be carrying 'freight' for the homeland. I happened to notice that as 'freight' there were carpets and other expensive items that in no way could be considered as 'military goods', but rather were purely for private purposes. Personnel from the *Luftgauarzt* (Air Adminstrative Region Medical Section) were among those in the party. I saw to it that action was taken. There were also some swift reassignments made. As to what was going on, somebody had already whispered in my ear when I arrived in Rostov. Such items could not have been purchased with military funds. And it was not booty; the whole thing stank. I thus made sure things were corrected.[42]

Forty-five kilometres away, Fiebig made a fleeting visit to see von Richthofen at Novocherkassk, who told him that a final decision was awaited on a possible breakout, but that in the meantime 6.*Armee* had stated its requirement as being 1,800 tons of rations and 4,000 tons of fuel. Fiebig admitted that 'It was impossible to accomplish. One cannot see how things will develop'. Von Richthofen's exasperation only grew at the latest news from Germany:

> The *Führer* decided that Stalingrad has to be held. In relation to this, I was informed via Manstein and Zeitzler that in a decisive briefing the Reichsmarschall had said that the provisions situation there is not all that depressing. Quite apart from the fact that his waistline would be done a world of good were he to be located in the pocket, my reports have therefore either not been put forward or are not being taken seriously. In former times, consequences would have resulted from that, but at the present time, one is treated like a stupid ass and is unable to do anything about it.[43]

Meanwhile, on the 20th, elements of LVII.*Panzerkorps'* 6. and 17.*Panzer-Divisions* had finally managed to cross the Myshkova River to the northern bank and were tenuously holding bridgeheads against the Soviet Second Guards Army at Vasil'evka and Nizhne-Kumskii, respectively. From here, German soldiers could see the glow of gunfire around the perimeter of the Stalingrad pocket.[44] But to the west, the German front along the Chir was under severe pressure. Fiebig had asked *Luftflotte* 4 for urgent instructions but had received no response;

von Richthofen did not, at this point, consider what were reported to be a few enemy tanks heading south to be a danger. On the 20th, however, Fiebig ordered the He 111s of KG 27 to pull out of Millerovo. At Tatsinskaya, with no direction from the air fleet, he was becoming increasingly worried:

> It is unthinkable what may happen if the Chir front breaks. One asks oneself whether the *Führer* knows the facts and is kept informed on the condition of the troops and their capacities, and whether we did not again underestimate the strength of the Russians.[45]

Fiebig would also probably have been worried about the advanced *Gefechtsstand* (battle headquarters) of VIII.*Fliegerkorps* which had recently been set up at Skosyrskaya, on the River Bystraya, some 50 km to the north-east of 'Tazi' and a midway point between Tatsinskaya and Morosowskaya. Alarmingly, at 1600 hrs, the *Gefechtsstand* had reported an enemy tank breakthrough on the Chir, resulting in, according to air reconnaissance, Soviet armour having advanced to within 50 km north of the *Korps* HQ.[46] At that point the HQ was under the command of the *Korps'* highly experienced Chief of Staff, Oberstleutnant Lothar von Heinemann, and his small staff.

The next day Fiebig's concerns as to the safety of Tatsinskaya and Morosowskaya became only greater: if an airfield was lost, it could be recaptured – possibly. But it would be impossible to replace aircraft destroyed in any such action if an evacuation was left too late. Yet it was von Richthofen's view that the 'trickle' of enemy tanks heading south generated 'endless false reports, which in the hours of darkness and fog can naturally not be verified.'[47] Thus, despite his repeated requests to the air fleet, Fiebig took matters into his own hands:

> The situation is very critical. No word from the *Luftflotte* to the effect of what will happen if the units are forced to abandon the fields. We have our own ideas. I informed Oberst Förster and the executive officers and ask Oberst [Walther] Wenck [Chief of Staff, LVII.*Panzerkorps*] about the situation.

A short while later, VVS Bostons from 221st BAD bombed Tatsinskaya and Morosowskaya. Three Ju 86s are believed to have been damaged on the ground.

'Supply continues', noted Fiebig. In the air, the Heinkel was found to be the aircraft that was both more resilient to Soviet fighters during hours of daylight as well as more reliable in adverse weather. This was borne out when, from around 1030 hrs, some 40 He 111s, despite their smaller load capacity, delivered a little less than the all-time peak delivery.[48] Fiebig recorded that day, 'Fog did not allow it earlier. Weather does not permit any Ju transports'.[49] Pickert noted how, 'With great skill and braving much danger the splendid supply force again succeeded in flying in'.[50]

That may have been the case, but by the 21st, advanced units of the Red Army's full-strength 24th Tank Corps were already way south of Millerovo and had reached Degtovo, less than 100 km from their objective – Tatsinskaya airfield.[51]

13

'General, We Must Get Out of Here!' Disaster at Tatsinskaya

22 December 1942–8 January 1943

What does the Führer want to prove by the fate of this army?
GENERALLEUTNANT MARTIN FIEBIG, 26 December 1942

The air lifeline itself was now under threat. In reaction to the Russian attack, in the first minutes of 22 December, Hitler issued orders to *Heeresgruppe Don* that the railheads at Morosowskaya and Millerovo were to be held 'firmly' to allow for – apparently – the arrival of 'new and even stronger units' for the defence of the Don and Chir areas. As well, the key Rostov–Millerovo rail supply line had to be held.[1] Without these facilities, supplies would not get through to the airfields, and thus 6.*Armee* would suffer further. Later in the day, having been unable to consult with *Heeresgruppe Don*, a weary von Richthofen issued instructions to Fiebig and VIII.*Fliegerkorps* on the measures to be adopted for the defence of Tatsinskaya and Morosowskaya, where *Armeegruppe Hollidt* was responsible for the provision and loading of supplies. 'The *Heeresgruppe* becomes ever more despondent', the air fleet commander bemoaned, 'they are unable to do anything more, as they have no more strength'.[2]

Von Richthofen was right to be concerned; these two airfields were the bases for the bulk of the air supply force. The Ju 52/3m *Gruppen* still operational at Tatsinskaya were KGr.z.b.V.50, KGr.z.b.V.102, KGr.z.b.V.105, KGr.z.b.V.172, KGr.z.b.V.500, KGr.z.b.V.700 and KGr.z.b.V.900. The He 111 units at Morosowskaya were I., II. and III./KG 55 and KGr.z.b.V.5, while the Heinkels of I. and II./KG 27 had been relocated to Urasow and the Ju 52/3ms of I./KG.z.b.V.1 had pulled back to Novocherkassk. For the time being, the Ju 86s of KGr.z.b.V.21 and KGr.z.b.V.22 switched between Tatsinskaya and Morosowskaya as required and/or as able.[3]

Von Richthofen told Fiebig to use his Flak guns and all ground personnel to effect an emergency defence at both locations if needed. In this regard, for defence, Tatsinskaya had around seven 88 mm and six 20 mm Flak guns, two batteries of 75 mm Romanian Flak guns and some captured Russian guns. In terms of personnel, there were troops from the airfield command, a Luftwaffe construction company, two companies of airfield servicing troops, around 150 Romanian soldiers and the same number of exhausted German troops which had fallen back from Skosyrskaya in the face of the Russian advance – altogether some 400 men. The crews from the aircraft, and their mechanics, could not be enlisted for airfield defence as they were on standby for immediate evacuation.[4]

Fiebig was also to prepare for an evacuation of both fields sooner rather than later, if necessary, so that vital equipment such as engine-warmers, fuel tankers, engine parts, freight containers and weapons could be driven away or airlifted out. These were now in short supply after the loss of the airfields east of the Chir in the wake of *Uranus*.[5] The following day (23 December) brought fog which severely restricted any flying by Ju 52/3ms. On the ground, armour of the Soviet 24th Tank Corps was now approaching VIII.*Fliegerkorps'* command post at Skosyrskaya, where things were in 'disarray' according to von Richthofen. Fiebig had told him that he felt the post could no longer be held. 'Tatsinskaya will be threatened tomorrow. If fog continues, then it is doubtful whether any more materiel can be saved'.

The air fleet commander now recognised that with very weak forces in front of Tatsinskaya, the supply airfield for 6.*Armee* was in serious danger. He contacted the Ob.d.L. for guidance, to be informed that Göring had issued strict orders that Tatsinskaya should be held at all costs, and only if and when enemy fire hit the airfield could it be vacated. Reluctantly, von Richthofen relayed the instruction to Fiebig, who noted in his diary, 'I see disaster ahead for us, but orders are orders'.[6]

That same day von Manstein advised Hitler that in his opinion there was a need to move one Panzer division, possibly two, from LVII.*Panzerkorps* west to shore up his army group's threatened left flank. But that would mean depleting *Wintergewitter* and either risking 6.*Armee* or at least introducing the possibility of a long-term air supply operation. If an airlift could not be maintained, then a breakout by 6.*Armee* was the only solution.[7] That evening, von Richthofen had several telephone conversations with Jeschonnek, during which he advanced the explosive proposal that the Caucasus should be given up. He also requested that Fiebig be awarded the Oak Leaves to his Knight's Cross for his exemplary command of VIII.*Fliegerkorps*: 'This is absolutely necessary in order to raise morale. He has long earned it'.

★　★　★

Forty-six-year-old Maj Gen Vasily Mikhailovich Badanov had led the Red Army's 24th Tank Corps since 19 April 1942. A native of Verkhnyaya Yakushka, a settlement just east of the Volga River and 900 km north of Stalingrad, he was a solid soldier, having been conscripted firstly into the Russian Army in 1916 and then into the Red Army in 1919. There followed an impeccable military career in which Badanov fought against Kolchak, and served in the Cheka (Soviet secret police) and the OGPU (Joint State Political Directorate – Soviet intelligence service and secret police from 1923 to 1934) during the 1920s, before retraining as an armoured warfare specialist.

In May 1931, Badanov became a battalion commander at the Saratov Armoured School, and despite once serving as a former Imperialist officer, he avoided Stalin's purges. Following the fascist invasion of the Soviet Union in June 1941, Badanov was given command of 55th Tank Division at the battle of Smolensk. He then led 12th Tank Brigade and served as acting Chief of Staff of the 56th Army, all with distinction. Upon taking command of 24th Tank Corps, Badanov led the formation in the defensive battles around Voronezh and the Don Bend. At this time a Soviet tank corps comprised three tank brigades, each made up of two battalions with 23 tanks in each plus a motorised rifle battalion. The corps also had a motorised rifle brigade and two self-propelled artillery regiments.[8]

Badanov was not a reckless man, but his tactical acumen, situational awareness and frontline experience meant that he recognised opportunity. The Axis position south of the Don and west of the Chir was not looking good. By late on 18 December, his T-34 and T-70 tanks, meshed in with the Corps' motorised riflemen, had found 'operational space' and crossed the Bogucharka River on their course to capture, as instructed, Tatsinskaya airfield by the 23rd. Within the first 36 hours of *Malyy Saturn*, the Corps, a component of Kuznetzov's 1st Guards Army of the Southwestern Front, had pushed through 30 km of territory held by patchy Italian and Romanian forces. But, sensibly, Badanov resisted the temptation to 'charge' on, and sent out reconnaissance to check that the way ahead towards Tatsinskaya was clear. It was. By the 19th, his tanks had doubled their depth of penetration, and it was clear there was still no significant opposition waiting for them. So Badanov ordered his crews to continue their drive south, heading for the Bystraya River. By the 22nd, his tanks were fighting around the Bolshinka-Ilinka area and moving so fast that the corps' 24th Motorised Rifle Brigade, unable to keep pace, had fallen some 100 km behind the armour, while their supply base now lay 240 km behind them.[9]

★   ★   ★

Not unexpectedly, during December the Russians considerably strengthened their anti-aircraft batteries in the area between the western and south-western edges of the Stalingrad pocket and 4.*Panzerarmee*. This was a shrewd move in more ways than one: it meant that the transport crews had to continually amend their flight routes, which, in turn, had the adverse effect of increasing flight duration and thus fuel consumption. Once the Soviet commanders had recognised the changes in course, they simply moved their guns. Anti-aircraft batteries were also set up along the line of the Pitomnik radio beam, which forced the transports to adopt longer routes to avoid ground fire.[10]

VVS fighters were also becoming more of a problem for the slower, less manoeuvrable and poorly armed Ju 52/3ms and Ju 86s, although less so for the crews of the He 111s, who were used to flying in disciplined formation with mutual fire support from their defensive armament. When it came to the

Heinkels, as mentioned previously, Soviet fighter pilots tended to shy away more.[11]

The Ju 86 soon proved to be wholly unsuitable for the airlift operation, and the fact that it had been brought in in the first place simply illustrated how precarious things were. Aside from the fact that this type was no longer deployed elsewhere at the front, which caused 'enormous difficulties due to a lack of spare parts and tools', its range was prohibitive and in strong winds it either required an interim landing spot on a forward airfield or could not be used at all. To these issues could be added the crucial point that the Ju 86's limited transport payload of 0.8 tons meant that the effort and risks involved in deploying such aircraft far outweighed any benefit. Despite this, with insufficient numbers of serviceable Ju 52/3ms and He 111s available, it was still needed.[12]

Nevertheless, as Schulz recalled, the real enemy was not even the VVS:

> As uncomfortable as enemy countermeasures became, and despite the losses and damage they caused to our aircraft, in comparison to meteorological difficulties, their effects were insignificant. Entire days with good visibility over the whole region hardly ever happened. Either the supply airfields were covered by fog so that take-offs could not take place or it was present over the airfields in the pocket so that no landings could be made. Particularly common were clouds of great magnitude with ice in the interim layers which did not permit penetration or flying over, even though the weather in the pocket may have remained good. Such weather conditions, which could not be seen from the pocket, often led to conflicts. To force supply flights in such weather conditions often led to the loss of entire *Staffeln*. Furthermore, the weather changed very quickly during the course of a day, so that even with very flexible aircraft management it was not always possible to master every situation. In effect though, for the units, the demand was always to carry out bad weather flying; the high total losses arising and the often very long waiting for a mission was particularly stressful for the crews. Losses in aircraft due to the effects of weather rose by far over losses caused by enemy action.[13]

During periods of anticipated very low temperatures, the transport *Gruppen* were informed of planned operations as far in advance as possible so that the groundcrews could be ready to commence the difficult and protracted task of starting engines and de-icing wings and equipment in order to avoid delays to take-offs. On (the rare) occasions when early morning and night temperatures rose above zero, the airfields were hurriedly steamrollered so that when the next frost came, the runway would become rock firm.

As an aid, the VIII.*Fliegerkorps* outpost within the pocket transmitted half-hourly weather updates, and similar updates were given for the Oblivskaya, Kotelnikovo and Ssalsk areas.

As mentioned by Fiebig, fog was often present before dawn, and in such instances take-off for more experienced aircrews would be shifted back to the hours of darkness. While on the outward flight to the pocket, during the unloading of the aircraft and during the return flight, weather at the base airfield would often improve, and as a result any decline in a unit's sorties would hopefully be avoided. Time-usage was also optimised, since it was possible that the more experienced crews could fly a further mission. When the weather was particularly foul, however, it was often only the veteran crews who were able to fly at all. In such instances when fewer aircraft operated, the priority was to take food into the pocket, although it was common that the bad weather also affected conditions over the pocket, or it deteriorated even further, which meant that aircraft were unable to land.

Changing and adverse weather would also preclude the use of alternative landing grounds upon returning from Stalingrad, but in any case these tended to be avoided as they were so far away from the immediate flying zone that units would become scattered, resulting in a decrease in sorties the following day. Wherever possible, the younger and least experienced crews would be allowed to take off first to give them ample time to return to their base landing ground.[14]

At Tatsinskaya things were particularly challenging for the Ju 52/3m units. On 22 December Ju 52/3ms went out to Stalingrad under the cover of darkness at 2200 hrs. This was, necessarily, becoming an increasing occurrence, imposed upon Förster's crews by greater numbers of VVS fighters operating around the pocket in daylight.[15] Morzik spelled out the risks in a report to VIII.*Fliegerkorps* in February 1943:

> Because of Russian fighter attacks, missions by day were only possible under protection from our own fighters. With experienced aircrews, execution was faultless, with the escort in close formation. Newer, inexperienced crews in formation flight, however, caused the escorts to become dispersed, made fighter protection more difficult, and endangered secure execution of the mission.
>
> Deployment of regular aircrews was faultless. The use of various new crews without any war or mission experience, together with the difficulties of flying missions at night, in bad weather and blind-flying, led to a reduction in the number of missions flown. Long instructional periods proved necessary and, as a result, became a burden on the highly-taxed regular crews who had been in operation over a long period of time. Due to their lack of training, less experience in blind-flying, as well as less self-confidence, the newer crews displayed somewhat less enthusiasm for their missions. But the authorities back home arranged to send us partly trained, night-blind and civilian crews to the Stalingrad theatre.
>
> For transport units, the challenges of their missions and the great flying and navigational demands involved, require well-trained, experienced crews, similar to the bomber units. Since it cannot be foreseen in what way tasks may change or become more difficult, it would be misguided to assume that crews who have proved to be unsuitable for other units can be transferred to transport units.[16]

In a post-war reflection on the performance of the Morosowskaya-based He 111 units in the Stalingrad airlift, Ernst Kühl noted:

Experience has shown that:

1 Newly formed *Transportstaffeln* without experience of contact with the enemy should be incorporated in bomber units or in experienced transport units so that they can gradually achieve a successful level of performance which then avoids high losses.

2 Newly assigned 'z.b.V.' *Gruppen*, when selected for operations over enemy territory, are:

   a Adequate in terms of personnel and equipment and are at least comparable to the more established z.b.V. *Gruppen*, but they must be equipped quantitively and qualitatively.

   b They must be given at least a few days to assemble crews.

3 Also, independent transport units which already possess a certain amount of operational experience in such difficult supply tasks as at Stalingrad must be placed, if at all possible, under the command of bomber units in order to be correctly deployed tactically and so from operational experience, they will gain encouragement.[17]

On 23 December, *Heeresgruppe Don* signalled Zeitzler with its latest estimates on 6.*Armee*'s supply requirements. In the prevailing bitter weather conditions it calculated that the minimum required to maintain the fighting strength of the men in the pocket was 2,500 calories per man per day, comprising 500 grammes of bread, 90 grammes of tinned meat, 100 grammes of vegetables, 90 grammes for an evening meal, 50 grammes of fats, 50 grammes of sugar, 20 grammes of salt and seasoning, 15 grammes of drinks and 25 grammes of tobacco, which equated to a total, including packing, of 1,130 grammes. For a ration strength of 250,000 men, this amounted to 282.5 tons per day.

There were also 7,300 troop horses and 15,700 pack and transport animals in the pocket. If all these animals were to be slaughtered, 6.*Armee* believed it would then have enough meat to last until 15 January, and that no tinned meat would be required before that date. This would serve to reduce the daily airlift requirement to 255 tons. However, if a slaughter was to take place, the Army's infantry divisions would become immobilised (except for any assistance that might be rendered from mobile units), and therefore the preservation of the horses was considered highly prudent, especially to maintain the mobility of at least a quantity of heavy weapons and divisional artillery – the items which Hitler and Zeitzler particularly wished to save. This would necessitate supply by air of 22 tons (three kilos per horse) of fodder per day. The period during which horse flesh would provide the meat ration would be proportionately decreased.

In terms of ammunition, a daily quantity of 100 tons was needed just to defend the pocket; that did not allow for any unexpected 'major action', while in order to distribute supplies within the *Kessel*, as well as to power Panzer and Flak units, 75 tons of fuel would be required daily. The signal concluded that 6.*Armee* would need 550 tons per day to maintain its fortress position.[18]

By late December, with Tatsinskaya and other airfields overcrowded from the influx of transport aircraft, the airfield infrastructures struggled to cope, which affected performance and efficiency. Besides the high density of air transport units, there were service units, signals units and medical units to handle and treat the wounded being airlifted out of the pocket.[19] There were also several supply dumps and their associated vehicles. There was insufficient space for aircraft repairs, maintenance or parking, nor were the necessary personnel for such available. In addition, there was a continual lack of spare parts. Technical supervision and maintenance – and thus operational readiness – suffered as a result of aircraft being relocated or simply being returned because the units, without their assigned *Feldbetriebskompanie*, could attain only a 35–45 per cent serviceability rate. Those groundcrews who had been drafted in lacked the tools for the Ju 52/3m and were not suitably trained personnel. Furthermore, the influence of the weather considerably hindered work carried out in the open, so that the duration of repairs bore no relation to the work involved.

In a report compiled a few days after the airlift, Major Fritz Uhl, *Kommandeur* of KGr.z.b.V.5, wrote an honest description of the conditions faced by his unit and others:

The continual relocations and the associated change in the personnel of the airfield servicing companies and workshops had a very detrimental effect on operational readiness. Likewise the transfers to different airfields which are in no way prepared and equipped for the arrival of several units simultaneously. Special winter equipment troops were almost never available in sufficient numbers at any airfield, and almost all work had to be undertaken outdoors with the help of a warming cart. The assignment of a dedicated winter special equipment unit proved to be very beneficial. The maintenance of equipment is better and their deployment can be controlled more appropriately.

When it is very cold, the efficiency of the technical personnel is significantly lower. Machines returning from daylight operations could seldom be cleared again by the next morning, since most of the work could not be carried out at night and without adequate lighting. Therefore, night missions were a much better prospect from a technical point of view.

Some aircraft which were newly assigned from the Reich or newly arrived with a new squadron, were delivered without the required equipment, so that they were out of action for several days or had to be transferred to another location for upgrading. Regarding the inadequate technical equipment of the machines and crews, this meant a lack of pistols, machine guns, flashlights, prismatic compasses, etc.[20]

Beyond the question of *why* the airlift took place, many commentators, including those who were involved and those with the benefit of post-war hindsight, point their fingers at Göring, Jeschonnek and the RLM for the failings in the mechanics and logistics of the operation. Intriguingly, Karl–Heinrich Schulz felt that such finger-pointing may have been unduly harsh. In his opinion, Göring worked hard and quickly to introduce various measures to secure aircraft, servicing units, equipment, winter–weather aids and fuel.[21]

In reality, however, around 60 per cent of the Ju 52/3ms arriving from the Reich to bolster the airlift were not operationally fit for purpose and simply became an additional burden to the already overstretched and exhausted groundcrews. The litany of shortcomings included aircraft fitted only for administration flights and without any equipment installed for frontline operations, or calibration documents for radio or direction-finding equipment; aircraft with no winter protective coverings; aircraft with no armament or parachutes; aircraft arriving with excessive flying hours so that it was necessary to send them back for partial overhaul; aircraft with a total flying time of just four hours; aircraft with special installations, precluding them from being used on frontline missions; and aircraft with engine defects, damage to radios, and defective exhausts which, according to their crews, had already been encountered and reported in the Reich.

Machines arriving in these states served only to increase the inventory without bringing any benefit, thus crowding the airfield and leading to a *reduction* in operational readiness. Fritz Morzik noted at the time:

> It is a false assumption on the part of the service commands back home that operations can be guaranteed with 500 aircraft when some of them are in an unacceptable condition. The number of hot air warmers and starter carts delivered from the Reich and from the rear area airfields has increased continually. This would have been fine if the aircraft on hand had fully satisfied the agreed requirements.[22]

A major problem came when it was necessary to transport aircraft, personnel and equipment from the Reich to Russia. The capacity of the Polish rail system, for example, was woefully inadequate and supply trains were often held up en route to the frontline flying units. During the airlift period, the Luftwaffe had an allocation of only four trains per day, which had to supply all Luftwaffe units in the Don area and in the Caucasus; and on the trains that did run, priority had to be given to fuel, ammunition and air-drop containers.

The Luftwaffe's Quartermaster General, General der Flieger Hans-Georg Seidel, endeavoured to sort things out by sending officers from his staff to *Luftflotte* 4 as 'Supply Commissars'. Whilst these officers did serve to defend the air fleet staff against unreasonable reprovals from Berlin, ultimately they produced no practical benefits or improvements. In his study of Luftwaffe operations in Russia in 1942, Hermann Plocher, indulged in his own finger-pointing:

> Von Seidel should have oriented himself on the spot concerning the adverse supply situation and critical military situation in general in the Stalingrad area. It would have been advisable for him to have then flown an experienced staff

officer, conversant with air transport, supply and ground service problems, into the pocket.[23]

This can only have been a thinly veiled reference to Oberst Fritz Morzik.

For sorties from Morosowskaya, the existing radio beacons at Morosowskaya, Tatsinskaya and Zymlianskaya, and at Pitomnik and Basargino in the pocket, were sufficient to ensure flight safety on long- and shortwave frequencies, plus *Peiler* (direction-finders) at Morosowskaya and Pitomnik were used with the beacon at Zymlianskaya for take-offs and approaches. However, Kühl recalled how:

> The light beacons were very often interrupted and overlapped, so that they were completely unserviceable for *Eigenpeilung* [self-direction-finding]. It is proposed that for new missions the frequencies of the *Zielfunkfeuer* [target direction finder] be changed several times daily.
>
> Targeting of the beacon in the *Festung* through blind-calling did not function. The same applied for the proposed ground-to-aircraft wireless traffic, which did not function with the He 111. It is proposed that in future to adopt UKW [ultra-shortwave] wireless traffic.[24]

By contrast, the direction-finder at Pitomnik functioned well despite heavy use, but aircraft fitted with older FuG VII radio equipment could not use it and were forced to turn back. Kühl's staff recommended that aircraft should be assigned and directed towards a specific direction-finder depending on their installed equipment.

Signals communication between the pocket and the airfields was vital and, according to Kühl, generally it worked 'very well until the last day'. Remarkably, the Luftwaffe signals teams in the pocket, working with their opposite numbers outside, even managed to establish a telephone link from Pickert's command post to the headquarters of VIII. *Fliegerkorps*.[25]

★   ★   ★

By 23 December Badanov's tanks were just 20 km from Tatsinskaya, although they still needed to cross the Bystraya River. But here the way ahead was defended by only a weak and overstretched German defence. Officers of 24th Tank Corps quickly reconnoitred the area and located a crossing point at Kryukov. Pushing on past Skosyrskaya and the VIII. *Fliegerkorps'* command post, a five-hour battle ensued which forced the German defenders to eventually pull back. The Russian tanks were now low on fuel and ammunition, but instead of waiting for their infantry to catch up with them, they kept moving south towards Tatsinskaya. At this point the airfield finally received orders to evacuate, but VIII. *Fliegerkorps'* Chief of Staff, Oberstleutnant Lothar von Heinemann, had already departed Skosyrskaya for Tatsinskaya in order to set up new quarters there, leaving a skeleton staff to handle immediate matters.

Fiebig despatched some of VIII. *Fliegerkorps'* Ju 87s to attack enemy armour following reconnaissance reports that another 40 tanks had been reported approaching Skosyrskaya from the north. In the meantime, Tatsinskaya was, as Fiebig described it, on 'the highest state of alert'. However, he was forced to relieve the colonel in charge of the airfield's defences as he proved unable to cope with the task. Fiebig next talked with the *Lufttransportführer*, Oberst Förster, and arranged that the Ju 52/3m crews were to be at readiness to take off from 1600 hrs. Later that evening he called Oberst Kühl, the *Kommodore* of KG 55, acting as the *Lufttransportführer* at Morosowskaya, to discuss what would happen in the eventuality that communications were cut between the two airfields:

> It is still not clear what the tanks will do − whether they will turn against Tatsinskaya or Morosowskaya. There has been a report of three tanks at the railway between Tatsinskaya and Morosowskaya.

Fiebig and Kühl agreed that, if necessary, a Storch liaison aircraft would have to shuttle between the two fields for communications purposes, but in the meantime, from the following day, and until further notice, Kühl was to take command of an ad hoc battle formation, *Gefechtsverband Kühl*, controlling all VIII. *Fliegerkorps'* Ju 87, fighter, ground-attack and short-range reconnaissance units based in the Morosowskaya area.[26]

One glimmer of good news was that Hitler had agreed to von Manstein's request for the transfer of one armoured division from LVII. *Panzerkorps* to help block the Soviet advance towards Morosowskaya. That night, following an exhausting March through the darkness with the temperature at -20°C, advance elements of 11. *Panzer-Division* moved into the area of the 3rd Romanian Army and were deployed to the west of Morosowskaya-West airfield where the threat appeared greatest.[27] Because of this, the dwindling number of Bf 109 fighters of *Stab*/JG 3 under Oberst Wolf-Dietrich Wilcke and Major Klaus Quaet-Faslem's I./JG 3 were transferred from the West airfield to Morosowskaya-South. Here, they would join II. *Gruppe* under Major Kurt Brändle, although some of this latter unit's machines remained in the Stalingrad pocket at Pitomnik as a *Platzschutzstaffel* formed from pilots of all of JG 3's *Gruppen*.

The weather also cleared a little − sufficiently so to prompt Fiebig to suggest to von Richthofen that 30 Ju 52/3ms, which would not be required to carry equipment and personnel out of Tatsinskaya, be evacuated immediately west to the airfield at Ssalsk in the northern Caucasus, 165 km east-south-east of Rostov. Von Richthofen agreed, but because of rapidly changing and deteriorating conditions, ultimately only four Junkers managed to leave Tatsinskaya safely, of which just two made it to Ssalsk. Of the other aircraft assigned to take off, three crash-landed elsewhere and four crashed over Tatsinskaya itself.

Exhausted, as the spearheads of the Red Army's 24th Tank Corps approached the village of Tatsinskaya and the perimeter of its airfield, Fiebig lay down on his bunk at 2230 hrs and soon fell into a deep sleep.[28]

★ ★ ★

At 0200 hrs on the 24th Oberst von Below, Hitler's Luftwaffe adjutant, telephoned von Richthofen to advise that the Oak Leaves to the Knight's

Cross had been officially awarded to Fiebig. Von Richthofen was genuinely pleased for his corps commander and called to congratulate him personally. Fiebig was already awake again but was not cheery. 'A bitter moment to receive a decoration', he recorded, 'at such a low point in the military situation. I reported briefly on the enemy situation so far as it can be made out'.

In any case Fiebig had little time to savour the news of his award, for some 90 minutes later Soviet shells began blasting Tatsinskaya as Badanov's light field guns and rocket-launchers opened fire. Completely undetected, and after having advanced 240 km, 24th Tank Corps, with its artillery in train, had closed in on Tatsinskaya village, its railway station (thus cutting the Likhaya–Stalingrad line) and the airfield. But his audacious 'gallop' had left Badanov with just 58 tanks and limited supplies of fuel and ammunition even before the corps had reached its target destination.[29] Nevertheless, Badanov and the crews still with him were ebullient: the tanks of the Corps' 130th, 54th and 4th Tank Brigades split up in readiness for an attack, but held back to let the guns lay down a barrage first, their shells and rockets cratering the airfield and destroying or damaging several parked Luftwaffe transports.

The German writer Paul Carell refers to Badanov stating that his troops found the German defensive guns unmanned, their crews still asleep in their bunkers.[30] Regardless, caught by surprise as they had not been able to fully track the Russians' progress due to the darkness and fog, for the Germans, what happened over the next few hours was apocalyptic. It was perhaps the fear of raising Göring's ire (and no doubt his blood pressure) that no practical steps had been taken to prepare to evacuate aircraft and airfield equipment, such as heaters, generators and spares. Fiebig had hesitated, maintaining his view that no matter how absurd, orders were orders, and the transports were to stay on the ground.

Shortly after the guns ceased firing, T-34s began to clatter through the dense gloom and onto the airfield. Visibility was down to 500 m but this did not stop the Russian tanks from opening fire. The German and Romanian troops in the north of Tatsinskaya, together with some 88 mm Flak guns, were quickly swamped by the overwhelming enemy force and the speed and ferocity of its attack. Almost immediately a T-34 collided with a Ju 52/3m as it taxied towards the runway, causing both to explode in a sheet of flame. 'The approaching tanks could not be heard because of the noise of [aircraft] engines', Fiebig later explained in his diary. 'Anyway, it was the heavy fog that made it impossible to fight the approaching tanks successfully, and to prevent them from overrunning us'. A tank shell also struck the Wehrmacht's communications centre.[31] 'Now all communications are gone', Fiebig jotted desperately in his diary.

At 0415 hrs, Fiebig trudged out into the snow and darkness, passing through the empty village, to take a look at the airfield as best he could. Flames licked up into the sky from the burning communications centre and the Russian tanks seemed to have pulled back. He made his way to a command bunker, where he asked his staff which other airfields could be used as safe landing sites for the transports to head to in the prevailing weather. He established that the weather ceiling over

Novocherkassk, 36 km north-east of Rostov, was at 60 m and visibility at one to two kilometres. That would do.[32]

An hour later, another salvo of Russian artillery fire suddenly rained down on the northern edge of the airfield. One Ju 52/3m burst into flames and another aircraft already out on the runway also caught fire, lighting up the night sky. It took Fiebig's Chief of Staff, Heinemann, and the Chief of Staff of *Luftflotte* 4, von Rohden, who was also present, to urgently convince Fiebig to overcome his hesitation and reluctance and order all the remaining Ju 52/3ms and Ju 86s to take off immediately for Novocherkassk – or *anywhere* that was safe, and to where their fuel would take them.[33] Many of the transports subsequently landed scattered over a wide area at different airfields west of the Don or even on the open steppe beyond the Manych River between Novocherkassk and Ssalsk – but at least they escaped the Russian tanks. 'The transport aircraft crews should be given recognition for having overcome the weather conditions', noted Fiebig. 'A total of 108 Ju 52s and 16 Ju 86s were saved – almost unbelievable. It was a frenzied take-off. The only appropriate slogan for the situation is, "*Survival in the face of all opposition*"'.

However, the war diary of the *Luftgaukommando Rostov* noted:

The evacuation of the Tazi airfield by the flying units and their associated ground services would not have had an encouraging effect on the elements ordered to stay, and it risked the splintering of these remaining units.[34]

Fiebig's act of 'disobedience' saved the transports from annihilation, although he ordered one Junkers to be held back to fly himself and his staff out when the right moment came. Its NCO pilot, Feldwebel Ruppert, hurriedly began to load personal baggage into the aircraft.

At 0550, Fiebig was in another bunker:

Tried to use the direction-finder to get a message to the *Luftflotte* about my order to have the units take off. No idea whether it worked. I give orders that a powerful radio set should be kept operating continuously.

Fiebig cautiously left the shelter of the bunker, noting 'Shooting all across the field. A ration dump and other bunkers are on fire'.

As T-34s roamed across the airfield as far as the south-eastern corner of the runway, so they continued firing at the Ju 52/3ms as they taxied and took off. Several aircraft were hit very quickly, but it was due to the skill of their pilots that most managed to get airborne and escape. By 0600 hrs, as a Russian tank rolled towards them, one of Fiebig's staff, the Knight's Cross-holder and veteran Stuka pilot Hauptmann Dieter Pekrun, turned to the *Korps* commander and urged him, 'General, we must get out of here!' Seven minutes later an officer from 16.*Panzer-Division* rushed into the bunker and reported that the area beyond the airfield was in a state of 'wild confusion, full of enemy tanks and infantry. We cannot hold out any longer'.

Near the airfield, more T-34s were firing at rail wagons laden with supplies for 6.*Armee*. At 0610 hrs, Fiebig noted:

> No clear idea of the situation. Constant artillery fire on the runway. The sound of more enemy tanks. I ordered Feldwebel Ruppert to take off in the Ju 52.

Thus, finally, at 0615 hrs Fiebig and seven officers from the staff of VIII.*Fliegerkorps* scrambled on board the last Ju 52/3m remaining on the field. Ruppert applied full throttle and clouds of snow sprayed out from behind the aircraft as it lumbered down the runway and lifted slowly into the air, its starboard engine emitting a worrying 'knocking' sound.[35] Visibility was 500 m, ceiling 30 m. 'It was impossible to get above the clouds', wrote Fiebig. The *Korps'* senior engineering officer followed behind, bravely, in a little Storch.

Thirty kilometres to the east, Morosowskaya was also under threat. Oberleutnant Rudolf Müller, pilot and Technical Officer with the He 111 transport unit KGr.z.b.V.5, described the airfield that morning in a letter home:

> We are on a large airfield on the Russian steppe – 300 km from Stalingrad. Actually, everything is an airfield here, especially now in winter when everything is covered in snow. In this vast area you won't find a tree or a bush, just a few poor little villages, that's all. Everything is snow-covered steppe and there could be an airfield anywhere. Here, where we are now, holes have been dug in the earth – the mole shelters of the crews who fly supplies to Stalingrad in He 111s. Just a couple of tents and a few barracks are above ground. Otherwise, only the two- and three-engined aircraft betray the importance of this airfield. You can hardly see them today, it's so dim. The sky is heavily overcast. The snow clouds hang down almost to the ground. Surely they will collapse at any moment.
>
> And yet it is always day, even when the sun is unable to penetrate the clouds. It is always day, even on an airfield on the Russian steppe, where you feel abandoned by civilisation.

But here Oberst Kühl acted on his own initiative. As soon as he received news that Tatsinskaya had been evacuated, he ordered the He 111s and the Ju 87s at Morosowskaya to also leave for Novocherkassk, while he remained behind in the hope that his units might, at some point, be able to return. His hope would be rewarded.[36] In the meantime, as Rudolf Müller recorded:

> The tank alarm call. Soviet tanks have surrounded the field. In addition to the well-known engine noise, there is a noise like a thousand chains being rattled. There they are, the dreaded iron 'steppe wolves' who fire at our aircraft when we can't get them up into the air.
>
> We are only free in the air. We can't defend ourselves here on the ground. But how do you get up in this weather? We all run to our aircraft. Soon the engines are running everywhere. We can't see each other. Despite all

the inherent danger, we are lucky once again. The tanks seem to remain somewhere in the area, but they are just waiting for better visibility. They don't want to shoot blind.

We have to use this respite and be ready to start, to jump into the grey nothingness as soon as the cloud cover rises even just a few metres. But to fly where? Yesterday, the plan was that in the event of imminent danger, our alternative airfield would be Novocherkassk. No one knows what the weather is like there today and what it will be like on the way there or whether we can even find out by radio.

Müller's was one of the last He 111s of a total of 42 to take off from Morosowskaya. By that point, visibility had extended to about 500 m, and already enemy tanks were rumbling onto the airfield firing in rapid succession. But Müller was forced to fly low in order to hold onto the visibility:

> Only one thing is reassuring and that is that we do not have to reckon with trees, chimneys, telegraph poles or other obstacles at low altitude. But what an effort that means for the eyes, without any horizon! Only now and then does a tuft of steppe grass or an isolated clod of earth stick out of the white. It seems our lives are no longer worth a whistle on this Christmas Eve 1942.
>
> After half-an-hour of awkward ground-crabbing, we at last climb five to ten metres higher, but always close to the snow-laden clouds. We have no radio connection. I keep an approximate compass course in the direction of Novocherkassk. In the vicinity of Novocherkassk there are hills of up to 150 m in height. That is all I know. The weather is not getting any better. Suddenly the clouds are completely on top of us again. I don't change altitude. My eyes are out on stalks from their hollows. The crew is tense. Finally the fog clears once more and we have visibility of 1,000 m, so I speed ahead at 300 km/h.

Exhausted, Müller managed to avoid the hills and finally set the Heinkel down, much to the relief of his crew. He also avoided collision on the ground on the now-crowded airfield:

> Forty-two aircraft took off from Morozovskaya to here. Two had accidents at take-off in the fog. Two others collided. Several had to make emergency landings on the way.
>
> I just want to fall asleep on the spot, here, still in the aircraft. But an empty factory hall with broken windows welcomes us for this Christmas Eve. We sink to the cold floor, roll ourselves in blankets and sleep and dream of snowflakes . . . tanks . . . falling aircraft . . . of home and of those cut-off in Stalingrad whom we should be helping.

The drama was not over for those on board the lone Ju 52/3m carrying Fiebig and his staff as its faulty engine continued to knock away for the duration of the flight to Rostov. Even at 2,400 m they could not reach the upper limits of the cloud. With calm skill, however, Ruppert flew to Rostov using only his instruments. Fiebig was grateful for one thing: 'No ice – what a lucky break!'

Meanwhile, they left behind an airfield littered with the charred wreckage of 46 of Fiebig's transport aircraft. It was fortunate that as many as 108 of his 130 Ju 52/3ms had managed to fly out, along with 16 of the 40 Ju 86s. This represented a 27 per cent loss to his force of 170 machines. Also lost was a large quantity of supplies and equipment belonging to VIII.*Fliegerkorps*, as well as two precious days of supplies for 6.*Armee*.

Fiebig's Ju 52/3m touched down at Rostov-West at 0725 hrs, and 20 minutes later he reported to von Richthofen, relating what had happened at Tatsinskaya and his subsequent order to evacuate. The *Luftflotte* commander agreed with Fiebig's course of action.[37] 'Fiebig is very despondent and dejected', penned von Richthofen later that night, 'and his Staff moans a fair bit'.[38] Fiebig was actually concerned about his actions at Tatsinskaya being interpreted and judged wrongly by the likes of Hitler, Göring and Jeschonnek. He wrote unsparingly in his diary that evening:

> If it really turns out that one or the other of the airfields was cut off and the defence did not function properly, it was solely the fault of the Supreme Command who asked for this kind of situation with the orders they issued. Subordinates who may have committed errors should not be the ones to be punished in this case; that would be a gross miscarriage of justice.

However, even as the wrecks of Luftwaffe transports lay smouldering in the freezing air back at Tatsinskaya, groups of German soldiers were taking up position north of the airfield and around Morosowskaya to hold off any further attacks and to isolate 24th Tank Corps. But, as Fiebig intonates, that this fiasco had occurred at all was attributable to Hitler's and Göring's intransigence to let the airfield go unless it was under direct enemy fire. Even if Fiebig had been able to evacuate as late as the evening of the 23rd, heavy losses in aircraft and equipment could have been avoided.[39]

Meanwhile, in a supreme effort of logistics, from their interim landing points, one-by-one the German transports flew into Ssalsk and Novocherkassk airfields, from where they would continue the airlift. When the He 111s of KGr.z.b.V.5 landed at the latter field no accommodation was available for their crews, and so they were directed to a stone building in the town devoid of lighting, heating or water, with no furniture, the only comfort being straw on the floor. Nevertheless, food was made available at the *Luftflotte* kitchen, where some meagre Christmas celebrations were had sitting around a Christmas tree.

Fiebig summoned his energy for the task in hand: 'Now to rescue 6.*Armee* from Ssalsk, from which point we will have to carry on our supply operations'. Ssalsk, to the south of the Manych River, was poorly equipped to handle the Ju 52/3m units, aside from the fact that it lay under deep snow which had to be cleared. Here, the provision and loading of supplies fell under the jurisdiction of

Heeresgruppe Don.[40] The run to Stalingrad was 400 km, almost at the maximum range of the Junkers.

Typical of the units operating out of Ssalsk was II./KG.z.b.V.1 under Hauptmann Guido Neundlinger. The *Gruppe* had seen service in the Balkans and North Africa, and so when called to take part in the airlift on 24 December its aircraft and crews were relocated to Berlin-Staaken, where they underwent hurried preparations for winter operations. Leaving Staaken on the 28th, its first crews reached Ssalsk two days later. Having been used to the climate of North Africa, they were quartered in a wood-lined bunker at the southern edge of the field where there was some rudimentary heating, while outside the temperature rarely rose above 0°C. The *Gruppe* would commence its supply runs on the 31st.[41]

In the pocket that afternoon, Generalmajor Pickert once again made the rounds of his Flak batteries, doing his best to bestow some Christmas morale:

> It is uplifting to observe the wonderful inner confidence and resolution of our men. The weather is bad, with snow, fog, storms, drifts, no air supplies. We are greatly concerned about our airlift base, which the enemy is threatening from the north. The strangest Christmas I have ever experienced.[42]

Helmut Bieber was a member of 1./37, a heavy Flak battery based at Pitomnik airfield. He recalled:

> The batteries had the task of positioning themselves in such a way that, in addition to air targets, ground targets could also be engaged if necessary. We knew that Manstein's Panzer Army was fighting its way from the south. On 20 December, the spearhead was said to have been about 60 km away. The XIV.*Panzerkorps* had orders to push through to the south with a combat group to establish a connection. To accompany and support the attack, a *Flakkampfgruppe* [Flak Battle Group] was put together, to which 1./37 also belonged. Our heavy battery was ready to march on 21 December and waited for orders. The attack was eventually cancelled because the *Panzerarmee* – in danger of being trapped – had to turn to the southwest. Our hopes were thus dashed.
>
> However, the Russian air attacks increased. There were constant nuisance attacks, even at night. Since the Army's supplies of food and ammunition were low or used up, the deployment of our transport units was stepped up. The Russians, who kept an eye out for the approach of our transport units, carried out their attacks mostly during the landing and take-off times. Our Flak was therefore always ready to fire when more than three machines were taking off or landing. Cooperation with our fighter pilots [of JG 3] went smoothly. The Flak guns had permission to fire until our fighters were obviously ready to attack. Often one transport unit wanted to land while another took off, and at that moment Russian aircraft would attack. The incoming unit would be directed to a waiting area, away from the airfield, and hold there at high altitude. We would open fire on the Soviet aircraft regardless of where our own fighters

were. Sometimes, for example, a He 111 would be attacked by an Il-2 or Pe-2, and the Russian aircraft would be repulsed by the Heinkel's gunner and also by our Flak, while at the same time a German fighter would engage. If our fighter got itself into a close attack position, our firing would stop. Our fighters could also be alerted to departing Russian aircraft by our shooting in their direction.

Individual He 111s were able to defend themselves successfully against attack through the energetic defence of their gunners and their pilot's flying skills. The performance of transport aircraft at night was greatly admired. Some crews flew into the 'fortress' two or three times and took off or landed in the dark despite the bomb damage. As far as I can remember, the maximum number of machines used in one night was 79.

Bieber was wounded the following month and would fly out of the pocket on 15 January on one of the last two Ju 52/3ms able to leave from Pitomnik for Ssalsk.[43]

Meanwhile, at 1830 hrs on 24 December, Maj Gen Badanov radioed the headquarters of Southwestern Front and 1st Guards Army that Tatsinskaya had been taken. If that were not bad enough for the Germans, the neighbouring Soviet 25th Tank Corps had closed into artillery range of the He 111 base at Morosowskaya – albeit two days later than originally ordered.[44]

That Christmas Eve, von Richthofen assembled his own staff and the officers of VIII. *Fliegerkorps* in the dining car of his headquarters train at Rostov for a seasonal meal and celebration. Although the food was good, the mood was downbeat and was not dispelled by the singing of carols or the consumption of some festive alcohol. Fiebig was not in the mood for a party, however, and chose to go to bed: 'I was at the end of my strength and went to sleep early'. Later, von Richthofen sat up writing up his diary. One paragraph was telling:

> Once more I had the most serious telephone conversations with Jeschonnek and Zeitzler. They have still not yet recognised the situation here and they believe that small measures are still of help. Zeitzler maintains that he shares my assessment. From the way he rambled on, however, I get the impression that he is not supporting things, nor pushing things forward. Jeschonnek appears only to be repeating what comes from the mouth of the very highest. I request both of them to mention my name to the Reichsmarschall, who, up to now, likewise, has only exerted himself in terms of small solutions. But I fear it has now become too late for even more wide-ranging solutions.[45]

★ ★ ★

Christmas morning dawned clear but bitterly cold and windy. Fiebig took a flight in a Storch from Rostov with Pekrun, passing over Shakhty and, despite being buffeted by the wind in the little aircraft and the constant danger from below, he flew on towards Tatsinskaya. He put down in a field on some high ground occupied by a Wehrmacht reconnaissance patrol and watched his *Korps'*

He 111s bombing the area around the supply base while ground forces clashed north and south of the railway. Climbing back into the Storch, he pressed on towards Morosowskaya, where he landed. Meeting with Wenck and Kühl, he was left a little more reassured by the situation there as the newly arrived 6. *Panzer-Division* had taken the area north of Tatsinskaya and was shoring up the defences, although enemy pressure from the north remained considerable. The word from 6. *Armee* was that Paulus and his staff felt they had enough horsemeat to last until 15 January, but no one knew what would happen after that.

In the *Festung* at Stalingrad, there was a sense among most of the soldiers that this would quite probably be their last Christmas. The Russians preyed on their exhaustion, cold, frayed nerves and hunger. It was psychological warfare. At one place at least they set up a Christmas tree and played seasonal German hymns and songs across the ruins from giant loudspeakers. They broadcast messages, imploring the Germans to surrender, promising them fair treatment, food and clean clothes. The 3,500 Russian prisoners of war still trapped there in makeshift camps at Voroponovo and Gumrak received hardly any food. 6. *Armee's* surgeon-general refused to allow the evacuation of men with frostbite since there could be a case for a self-inflicted condition as a ruse to avoid fighting.[46]

On his return flight Fiebig passed Tatsinskaya again. 'A fuel train is on fire', he noted. 'Russian tanks are feeling their way forward on the road south'. Down on the airfield, however, Badanov reported just 39 T-34s and 19 T-70s left from his tank corps, and very limited fuel and ammunition.

The temperature was down to -25°C. The water in rivers, storage tanks and in shell holes froze solid. At the German airfields west of the Don a few small Christmas gatherings took place in tents, wooden huts and shattered buildings so that men could take mass or communion, but it was hard to address a congregation above the biting wind.

On return to Rostov, Fiebig visited von Richthofen, and the two men exchanged seasonal greetings. Fiebig learned that during the fighting with the Soviet 24th Tank Corps at Skosyrskaya on the 24th, VIII. *Fliegerkorps* headquarters staff had lost three dead, 17 missing and 15 wounded. 'The Staff's ability to function has to be restored before we can take back on any combat operations', Fiebig wrote in his diary. 'I hope that one or more of the missing men may still return'.[47] 'I attempt to raise Fiebig's downturned, pessimistic face', wrote von Richthofen. 'He is of the belief that the stubborn defence of Tatsinskaya was some kind of private joke of mine'. The air fleet commander was taken aback by this, so, 'I showed him the *Führer* order'.[48]

And as darkness fell on Christmas Day, the new supply airfield at Ssalsk, although poorly equipped for continuous operations by several units simultaneously, was – somehow – brought up to a functioning status.[49] At their dispersal area at the edge of Pitomnik airfield, the fighter pilots of JG 3 were becoming increasingly concerned for Leutnant Georg Schentke of 2./JG 3 who had failed to return from a sortie over the northern edge of the pocket towards the end of the day. 'He bailed out', noted Feldwebel Kurt Ebener of 4./JG 3. 'The wind drove his parachute over the railway line near Kotluban in enemy territory'. Schentke, who was credited with 71 aerial victories, was not seen again.

At 0500 hrs that morning, at Tatsinskaya, Badanov's force had been given a boost when a column of five tanks and six trucks laden with ammunition, under escort from five T-34s, reached 24th Tank Corps' outer positions in the morning darkness. Behind them also, at last, came 24th Motorised Rifle Brigade, finally rejoining the rest of the Corps. An hour later, a radio message informed Badanov that 24th Tank Corps had been renamed 2nd Guards Tank Corps and assigned the honour title *Tatsinskaya* in recognition of its contribution to the destruction of German forces in the Don–Bystraya area and the disruption it had inflicted on the Luftwaffe's airlift effort. Badanov was also awarded the new Order of Suvorov 2nd Class – the first such recipient. There was little time for celebration, however, for the tables had begun to turn on the stranded Soviet corps. That afternoon Badanov signalled Southwestern Front and the Army HQ asking for further urgent replenishment of fuel and ammunition, the latter to be dropped by air.[50]

Badanov was not the only one in need of urgent supplies. From Stalingrad that night Paulus signalled *Heeresgruppe Don* the bleak, but not unexpected news that losses, cold weather and inadequate supplies had seriously impacted 6.*Armee*'s ability to continue to fight all but the smallest skirmishes and 'local crises'. Furthermore, the *Armee* was now unable to break out unless a corridor was already prepared and supplied with protective forces. Paulus did the nearest thing in his character to demand relief, but he tempered his demand by stating his acceptance that such a relief operation may not be possible, and that his Army may therefore have to be sacrificed. Whatever the case, he assured *Heeresgruppe Don* that 6.*Armee* would hold out until the last moment. He also advised that just 70 tons of bread had reached the pocket that day, some of his corps would exhaust their supplies the following day and supplies of fats were expected to run out that night. The army commander concluded by stating that urgent, radical measures were needed. *Heeresgruppe Don* relayed the signal to the OKH.[51] Indeed, according to the senior Luftwaffe officer in the pocket, Wolfgang Pickert, fuel and food were almost used up, and that day's bombing of Pitomnik by the VVS had made the air supply operation even more precarious.

At the new headquarters of VIII.*Fliegerkorps* in Rostov that night, Fiebig was trying to come to terms with the situation facing German forces on the Volga:

What could the *Führer*'s idea be? 250,000 men are involved here and we cannot sacrifice them just like that, because we cannot replace them. What are the Russians going to do with 250,000 men? They will only drive them into death because they can't feed them. It will be wholesale death. Every man should use his last bullet for himself. But what does the *Führer* want to prove by the fate of this army? It must have some meaning – or one could lose faith.[52]

In the meantime, German army units were slowly surrounding Tatsinskaya airfield and had repelled several Soviet relief attempts for 24th Tank Corps. They had also been strengthened by the arrival of 6.*Panzer-Division* from the east, which took up blocking positions along the Bystraya.

General Badanov found himself in a precarious position. His corps was cut off, weakened and exhausted from its long thrust down from the Don. He was also having to fight off determined attacks from 6. and 11.*Panzer-Divisions*. His tanks were fast becoming outnumbered and, once again, their ammunition was almost expended. Tatsinskaya had become a landscape of destruction, the snow-covered ground lit up by the burning grain silos and storage dumps, while the runway was littered with knocked out tanks and anti-tank guns, crushed and wrecked aircraft and frozen, twisted corpses – the legacy of close-quarter combat. At 1800 hrs on the evening of 27 December, Badanov radioed Southwestern Front that the situation 24th Tank Corps faced was 'serious', and that he had, '*No shells. No tanks. Heavy losses in personnel. Can no longer hold Tatsinskaya. Request permission to break out of encirclement*'.

The Front Commander, Lt Gen Vatutin, ordered Badanov to hold out, and at 2300 hrs the VVS air-dropped ammunition. But during the night, as Vatutin kept Stalin and Zhukov appraised of developments, the latter enforced upon the Front commander that he was not to allow 24th Tank Corps to be destroyed, and that appropriate forces should be despatched immediately to relieve him. Vatutin was to get Badanov 'out at any cost'.[53]

With Ssalsk airfield ready, this meant that on the 27th, in clear skies and temperatures of -20°C, 40 Heinkels and Junkers recommenced supply operations to Stalingrad from there.[54] Meanwhile, He 111H-6s from I./KG 100, which had been able to return to Morosowskaya on the 25th following a German counter-attack against Pavlov's 25th Tank Corps, also flew to Stalingrad. Each Heinkel carried a container of rations, three smaller containers of meat, 18 cases of butter, six bundles of blankets and two sacks of peas. Once the aircraft had landed and been unloaded, wounded were flown out.[55] This counted for little in the ruins of the city, however: there, the men of Seydlitz' LI.*Armeekorps* lived a subterranean existence in cellars, seeing little daylight, covered in brick dust and eating meagre supplies of horse flesh.[56] The standard daily rations by the 19th amounted to 200 grammes of bread, 15 grammes of fat and 40 grammes of honey substitute. Even horsemeat had become rare and, because there was no firewood on the steppe, what there was could only be eaten raw.[57]

But Fiebig was wary about the situation at Morosowskaya. 'It is not a good one. It can easily turn into a crisis like the one in Tatsinskaya on the 24th. After checking with von Richthofen, the order has been given to withdraw only if the field is under fire'.[58]

11.*Panzer-Division* was able to retake most of Tatsinskaya in a counter-attack on the 28th aided by strikes from the Luftwaffe. 'Tatsinskaya is back in our hands', noted von Richthofen, no doubt with relief. 'The airfield has once more been put into operation and work on the railway is being energetically pursued'.[59] Nevertheless, Badanov still clung on to a small part of the perimeter ground and the Russians continued to apply pressure on the German line east of Morosowskaya. Yet if this news reached Rastenburg, it did little to lift what Gerhard Engel has described as the 'deepest depression' pervading there. It seemed everyone was 'hoping against hope' that Paulus would break out, despite the *Führer's* instructions otherwise; even Jodl seemed to want it. But according to Engel, 'Nobody knows what should be done next at Stalingrad. *Führer* very quiet and is almost never seen except at daily situation conference'.[60]

During the morning von Richthofen flew to Ssalsk, where he met with Oberst Förster and his staff. Von Richthofen presented Förster with the Knight's Cross in recognition of his role as the Ju 52/3m *Lufttransportführer* for the Stalingrad airlift, as well as his stalwart service as a transport pilot. To 21 December 1942 he had flown 107 operational missions.[61] However, von Richthofen harboured some concerns about how the transport organisation was functioning at Ssalsk and set up a 'pep talk' between Fiebig and Förster for the next day.

Only Ju 52/3ms flew to Stalingrad on the 28th, taking barely 100 tons. 6.*Armee* had suffered the loss of 30,000 men since it had become encircled, but there were still 117 'average battalions' to supply, plus tank battalions and artillery and mortar batteries.[62]

The Bf 109s of the *Platzschutzstaffel Pitomnik* were in action over the pocket, and Feldwebel Kurt Ebener had a narrow escape when he and Feldwebel Frese encountered some LaGG-3s. Ebener attacked one of the Soviet fighters but without success:

Too much speed in the second attack I make from behind and above, so that I bank a little when intercepting and ram the Russian's vertical stabiliser. The underside of my Messerschmitt is slit open along the side. The crate has to go to the workshop and I'll fly it alone to Moro in the afternoon, and report to the *Kommandeur*.[63]

Twenty-two-year-old Ebener, a Thuringian by birth, had volunteered to serve in the *Platzschutzstaffel* greatly motivated by the fact that his older brother, Helmut, was a company commander in a *Panzer-Jäger* (tank-destroyer) regiment of 414.*Panzer-Division*. Ebener's eldest brother had been killed in action on the Eastern Front, and as such, Kurt was determined to protect Helmut. Ebener had flown into Pitomnik on the 16th to find that the *Platzschutzstaffel* had only three grimy and exhaust-stained Bf 109Gs that remained serviceable. The others had been cannibalised for spares as the transports were unable to carry parts that would be used for routine fighter operations. The *Staffel's* mechanics had to make do with whatever was available – one way or another.

Ebener threw himself into the operations of the *Staffel*. On the 19th he had flown four sorties, almost continuously, for five hours, during which he landed only to refuel and rearm. His missions included a fighter sweep, escort for an Fw 189 reconnaissance aircraft and escort for the transports. On one mission, he and his wingman bounced a formation of LaGG-3s. Although outnumbered four-to-one, the Luftwaffe pilots made the best of it and Ebener scored the first of more than 30 kills he would claim over Stalingrad. His victim smashed nose first into the ground south of Karpovka. Airborne again 40 minutes later, he shot down two more Soviet fighters before attacking a flight of Pe-2s and accounting for two of them, as well as breaking up their formation. By the time he landed at Pitomnik again, Ebener was physically and mentally exhausted.[64]

At 0130 hrs in the morning of 29 December, Vatutin signalled Badanov that he should make an 'independent breakout' from the little ground he continued to hold at Tatsinskaya. Although Maj Gen Pavlov's 25th Tank Corps was fighting in the Morosowskaya area, it was unable to make contact with Badanov's Corps. At around 0200 hrs Badanov issued orders to his brigades to break out. To overcome the shortage in fuel, they took fuel oil pre-heated in tin cans and aviation octane drawn from the remaining German stocks, pouring the mixture into the near empty tanks of their surviving T-34s and T-70s. Forming into an armoured 'spike', 24th Tank Corps fought its way through the German line and fanned out, its tanks heading for the Corps' operating base at Ilinka. The remaining ammunition was used to provide covering fire for the Corps' wounded and soft-skinned vehicles to stage via Nadezhevka to Ilinka. They did so under attack from German aircraft and ground units. At last, on the 30th, Badanov's battered tank corps linked up with Pavlov's 25th Tank Corps. Both had been reduced to fewer than 20 tanks each.[65]

At Tatsinskaya, *Luftflotte* 4 moved quickly to replenish its supply dumps in order to continue the airlift, but as Morzik has recounted:

> The consequences [of the Tatsinskaya 'raid'] were not long in making themselves felt, and the units were the ones who had to suffer. Germany's war leaders were unimpressed by the fact that the operational readiness of the transport forces had sunk to less than 25 per cent; the important thing was to meet the increased demand for supply tonnage. Whatever else happened, the supply missions had to go on, and the transport units continued to do their duty.[66]

Paradoxically, based on decrypted German radio traffic, in Britain, the Air Ministry's Intelligence Branch calculated with some authority that by 10 December approximately 200 transport aircraft had been transferred from Russia to the Mediterranean to ferry supplies needed by the *Afrika Korps* in Tunisia. But by the 26th, no fewer than 150 aircraft had been sent back to the East over a period of six days. The British concluded that had it not been for the high numbers of transports lost over the Mediterranean on their way to Tunisia and on airfields in North Africa, more would have been returned to Russia. Much of the intelligence gathered from intercepted signals was sent by London to Moscow after the commencement of *Malvyy Saturn*.[67] On the 27th, Hitler told von Manstein that at least two *Gruppen* would be added to the strength of *Luftwaffenkommando Don*, and that a further 220 Ju 52/3ms and 50 He 111s were to be assigned to *Luftflotte* 4 'for transport purposes'. One hundred alone were being brought in from North Africa, while others were being stripped from the training schools, civilian and government flights in the Reich and other sectors of the Eastern Front. They would be fully equipped for winter deployment at Kirovograd, Zaporozhye and Warsaw.[68]

Pursuant to von Richthofen's actions of the previous day, Fiebig flew to Ssalsk to meet with Förster to review how flights from Ssalsk and Novocherkassk would be carried out. Fiebig noted that, 'Additional transports have arrived. The supply of 6.*Armee* is to be carried out with all available means. Therefore, there must still be some intention of relieving it. But what are the intentions? Nobody knows'.[69]

Meanwhile, however, *Wintergewitter* had faltered: Hoth's 4.*Panzerarmee*, weakened from giving up some of its forces to launch the counter-attacks further west at Tatsinskaya and Morosowskaya, began to be pushed back from its drive towards Stalingrad. On the 28th von Manstein advised Hitler that 4.*Panzerarmee* could no longer hold the front south of the Don, and that the neighbouring *Armeeabteilung Hollidt* was also vulnerable to enemy attack from north or south. Von Manstein planned to wheel Hoth's army east, beyond the Sal River, so as to protect *Heeresgruppe* A, but there was a risk that forces from Yeremenko's Stalingrad Front could break through the narrow gap between the two rivers.[70]

Where would this leave 6.*Armee*? Von Manstein's biographer, Mungo Melvin, has commented that von Manstein was vague and ambiguous in his instructions regarding *Donnerschlag* and *Wintergewitter* in an important order to *Heeresgruppe Don* on the 19th in which he endeavoured to coax Paulus to break out 'sector by sector' towards a revised and more southerly link point with 4.*Panzerarmee* on the Myshkova. Von Manstein knew well that 6.*Armee* lacked the force to break out towards the south-west unless it used most of its strength in one move rather than sector by sector. He gave no direction to Hoth on deployment of LVII.*Armeekorps* or to the Luftwaffe to rush fuel into the pocket in preparation for a breakout, or to prepare for attacks on Soviet ground forces around the pocket. Finally, he had no plan for how a 50 km gap between 4.*Panzerarmee* and 6.*Armee* could be effectively closed when the latter had already advised it had fuel reserves for only 30 km.[71]

Notwithstanding this, in a momentous move, over 28–29 December, following Hitler's reluctant decision to give up the territory beyond the Don, OKH authorised the withdrawal of *Heeresgruppe* A from the Caucasus and its relocation to the Crimea and the southern Ukraine.[72] Hand-in-hand with this, Hitler still believed that by keeping 6.*Armee* on the Volga, several Soviet armies would be tied up. Nevertheless, this would mean that both *Heeresgruppen* would be pulled back 240 km west of Stalingrad, leaving the pocket increasingly isolated and at the extremity of Luftwaffe airlift capability. As for Hoth, he pulled his 4.*Panzerarmee* back stage-by-stage across four rivers, fighting all the way: firstly the Myshkova, then the Aksai, then to the Sal, passing Kotelnikovo, the starting point for *Wintergewitter*, and finally the Kuberle.[73]

The mix of retreat, failure of mission and the abandonment of 6.*Armee* must have been dispiriting for Hoth and his troops. As Zhukov wrote after the war, understandably the failure of von Manstein's relief operation had an adverse psychological impact on the men in the pocket: 'Despair and a desire to save themselves from inevitable catastrophe were widespread. Now that their hopes for relief had been frustrated, deep disappointment set in'.[74]

To cover these various movements, the Luftwaffe flew He 111s back into Morosowskaya, together with the Ju 87s of St.G 2, the Bf 109s of JG 3 and the Bf 109s, Hs 123s and Hs 129s of Sch.G 1. They soon went into action against Soviet forces from there.

On the 29th, the He 111s of I./KG 100 returned to the pocket, flying two supply missions during which a flight engineer of 2.*Staffel* was wounded by anti-aircraft fire. The *Gruppe* was airborne, bound again for Stalingrad the next day, and again on the 31st when the crew of Unteroffizier Josef Reif of 1.*Staffel* went missing while flying a Ju 52/3m with KGr.z.b.V.5.[75] Hauptmann Hansgeorg Bätcher, *Kapitän* of 1./KG 100, recalled one of the missions at this time:

On 29 December, I landed my Heinkel 111 at Pitomnik at 1010 hrs, carrying butter, salt, mail, and 600 litres of fuel in my 'supply bombs'. Wounded were loaded and an hour later we took off for the flight back to Morosowskaya. We had barely left the ground before we came under attack from a string of fighters. My skilful gunners were able to ward off most of their attacks, but the Russians did not relent. They were very aggressive and each of them made eight to ten individual attacks. Time and again, my aeroplane was hit by their fire – and this included five cannon shells. Several of the wounded soldiers on board received additional injuries, and I wanted to land as quickly as possible in order to have their wounds seen to. But when the soldiers heard of my intentions, they pleaded with me to fly on to the main base. They wanted to get as far away from Stalingrad as possible![76]

Returning to Pitomnik that day from Morosowskaya with his repaired Bf 109 was Feldwebel Kurt Ebener of 4./JG 3. He had successfully managed to avoid agreeing to his *Gruppenkommandeur's* suggestion over cigars that he stop flying. Instead, he loaded his fighter with as much food as he could for his brother and his comrades in their *Panzer-Jäger* regiment also based in the pocket.[77]

29 December also saw no less a figure than General der Panzertruppe Hube, commander of XIV.*Panzerkorps* and probably Paulus' most forthright and competent corps commander at Stalingrad, fly out of the pocket. He had been summoned by Hitler, who wanted facts about what was really going on at Stalingrad from a straight-talking, highly decorated, combat-seasoned soldier whom he trusted. Such was the value that he placed in Hube's opinion that he sent his personal pilot, Hans Baur, to collect the general. Hube spoke plainly, but it seems even he fell prey to the *Führer's* calm and convincing rhetoric that all would be well and that there was a masterstroke in preparation to relieve the pocket once and for all. 6.*Armee* would just need to hold out until late February.[78] The reality was that Hube had little option but to accept this, whether he believed it or not.

On the 30th, 180 tons of supplies were flown to the pocket which at that point stretched from the northern edge of Stalingrad, 50 km to the west, bending south as far as Betekovka and back towards the city.[79] That day, Fiebig was informed that VIII.*Fliegerkorps'* principal mission would revert to the air supply of the 'fortress' once again, and that as such the *Korps* would soon receive reinforcements, this time in the shape of larger transport aircraft – four-engined Ju 90s, Ju 290s and Fw 200s. Further support came from conventional bomber units, such as the He 111s of I. and II./KG 27, which had been carrying out bombing operations from Urasow. They flew into Novocherkassk on the morning of 30 December and the first runs to Pitomnik, amidst foul weather and enemy anti-aircraft fire, took place as early as 1300 hrs that afternoon.

For the Heinkel crews, the greatest challenge was to land at night on an unfamiliar field with minimal lighting and with no beacon or radio guidance in dreadful weather and then to take off again in the same conditions with wounded on board.[80] The *Kommandeur* of KGr.z.b.V.5, Fritz Uhl, emphasised in a report written after the experiences of the Stalingrad supply operation that it was very important that gunners and radio operators in He 111s be allowed sufficient freedom of movement within the aircraft in order to quickly move, aim and fire the aircraft's defensive guns in case of an enemy fighter attack. 'This must be taken into account when carrying wounded on a return flight', Uhl noted. 'Overfilling the aircraft has been found to be very disadvantageous'.[81] In any case, He 111s would often depart the pocket not fully laden with wounded because it happened that a large number of Ju 52/3ms and/or Fw 200s had left earlier and all the wounded assigned for evacuation had been loaded. Waiting for further casualties was not an option as this would jeopardise the prospect of a second or even third mission in a night or day.[82]

Whilst the reinforcements were, in theory, a positive move, Fiebig confessed to his diary, 'I don't know yet how to manage to supply the requested 550 tons daily'. He believed that it would take one to one-and-a-half months for there to be any positive effect on the men at Stalingrad. In the last week of December, just 19 tons of ammunition was delivered to Stalingrad – a figure which was actually 2.2 per cent of the quantity expended during that period. Worse was fuel, where, by 27 December, stocks had depleted to 15 cbm of diesel.[83]

In the early hours of the following day, New Year's Eve, there was more bad news. Due to continuing pressure from Vatutin's Southwest Front, *Heeresgruppe Don* had decided to give up Morosowskaya and withdraw to a line 20 km east of Tatsinskaya, or possibly even as far back as the Donets. This would have a significant effect on the Luftwaffe's ability to supply Stalingrad, and if Tatsinskaya was to follow, the use of Ju 52/3ms would be 'uncertain' as Fiebig put it. Even von Richthofen conceded that the army group's decision would have 'severe consequences for us in the Morozovskaya–Tatsinskaya area'. He met immediately with Schulz and his senior operations officer to discuss relocation options and orders.

There was a great and sad irony to this, for in the Stalingrad pocket that day, Paulus had despatched Hauptmann Günter Toepke as his supply emissary to *Heeresgruppe Don* at Taganrog. Evidently Paulus and his staff were not satisfied with the way that the supply fields were handling cargo space. Toepke's orders were to report to von Manstein and then to closely monitor the loading methods being used. Incredibly, Toepke was advised by the *Armee's* Chief of Staff, Generalmajor Schmidt:

> The Army Group must stop sending dozens of He 111s to the abandoned Tatsinskaya airfield. Our soldiers are threatened with death by starvation. Report back to us when we can expect a better supply service![84]

In fact, although Tatsinskaya had been taken back by determined efforts, dangerous levels of attrition caused by the airlift operation were eating away at the Ju 52/3ms and their crews: losses in the period 28 December to 4 January stood at 62 aircraft, of which 15 were classified as missing, while 12 aircrew had been killed, with 52 missing and a further 20 wounded. Around half of the casualties – both men and machines – had been caused by the weather.[85] If the period is widened from 30 November to 5 January, the number of lost aircraft climbs dramatically to 254 machines.[86]

Furthermore, given the loss of all supplies on 24–25 December, it was an impressive accomplishment that the Luftwaffe averaged a daily delivery of 100 tons between 24 December and 11 January.[87] But according to Wilhelm Adam, in a bizarre move in early January, two transports landed in the pocket with fresh troops in a hopelessly pointless gesture. It simply meant more mouths to feed; the space on the aircraft would have been better used by sending in food or fuel or ammunition.[88]

Meanwhile, on the afternoon of 31 December, more Junkers went out from Ssalsk. Ahead of their mission, at midday, 50+ pilots and radio operators drawn from at least ten Ju 52/3m *Gruppen* were called in for a briefing. Many of them were already old acquaintances from pre-war service with Lufthansa, being highly experienced aviators; one former *Flugkapitän* had clocked up more than two million flight kilometres. They listened attentively as the meteorologists, technicians and liaison officers from *Heeresgruppe Don* discussed the anticipated weather conditions on the route to, and over, Stalingrad, the conditions to be expected at the Pitomnik and Basargino landing grounds in the pocket, details of the radio beacons and locations of enemy anti-aircraft guns and searchlights, and gave helpful tips to the newly arrived crews.

Leutnant Franz Lankenau, a pilot in II./KG.z.b.V.1 on his first flight to Stalingrad, recounted, 'A difficult flight lay ahead of us'. His unit's Ju 52/3ms climbed to around 3,000 m and then their crews faced flying more than 300 km into enemy territory. Under guidance from a radio beacon, they made their approach to the pocket, where they would have to land within a confined area with the most rudimentary lighting in the wintery darkness. Lankenau recalled:

> Three kerosene lamps – a green one on the landing cross, a white one in the centre of the field and a red one at the end; that is the entire field illumination. These lamps are only visible for a short time on landing and then immediately covered again because of the enemy's night bombers. The weather on this

New Year's Eve is relatively good. There is a cloud layer with a lower limit of 500 m above Stalingrad. The crew take care of unloading the fuel drums and then help the wounded soldiers on board, who are wrapped in paper against the cold. It's cosy and warm in the flight control bunker, but my frozen fingertips ache. We report in, unload and start up again, but without a long stay. We wind our way up over the pocket to 2,500 m and then make course back to Ssalsk. The anti-aircraft searchlights cannot reach us above the clouds.[89]

And no sooner had Lankenau and his comrades landed back at Ssalsk than the wounded were helped off the aircraft and the Junkers reloaded and refuelled for a second mission. As they climbed up into the night sky, there was silence in the aircraft as thoughts turned to home on New Year's Eve. The quiet was interspersed only when the flight engineer gave bearings to the radio operator. Once down in the pocket, it was a repeat of the process. Then, as Lankenau, exhausted from two sorties, and with an aeroplane-load of wounded troops, returned once more to Ssalsk at 0605 hrs, the sun was rising.

One crew was not so fortunate. As an indication of just how wide the Luftwaffe was having to cast its net for aircraft, a Ju 52/3m brought in from the *Kurierstaffel der OKM* (the Liaison Flight of the Naval High Command) and flown by Oberfeldwebel Oskar Paust failed to return from a supply flight that night.

Both Fiebig and von Richthofen were also exhausted: before he went to bed that night Fiebig wondered, 'What will 1943 bring?' and he jotted down an order of the day for 1 January that he would send to all his units the next morning: 'In spite of all the opposition facing us, we must keep 6.*Armee* alive'. Von Manstein evidently agreed. He told Paulus that evening that it remained the prime objective of *Heeresgruppe Don* to free 6.*Armee*, but that the Army must be ready to hold out for a while longer. He also let Paulus know that Hitler had told him he had instructed Göring to increase the daily air supply to at least 300 tons, and that larger aircraft were on the way so as to facilitate this. To meet the *Führer's* demands, there was now available a total of 567 Ju 52/3ms and He 111s, although how many of these were serviceable, let alone immediately operationally ready, was another matter altogether.[90]

Von Richthofen retired at 0030 hrs, having spoken with both Jeschonnek and von Manstein: 'Turned-in tired. The New Year is starting off well; it will be a turbulent one!'

On New Year's Day, Hitler signalled Paulus, extending his and the German people's good wishes to the valiant 6.*Armee*. The *Führer* acknowledged the hardship and adversity that 6.*Armee* faced, and that he held its soldiers in the highest of respect. 'I and the whole German Wehrmacht', he promised, 'will do everything in our power to relieve the defenders of Stalingrad'. He then announced that he intended sending an ostensibly powerful, elite grouping of the army's *Grossdeutschland Division* and the 1.SS *Panzer-Division 'Leibstandarte Adolf Hitler'*, 2.SS *Panzer-Division 'Das Reich'* and 3.SS *Panzer-Division 'Totenkopf'* to relieve the pocket. These divisions would apparently be deployed from the Kharkov area in mid–February, but this overlooked the fact that they were still refitting, and the limited capacity of the Russian railway system would deal its hand once again.[91]

Against this was the fact the improved weather at Morosowskaya took a turn for the worse, and there was more fog and ice, which allowed Russian tank units to resume their attack on the airfield (no fewer than 32 enemy tanks had been reported destroyed near the town by 6.*Panzer-Division* on the 1st).[92] The decision was therefore taken to evacuate the airfield. KG 55 and its assigned units were to relocate to Novocherkassk, while the more mobile close-combat units of VIII.*Fliegerkorps* were to move to that field the following day.

That afternoon (1 January) von Richthofen and Fiebig met for tea at *Luftflotte* 4's headquarters and held a long, confidential and frank discussion. Von Richthofen conceded that, 'It's really very bad', while Fiebig felt that:

> The situation would not be so difficult were it not for the fact that the fate of 6.*Armee* is a spectre which influences all the decisions that have to be made. Why does Russia not pluck the ripe fruit? Do the Russians want to capture Rostov first as their strategic objective?
>
> The *Führer* must be under heavy pressure. Why didn't they let 6.*Armee* withdraw from Stalingrad and the Volga or else give up the Caucasus? Now we have to do the latter anyway, without being able to help 6.*Armee*. Whatever caused this action is very difficult to comprehend because the losses it has brought on us are very great.[93]

The next day, from out of the fog, Russian tanks and infantry mounted an attack on Morosowskaya. In order to avoid being overrun in a repeat of Tatsinskaya, the He 111s of KG 55 were forced to take off in weather conditions of the worst possible kind, with the fog reducing visibility to almost zero, while the close-support units also withdrew to Tatsinskaya as planned.[94] As the enemy tanks rolled onto the field, German engineers blew up the unserviceable aircraft, including five Bf 109G-2s from I./JG 3, a pair of Bf 109G-2s from III./JG 3, five Ju 87Bs from I./St.G 2, three Hs 123 biplanes from 7./Schl.G 1, three He 111s from KGr.z.b.V.20 and a Ju 86 from KGr.z.b.V.21.[95] The Luftwaffe was also forced to abandon its last stock of 'Type 1000' air-drop containers there.[96]

The move to Novocherkassk, 330 km distant from Stalingrad, added another 225 km and reduced the number of sorties flown by one aircraft to one per day. Besides the detrimental impact on sortie rates, there was an inherent impact on fuel consumption and aircraft serviceability, as well as, understandably, a negative effect on the men in the pocket.[97] Schulz described the predicament the Luftwaffe now faced at Novocherkassk and Ssalsk:

> The difficulties were enormous. Fighter escort was no longer available because the forward fighter airfields had to be abandoned. Ju 52 missions had to be conducted only at night and the He 111 units had to fly without any fighter protection. Due to lack of range, the Ju 86 units had to be dispensed with. The last remaining AB 1000 containers, particularly valuable

because of their load–carrying capacity, had fallen into enemy hands at Morosowskaya. Due to the longer flying distance [320 km], which brought the Ju 52 to the limit of its range, the required mission performance rose per tonne of air supply. In addition, brief improvements in the weather were no longer able to be exploited.[98]

In the first few days of January operating conditions for the transport units reached a nadir. Temperatures fell to -45°C. Engines froze, fuel froze, wings iced and tyres and cables split and burst. The warming carts could not cope with such extremes.[99] Despite this, there was a major effort to fly in supplies on the 3rd. 'Everybody is trying as hard as possible', wrote Fiebig. The next day, accompanied by Morzik, he flew to Ssalsk to meet with Förster, where they 'talked over technicalities of the Ju 52 commitment' and the feasibility of using a new airfield at Sverovo.

I./KG 100 managed to fly two supply flights on the 4th, although Heinkel operations were generally hampered by the softening of the runway at Novocherkassk. This led to difficulties with loading the transports. 'I took measures', Fiebig noted, 'with 250 tons flown in [on the 3rd]'.[100]

In the period 28 December to 4 January, Ju 52/3m losses amounted to 62 aircraft, including 15 missing. Of their crews, 12 were confirmed dead, 52 posted as missing and 20 wounded. Approximately 50 per cent of the losses were due to the weather.[101] It was, understandably, a particular blow when an aircraft had made it all the way to Stalingrad, where it unloaded, but was then lost on its return flight with wounded on board. For example, the He 111 flown by 26-year-old Feldwebel Willi Wunderlich of 2./KG 27 landed at Pitomnik in the late morning of 3 January and flew out of the pocket carrying seven wounded soldiers. It was attacked by two Russian fighters south of Kalach on its return to Novocherkassk and seen to veer over on its right wing and crash, but with no fire on impact with the ground. Wunderlich, his crew and the seven wounded were posted missing.

Late the following afternoon, Feldwebel Dieter of 3./KG 27 was forced to make an emergency landing following an encounter with a VVS fighter on its return from Stalingrad. His He 111 came down in open country three kilometres from the village of Paptschino. It was pitch dark and raining. The observer and flight engineer were killed, while the gunner, Obergefreiter Ernst Gröning, remained alive but trapped in the aircraft's ventral gondola, with his feet crushed between some of the buckled armour plating. During the landing impact, several full drums of machine-gun ammunition were torn away from their stowage brackets and also fell on top of him. Almost immediately after the aircraft had landed, the rain began to form a layer of ice. The radio operator, Obergefreiter Wilhelm Rinka, managed to establish radio contact with Novocherkassk and advise of their situation, but even after firing emergency flares, they were not found. Dieter, Gröning and Rinka were forced to spend the night in the cold, wet wreckage of their Heinkel, during which Gröning developed frostbite in his feet and legs. They were eventually rescued, but on the 7th Gröning's right leg was amputated at the military hospital in Rostov.[102]

Only 21 He 111s were able to take off on the 5th, while the Ju 52/3ms were prevented from operating because of icing in the air and on the ground. In the pocket, a winter storm howled in from across the eastern steppes. 'The weather is horrible', noted Pickert. 'Snowdrifts reduce visibility to less than 100 m, but the sky is blue'.[103]

On the 6th, both the Ju 52/3ms from Ssalsk and the He 111s from Novocherkassk were again hindered by fog, and those that made it to Stalingrad were forced to stay on the ground in the pocket until noon when conditions cleared. Some Ju 52/3m crews of II./KG.z.b.V.1 attempted to use the cloud as cover, but while on the way out to Stalingrad the conditions proved fickle and the cloud cleared. In clears skies the Junkers were attacked by Soviet fighters: some escaped, but at least one was shot down over the pocket. Only a gunner survived, having suffered the loss of an arm and a leg.[104]

At this time, there was a 30 per cent failure rate in attempted supply missions. Fiebig explained the situation:

General weather conditions have been particularly unfavourable for days. We are situated on the water borderline between warm and cold weather, and therefore we have very low clouds; sometimes the clouds are so low as to become fog. We have poor visibility, icing on the ground and in the air, snow flurries and changing conditions between take-off and landing fields.

In such conditions, mass take-offs would not normally be attempted, but as Fiebig commented, 'We know what is at stake!' However concerned and conscientious he was, the fact was that by the 6th, Wolfgang Pickert recorded that there was no bread left in the pocket for the following day. According to Fiebig, by 7 January:

He 111s are taking off both day and night. During the night only air-dropping is possible. The situation in the fortress is very grave as a result of the small amounts flown in during the recent bad weather. We must prevent losing the field and the He 111s at Novocherkassk. Without He 111 supply the fate of the fortress would be sealed in one stroke.[105]

Snowfalls at Ssalsk stopped the Ju 52/3ms from getting out, but while fog blanketed the runways at Novocherkassk during the morning, I./KG 100 went to Stalingrad despite the weather. In the process the He 111H-6 of Leutnant Heinz Fischer of 3.Staffel was shot down.[106] Another factor that came into play was a technical breakdown in one of the main radio markers during the night of 6–7 January, while Soviet jamming measures had increased significantly, which confounded the less experienced crews and forced many to turn back. When the Heinkel crews found it difficult to locate groups of German soldiers below them, they resorted to dropping the containers they still had randomly over a wide area in the hope that something, somewhere would be retrieved. But this, in reality, rarely happened.[107] In the pocket, the troops lacked the energy to haul the containers from the deep snow, and their vehicles had no fuel to be able to transport them.

General Hube flew back into to the pocket from his meeting with Hitler at Rastenburg, landing at Pitomnik on the 7th. He now wore the Knight's Cross with Oak Leaves and Swords around his neck, awarded to him for his typically bold thrust to the Volga River north of Stalingrad earlier in the year, and the subsequent defence there against repeated and fierce Soviet counter-attacks. Hube drove through the snow and ice straight to Paulus and told him that a new relief effort was in preparation that would be much stronger in force than anything Hoth had. Things were scheduled for mid-February.[108]

Back at VIII.*Fliegerkorps* headquarters, this was far from Fiebig's mind. There were more pressing and immediate matters to attend to. As he confessed to his diary:

The worry about the supply situation in the fortress is very hard on my nerves now because the situation is very tight, and despite all our efforts we are not able to deliver more than very small quantities. Weather conditions render us completely powerless. We are too far away from our target fields. Just when take-offs become possible, as a result of fog, heavy clouds and snow flurries, Pitomnik and Basargino are closed down.[109]

On 8 January, despite more favourable weather, I./KG 100 managed just one supply sortie[110], and to add to the pressure, more He 111s were required for combat operations on the Don Front.[111] The situation was grim even to von Richthofen:

The supply flights are proceeding with all the means available. Because of Russian advances, there exists a serious danger for the airfields at Ssalsk and Novocherkassk. We are forced to also withdraw from there, hence our supply performance sinks to a minimum. Since up to now we have only been able to cover 25 to 30 per cent of the supply needs, and due to our withdrawal relocations, performance has sunk by 50 per cent. This results immediately to the conclusion that the fate of 6.*Armee* is sealed.[112]

14

The Giants of Stalingrad

On 8 January, Fiebig received word that some of the Luftwaffe's largest aircraft were en route to join the airlift: 'Tomorrow Fw 200s will start supply operations; they can carry 5-6 tons'.[1]

This must have raised his eyebrows. The Focke-Wulf Fw 200 was a big, elegant, adapted airliner with four engines. Known as the Condor, it boasted a wingspan of more than 32 m. In theory, it was an ideal machine for the airlift. However, while its internal payload offered improvement over the Ju 52/3m, Ju 86 and He 111, it would require more servicing and parts per aircraft on account of its number of engines (particularly in the hostile conditions of Russia), and a unit equipped with such aircraft would require a large airfield from which to operate. The likelihood is that in the corridors of the RLM in Berlin, there was a crude assumption that 'big' equalled 'more tonnage space'. Yet from a military perspective, the small number of Fw 200s operated by the Luftwaffe were needed in France, where they were engaged in prosecuting the anti-shipping campaign over the Atlantic – a campaign that was steadily being lost.

Notwithstanding strategic demands, the initiative for the move of Fw 200s to the East had begun less than a week earlier when, during the night of 2–3 January, Major Hans-Jürgen Willers, the *Staffelkapitän* of 11./KG 40 based at Châteaudun, in north-west France, received a telephone call unexpectedly ordering him to report to the Luftwaffe's *Generalstab* in Berlin. Willers was an experienced bomber pilot who had flown He 111s with KGs 4 and 54, and who carried the unwanted distinction of having once been shot down by 'neutral' Swedish ground fire. He had also been wounded on more than one occasion and, as such, wore the Wound Badge in Silver. Willers' unit was equipped with Fw 200s, each carrying a crew of up to six, and it served as a component *Staffel* of the operational training *Gruppe* of KG 40.

Since the summer of 1940, the Fw 200 had equipped the *Stab*, I., III. and IV.(Erg.)/KG 40, based at Trondheim-Vaernes, in Norway, Bordeaux-Mérignac in western France and Châteaudun, respectively. These *Gruppen* had deployed the Focke-Wulf over the North Sea, the Atlantic and the Bay of Biscay, with some success. Aside from offensive action against Allied shipping, the Condors performed the additional roles of maritime reconnaissance and the 'shadowing' of convoys on behalf of the U-boats.

Like other multi-engined Luftwaffe aircraft, the origins of the Fw 200 lay in a design for a civilian airliner. Designed by Professor Kurt Tank, the eminent Chief Executive and Technical Director of Focke-Wulf at Bremen, shortly before the outbreak of World War II, the Condor became a beacon for German aeronautics. On 10 August 1938, an Fw 200 of Deutsche Lufthansa flew from Berlin-Staaken to New York, having flown non-stop for 24 hrs 56 min – a record-breaking flight of 6,370 km. Aside from Lufthansa, the Condor was used by airlines in Denmark, Brazil and Japan.

From 1940, in addition to maritime reconnaissance, the Fw 200 gained for itself a formidable reputation as an anti-shipping strike aircraft. From their bases in western France and Norway, Condors from KG 40 – the principle operator – waged war against Allied shipping and convoys from Iceland in the north, to the west of Ireland and south to the Mediterranean. A report from June 1941 stated that I./KG 40 alone had sunk 109 ships and damaged a further 63 since mid-April 1940. But by 1942, attrition had started to gnaw away at KG 40 as the Allies devised ways to improve convoy protection through increased surface escort, radar and carrier-based air cover. That year, KG 40 lost no fewer than 26 Condors on operations.[2]

This was the backdrop when Willers reported to a Major Schmidt in Berlin on the morning of 3 January. He was told that he was to take command of a new *Gruppe*, designated with immediate effect as KGr.z.b.V.200, which would have the specific task of flying supplies into the Stalingrad pocket using the Fw 200 from the Luftwaffe airfield at Stalino, 167 km north-west of Rostov in eastern Ukraine. Willers harboured some doubts about his new assignment: because of the construction of the aircraft's fuselage and its notoriously weak landing gear, the Condor's maximum safe landing weight when loaded was 19 tons. But in terms of payload and efficiency as an airlift aircraft, according to Willers, it was a different story. 'Heavier loads were out of the question. There was usually something small to repair on the Fw 200 after each landing'.

To form the new unit, aircraft and air- and groundcrews were on their way to Berlin-Staaken, being drawn from III. and IV./KG 40 in France and the 2.*Staffel* of I./KG 40 in Norway.[3] At Staaken, the aircraft would be quickly modified for transport use by specialists from Focke-Wulf. This process would entail, amongst other things, the removal of some fuel tanks to allow for more cargo and the application of yellow Eastern Front identification markings.

Willers would have a small *Gruppe* staff, and two *Staffeln* were to be established: 1./KGr.z.b.V.200, with 50 flying and 66 ground personnel from France under Oberleutnant Franz Schulte-Vogelheim of IV./KG 40 as *Staffelführer*, and 2./KGr.z.b.V.200, with 61 flying and 62 ground personnel from Norway under Oberleutnant Karl-Heinz Hausknecht, who had come from I./KG 40. The men arriving from Norway would bring with them experience of flying in winter conditions, and as such, it was planned that they would very much 'lead' the operation. Both *Staffelführer* were experienced Condor pilots. Each *Staffel* was assigned nine aircraft, with 2.*Staffel* also allocated a single Ju 52/3m for the transport of bulky equipment. The unit's personnel were to be assigned with all urgency to the collection and loading of the required equipment and spares from across the Reich that would be needed for the forthcoming mission. Given the urgency of the situation at Stalingrad, the *Gruppe* was to move to Stalino as soon as possible.

Thus, amidst conditions of considerable haste, it was recognised that the two *Staffeln* would be required to be self-supportive and would need to operate in the East in adverse conditions for a period of several weeks, despite the known complexities and fragility of the Fw 200.[4] They were given full authority to work directly with industry and Luftwaffe supply parks to obtain what they needed ahead of their departure to the East. Willers must have pulled strings, for astonishingly the men of KGr.z.b.V.200 were at least *assigned* stocks of additional weapons and winter equipment such as lined overalls, felt boots, fur hats, blankets, lined coats, gloves, bandages, earmuffs and vests – although how many, if any, of these items arrived before their move to Russia is not known.

But there were problems from the outset: the nine Fw 200s and personnel intended to form 2./KGr.z.b.V.200 were delayed at Trondheim because of bad weather, and so there was insufficient time to gather enough basic equipment. However, at 0915 hrs on 3 January, they finally left Norway, although the aircraft of Leutnant Heinz Küchenmeister suffered damage on take-off and so he had to fly to Staaken in a Ju 52/3m via Aalborg, in Denmark. The Junkers carried the vital aircraft jacking device to be used in cases where an Fw 200 suffered undercarriage collapse. The remaining Condors, landed at Staaken in heavy snow showers.

In the apparent absence of Hausknecht, and aware of the conditions that lay ahead, Küchenmeister set about hurriedly procuring as much equipment and as many parts as possible whilst at Staaken. This included spare wheels and wheel parts, oil coolers, engine 'blankets', pipes and tubes, split flap switches and cylinders, pressure accumulators, shut-off valves, spark plugs, fuel tank fittings and their parts, fuselage rivets, oil temperature sensors, pressure gauges, electric meters, lighting equipment, specialist tools, engine parts, weapons and spares, hydraulic oil, grease, screws and other items of which the unit was short.[5] Yet despite aircraft being knowingly overloaded at the time of the *Gruppe*'s departure, because of the weights involved and a lack of space, large quantities of the spares and technical equipment had to remain in Staaken and would supposedly follow on as freight on the highly restricted and inefficient Russian rail network. By the time the unit left, however, other items had still not even arrived in Staaken by rail.

1./KGr.z.b.V.200 was assigned ten crews, of which three had long-range bombing and reconnaissance experience on the Fw 200 with KG 40 over the Atlantic, while the others had been undergoing training with that *Geschwader*'s IV. *Gruppe*. In terms of the *Staffel*'s key technical support, the assigned personnel were woefully inadequate, and included an Oberwerkmeister assisted by an aircraft specialist, just three mechanics, three engine specialists and three electricians.

Aside from the personnel issues, Willers had been assigned a number of ageing and heavily used former training aircraft from IV./KG 40 that lacked any structural strengthening and which had been used at the *Gruppe's* bases at Bordeaux-Mérignac and Châteaudun, in France, to train crews in how to take off and land in the Fw 200. Flown from dawn to dusk, the aircraft had been routinely over-revved during such flights, imposing excessive strain on their engines, whilst hard-landings had inflicted damage to undercarriages. The supposed 'winter preparation' implemented by IV./KG 40's groundcrews was either non-existent or rudimentary at best. According to Schulte-Vogelheim, some of the aircraft assigned to 1.*Staffel* had been out of operational service for at least a year. The single example of a new Fw 200 variant with an improved dorsal gun turret, which had been given up by 8./KG 40 for service with 1./KGr.z.b.V.200, was subsequently 'intercepted' and commandeered by the *Kommandeur* of IV./KG 40, Major Roman Dawczynski, who then handed over his own *old* aircraft for use at Stalingrad.

As Willers recounted:

You can imagine my tremendous concern. For example, I had an old training machine which, as a *Staffelkapitän* in IV.*Gruppe*, I knew had been continually declared as unserviceable, but it came out to Stalino with me. After its first landing in Russia it spent three weeks being repaired and then had to be sent back to Staaken. Despite all the obstacles, compared to conditions in Bordeaux (where I had my own mechanics and workshop sections, as well as better weather conditions, etc.), I had six times as many aircraft under the most primitive conditions in Russia. But don't ask what Stalingrad was like for us in terms of operations. The fact that anything was achieved at all was thanks to Oberwerkmeister Glaser and his excellent mechanics who worked so hard.

It would take a considerable amount of time for the Fw 200s to fly to Stalino, the long flight to Russia requiring a staging point at Radom, in Poland, with delays caused by more adverse weather and snowdrifts.[6] The first Condor took off for Radom at 1100 hrs on the 5th, followed by 15 more at three-minute intervals. The aircraft flew a course from Staaken towards Nauen, where they turned south and then followed the route of the Autobahn towards Frankfurt-an-der-Oder and from there to Radom, where they had all landed by 1500 hrs. The following day, the weather worsened and the aircraft suffered from overnight icing to their control surfaces, although one machine piloted by Leutnant Gilbert bravely flew on to Stalino carrying the *Gruppe's* advance detachment.

On the morning of the 7th, with the temperature plunging to -22°C, the remaining Fw 200s took off for Stalino. Seven Condors made it to their destination, but three were forced to land at Zaporozhye due to bad weather. They arrived in Stalino on the 8th, and all aircraft were unloaded immediately, with items of equipment being stored outside under tarpaulins. It was less than ideal. One Condor remained at Staaken awaiting an engine change.

Conditions at Stalino at that time of year were much like those at Tatsinskaya, Morosowskaya and Novocherkassk – overcrowded, although at Stalino heavy snowdrifts also hampered operations. However, KGr.z.b.V.200 was at least allocated its own dispersal area. Both air- and groundcrews were billeted in rudimentary, windowless buildings some three to four kilometres from the airfield, where there were no stoves and the men had to sleep huddled together under single blankets on meagre layers of straw. The less-than-ideal location of the accommodation meant starting the engines of trucks and buses in the freezing darkness for transport to and from the airfield. These vehicles would often get stuck in snowdrifts. A lack of timber meant that it was not possible to build a sufficient number of windbreaks to shelter the groundcrews working in the open. The *Staffelkapitäne* sought out as much winter clothing as they could from local stocks, with some being sent from Luftwaffe units in Norway, and also made sure that the groundcrews were regularly supplied with hot drinks.[7] As Willers described:

Working on the aircraft at -30°C in snowstorms, without any protection, was hopeless. On several occasions we had to use the warming carts to thaw out the mechanics who had become frozen to the aircraft with wrenches in their hands. Furthermore, the heating carts were only sufficient for three engines, so another was needed for the fourth engine, and often to release frozen tail wheels.

In addition, trying to protect such large aircraft from the elements was a futile affair, since if a tarpaulin of sufficient size was found, it was invariably torn by the act of handling it in such icy weather or the wind would tear it apart. Either that, or three engines would have to be left running idle while the cart was refuelled. It was also an extreme and difficult process of acclimatisation for our personnel to go from +20°C at the previous base at Bordeaux to -30°C at Stalino and Zaporozhye.

In 1.*Staffel* there was an excess of radio, weapons and bomb specialists who, according to Schulte-Vogelheim, simply took up room aboard the aircraft during the transfer flights to Russia and who later had to be re-employed as 'emergency' mechanics – as he recalled, 'Many of the other technical staff were worthless, and without sufficient training they were capable only of "handy-man" work'. Another problem was that one Fw 200 required a team of four groundcrew to carry out standard maintenance, but because of the restricted carrying space, each aircraft could only carry two groundcrew to Russia – this despite the size and complexity of the Condor.

No sooner had KGr.z.b.V.200 arrived at Stalino than in addition to his function as *Gruppenkommandeur*, Willers was appointed by Fiebig as the *Lufttransportführer Stalino*. This was an expedient measure because another even larger aircraft was shortly to make its debut over Stalingrad, operating alongside the Condors, and Fiebig wanted Willers to coordinate the efforts of both types. Indeed, a single, colossal Junkers Ju 290 had already been flown into Stalino from Germany, via Wiener-Neustadt, on 28 December, piloted by Flugkapitän Walter Hänig, a Junkers test pilot, along with his radio operator and flight engineer.

Of the four larger aircraft types sent, or intended to be sent, to Russia for the airlift, the aircraft which Willers viewed as perhaps the most suitable for the task was the Ju 290. This big, purpose-built transport was capable of carrying in ten tons of supplies or flying out up to 80 wounded men.

In April 1936, the designer of the Ju 52/3m, Ernst Zindel, put forward plans for a large, four-engined, low-wing *Transozeanflugzeug* (pan-oceanic transport) or *Schweretransporter* (heavy transport).[8] Certainly, at the time of its release, with its wingspan of 35.27 m and length of 26.45 m, the first prototype of what became the Ju 90 was the largest aircraft in Germany. The Ju 90V1 made its inaugural flight on 28 August 1937, but it crashed after tests on 7 February 1938. The V2 first took to the skies on 2 December 1937 powered by four 830 hp BMW 132H radials. Six months later, the aircraft was tested by Lufthansa as an airliner. It was, undeniably, an impressive machine, and elegant for its size. Passengers could be accommodated four-abreast in facing rows on either side of a central aisle in a roomy cabin which was augmented by two toilets, a mail compartment, a food storage area and baggage hold. The seats could be converted into berths for night travel. However, it crashed at Bathurst, in the Gambia, as a result of engine failure, killing 12 of the 15 people on board.

A run of ten production machines was planned, but despite interest in the aircraft from Lufthansa and South African Airways, this did not progress, and the outbreak of war prevented further civil use. Undaunted, however, the Luftwaffe, continued assessment with a small number of prototypes. In 1940, it was decided to further exploit the design in order to create an even larger military aircraft able to undertake long-range transport and reconnaissance operations. But it was not until 11 February 1941 that the Ju 90V11 was assigned for this purpose. Given an increased span of 42 m, the aircraft was a little longer than the standard Ju 90, measuring 28.68 m in length. It was also fitted with the innovative *Transporterklappe*, a hydraulically operated ventral loading ramp which would enable military vehicles and guns to be driven directly into the fuselage, as well as allowing the dropping of large quantities of supplies by parachute. Powered by four 1,560 hp BMW 801A engines, the enhanced variant emerged as the new Ju 290V1.

It commenced flight-testing on 16 July 1942, and was one of the largest land aircraft in the German inventory; the Ju 290V1's span was almost ten metres greater than the Fw 200. Within the first three months of 1943 four Ju 290A-1s were produced, representing the entire sub-series. These aircraft were assigned, officially, a crew of eight and were fitted with a hydraulically operated dorsal gun turret with a 15 mm MG 151 cannon, further such weapons mounted forward and aft in a ventral gondola, and a fourth MG 151 in the tail. A single cannon could also be installed on remotely controlled mounts on either side of the fuselage. Aircrew found the Ju 290 a comfortable and stable aircraft to fly.[9]

However, in being despatched to Stalino to partake in the airlift to Stalingrad, the Ju 290V1's 'baptism of fire' would, very much unexpectedly, take place amidst some of the most demanding conditions imaginable – especially for a still largely untried aircraft.

Meanwhile, KGr.z.b.V.200 flew its first mission to Stalingrad in the morning of 9 January, sending out nine Condors, their tanks loaded with 3,500 litres of fuel and carrying supplies, fuel and ammunition for 6.*Armee*. However, Leutnant Küchenmeister was forced to abort the mission when one of his engines failed and the aircraft of Oberfeldwebel Hätzold received a Flak hit to its cockpit, which damaged the hydraulics system. He too had to abort. Landing at Pitomnik for the remaining seven Condors was tricky because of the numbers of Ju 52/3ms and He 111s already there. 'A particularly high risk of collision!' Willers noted afterwards. The eight Focke-Wulfs spent the morning unloading. According to the *Gruppe's* war diary:

> The soldiers in the fortress eagerly help with unloading, and there is great joy and gratitude on their part when an aircraft can be unloaded. Despite the extreme shortage of food (200 grams of bread per day), the troops show a good military bearing and are full of confidence. The Russians try to break into the fortress from the west and south-west with mass tank attacks. There is light, medium and heavy Flak on the flight route and at the edge of the fortress. Some good hits!

Once the supplies had been unloaded, the wounded embarked, with each aircraft taking between 15 and 20 men. All the Fw 200s returned, but not without damage to their engines. This placed even greater demand on the fatigued, cold and insufficiently trained groundcrews at Stalino. That night, Oberleutnant Schulte-Vogelheim and Leutnant Franz-Fritz Kollonitsch of 2.*Staffel* flew two more sorties. Altogether, on its debut operation, KGr.z.b.V.200 had delivered 22.5 tons of supplies, nine tons of ammunition and 4.5 tons of fuel to 6.*Armee* and brought out 156 wounded. As soon as the wounded had been taken off at Stalino, the mechanics went to work refuelling and repairing the damage to the Condors in preparation for the following day's mission.

The first aircraft airborne on the morning of the 10th was the Fw 200 flown by Oberfeldwebel Alfred Weyer of 2./KGr.z.b.V.200, which left Stalino in darkness at 0652 hrs. Weyer touched down at Pitomnik in dim winter light just under two hours later at 0845 hrs. Another six Focke-Wulfs attempted the trip, but the aircraft of Schulte-Vogelheim suffered an engine failure and Soviet anti-aircraft fire once again proved a menace: Weyer's aircraft was hit in one of its propellers and Oberfeldwebel Hartig's Fw 200 suffered shrapnel damage to an engine and an elevator, but they both returned. Less fortunate was Oberfeldwebel Reck, whose Condor was shot down on the return flight with 21 wounded on board, while Leutnant Wilhelm Stoye and his crew from 1.*Staffel* were forced to remain at Pitomnik as a result of engine and instrument failure.

Crews not only had to contend with intense anti-aircraft fire, but also VVS fighters patrolling the skies over the pocket. Fortunately, their attacks were inaccurate, although worryingly the Bf 109s of JG 3 based at Pitomnik were unable to offer escort cover for the Condors because of a lack of fuel.

Flying its first mission later that morning (10 January) was the Ju 290V1, piloted by Flugkapitän Hänig. The aircraft went out alone, but the flight went smoothly, despite encountering anti-aircraft fire, and the big Junkers returned to Stalino safely during the late afternoon carrying 78 wounded men.

Another night operation went out guided by the radio beacons, although of the four Condors involved, one piloted by Oberfeldwebel Boeck suffered engine failure, two flown by Oberfeldwebel Hartig (on his second mission) and Oberfeldwebel Löffler experienced radio failures and landed on return at Ssalsk, while the aircraft of Oberfeldwebel Brune was unable to land at Pitomnik due to bad weather, and it also took a Flak hit in the fuselage. It too landed at Ssalsk. In total, 19 tons of supplies, ten tons of ammunition and 16 tons of fuel were safely delivered, and 138 wounded, one doctor and two sacks of mail were lifted out.

Despite the losses, Fiebig was prompted to note, 'The long-range Fw 200s are giving a good account of themselves'. Indeed, two Luftwaffe liaison officers had returned from the pocket that day and told Fiebig that they were 'jubilant about the long-distance aircraft'. But Major Willers would soon be faced with the arrival of yet more 'giants' sent from Germany, and this time they would be in the form of one of the most unreliable, accident-prone and downright dangerous aircraft in the Luftwaffe's inventory.

PART III

Catastrophe

There shall he pause, with horrent brow, to rate
What millions died—that Caesar might be great!
THOMAS CAMPBELL, *THE PLEASURES OF HOPE*, 1799

15

'No Hearts Beat Stronger'

8–16 January 1943

The victorious advances of our ground forces and their indomitable resistance within their defensive battles are inextricably linked with the unsurpassable achievements that you, my transport flyers, have achieved in all theatres of war and at all times of year. In particular, your deployment in the winter fighting on the Eastern Front will always remain an immortal glory in your history, as well as in the annals of the entire Luftwaffe. For this you deserve thanks and appreciation; as before, the Führer will assign the highest awards for your deeds on operations.

Today, in the current stage of the battle for the Stalingrad fortress, I call upon you again, my airmen, and expect from you the final and greatest commitment of your flying skills, your will of steel and the bravery that you have shown so often. Always bear in mind that at these times the fate of thousands of your comrades depends on you; the will to resist shown by your comrades fighting on the ground should be fostered within your own heroism. It is the honour of my Luftwaffe, despite all the resistance levelled against it, the unfavourable weather, and enemy action, to ensure that we supply the fortress of Stalingrad until it is liberated. That is why a last and greatest effort is required, as we gave our word and we must stand with our conscience. I want everyone who takes-off within the Eastern area of operations to supply the troops fighting around Stalingrad to be aware of my appeal.

The Commander-in-Chief of the Luftwaffe
Göring

Reichsmarschall
Tgb.Nr.86/43
11.1.43.

At 1000 on the morning of 8 January 1943, under a prior agreement made over the radio between Lt Gen Rokossovsky's Don Front and 6.*Armee*, two Soviet officers – from Red Army Intelligence and the NKVD (People's Commissariat for Internal Affairs), respectively – left Russian lines and trudged their way cautiously on foot along the railway line between Karpovka and Sovetsky towards Marinovka at the extreme western 'nose' of the Stalingrad pocket. They were accompanied by a corporal waving a white flag and blowing a warning trumpet. They eventually approached the forward positions of 3.*Infanterie-Division (mot.)*.

They were greeted cautiously, then blindfolded and escorted to the headquarters of the divisional commander, to whom the Russian emissaries handed over a document addressed to Paulus. It was an ultimatum to surrender, and it told Paulus, in no uncertain terms, that the forces sent to relieve his army had been beaten and were hastening back towards Rostov. Furthermore, the Luftwaffe's transport units trying to supply his surrounded troops had suffered debilitating losses and the whole airlift operation was now an unrealistic prospect. And all this on top of the extreme Russian winter that was only just beginning, and which, in any case, would probably finish off his starving, freezing, disease-ridden and rat-infested men even if the Red Army did not. The situation was hopeless.[1]

Paulus contacted Hitler, who refused to even consider such a thing. The Russians resorted to dropping propaganda leaflets aimed at convincing the weary defenders that the game was up and broadcast the surrender terms at volume through loudspeakers aimed towards the German lines. However, the ultimatum – in all its forms – was ignored.

So it was that on the morning of the 10th the Russians launched Operation *Koltso* ('Ring'), an attack by seven armies against the German positions intended to eliminate the pocket once and for all. Specifically for this purpose, on 30 December, the *Stavka* had transferred 62nd, 64th and 57th Armies of the Stalingrad Front (reformed on 1 January as the Southern Front) to supplement the four armies of the Don Front.

For several hours a massive, rolling artillery barrage fell on 6.*Armee*'s westernmost and southern positions, made even more terrifying by streams of rockets raining down from *Katyusha* launchers, although mortar shells and rockets simply bounced off the frozen ground and exploded in the air, showering lethal fragments. The shells and rockets were followed by waves of infantry drawn from some 17 divisions – thousands of men with bayonets fixed – and around 160 tanks advancing under fluttering Red banners. 6.*Armee* endured it, but was unable to respond because of ammunition shortages. The Soviet 65th Army pushed eight kilometres into the German lines in the first day. In their foxholes, dugouts and trenches, the defenders were so badly afflicted by frostbite that they found it difficult and painful to jam their fingers into the trigger guards of their weapons.

Paulus signalled that if the Russians maintained such ferocious attacks there was no way the 'fortress' could hold out for more than a few days, let alone until mid-February. At the very least the supply tonnage promised by Rastenburg as well as replacement battalions would have to be flown in immediately.[2]

As the first day of the Russian attack got underway, He 111s from I./KG 100 flew into Pitomnik, but as it took off on its return flight, the H-6 of Feldwebel

Karl Meyer of 1.*Staffel* experienced difficulties, hit the ground and overturned several times. Meyer and his observer were removed dead from the wreckage. The radio operator and gunner were later flown out, wounded, from the pocket.[3] From 10 January, the situation for the He 111 units at Novocherkassk became increasingly precarious: the VVS flew 676 sorties over the Stalingrad area as the Red Army approached from the south against the Don. It therefore became an unavoidable decision to move the Heinkels back to Taganrog. From there, the distance to Stalingrad extended to 405 km. Undaunted, however, the crews set about recommencing their flights as soon as possible.[4]

Five Ju 52/3ms crashed undertaking airlift flights during the night of 9–10 January, but the following day conditions were sufficiently acceptable to send out 87 aircraft of all kinds, including, as mentioned in the previous chapters, Fw 200s and, for the first time, a Ju 290, although 31 Ju 52/3ms were forced to turn back at 2200 hrs. Once again the weather was the main enemy, meaning 60 tons of the intended supplies failed to get delivered. 'One is powerless!' wrote Fiebig. 'It is a hand-to-mouth operation'. That night Jeschonnek, unusually, and clearly worried, called Fiebig promising another 100 Ju 52/3ms, ten Fw 200s and a He 177. He also told Fiebig that he would be visiting him shortly, and that any requests should be sent directly for his personal attention. Perhaps von Richthofen's voice was finally being heard.[5]

This seems to have been the first time that Fiebig would have been made aware of plans to further augment the airlift with another type of large aircraft – and it did not augur well. At 20.4 m in length and with a wingspan of 31.44 m, a crew of six and a maximum internal bombload of 7,000 kg, the monstrous Heinkel He 177 had been conceived as a much-needed, new generation strategic bomber for the Luftwaffe. It featured the radical and overly complex attribute of coupled engines sitting directly over sets of twin mainwheels, giving what was effectively a four-engined aircraft the appearance of a twin-engined machine. The idea was that by coupling two engines together around one shaft to which was fitted a single, three-bladed propeller, effectively double the power could be achieved in one unit while maintaining drag levels of one engine. The resulting Daimler-Benz DB 606 comprised twin 12-cylinder, liquid-cooled, 1,085 hp DB 601 engines mounted either side of the gearing system.

Featuring this technology, work began on what would become the He 177 in 1937, and after considerable delay, the initial prototype first flew in November 1939. Despite the fatal crash of the second prototype in June 1940, pressure from the RLM pushed things forward. There were more delays and more crashes. At one point in mid-1942 there was only one prototype left flying. Ready or not, the ungainly He 177 eventually found its way into Luftwaffe service. By mid-1942, three test aircraft had been lost in crashes, and at one point only two aircraft remained.

In July 1942, however, a new He 177 bomber *Gruppe*, I./*Fernkampfgeschwader* (FKG) 50, was established at Brandenburg-Briest under Major Kurt Schede, a staff officer with little operational experience. Shortly after its formation, I./FKG 50 received some new He 177A-1s, and Schede was assisted greatly in the organising of the unit and its tasks by the *Kapitän* of 1.*Staffel*, Hauptmann Heinrich Schlosser, who had been awarded the Knight's Cross on 18 September 1941 for his personal involvement in sinking 55,000 GRT of enemy shipping while flying the Fw 200 with 2./KG 40.

In August, I./FKG 50 received a small number of He 177s modified with dual controls, and aided by Schlosser's expertise, Schede was able to train up the *Gruppe's* pilots. Several crashes ensued, often for reasons unknown, and by the autumn Schede was forced to report that the aircraft was not suitable for operations in its 'present form'. Notwithstanding this, Schede was allocated the airfield at Zaporozhye-Süd in south-east Ukraine as a suitable base for trial bomber operations in the East by up to 12 He 177A-1s. By December, the *Gruppe's* strength stood at 33 Heinkels, including 20 new A-3s, 22 m in length, of which only ten were serviceable.

By then, this small number of aircraft had managed to attain 290 flying hours, most of which had been taken up by bombing and conversion training. They had been fitted with a supply-dropping modification in their bomb-bays. However, while for combat missions the He 177 could carry a payload of six 1,000-kg bombs, it could for technical reasons accommodate only two 1,000-kg *Mischlastabwurfbehälter* of supplies and between four and six 250-kg containers of food internally. This was because the underwing bomb suspension lugs were fitted closely together, which meant that while a pair of bombs could be suspended under each wing, a pair of the more robust, thicker-walled *Mischlastabwurfbehälter* could not.

A reserve of DB 606 engines for the Heinkels was created by stripping engines from 50 newly manufactured aircraft. Despite this, only nine crews had been fully familiarised with the mission, mainly due to adverse winter weather.

In early January, the He 177s started to fly to Russia. At Zaporozhye-Süd there was hangar accommodation for only five aircraft. Furthermore, transporting the *Gruppe's* equipment from the railhead amidst extreme temperatures and deep snowdrifts proved very challenging. Moving the 16-ton Heinkels to a 'suitable' dispersal took half a day, despite the availability of a tractor and men. Soon there were ominous signs, such as when a connecting rod in an engine of a He 177 broke through its casing, setting the engine on fire.

The man responsible for overseeing I./FKG 50's operations, the *Lufttransportführer Stalino*, Major Willers, viewed the He 177 as 'a marvel of technology, but it couldn't fly because of its [lack of] power. Also known as the *"Reichsfeuerzeug"* ("Reich cigarette lighter") of the Luftwaffe, it was one of the most evil aircraft we had'. The unfortunate moniker was, indeed, a reference to the terrible reputation the Heinkel's double-engine arrangement had for its tendency to catch fire.

On the 11th snow flurries swept across the Stalingrad supply bases and then fog pressed in once more. Some He 111s attempted to go out but were forced to turn back and their formations split up. The Ju 52/3m units also tried to operate but were not successful. 'If the weather remains as it is', Fiebig noted, 'and it does not seem that it is going to change materially, 6.*Armee* will have to give up. We cannot do any better with respect to organisation and flying. Everybody knows what is at stake and gives everything he can. I can only repeat that everything possible is being done'.[6]

In the pocket, Pickert was becoming increasingly worried about the ability to hold onto the airfield at Pitomnik:

The situation is serious. If the enemy achieves a deep penetration we shall have to shift the base for the airlift. This will require a tremendous amount of manpower and fuel. We can hardly spare either. And if we are pushed back once more, it will all be over, because it is impossible to supply an army with either food or ammunition entirely by dropping supplies.[7]

The *Kommandeur* of KGr.z.b.V.5, Major Uhl, stressed that:

When conducting intensive night operations to destinations with limited space it is important that the approach and return altitudes of respective transport units are coordinated and that landing times are regulated in such a way that formations do not arrive at the landing ground at the same time. It must be ordered that all landings must be undertaken using identification lights, otherwise there is an increased risk of collision. It has only been due to fortunate circumstances that we have avoided losses in this regard.[8]

Oberst Dr. Kühl, *Kommodore* of KG 55, wrote of Pitomnik:

As long as 6.*Armee* retained use of Pitomnik, supply flights to, and evacuation flights from, the pocket could be undertaken by day and night, even, to some extent, in bad weather. The success and efficiency of a landing in terms of accurate and safe delivery was around three times greater than that of an air-drop. Initially, air-drops were only intended to be undertaken at night if the airfield had been bombed and safe landings were deemed to be hazardous or the direction-finder prohibited landing. Daylight drops in cloud were also attempted with the aid of guidance from a radio beacon, but this method was not generally satisfactory.

Air-drops were carried out in accordance with specially lit recognition fires or through primitive airfield illumination. If such fires or illumination were not possible, drops would be made over the eastern perimeter of Pitomnik. While in most cases it was possible to retrieve the drop containers from this area, it was not a task favoured by the Army since motor fuel to transport them was in critically low supply, and also because the light colour of their parachutes precluded their landing locations from being easily spotted against the white of the snow.

Because of this state of affairs, air-drops tended to be made only if and when 6.*Armee* made a firm request, especially in the final stages of the airlift after Pitomnik had been lost.[9]

Uhl amplified this in a report written shortly after the air-supply operation:

> A prerequisite for the success of the dropping of supply containers is that due to the proximity of the enemy, the drop-point should not be clearly marked, but rather an electrical lighting system must be created and switched on each time a machine approaches, which, itself, should fire a recognition signal on approach.[10]

Indeed, as the German front around Stalingrad began to contract, which, in turn, saw the loss of the small number of airfields available to 6.*Armee*, the increasing dependency on air-drops presented problems to the Luftwaffe supply operation. As Fritz Morzik explained:

> Taking into consideration the operational time we had available, limits had to be set for the number of aircraft that could be used. The use of 60 aircraft with a take-off gap of only five minutes led to more impediments at night and a massing over the target since, for the most part, four-five approach flights each of ten minutes for jettison time were necessary.[11]

Over the 11th and 12th the Soviet 16th VA carried out intensive bombing and strafing attacks against the Stalingrad pocket, mounting 900 sorties over the two days. Pitomnik was bombed and at least one He 111 was destroyed.[12] The small number of Bf 109s from the *Platzschutzstaffel* of JG 3 at Pitomnik were in the air, desperately trying to make some impact on the Red onslaught. On the 10th, Feldwebel Kurt Ebener of 4./JG 3 shot down three Il-2s and a LaGG-3.[13] Two days later, Leutnant Franz Daspelgruber of 1./JG 3 and Ebener each claimed three Russian aircraft shot down from 16th VA.[14] Ebener became the most successful fighter pilot over the Stalingrad pocket, being credited with 32 victories in under a month, including multiple kills on several days.

In the period from 25 November to 11 January, daily delivery averages were as follows:[15]

Total supplies = 102 tons
Motor fuel = 34.4 cbm
Ammunition = 21.5 tons
Food supplies = 42 tons
Wounded evacuated = 520 men
Average per aircraft = 53 tons

In roughly the same period, the He 111s of KG 55 alone flew 1,766 sorties carrying 1,245 tons of food, plus ammunition and motor fuel.[16] Between 22 December and 11 January, as the Soviets attacked 6.*Armee*'s position, the supply units delivered 2,414 tons of supplies.[17]

At 1600 hrs on the 12th, acting under orders from an increasingly anxious Paulus, Pickert flew out of the *Festung* in a He 111 bound for Taganrog for a meeting with von Richthofen and von Manstein. He was due to brief them on the latest situation and to try to make the case for an increased airlift effort. As the Heinkel climbed up through the twilight, the Flak general peered out from a window in the bomber's fuselage towards the ground below and watched the flashes from Russian guns encircling the pocket. He landed 80 minutes later, and told his senior officers that based on what Generalleutnant Schmidt, 6.*Armee*'s Chief of Staff, had told him, the collapse of the pocket was only days away, and that it was beyond saving. Von Richthofen found what Pickert had to say 'shocking'. Pickert then left for a long meeting with Fiebig that evening at Novocherkassk.[18]

Later that night, Fiebig sat down and attempted to come to terms with what had happened – to try to reconcile his personal performance and that of his staff and his units within the context of the gargantuan, draining, horrific and almost impossible task which had been enforced upon them. He wrote:

> The 6.*Armee* is fighting its last battle. It may be six days or only two days until the end comes. There are no reserves of ammunition or fuel left. Shifting of forces is no longer possible. Our troops are at the end of their strength. From the 13th onwards, every man will defend himself with his weapon, where he stands, down to his last bullet.
>
> Pickert told me that the transport units have done everything in their power. Everybody in the pocket is convinced that the flying has been carried out in an unbelievable manner. The loss of 250 aircraft is the best proof of it. I believe that no hearts beat more strongly for the fate of 6.*Armee* than those of the men who are charged with the organisation and with the carrying out of the airlift. We have done our best. If I judge myself, I don't know of any fault of my own or what I could have done differently or better. How long will this time of sorrow continue for 6.*Armee*? What good or noble thing will be born of it?[19]

According to Warlimont, at OKH headquarters, Zeitzler had become increasingly despairing over the situation at Stalingrad. In some kind of eye-catching act of penitence, he placed himself and members of his staff on the same daily rations afforded to the soldiers of 6.*Armee*. By mid-January, that ration had been reduced further and comprised 70 grammes of bread, 185 grammes of horsemeat, 15 grammes of fat, 15 grammes of sugar and one cigarette.[20]

The conditions at Pitomnik and Gumrak airfields – the latter still under preparation – were nothing short of infernal. They had been under constant enemy fire for three days. On the 12th a report reached Paulus' headquarters that Pitomnik had actually been abandoned in the face of Russian tanks. Schmidt was furious and sent out a reconnaissance patrol to ascertain whether this was true. It transpired that at the sight of a Soviet reconnaissance unit west of the airfield, soldiers, airmen, doctors and wounded began to make off to the south and east as fast as they could. It was later established that the Russians had withdrawn, but a German officer returning from the airfield recounted how at the mention of the enemy, men in tattered, filthy uniforms rushed or hobbled on sticks or rifles out from their tents and bunkers, trampling in panic over the seriously wounded. Some simply collapsed into the snow, while others fought for space on what few vehicles there were. The dead on the trucks were hauled off and thrown to the ground. The corpses began to pile up by the side of the road. Discipline and order had finally broken down.

Of Gumrak Oberst Dr. Kühl wrote:

Gumrak was supposed to be a rolled landing strip measuring 50 x 800 m, but conditions there were far from ideal. Ruptures in the ground surface caused problems during landings and at times the surface was pocked with shell craters. During take-offs, pilots sometimes failed to notice where a crater had been recently filled in, resulting in the aircraft sinking into the ground and remaining there stranded. Initially, at night, there were only three lights available to illuminate the strip. Furthermore, Russian shelling and air attack destroyed many aircraft. Because of these prevailing conditions, crews attempting to land in daylight would take-off as soon as possible after landing, only to be attacked by marauding VVS fighters. Twenty He 111s landed at Gumrak in total.[21]

Persistent rain over the night of 11–12 January meant that the Ju 52/3ms were unable to fly. For their part, the Heinkels continued to undertake missions despite blizzards, although a He 111H-14 of 1./KG 100, damaged by ground fire, had to be destroyed on the airfield rather than risk giving it up to the Russians. However, as Fiebig observed, 'if the Novocherkassk base is cleared of He 111s, then the supply of the fortress is correspondingly endangered. Therefore we cannot leave except in a case of dire emergency'.[22]

For the crews, added to the danger of the flights were the harrowing scenes that now greeted them at the airfields. As soon as a transport landed, ragged, ghostly figures of German soldiers would appear from out of the gloom, stumbling towards the aircraft, desperate for food or hoping to climb aboard to fly out of the pocket. As the side door of a Junkers was opened, soldiers would attempt to clamber up into the fuselage, and they had to be pushed or kicked away by the crew as the supplies were quickly thrown out into the snow. Frozen hands would frantically claw open the parcels as they landed while squads of military police fired their weapons into the air in an effort to retain order.[23]

One aircraft to fly into the pocket on the morning of the 12th was the He 111 piloted by Unteroffizier Peter Adrian of III./KG 55. Adrian took off from Novocherkassk at 0745 hrs and landed at Pitomnik at 0955 hrs, his aircraft carrying mainly food supplies. Aboard the Heinkel as flight engineer was KG 55 veteran Unteroffizier Michael Deiml. Hailing from Bavaria, 24-year-old Deiml was an experienced crewman, having flown 20 bombing missions over France and nine over England in 1940. He later saw service in Russia, undertaking many flights over enemy territory. Although he had been flying bombing missions to the Stalingrad area since August, his first supply flight took place on 12 January

1943; it was Deiml's 198th operational sortie. He subsequently recalled his experience of landing in the pocket:

> There were masses of wounded German soldiers, also *Organisation Todt* [OT] people, nearly all of whom were middle-aged. They wore a light olive-green uniform. When asked how they came to be trapped in the Pocket, they said they had been repairing the road between Kalach and Stalingrad. After setting down an Army Obergefreiter who had brought some spare parts for his unit from Germany, we began unloading the food containers with the help of the OT men. After that we off-loaded about 20 sacks of large loaves and distributed them there. Eight wounded and a war correspondent were brought aboard, then we rolled out to the airstrip.
>
> Although the aircraft had been seriously damaged by heavy AA fire on the way in – the tail unit and rear fuselage had been holed by 50 AA shells – it could still fly! The machine was not a transport, but a bomber with bomb-bays, supplementary tanks etc, in the interior, and we could only take eight passengers. We left Pitomnik at 1050 hrs and landed at Novocherkassk at 1210 hrs.[24]

On the night of 12–13 January, all 51 available Ju 52/3ms were prepared for night commitment, but only 44 were able to take off because of difficulties in starting up in the bitter cold (recorded at -26°C at Ssalsk). Hauptmann Guido Neundlinger's Ssalsk-based II./KG.z.b.V.1 had recently been bolstered by the arrival of a few more aircraft and new crews. The front was now dangerously close to the airfield, and as the *Gruppe's* aircraft took off on course for Basargino, they had to endure Russian light anti-aircraft fire. Leutnant Franz Lankenau flew with a newly arrived crew in the second Ju 52/3m to land at Basargino that night, the aircraft laden with drums of fuel:

> We were wary of enemy bombers. In the flight control (a dug-out bunker) we quickly drank a cup of hot coffee and then started on the homeward flight. We carried 11 badly wounded soldiers. At Ssalsk all was dark on the airfield – the Russians were there. We had to go to the holding area. After ten minutes we were allowed to land; only a few bombs fell without causing damage.[25]

Just 28 Ju 52/3ms completed the mission; 12 were forced to return, eight with seized engines.

The 13th did not prove a fortunate day for the airlift: attacks by the VVS claimed 29 German aircraft destroyed on the ground at Pitomnik and other landing fields in the pocket. In the dark early morning hours Flugkapitän Hänig tried to take off from Pitomnik in the Ju 290V1 on the return leg of his second supply flight, but as the heavy aircraft attempted to climb out of the pocket at 0045 hrs, it quickly crashed back down into the snow and ice.

Hänig, along with his Junkers flight engineer, Flieger-Obering Robert Stiefel, and three of his crewmembers, together with 40 of the 75 wounded troops on board, were killed. In Willer's view:

> My personal opinion is that after take-off from Pitomnik, Hänig had to cross over enemy territory, and he took a direct hit in the cockpit. In a convulsion of death, he probably wrenched the steering column up to his chest, the Ju 290 reared up, the wounded slid towards the rear of the aircraft and so a crash followed.

It was a grim beginning for the Ju 290. Despite their valuable load capacities, and the obvious advantages of the *Trapoklappe* loading system over the more makeshift capabilities of the Fw 200, the second such example of the big aircraft to operate over Stalingrad proved an easy target for Soviet fighters. Indeed, the flight of the sole Ju 290A-1 variant to the pocket on the 13th would be its only one. The aircraft was flown by the very experienced Major Hugo Wiskandt, who had joined Junkers in 1925 and later served as *Staffelkapitän* of 1./KG.z.b.V.172. The aircraft took off from Stalino in refreshingly clear winter skies, en route for Pitomnik, accompanied by an Fw 200. But a short while into their flight the German aircraft were attacked by a formation of five Soviet LaGG fighters. The Ju 290 received multiple hits but was able to make it to Pitomnik, where an inspection revealed that the aircraft's fuel feed system had been damaged.

Despite the airfield being bombed and strafed by VVS aircraft, the Junkers unloaded its supplies and then took on wounded. After some hasty and temporary repairs, the Ju 290 took off again to return to Stalino, but with a restricted load of only some ten badly wounded soldiers. The aircraft reached its destination, where groundcrew calculated that the Ju 290 had been hit no fewer than 123 times. Under such circumstances, no further operations were considered possible, and so on 17 January, following orders from the RLM, the aircraft undertook a 5.5-hour direct flight back to Rangsdorf, in Germany. From there it flew to Berlin-Tempelhof for major repair work.[26] It marked the end of the Ju 290's brief attempts to supply Stalingrad.

13 January was also the date that the dubious He 177s of I./FKG 50 made their inauspicious debut in the airlift. Oberleutnant Lawatschek's Heinkel crashed on its return from the pocket when both a fuel pump and the de-icing system on the horizontal stabiliser failed. The 'giants' had taken in 10.5 tons of ammunition, two tons of fuel, half-a-ton of medical supplies, 33 sacks of mail and two doctors. Together, the Ju 290 and the Fw 200 airlifted 87 wounded from the pocket on that date.[27]

Major Willer's executive officers and *Staffelkapitäne* in KGr.z.b.V.200 had experience flying in foul weather over the Atlantic with KG 40 and also with navigation in adverse conditions. With the conditions prevailing in Russia, Willers viewed this as 'a life insurance for the crew of a big, slow Condor'. Whenever possible, missions were flown at night, because flights made in daylight, without cloud cover, resulted in the Fw 200s suffering significant losses at the hands of VVS fighters. Willers explained his flight tactics once he reached the pocket:

> Since, in the final phase of the battle of Stalingrad, the Russians had covered the main guidance beacon with strong Flak, I succeeded in finding a new flightpath for my *Gruppe* using the secondary beacons north and south of the main beacon. I would reach the pocket at 90 degrees, then fly for five or ten minutes further (depending on wind strength) past Stalingrad, turn 90 degrees to the right or left of the main beam, then fly with throttled engines in a gliding flight over the Volga and into the pocket. For the return flight, we used the same method. This way, we were never shot at.

Despite the fragility of the Condor's landing gear, the Fw 200s were regularly overloaded by four to five tons, and yet they still managed to land in the pocket in very bad weather. As Willers has commented:

> The fact that these missions were carried out without damage is due to the exceptional flying skills of the crews, and because the snow had an advantageous effect on landing in as much as its coldness reduced the frictional heat of the tyres as they made contact with the ground, thereby preventing them from bursting.
>
> But there was also a particular difficulty when we could no longer land. We would drop our food bombs and still have 300–400 30 x 30 x 30 cm parcels, each weighing 7.5 kg, in the fuselage. These parcels had to be thrown individually from the Condor from a height of 200 m. In continuous turns, this took one-and-a-half to two hours, and the aircraft could be held in Russian searchlights and fired at by AA guns. Yet no losses occurred during these manoeuvres.[28]

Leutnant Heinz Küchenmeister of 2./KGr.z.b.V.200 recounted bags weighing up to 15 kg, and at such weight and with a turn radius of two kilometres, it took at least two hours to drop them all: 'In my opinion, the safe return of the aircraft only seems to be due to the fact that the enemy himself was as much concerned with getting hold of the food'.[29]

The large, slow Focke-Wulf, Heinkel and Junkers transports were often promised fighter escort, but this never materialised, although on one occasion two Fw 190s apparently arrived at Zaporozhye fitted with long-range tanks. Unfortunately, however, both aircraft were badly damaged on landing and the prospect of any escort had to be forgotten.

The night of 13–14 January was refreshingly clear, but the thermometer plunged to -25°C and the cold brought considerable difficulties in maintaining the operational readiness of aircraft. Only 55 Ju 52/3ms were able to take off, ten of which failed to make it as far as Stalingrad because of technical problems. While 43 He 111s managed to get airborne, two did not make it as far as the pocket. Thus, only 160 tons were delivered over the previous 24 hours.[30]

The Germans now faced threats to both the pocket and – once more – the airlift bases. The Russians were only 35 km east of Ssalsk and the pocket was being squeezed further by *Koltso*: Pitomnik airfield was under threat and 6.*Armee* signalled that it would only be useable until the following day. Plans were being put in place to make Gumrak a workable alternative field, but this was a reactive move rather than a proactive one, and the question remained in Fiebig's mind as to why it had not already been prepared.[31] In fairness, it had been inoperable initially because of aircraft wreckage, trenches, shell holes and deep snow.

The Luftwaffe personnel in the pocket struggled to clear fields in a makeshift manner with just a few trucks, as they had no equipment for snow removal or with which to level the ground or to remove large items of wreckage and other debris. However, much was done, as Pickert recalled, using 'shovels in the hands of exhausted men'.[32]

During the 14th the Fw 200s of KGr.z.b.V.200 mounted four sorties to the pocket, although on his first attempt in daylight, Leutnant Gilbert had to abort due to electrical failure. He went out again that night, along with two other Condors, during which the aircraft of Oberfeldwebel Löffler was hit by light anti-aircraft fire. The Focke-Wulfs delivered 3.5 tons of supplies, 4.5 tons of ammunition and 14 sacks of mail, and carried out 37 wounded, two officers and the crew of an He 111.[33]

Major Schede reported to Fiebig on the operational status of I./FKG 50. It was not good news. Of 30 He 177s that had made it to Zaporozhye-Süd, ten had broken down. Fiebig was exasperated:

This type of aircraft does not accomplish anything! They only dropped eight 250-kg containers, which equates to eight loads of 140 kg which equates to 1,120 kg. They consume 4,000 litres of fuel for their mission. This aircraft cannot land because there is too great a danger of them being damaged, so they would have to stay in the pocket.[34]

Luftflotte 4's headquarters remained unimpressed as well, noting that the He 177s 'eat too much fuel and carry too little'. Von Richthofen decided that the only way to use the aircraft to any effect at all was to air-drop from it.

Another flawed proposal which refused to die was the use of towed DFS 230, Go 242 and Me 321 cargo gliders, which had been employed with some success during the air supply for Kholm, and also by VIII.*Fliegerkorps* to supply air and ground forces on the Don during Operation *Blau*. Therefore, as far as the Ob.d.L. was concerned, there were precedents for this notion. For the Ob.d.L., the instant appeal lay in the cargo capacity of these cheap craft built of steel tubing, wood and doped canvas. The smaller DFS 230 had been built as an assault glider to carry nine men, but it could also carry up to one ton of cargo. Communication was maintained between the tow-aeroplane and the glider in flight via a cable which ran along the tow rope. The DFS 230 landed by means of a skid.

With a wingspan of 24.5 m and a stubby, box-like fuselage from which extended twin booms, the Gotha Go 242 had been seen as a potential successor to the DFS 230. It was intended for the transport of 21 troops with personal equipment, or of smaller motor vehicles such as a *Kübelwagen*. But the Go 242 proved too dangerous for the carrying of men and so was used solely for cargo.

The Messerschmitt Me 321 Gigant was an enormous heavy-lift glider originally built for the planned invasion of Britain with a capacity to carry 21 tons, loaded through vast clamshell doors in its nose. But with a wingspan of 55 m, a length of 28 m and a height of more than ten metres at its highest point off the ground, the problem was that there was a need for an aircraft powerful enough to be able to tow the machine into the air. With the Me 321 weighing 34,400 kg when fully loaded, there was no single type in the Luftwaffe inventory capable of hauling the Gigant aloft. In order to solve this problem, the extraordinary He 111Z Zwilling (Twin) was created – two standard He 111H-6 airframes joined by a rectangular wing section between them, onto which was mounted a fifth engine.

In mid-December 1942, the Ob.d.L. ordered General Kurt Student's specialist paratroop and air-landing command, XI. *Fliegerkorps*, under which the glider units operated, to establish a glider command headquarters at Makejewka, with operational airfields at Stalino, Taganrog, Rostov and Novocherkassk. In this regard, on 9 January 1943, an advance detachment from *Luftlandegeschwader* (LLG) 1 (Air Landing Wing 1) under Leutnant Gerhard Raschke departed Hildesheim and staged in bad weather with its Do 17/DFS 230 tow combinations via Berlin-Staaken to Zaporoshye, where it arrived four days later. Already at Zaporoshye were the He 111/DFS 230 combinations of the *Verbindungskommando* (S) 4, and this unit would fall under the tactical direction of LLG 1, led by Oberst Dr. Hans Eggersh – he had arrived in Russia with his staff a short while after the advanced detachment under Raschke.[35]

On the 14th, Major Walter Kiess from the staff of XI. *Fliegerkorps* arrived at the headquarters of *Luftflotte* 4, to which he had been sent as a liaison officer with responsibility for glider operations. Kiess had been awarded the Knight's Cross for his role as a glider commander during the famous air-landing operation at Eben Emael and the Albert Canal in May 1940. It seems, however, that Kiess was given short shrift by von Richthofen as to the notion of glider supply flights for Stalingrad, the latter noting cynically:

> Announced with a great fanfare by the Ob.d.L., Major Kiess, the expert on towed aircraft matters, reports his arrival. The Ob.d.L. has constantly accused me that when it comes to towed units, I have harboured prejudices and am indifferent to the whole thing. This great specialist tells me that my attitude towards deployment is still too frivolous. He was, however, somewhat 'taken aback' by the local situation here. I shall now send him to Jeschonnek to

make a report, since it would, of course, appear to serve no purpose to express any kind of views from here.[36]

According to Fiebig:

Report by Major Kiess of the *Schleppgeschwader* [Tow Wing]. Missions cannot operate continuously because there is no possibility of taking off from the pocket. Preparations are being made for one-time commitment in case of dire emergency, in which case the aircraft would have to remain in the fortress. Because of the distance, only medium and heavy gliders could be used [three and 12 tons]: small gliders can no longer reach the fortress. As for He 111Es and Fs, and Ju 86s, they aren't accomplishing much either, and only make things more difficult. These operations are not well thought out. They were carried out in too much of a hurry. They just cost materials and jeopardise the training programme.[37]

In the meantime, Raschke's *Kommando* was ordered to relocate to Sverevo, where Oberst Fritz Morzik, the *Lufttransportführer Stalingrad*, was based. Sverevo was just a cornfield close to a Cossack village off the spur railway line running north from Shakhty. It had no ground facilities, but it would suffice even if it meant that all maintenance and handling had to be conducted in the open, leaving groundcrews exposed to the vicious sub-zero elements. Initially, the only quarters available to air and ground personnel were snow huts, but these were eventually replaced by tents and crude wooden shelters. One take-off and landing strip, just over 600 m in length, was created out of hard, compacted snow. The laborious task of moving ground equipment in the air or along frozen, snow-laden 'roads', tested aircraft, vehicles and men to their limit. There was no other option: Sverevo was the only field from which the Ju 52/3ms could reach Stalingrad – just – and yet as Schulz recalled:

Hardly had these difficulties been overcome and the missions once again got underway, when a snowstorm with snowdrifts up to six metres in height brought Sverevo airfield to a standstill for days; this was a new problem which repeated itself several times until the conclusion of air supply.[38]

The Do 17/DFS 230 combinations flying in clear winter skies to Sverevo via Stalino – a distance of some 200 km – must have been quite a sight, let alone the sight of them landing there. The Do 17s released the gliders as they approached Sverevo, allowing them to land first and slide on their skids along the single, 50 m-wide snow runway. Once they were down and stopped, they were immediately hauled into revetments shovelled out of the walls of snow on either side of the runway. The Do 17s then dropped their tow cables and came into land. A few hours later Raschke reported to Morzik and outlined the Ob.d.L.'s order to use the gliders to fly to Stalingrad. The *Lufttransportführer* rejected the order as being impracticable.

Morzik believed firmly that the additional ground facilities required to operate gliders did not exist, and that they could not simply be conjured up in time. Furthermore, the introduction of gliders would have served to disrupt, or even bring to a stop, the handling of motorised transports at Pitomnik. Gliders could only be deployed in favourable weather conditions, ideally with a fighter escort, which was not even available for the powered transports.[39] Finally, the range of the Do 17 was insufficient, and the existing Ju 52/3ms did not offer an alternative because they had no tow couplings and their engines were too worn out to undertake glider-tug take-offs and flights.[40]

Attrition ravaged the few remaining combat aircraft still operating within the pocket. On the 14th Feldwebel Ebener and Unteroffizier Richard Eisele from 3./JG 3 were ordered up in their Bf 109Gs to strafe enemy incursions on the perimeter of the pocket. As Ebener described:

The noise of the battle can be heard from the west. Stukas, of which only three are left, fly non-stop. Attacks come in at the break-in points. Unteroffizier Eisele is to start with me. His 109 starts up, and then the only available warming cart has to function again for me. Eisele starts ahead, but my engine runs too hot. He's waiting for me 500 m above the field. I see black dots in the sky coming closer and scream in the radio. Too late. Tracer heads towards him. Eisele falls like a stone and crashes in flames on the western edge of the field.

Bombers from the VVS's 17th AD claimed six Ju 52/3ms destroyed on the ground at Pitomnik during the night of 14–15 January. Worst still was the loss of the landing ground at Basargino, which was taken by the Russians during the 15th. In effect, only two practicable fields remained – Pitomnik and, in theory, Gumrak, which was declared ready to receive aircraft officially on 16 January using a small number of groundcrew from the former field.[41]

As of the 15th, the *Luftflotte* 4 repair workshops reported that:[42]

14 Ju 52/3ms would be available in three days' time
40 ready between 3–14 days
19 requiring more than 14 days repair work
19 ferried back to the Reich for further repair

That evening, von Richthofen noted bleakly, 'At Stalingrad, it now really appears to be approaching the end. The Russians are nearing the few landing possibilities. There's no more food and no ammunition. General dissolution'.

As 4.*Panzerarmee* yielded to Red Army pressure, so it fell back from the Manych Line, which meant that the only operable base for the Ju 52/3ms at Ssalsk, just south of the Manych, had to be evacuated. Junkers pilot Franz Lankenau of II./KG.z.b.V.1 watched herds of cattle being driven west past the airfield, and noticed that all the trains were heading west too: 'It was clear to us that we were going to have to evacuate'.[43]

Luftflotte 4 began to search for a new, viable location, but the problem was that because of a lack of manpower and materials at the time, few sites had been prepared west of the Donets during the summer, as the emphasis was on temporary forward airfields close to the front as *Blau* had progressed. The only option was Sverevo. At 0945 hrs on 15 January, *Luftflotte* 4 ordered the evacuation of Ssalsk, with the requirement that the move be completed by the following morning.

One Ju 52/3m unit to make the move north from Ssalsk to Sverevo was II./KG.z.b.V.1, whose aircraft arrived on 15 January, having staged via Rostov. When he landed his Junkers there, Franz Lankenau was disconsolate at the *Gruppe*'s new base:

> The runway is under a metre of snow. The distance by air to the Stalingrad pocket is 400 km. Sverevo field is not an airfield like Ssalsk, but just a cornfield in the snow. No hangars, no on-site accommodation for our technical personnel, an old unheated bus houses the flight control. Dispersals for the aircraft are scarce and some aircraft which are supposed to fly at night come in from Taganrog and Mariupol, but they have to be refuelled and loaded at Sverevo.

The *Gruppe*'s crews were accommodated in a nearby village, living under the same roofs as their occupants. On his first day at Sverevo, Leutnant Lankenau had to sit in the cold bus waiting for the arrival of aircraft that had left Ssalsk to fly to Stalingrad and then return to Sverevo. 'At 0300 I am relieved and have to walk, completely frozen, to my accommodation in the village two kilometres away'. Lankenau enjoyed just four hours' sleep before being rudely awoken by a Russian bombing raid that blew out the window of his room when ordnance landed 15 m away.[44]

However, no sooner had the move of several *Gruppen* been completed than the 'weather Gods' dealt their cruel hand again: as described by Schulz, a heavy snowstorm blew in to Sverevo, bringing all movement to a halt.[45] If there was ever a moment at which those who believed in the airlift and believed it would be successful should have realised they were wrong, this was it. Deliveries to the pocket plummeted.

Things could not have got worse – but they did. That day (15th), the southern perimeter of the pocket gave way under Soviet pressure, allowing enemy troops to move close to the airfield at Pitomnik. Furthermore, during the night, VVS fighters prevented German aircraft from landing. There had been reluctance on the part of 6.*Armee* to prepare Gumrak sufficiently for increased air operations because of its proximity to the Army's command post and those of two of its corps. In addition, hospitals and supply installations were located nearby. Nevertheless, the fact that Gumrak and other smaller fields in the pocket had not been prepared in readiness by 6.*Armee* now became a real problem, and as Hermann Plocher states, 'Whether the field was well situated was beside the point, since there was no other choice. This act of negligence was to have serious consequences'.[46]

In his post-war study of Luftwaffe operations in Russia in 1942, Plocher absolves Generalmajor Wolfgang Pickert, as the senior Luftwaffe officer in the pocket, of any wrongdoing in this regard. He considers Pickert to have been 'well qualified as an artilleryman and commander of the 9th Flak Division', but that he was 'hardly a "fully competent" authority on matters involving aviation, especially air transportation'. Despite the presence of more junior, but more tactically and technically aware Luftwaffe officers in the pocket, Plocher felt that Pickert:

> . . . despite his good intentions and abilities, could not have influenced the execution of air operations originating from outside, or done anything to increase the amount of supplies flown into the pocket. Actually, any Luftwaffe general could only have been made a scapegoat for Paulus' unreasonable complaints, made without any appreciation of either the potentialities or capabilities of air power.[47]

Luftflotte 4 took immediate steps to overcome the threat by ordering all aircraft arriving in the vicinity after 0700 hrs to land at Gumrak rather than Pitomnik, while all dive-bombers, fighters and reconnaissance aircraft still at Pitomnik were to remain there until such time as Russian shelling forced a move to Gumrak.[48]

From their new base further west at Taganrog, the He 111s continued their flights, and up until the 16th this resulted in an increase from 60 tons to 78 tons delivered. After that point, the problems at Gumrak affected tonnages.[49]

An analysis of aircraft status in the repair shops over 15–16 January prepared by the Chief Engineer of *Luftflotte* 4, Generalingenieur Dr.-Ing. Hanns Weidinger, revealed as follows:

15 January

Ju 52/3m

14 ready to go out in three days' time
48 ready to go out in three to 14 days' time
18 requiring more than 14 days' repairs
19 ferried back to Germany

He 111

28 ready to go out immediately
55 ready in three days
9 ready in between three and 14 days
22 requiring more than 14 days' repairs
2 ferried back to Germany

Evening 16 January

Ju 52/3m

140, of which 91 were not serviceable, 27 evacuated from Ssalsk,
   15 ready for service, seven still out on mission

He 111

140, of which 98 were not serviceable, 27 evacuated from Ssalsk,
  41 ready for service, 11 still out on mission

Fw 200

20, of which 19 were not serviceable, 1 ready for service

Weidinger noted that 'The Focke-Wulfs are very subject to damage (tailskid) and very worn out'.[50]

The small number of Bf 109s of JG 3 inside the pocket were not sufficient to allow escort to incoming or outgoing flights of transport aircraft. Plocher claims that the lack of adequate servicing facilities for the Bf 109s was a contributory reason for 'the rapid attrition rate of German fighters operating from the pocket'.[51] Despite this, the *Platzschutzstaffel* claimed three victories each day on the 13th and 14th.

Meanwhile, regardless of the Herculean effort of maintaining some kind of air supply line to the pocket, and the inherent stress and pressures that that brought, relations between the Luftwaffe and 6.*Armee* were strained. From the historical record, there does seem to have been criticism of the Luftwaffe and a degree of resentment especially from Schmidt, 6.*Armee*'s Chief of Staff, who used his strength of personality to force opinions onto Paulus. However, as former Luftwaffe General Hermann Plocher has commented:

> Despite such statements as 'betrayed by the Luftwaffe', it is possible that Schmidt's lack of judgement and self-control was not just due to a petty desire to take revenge upon the Luftwaffe, but, rather, because of his wish to conceal his own feelings of guilt.[52]

And so it was in an attempt to investigate and hopefully address the continual stream of complaints arriving at his headquarters from Stalingrad that Hitler decided to turn to a 'fixer' – a man whom he believed he could trust and who would apply his customary logic and ruthlessness to achieve what neither the Luftwaffe or Army commanders at the front seemed able to – to deliver 300 tons per day to the *Festung*. Hitler had lost patience with Göring and the other generals.[53] The man to whom he turned at this hour of need was Generalfeldmarschall Erhard Milch, the blunt, intelligent and ambitious Inspector General of the Luftwaffe and State Secretary of Aviation.

On 15 January, Milch attended the evening situation conference at the *Führer*'s headquarters, where Hitler spelled it out that the Generalfeldmarschall was to travel to the Front and to have total authority, not just over all Luftwaffe commands and units in respect to the airlift, but also over all supply offices of the Army as well, although he would be required to consult with von Manstein when it came to *Heeresgruppe Don*.[54]

At Fiebig's headquarters in southern Russia that night, the moon shone from a cloudless sky, but there was an icy easterly wind. The temperature stood at -25°C. 'It is almost impossible to remain in the open', the *Korps* commander noted.

At 0700 on the morning of 16 January, five Bf 109s of the *Platzschutzstaffel* at Pitomnik managed to get airborne to transfer to Gumrak led by Hauptmann Rudolf Germeroth, the *Staffelkapitän* of 3./JG 3, but all five crashed on landing, turning over as they did so. 'That is a good indication that field is not ready', Fiebig noted acidly. The *Staffel* had claimed six kills the day before, but on the 16th it was forced to abandon around 11 unserviceable fighters at Pitomnik, as well as a Klemm 35B from the *Geschwaderstab*.[55] Other aircraft suffered a similar fate, including the Fw 200 flown to the pocket on the 10th by Leutnant Stoye from KGr.z.b.V.200, and were blown up to prevent capture. The Condor had received superficial repairs to make it flyable, but had then been damaged by Russian bombs. Willers arranged for Stoye and his crew to be evacuated from the pocket on board the two other Fw 200s that had flown into Pitomnik that day. They joined 36 wounded soldiers from 6.*Armee* crammed into the slender fuselages of the Focke-Wulfs.

On the morning of 16 January, Russian shells crashed down and exploded on Pitomnik airfield. Despite determined opposition, including a Luftwaffe Flak battery which fired its 88 mm guns at approaching T-34s until, literally, its last round, those German personnel – hundreds of them – who were still able and who could summon enough energy, hobbled away as fast as they could across the snow, blankets draped over their sunken shoulders. The dead and dying were left behind in and around the field hospital under the care of a single doctor and an orderly.

During the day, Major Schede led a formation of five He 177s from I./FKG 50 to Gumrak to drop supplies, but two aircraft had to return because of engine and technical issues. Worse was to come, when Schede's Heinkel crashed in flames near Poljakawa during the return flight. The *Gruppenkommandeur* was killed. The newly promoted Major Heinrich Schlosser took over command of the unit from Schede.

Another problem arising increasingly during night drops – recognised at an early stage by the He 111 crews of KGr.z.b.V.5 – was that the Russians became adept at setting up bogus drop-points and, according to one of the unit's officers, 'a lot of supplies ended up with the enemy that way'.[56] This was a problem that would only worsen as the Soviets gained more ground.

From their respective diaries, the situation in the pocket was evidently causing distress to the senior Luftwaffe commanders. At Rostov during the afternoon of the 15th, the commander of 9.*Flak-Division*, Generalmajor Wolfgang Pickert, had prepared to return to Stalingrad following his meetings with von Manstein, von Richthofen and Fiebig. Once there, he did not expect to return, and so he wrote farewell letters to his wife and children and entrusted them to General der Flieger Albert Vierling, the commander of the Rostov administrative air region. Pickert had come to terms with what he believed lay ahead. He wanted to end things honourably fighting alongside his Flak troops:

Vierling will turn my letters over when we have perished, as we shall, without a doubt. It was very difficult to write them, but when I had finished I was filled with a cheerful serenity, like a man who has inevitably reached the end of his days. Now I feel carefree, and all that is left is to do my duty to the end.

After bidding farewell to his staff, Pickert took off for Stalingrad from Novocherkassk at 2330 hrs:

I started out to into a clear-cut but brief future. At least that is what I thought would happen, but things turned out differently. The flight proceeded well. Once an enemy searchlight spotted us, but there was no firing. Below, we could see numerous enemy campfires. In the area of the fortress itself all was dark, only the explosions of bombs. We circled over the field [Pitomnik] for one-and-a-half hours, but kept getting the red light and radio signals to the effect that we must wait – the field was not clear. Then we had to fly back! I must say I felt deep regret that we hadn't made it, and that I would have to be separated from my men for yet another day.

Pickert's aircraft returned after spending four fruitless hours in the air. On the 16th, he radioed von Richthofen that he would attempt to fly to Gumrak that afternoon, but the air fleet commander ordered him to remain where he was. Saddened and vexed, Pickert wrote:

Gumrak has not been made suitable for landing. Attempts are being made to drop supplies. However, that can no longer avert the bitter end. And those excellent soldiers whom I am leaving behind there, both officers and men, are all fighting their last battles – all those who, again and again, I have encouraged and watched over, all those to whom I feel bound by such close ties . . . splendid people. It is unimaginable. And me, their divisional commander, is not with them![57]

An evidently depressed Martin Fiebig wrote of the situation, 'The last act of the tragedy is starting. One must not think of it; how all those exhausted men are now fighting their last, heroic battle'.

And as curious troops from the Soviet 21st Army's 51st Guards and 252nd Rifle Divisions moved warily across the airfield at Pitomnik, so they stopped briefly to inspect the charred, abandoned and snow-coated wreck of Leutnant Wilhelm Stoye's Fw 200, its nose up pointing towards the grey winter sky like some lonely memorial.[58]

It now remained to be seen if Generalfeldmarschall Milch would be able to work the miracles which Hitler believed he could.

16

Cometh the Hour

17–23 January 1943

'We must protect ourselves from the slanderous reproaches of the 6.Armee.'

GENERALLEUTNANT MARTIN FIEBIG TO GENERALFELDMARSCHALL
ERHARD MILCH, 18 JANUARY 1943

To advance and succeed at a high level of leadership within the Third Reich, one needed to be ambitious, shrewd, determined, ruthless, insensitive, stubborn and Machiavellian. Fifty-year-old Erhard Milch was a man blessed with these attributes by the bucket-load. Hailing from the port city of Wilhelmshaven, this former World War I artillery officer turned fighter pilot used such qualities to propel and bludgeon his career forward in the lean but opportunistic inter-war years in Germany. During the early 1920s he worked as joint-owner/manager of two small, pioneering airlines, but he subsequently joined Junkers-Luftverkehr at Dessau, the wholly owned air transport company of the Junkers aircraft concern, where he eventually became head of the management office. Milch was hard-headed, and he soon discovered he had differences with Professor Hugo Junkers, the firm's owner. Nevertheless, Junkers despatched Milch on company business to South America and New York, where he did well.

Deutsche Luft Hansa Aktiengesellschaft (DLH) was formed in Berlin in January 1926 from the merger of Junkers-Luftverkehr and Deutscher Aero Lloyd which operated airline services across Europe. Milch was soon appointed as a director. He harboured a vision for a single, leading, domestic and international 'flag carrier' and set about rationalising the airline's fleet, aiming for efficiency and profit. His view was that aircraft made money when they were flying, not on the ground, irrespective of light or darkness, or of good or bad weather. Aircraft had to work. Under Milch's leadership, DLH grew to become the most important airline in Europe – a 'beacon to the world', its aircraft flying further and carrying more passengers than its British, French and Italian competitors. Milch also understood that the 'customer was king', and placed emphasis on comfort. In 1928 stewards were introduced to serve drinks and snacks, and reclining seats were added to some aircraft.

But Milch was not afraid to pick fights with aircraft designers: his long enmity with Willy Messerschmitt, whose early passenger designs he did not trust, was such that it proved detrimental to the efficient functioning of the German aviation industry during World War II. He also continued to clash with his former employer, the ageing Hugo Junkers, whose company produced the Ju 52/3m. In a potentially fatal episode of irony, in July 1932 Milch happened to be aboard one as it approached Schleissheim airfield, near Munich, when a Udet biplane collided with it from below, striking the port engine and wing. The Ju 52/3m's engine was partly torn away but remained attached. Debris from the Udet penetrated the cabin space of the Junkers and flew over the passengers' heads, but there were no injuries. The tri-motor made a safe landing in a cornfield and was repaired.[1] According to David Irving in his biography of Milch, 'Milch staggered clear of the maimed aeroplane and lit a cigar, blood soaking into his Lufthansa uniform from a gash in his neck'.[2]

Shortly after Hitler came to power in January 1933, the new Reich Air Ministry was established and placed under the leadership of General Hermann Göring, with Milch, in the post of State Secretary for Air, responsible for procurement. Several historians have attributed Junkers' death to the increasing pressures placed upon him by Milch, for he set about constructively victimising Junkers' firm following the old man's resistance to his ambitious and demanding aircraft production programmes, which included placing all of Junkers' patents and factories at the disposal of the Reich. In a deliberate campaign of persecution, Milch ensured that every detail of certain financial irregularities connected with factories outside Germany were made public. Placed under house arrest, Junkers' reputation as a pacifist and democrat was tarnished still further by a public investigation which brought forward charges of association with various leftist and Jewish causes. The pressure proved too much and the professor finally yielded, selling the controlling interests in his company in October 1934 and resigning his directorships the following month. When Junkers died on 3 February 1935, his 76th birthday, Milch, hypocritically, sent a wreath.

Following the suicide of Ernst Udet on 17 November 1941, Milch was appointed the Generalluftzeugmeister (Inspector-General of the Luftwaffe and Chief of Procurement). In this position, he held no fear of reversing any plans for aircraft or initiatives with which he did not agree. One example, in January 1942, was his decision to halt the troubled production of Messerschmitt's twin-engined fighter, the Me 210, particularly as it was having an impact on vital production of the Bf 109 fighter.

Milch brought his head for business and the goal of optimum productivity to the RLM, and he saw little difference between the principles of running an airline and the development and organisation of an air force. Nevertheless, it is a measure of the importance – and possible desperation – with which he viewed the Stalingrad air supply mission that, in an unprecedented move, Hitler risked sending Erhard Milch, his Secretary of State, to oversee it. But before Milch departed on his mission, Göring issued instructions strictly forbidding him to fly into the pocket himself.[3]

* * *

Milch arrived at the headquarters of *Luftflotte* 4 at Taganrog on 16 January after a 2,100-km flight from Rastenburg in his personal Dornier, supposedly to achieve wonders. He was accompanied by his small staff, which became known as the *Sonderstab Milch* (Milch Special Staff) and which included his adjutant, Oberst Wilhelm Polte, a former DLH test pilot who had flown some of the earliest Ju 52/3m prototypes in the 1930s. There was also a medical specialist, his personal pilot, as well as Oberstartz Prof. Dr. Heinrich Kalk, who would maintain Milch's diary and Oberstleutnant Edgar Petersen, a Knight's Cross-holder who, as one-time *Kommodore* of KG 40, was one of the foremost anti-shipping commanders and presently the overall chief of the Luftwaffe's test centres. The *Sonderstab* duly took over the operations coach of the air fleet's Chief of Staff, Oberst Herhudt von Rohden, in von Richthofen's mobile command train, which had been shunted onto a siding close to Taganrog-Süd airfield.

Given the scale of the task which lay ahead, it was a remarkably small team, and unlikely, in itself, to be able to effect any great change to the airlift measures already in place. That a number of these officers had been absent from conditions at the front for some time was evident in the fact that one of them found it puzzling that the flushing mechanism in the toilet in one of the headquarters buildings had become frozen and failed to function.[4]

Typically, Milch quickly got down to business. As far as he was concerned, von Richthofen would remain in charge of *Luftflotte* 4's combat operations, while his job was to focus on the airlift and its apparent shortcomings. However, after von Richthofen and Schulz had given detailed presentations on various aspects of the operation, Milch was left in no doubt that as a result of icy winds, sub-zero temperatures, snowdrifts and a lack of heating equipment, there were far fewer aircraft available or operationally ready than had been assumed at the *Führer's* headquarters (there were 308 aircraft reported on the supply fields in total on the 16th).[5] Milch also quickly declared himself in favour of supplying increased quantities of fuel to the pocket.

The units committed to the airlift at this time were assigned as follows:[6]

Lufttransportführer Sverevo: Oberst Morzik (Ju 52/3m)
    I. and II./KGr.z.b.V.1
    KGr.z.b.V.9
    KGr.z.b.V.50
    KGr.z.b.V.102
    KGr.z.b.V.105
    KGr.z.b.V.172
    KGr.z.b.V.500

KGr.z.b.V.700
KGr.z.b.V.900

Lufttransportführer Novocherkassk: Oberst Kühl (He 111)
Stab, I. and III./KG 55
I., II. and III./KG 27
I./KG 100

Lufttransportführer Voroshilovgrad: Oberst von Beust (He 111)
Stab/KG 27
III./KG 4
II./KG 53
15./KG 6
KGr.z.b.V.20
KGr.z.b.V.23

Lufttransportführer Stalino: Major Willers
KGr.z.b.V.200 (Fw 200)
KGr.z.b.V.5 (He 111)
KGr.z.b.V.OBS (He 111)
KGr.z.b.V.21 (Ju 86 and He 111)

Lufttransportführer Zaporozhye: Major Schede (He 177)
I./FKG 50

Some of these units had only recently been deployed to bolster the supply effort. The Heinkel bombers of III./KG 4 under Major Werner Klosinski had been pulled out of the central sector of the Russian Front, where the *Gruppe* had suffered heavy losses and had been re-equipped with new He 111H-16 variants. The unit departed Smolensk-Nord on 10 January bound for Voroshilovgrad, from where it would commence supply runs to Stalingrad. Two days later, II./KG 53, under Oberstleutnant Hans Schulz-Müllensiefen, had flown into Voroshilovgrad from Greifswald, where, similarly, it too had been resting and re-equipping after losses over the central sector of the front. Twelve He 111s also arrived from 15./KG 6, a specialist pathfinder unit, and a small number from the transport squadron of the Supreme Commander of German Forces in the Mediterranean and North Africa.

From his diary entry on the evening of the 16th, Fiebig seems to have been sceptical about Milch's mission:

> He will not have to do much organising because only air-dropping of supplies can take place now. This means success is down to a matter of chance, and for the Ju 52s it is very problematic. Von Richthofen agrees with me that we have done everything humanly possible. Nobody can be blamed for any lack of action.[7]

Later that evening, Milch met with Fiebig, who had flown to Taganrog, and endeavoured to calm his concerns; he assured the Luftwaffe general that his despatch to Russia was not to be viewed as a lack of confidence in either von Richthofen or himself, but rather that 'the *Führer* wanted to make certain that nothing was overlooked, and that everything humanly possible will be done to carry out the supply operation'.[8]

Meanwhile, the day of Milch's arrival saw three He 111s from KG 55 land at Gumrak, measuring 1,000 x 100 m, which by this point was the only functioning strip in the pocket. Since no army teams were available, the crews had to unload the aircraft themselves. The crew of a Ju 88 reconnaissance aircraft gave a similar report later in the day.[9] Fiebig pointed the blame for this at 6.*Armee*'s reluctance to get the strip ready earlier, but Paulus apparently did not want to attract the enemy's attention since the site also housed a supply dump, command post and hospital.[10] As a result of initial discussions between Milch and von Richthofen, orders came through that from now on the Ju 52/3ms would have to air-drop supplies only – something which Fiebig considered would be 'very problematic'. That evening, of 141 available Ju 52/3ms, 91 were unserviceable, 27 had to be evacuated from Ssalsk and seven were 'still out'. Just 16 were otherwise ready for operations.[11] Forty-one He 111s were available out of 141, and just one Fw 200 out of 20.[12]

In the 21 days from the commencement of the failed *Wintergewitter* relief attempt (which ran from 22 December to 11 January), 2,214 tons of supplies had been delivered to the pocket, or an average of 105.4 tons per day, while in the four days to the abandonment of Pitomnik (12–16 January), 300 tons had been delivered, or an average of just 75 tons per day.[13] This was an unacceptable decline to Milch, and he demanded an increase in the Luftwaffe's sortie rate. On the afternoon of the 17th Fiebig called Milch to confirm that five Ju 52/3ms and 35 He 111s had been sent out into an icy wind of up to 60 km/h the previous bright and frosty moonlit night. The crews reported seeing no landing path, only an illuminated cross which was lit up intermittently. Fifteen Heinkels had so far flown in daylight that day. 'The refusal of 6.*Armee* to expand Gumrak airfield is exacting a heavy penalty now', Fiebig noted. But the Army in turn complained to *Heeresgruppe Don* that only ten tons of supplies had been dropped. Fiebig was indignant:

> The supply situation is catastrophic. The guilty should be brought to account. The decision to drop supplies was made in agreement with General von Richthofen and Generalfeldmarschall Milch. There was no alternative. We must remain reasonable, even though our hearts are burning. It is very hard on us not to be able to commit more aircraft, but it cannot be done due to the terrible weather conditions and icy winds. Acts of God are involved here.[14]

Two hours later Fiebig spoke with Milch again to advise him that nine Ju 52/3ms had been destroyed during an enemy bombing attack at Sverevo and 12 more damaged. Altogether, 12 Junkers were operationally ready. But another raid followed that night, leaving two more Ju 52/3ms destroyed and eight damaged. Furthermore, 42 aircraft were 'fit only to be ferried to the rear, no longer suitable for missions'.[15] By nightfall Fiebig was able to confirm that 19 He 111s had made it to Gumrak and three He 177s had dropped supplies. During the night, 32 He 111s went out from Novocherkassk and ten from Voroshilovgrad, while seven Ju 52/3ms also made the trip. One Junkers was posted missing.[16]

The next day Milch set out in a car from von Richthofen's command train to the airfield, from where he would make the two-hour flight from Taganrog to Novocherkassk. Amongst others, he wanted to meet with General Pickert there to find out what conditions were like in the pocket. Milch sat in the front passenger seat next to his driver as a blizzard swept across the flat, frozen landscape. The wipers brushed away at the windscreen but it was difficult to see very far ahead. As the car bumped over the lines at a railway crossing Milch happened to spot, fleetingly, a speeding, blurred shape through the frost-crusted side window. The Field Marshal shouted a warning to his driver, who braked as quickly and as hard as he could, but in doing so, the car's front wheels became wedged against the inside of the railway line. At that moment a Russian locomotive hit the car at around 65 km/h, pushing it off the track, across an embankment and into a wooden lineside hut, which fell apart under the impact. Two soldiers inside the hut were killed.

Milch was crushed, unconscious, inside the vehicle. Fortunately, an ambulance was called quickly and he was extracted carefully from the wreckage and driven to the VIII.*Fliegerkorps'* field hospital. He had suffered a severe injury to his head, lost blood and several of his ribs were broken. It was not the start he had envisaged, or wanted, to his mission, but within three hours he was helped from the hospital and back to the command train.[17]

Dr. Heinrich Potthoff on the medical staff of *Luftflotte* 4 recalls:

Immediately after the accident I received a telephone call from VIII.*Fliegerkorps'* motorised *Luftwaffensanitätsbereitschaft* [medical readiness team] asking me to go to the command train. I was soon there. Milch was lucky to have come away from it relatively unscathed. I examined the Generalfeldmarschall and established that he had suffered a fracture to his right collar bone. I arranged for the necessary medical attention.

I then got into a lengthy conversation with the Generalfeldmarschall, whom I had previously met in 1938 at the RLM in Berlin, about the medical situation and the care and attention [of the besieged troops], and transportation arrangements for airlifting them out of the *Kessel*, also the mood 'barometer' and so forth, which I was able to supply in detail. The Generalfeldmarschall gave me a 'fat' cigar which he had brought with him in a cigar box from Reichsmarschall Göring. It was good tobacco, was of extraordinary quality and unusually long. I put the cigar in my cap so as to smoke it later at leisure, since on account of my talking too much it would have gone out. The Generalfeldmarschall duly gave me another cigar for smoking there and then. I lit it and tried not to let it go out. During our forthcoming conversation, Milch was relaxed and convivial, and said how he was relieved that he had come away alive from the car accident.[18]

Afterwards, Potthoff briefed von Richthofen, who felt Milch should have remained in hospital. However, after receiving treatment, Milch had chosen to return to his command coach where, despite running a temperature, he continued with the task of overseeing the airlift. 'Everyone is in shock, but there were no bones broken', von Richthofen recorded somewhat inaccurately in his diary.[19]

Over the coming days, aching, occasionally light-headed, but undeterred from his near fatal accident, Milch monitored and involved himself in the day-to-day functions of the *Luftflotte* and air-supply command infrastructure, bringing what he saw as fresh ways and means to streamline the processes involved, as well as 'innovative' alternatives. One of his favourite initiatives, which he tirelessly and repeatedly promoted, was the deployment of cargo gliders. He had already arranged to draw on the craft that were in southern Russia, and had called in others from the Reich. By the 16th, there were 15 DFS 230s and 50 Go 242s of 1.(DFS) and 1.(Go)/ *Verbindungskommando* 4 under Hauptmann Schossig at Zaporozhye, with another 120 DFS gliders from *Luftlandegeschwader* (LLG) 1 in the process of arriving there by air and 60 more being delivered via the Luftwaffe's *Generalquartiermeister*. Ten Go 242 of Hauptmann Krug's I./LLG 2 were being air-towed in by He 111Zs, with another 16 due to arrive disassembled by rail and 60 more through the *Generalquartiermeister*. Five Me 321s of GS-*Kommando* 2 were also on their way to Voroshilovgrad, with another five due to follow after repairs. More than 130 tow aircraft were being gathered, including Do 17s, Hs 126s and Ar 65s.[20]

During a telephone conversation with Milch late on the afternoon of the 17th, Fiebig advised that of 50 transport gliders that were available, there were crews for only 20. Despite Fiebig stressing that landed gliders blocked the runways, Milch was resolute that they should be used on a 'one-way' basis, and that their crews should be flown out of the pocket in He 111s. But as the *Luftflotte*'s Senior Quartermaster, Oberst Karl-Heinrich Schulz, noted:

> The deployment of *Lastensegler* [load-carrying gliders] was examined in detail, but had to be discarded due to it being impracticable and unsuitable. Gliders could only be used in daylight in clear weather when, as a result of their slowness on such a long, long stretch, they would have been certain booty for enemy fighters or Flak. In addition, because of the increase in fuel consumption (slower, hence longer flight duration) in the glider's tow transport, deployment of the tow aircraft [on their own] would have been more economical. Attempts to make *Lastensegler* capable of blind-flying at the end of January 1943, despite the loss of landing possibilities and despite the difficulties experienced, appeared to be desirable, but did not come to a conclusion.[21]

In fact Schulz felt that at this point operations by cargo gliders 'could' have been 'useful', but that the time and effort to train their pilots in blind-flying would not have met with success.

The remaining handful of JG 3's Bf 109 pilots were flown out of Gumrak on the 17th to re-join I. and II. *Gruppen* at Shakhty. Feldwebel Hans Grünberg left a harrowing account of this process:

In January 1943 the cold was almost unbearable. There were days when our groundcrewmen, with temperatures at -25 to -30°C, were not able to start the available serviceable Me 109s. The reason was that the heating devices were almost all defective and ripe for the scrapheap.

On 17 January 1943, on the field and in our bunker, we could quite clearly hear the impacts of the enemy's artillery shells. We knew then that the Russians had broken through the western front of the pocket and could thus be expected to advance on the most important place in the pocket, Pitomnik. Of the succeeding sequence of events I can still remember everything with crystal clarity.

I was supposed to fly airfield protection the next morning. On the previous evening Oberleutnant Lukas, who had flown escort for supply aircraft and become involved in an aerial combat on the way, landed at Pitomnik. His Me 109 was no longer serviceable and there was thus no question of taking off again straightaway. Oberleutnant Lukas thus had to spend the night with us. His fighter was supposed to be the first Me 109 to be warmed up the next morning and made ready for take-off, for this one needed a lot of time as the temperatures hovered around -25°C. Finally, his Me 109 was started and Lukas took off. He wanted to fly protection over the field until my Me 109 was also ready to lift off. After a while Lukas flew off to the west.

At almost the same time the last Ju 87s took off, climbed to 300 m and dived on the southern boundary of the field, dropping their bombs. We pilots and groundcrew looked at each other and suddenly one of the mechanics said that the Russians were coming. I saw only soliders in white camouflage suits, but these were Russian infantrymen. My Me 109 would not start, and on the second attempt to get the engine to fire, one of the mechanics got hit by a bullet in the hand and shouted to me, "Quick, out of the aircraft, the Russians are here". The airfield had been over-run. Chaos followed. What happened next defies description.

German vehicles and tanks drove over wounded German soldiers. In their hundreds our emaciated infantrymen threw away their rifles, fell exhausted into the snow after a few metres and died. For a long time there had been nothing substantial to eat. We pilots received daily a loaf of bread between seven men and a tin of sardines in oil between three to four men. We could still take off and land on this, but it was no longer possible to turn tightly in the air or to become involved in an aerial combat. When turning we became dizzy and then could no longer see properly. The panic was now complete. All those who could still walk, departed for the field at Gumrak that was about 25 km away.

We marched through the freezing cold, through deep snow, with nothing to eat, and the journey was broken by attacks by enemy Il-2 ground-attack aircraft. A forced march like that was a real challenge for members of the Luftwaffe, but the will to survive made us strong and able to overcome such obstacles. On 18 January, shortly before it got dark, we reached Gumrak (six kilometres from Stalingrad).

On the night of 18–19 January some supply aircraft still managed to land at Pitomnik. On the Eastern Front outside of Stalingrad it was yet not known that the Russians had taken this airfield. The Russians did not shoot at the landing aircraft. The aircraft, and the supplies they carried, were gratefully received by them. When it became known that Pitomnik had fallen, the supply aircraft were rerouted to Gumrak. The aircrews had orders not to land, but to throw the supplies from the aircraft over Gumrak.

On 19 January in the early morning darkness a Ju 52/3m landed in Gumrak between the bomb craters. The crew was made up of four Unteroffizieren. According to their orders they were to take off immediately. I joined them, and now had a small hope to escape the hell of Stalingrad. I was able to be of great assistance to my fellow fliers from the Ju 52. I was able to explain to them that we would only be safe if we turned to the south and then flew at low-level across the steppes. Several times we shuddered with fright as we could see Russian aircraft above us. In the Caucasus [Krasnodar] we had to land to refuel. I then had to pursue my further journey to II./JG 3 on foot and by truck. After five days I reached the II. *Gruppe* in the Donets area.[22]

Despite his ordeal, Grünberg was among the fortunate: JG 3's loyal groundcrews had to be left behind, and by the end of the fighting at Stalingrad, 66 of them were reported missing.[23]

The intention for the 17th was for He 111s to attempt to land in the pocket in order to deliver fuel, which crews were to siphon from their tanks and cargo containers. If landing proved impossible, they were to drop the containers. But, as Fiebig recorded, the plan simply did not work:

> . . . operations carried out with 16 He 111s only. Take-off difficulties were encountered. The winter equipment is inadequate. The engines won't start. The weather is getting worse. Although the temperature is getting milder, the wind is growing stronger. Work on the aircraft becomes like torture, but it has to be done. KG 55 continues its runs.

According to Fiebig, one problem was that the more recently arrived variants of He 111s were not ready for use at Stalingrad (*Kesselklar*) in as much as some of the aircraft had to have extra fuel tanks built in to give them the necessary range. But he told Milch how their crews were flying in 'absolutely unbelievable weather conditions. This is indicated by the high number of losses'.[24] Fiebig was also resolute that his aircrews 'really are doing their best; merely flying without fighter escort is a heroic accomplishment. But now, as before, the position taken in the fortress is: *"These are our demands and we don't care how you meet them"*.'[25]

The crews of KG 55 which did manage to land at Gumrak's narrow strip returned to speak of the place being deserted. Furthermore, artillery and *Katyusha* rocket fire was being directed at the northern and south-eastern edges of the field. The Heinkel crews also reported sighting enemy infantry just two kilometres away to the west, and that not all air-dropped supplies had been gathered. The *Gruppenkommandeur* of II./KG 55, the highly experienced Hauptmann Heinrich Höfer, who concurrently acted as Operations Officer to the *Lufttransportführer*, Oberst Dr. Kühl, reported to Fiebig that during the evening two other Heinkels failed to find the field, despite trying to search for 20 minutes.[26] Milch issued orders that the first aircraft to Stalingrad on the 18th was to carry in runway lights and smoke-signal equipment.

During the day there had been a flurry of radio traffic concerning the suitability of Gumrak for landing aircraft. 6.*Armee* maintained that the 'airfield' was in an acceptable operable condition, but Luftwaffe officers sent there to assess the situation were of a different opinion. Larger formations of aircraft could not land there, and even single aircraft rotation and turnaround was slow. Furthermore, because of the cratered and debris-littered surface, only more experienced pilots could land, and even then only with extended distances between aircraft.[27] Von Richthofen decided that no further night landings would take place, and so when I./KG 100 flew an operation to Stalingrad that evening its aircraft only air-dropped containers.[28] But at 2020 hrs Paulus had signalled that Gumrak *was* ready to accept night landings. 6.*Armee* sent an indignant message to Hitler which Oberstleutnant Eckhard Christian from the *Luftwaffenführungsstab* read out to Milch in a telephone conversation during the evening of the 17th:

Your [Hitler's] orders to supply the army are not being carried out. Gumrak field has been in condition to receive aircraft since early on 16 January. Numerous objections from the Luftwaffe outside the *Festung*. Field has been reliably determined by Luftwaffe experts to be capable of receiving aircraft at night. There is ground organisation. Request action at the earliest possible moment, as there is very great danger.

Milch was not cowed by this. He replied:

Crews who have landed there report the conditions to be quite the opposite. I have ordered that landing shall take place there tonight providing there is reliable identification of the field by means of lights. Last night the Russians used German beacons and landing lights at Pitomnik field.

This was a problem: one unit commander reported that the Russians 'repeatedly' tried to induce German crews to drop containers into their territory by firing false identification flares, or by setting up fake rows of guide lamps.[29] Later on the 17th Fiebig advised Milch that the weather was expected to turn even worse. The ability for the Luftwaffe to forecast weather prospects had become increasingly difficult by this time, as Kühl wrote:

The loss of the Don basin and the loss of Kotelnikovo and Ssalsk had the result that weather reports covering an area of more than 300 km were lost. In addition, it meant that for increasingly longer periods the *Festung* received no transmissions. Developments in the *Festung* were such that by both day and night, flights and landings had to be made in weather conditions that could not be ascertained. This had the result that not only weather 'surprises' were encountered during flights, but also often involved adverse weather conditions [snowfall, snowstorm, fog, icing] of which the aircrews were already aware of prior to take-off, always earning them the highest praise.[30]

Sverevo airfield was under continual attack from VVS bombers (which, evidently, were able to venture out despite the conditions), with nine Ju 52/3ms having been destroyed so far. It was by no means clear how long the transport *Gruppen* could remain on airfields under threat from the Russians. Novocherkassk was at risk of encirclement, as Soviet armour had passed around it both to the north and south. Milch duly asked Jeschonnek for another fighter *Gruppe* to protect the supply bases, but there were none available as there was an urgent need for fighters in the northern sector of the Eastern Front around Leningrad. Credit to Milch, he immediately called von Manstein and told him:

> The maintenance of Sverevo and Novocherkassk airfields is of the utmost importance for the supply situation. In order not to interrupt the supply, I have delayed the shifting of units to Stalino and Voroshilovgrad. It is of great importance that the *Heeresgruppe* should inform the Luftwaffe as early as possible when a field is particularly threatened by the enemy so that the units can be evacuated to the rear in time.[31]

Milch was of the view that Novocherkassk should be held for as long as possible and operate as the new Ju 52/3m base, while the He 111s should eventually be shifted to Stalino, which he recognised was in a bad position in terms of exposure to weather. Novocherkassk, with its six hangars, was not of sufficient size to operate both types, while Voroshilovgrad, which had three double hangars, was already overcrowded and was under threat from the enemy.

In the meantime, the VVS mounted more attacks on Sverevo and left three more Ju 52/3ms burning. A telling line in the OKW war diary stated 'The supply situation for 6.*Armee* can no longer be mastered'.[32]

Thirty-four He 111s, eight Ju 52/3ms and two Fw 200s went out over the night of 17–18 January. Six Heinkels failed to complete the mission, as did five of the Junkers and both Focke-Wulfs – 10.3 tons of supplies, one ton of ammunition and 0.2 cbm of fuel were air-dropped. Two He 111s from Voroshilovgrad were posted missing.[33]

Despite his activity on the 17th, Milch 'officially' took over responsibility for the airlift on the 18th – a day which saw the removal of 30 Ju 52/3ms from the airlift effort because, aside from enemy air attacks, the extreme weather conditions at Sverevo did not permit servicing. Conditions, as Fiebig had warned, were terrible, with heavy snowdrifts blanketing all the supply fields. Despite this, the VVS still made its presence felt: ten more Junkers were destroyed on the ground as a result of bombing and strafing attacks, while another 20 were so damaged that they were slated for sending to the rear for repair.[34]

Pickert, who had flown from Novocherkassk to Taganrog to meet Milch, noted that the weather was 'icy cold'. He found Milch to be 'covered in bruises and extremely lucky'. Despite the discomfort from his injuries, and being heavily bandaged, Milch worked tirelessly from early morning until late at night based in the command train. The barrage of telephone calls, cables and signals was ceaseless. Jeschonnek complained to Milch that, 'Paulus is sending one urgent radio signal after another', while Hitler had become fixated on increasing the production of air-drop containers of all capacities. The latter was not something Milch could easily arrange from Taganrog, and he told Oberstleutnant Christian that there was 'no emergency as far as containers are concerned'. Nevertheless, he issued orders for his ministerial departments to increase the manufacture of the larger 1,000-kg variant. In all, he requested 13,000 250-kg and 7,000 1,000-kg containers to be manufactured urgently – this despite the fact Luftwaffe aircrews had advised that many containers were not being recovered after being dropped into the pocket, with most ending up in Russian hands.[35] As von Richthofen observed:

> The waves in relation to Stalingrad roll ever higher. They arrive from the highest levels with ever increased urgency. Poor Milch is, so to speak, sitting in the crossfire, and, essentially, can do nothing at all. He is not accustomed to taking hard and brutal decisions, since in technical and organisational work back at home, of course, one does not need to do so.[36]

Complaints continued to flood in from 6.*Armee* that aircraft were not landing in the pocket. Yet, according to *Luftflotte* 4 records, five out of 49 He 111s from Novocherkassk landed (the others air-dropped), as did a lone Fw 200 out of three despatched – another air-dropped and one aborted. The Heinkels brought back 11 wounded men. Only three of six Ju 52/3ms sent out completed their missions to drop 6.6 tons of ammunition.[37] Just two triangles of light could be found at Gumrak airfield, and crews had to circle for some 30 minutes as they waited and searched for further recognition signals or landing aids. Clearly aggrieved by ill-founded accusations, Fiebig noted, 'We must protect ourselves from the slanderous reproaches of the 6.*Armee*'.

According to Fiebig, the Luftwaffe was averaging 150–160 tons delivered to the pocket daily, while 6.*Armee* claimed the average was 110 tons. This difference, as mentioned, was explained by the fact that not all supplies dropped or unloaded were actually 'received' by the Army, and because, oddly, 6.*Armee* did not include supplies destined to the Luftwaffe units in the pocket. Furthermore, the Luftwaffe supply figures tallied with those of the Quartermaster of *Heeresgruppe Don*. In order to get to the truth of what was happening, Fiebig had arranged for Hauptmann Karl Mayer, the *Staffelkapitän* of 9./KG 27, to fly into the pocket to assess conditions at Gumrak. He would report his findings directly to Milch on his return.

It was a depressing situation at the adapted cornfield at Sverevo, where 1,000 tons of supplies, comprising canned goods, smoked sausage, cheese and lard, as well as 800 tons of ammunition, awaited carriage to Stalingrad: of 106 Ju 52/3ms there on the 18th, ten had been left burning from eight Russian air attacks, resulting in two of the aircraft being destroyed. Seven personnel had been killed and several more wounded. The number of aircraft needing to be ferried to the rear for repair had climbed to 48. Morzik told Milch that although the field was completely covered with drifted snow, an attempt was being made to build barracks there, but it was a difficult process as the ground was frozen to a depth of a metre everywhere. It had taken three-and-a-half hours to dig out one Ju 52/3m. According to Morzik:

> The morale of the flying crews is excellent. Some crews are beginning to show the strain of night missions. All crews say that these missions are the most difficult of any in which they have participated. The greatest strain is instrument flying. Morale among the groundcrews is good, and clothing is in good condition. So far there have been 10 to 15 cases of first- and second-degree frostbite.

At the rear Ju 52/3m base at Zaporozhye, where Oberst Ludwig Beckmann, commander of KGr.z.b.V.500, oversaw operations, only eight of 21 Junkers had been able to take off, of which five turned back, either with engine or radio trouble. Other aircraft had been destroyed or damaged by enemy bombing. The units there also had to contend with ground winds of up to 90 km/h which blew snow over everything, meaning aircraft had to be dug out and heating trucks could not get to them. However, when Milch asked Morzik if he needed more men, heating equipment or any other items, the senior *Lufttransportführer* replied 'I do not need anything'. Milch, who may have been peeved with Morzik over his negative stance on the deployment of gliders, was not convinced, and told Fiebig, 'I have the impression that operations are not being properly conducted under Oberst Morzik'.

On the occasion Morzik explained to Milch that despite requesting items, nothing had arrived, the latter erupted, 'Do you think that lets you off?' And when Morzik further explained that he lacked transport to collect supplies, Milch simply referred to the presence of some unutilised army trucks near the airfield. Morzik responded that it would be tantamount to larceny to commandeer them. Milch scoffed, 'The only larceny done around here is that somebody has made off with your brains'.[38] Milch also began to question the crews' morale.[39]

The He 177s soldiered on at this time from Zaporozhye, despite the fact that a logistics error had seen a special Heinkel repair shop unloaded at Kalinovka, far back in the rear, instead of at Zaporozhye as *Luftflotte* 4 had expected.

Twenty-seven-year-old Oberleutnant Adolf Spohr from Cuxhaven was the son of a fish auctioneer. After joining the Luftwaffe in the mid-1930s, he became an experienced military pilot and had flown transports in the Polish campaign. In December 1939 Spohr qualified as a flying instructor on multi-engined aircraft and served at schools in Germany and France, but in September 1942 he joined I./FKG 50 and underwent conversion as a bomber pilot on the He 177. As such, in January 1943, he found himself in southern Russia and flew his first air-drop supply mission to Stalingrad on the 17th. The following day he wrote home, offering a vivid picture of life with his unit at Zaporozhye:

Since the cold has receded a little and I no longer need to bury my hands in my coat pockets in my room the whole time, I wanted to finally send you my first letter from this desolate wasteland, since I hope one of our aircraft will leave for the Reich tomorrow. We have taken up quarters here on a Russian airfield. We found only empty rooms, which we have furnished ourselves in a rather spartan manner. We had to sweep the snow out of the rooms and install new windows. During our first nights here, of course, we had no sleep. But we have all chipped in, no matter whether officer or private. The worst aspects of our accommodation have been overcome. I even have a steam heater, although unfortunately it is not enough. I want to get a stove built in, so that I will at least be able to sleep after missions.

My greatest luxury is a desk. The view through the window looks out to a burnt barrack block. All in all, Russia is as I always imagined it. The coldness wouldn't really be so bad if this damned cutting wind weren't blowing constantly, which often pulls one's legs off the ground. For the time being my dwelling is still bug-free, but I believe that those nice little animals will be around as soon as I heat my bunker properly.

I completed my first real mission yesterday. Our sortie was to a hotly contested city here in the southern sector. My aircraft and crew gave a brilliant account of themselves. We arrived at 4,000 m altitude, then I turned the old crate around and went at a decent speed through the anti-aircraft barrage to drop our 'blessings'. It was tricky as we climbed away because the anti-aircraft fire became more accurate. At 4,000 m six fighters showed up and began a wild combat, chasing us from the Volga to the Don. But as soon as they became difficult, my gunners fired back at them, whereupon they dived away to make a new approach. This way, none of them managed to get a shot at us, and they left us alone after half-an-hour. I greatly admired my crew, who remained calm all the way through it and did not get flustered even when their guns jammed. So I can now look ahead to the next missions with complete calm. Of course, you also need some luck in everything, but I know that you will cross your fingers for me.

This morning brought us the joyful news that Hans Will, whom we had missed from a mission since yesterday, is on his way here by train. He had to bail out with his crew for some reason on their return flight and fortunately he found himself behind our lines. Unfortunately, there is still no news of Major Schede, who has been missing for three days.[40]

Indeed, the *Staffelkapitän* of 1./FKG 50, Oberleutnant Will, together with his crew, was fortunate to be able to escape his burning bomber near Zaporozhye on the 17th when it was attacked by enemy aircraft, while another machine was lost when two of its engines caught fire 100 km west of Stalino, the crew being forced to take to their parachutes.

As a result of Milch's endeavours, trains were already on the way from the Reich with more air-drop containers, although the 1,000-kg units were in short supply. More trains were bringing in DFS 230 and Go 242 gliders, and were due to arrive in the Stalino area between 23 and 27 January.

Unusually, it seems that Milch's appointment had rattled the self-confident and caustic von Richthofen. The Air Fleet commander felt it was:

> . . . ridiculous that Milch has been sent here to bear down on my neck and has issued orders over and above me when it comes to transport matters. I have never shirked away from responsibility when it lies within an overall framework of clearly defined and potentially workable boundaries.

His diary nevertheless hints at some bitterness:

> The current task, however, is so grotesque that it is best to have as little as possible to do with it.[41]

Indeed, Göring was bearing down on Milch's neck. In the early afternoon of the 18th, the Reichsmarschall called Milch, concerned that 'terrible reports' were coming in from Stalingrad. The claim was also being persisted that Gumrak was 'satisfactory'. Milch informed Göring that 14 aircraft had landed there in daylight, but that the field was not suitable for night landing. When Göring questioned why VIII.*Fliegerkorps'* combat aircraft were able to take off and the transports were not, Milch explained that the transport groundcrews had to dig their aircraft laboriously out of snowdrifts in 90 km/h surface winds at -12°C. It was also very foggy. Nevertheless, the engineers, workshops and groundcrews managed to bring enough aircraft to readiness to enable a plan for 17 He 111s from Novocherkassk, seven Ju 52/3ms from Sverevo and two Fw 200s from Stalino to fly to the pocket during the night.

Thankfully, the 19th would be a day of milder weather, but with heavy cloud. One of the first aircraft that went out to Stalingrad was an Fw 200 flown by Leutnant Gilbert of 2./KGr.z.b.V.200 from Stalino. The unit had received an urgent and special order by radio:

> On the orders of the *Führer*, an aircraft is to be despatched immediately, as General Hube is to fly to Generalfeldmarschall Milch tonight on the *Führer's* orders.[42]

Hitler wanted, once more, to hear from one of his favoured generals as to conditions inside the *Festung*.

Gilbert's Condor took off at 0520 hrs and landed at Gumrak at 0715 hrs with the help of navigational assistance from the ground and the firing of flares. As soon as the big aircraft had turned around, Hube, accompanied by Hauptmann Winrich Behr, a highly decorated veteran of the *Afrika Korps* who had been assigned to the Staff of 6.*Armee*, climbed up into the fuselage of the Focke-Wulf. But as the aircraft began to taxi down the airstrip for its return flight, its tailwheel became snagged in snowdrifts and broke away. It was decided to delay the flight until dusk, when the aircraft made a second, successful attempt to take off, towards the north, and this time with no tailwheel. Gilbert landed the Condor back at Stalino safely.

When Hube and Behr eventually reached Hitler's headquarters, they came with a vivid and alarming portrayal of the conditions facing the trapped army, and its predicament. In their view nothing more could be done and there was no hope. For once, Hitler listened, and was apparently deeply affected by the soldiers' reports.[43]

Also that day Fiebig recorded, 'Some of Kühl's He 111 units have landed at Gumrak, others dropped their supplies. Artillery fire covers the field. Landing is difficult, but possible'.[44] Milch did manage to make improvements at Gumrak by ordering up lighting equipment, smoke canisters and radios and by sending signals and traffic specialists into the pocket, although the airfield was still more dangerous at night than during daylight – in this final phase, 25 per cent of the He 111s destined for Gumrak either crashed or were damaged during landing or take-off. Pickert observed how 'the air supply assumed major proportions today – an exciting day – but it was high time! The bread supply was about to give out despite a 260-g cut in rations. The daily requirements of bread alone are 40 tons!'[45]

Meanwhile, during the afternoon of the 19th, Kühl and Oberstleutnant *Freiherr* von Beust, the *Kommodore* of KG 27 and, since 9 January, also the *Lufttransportführer II Voroshilovgrad*, met with Milch in *Luftflotte* 4's command train at Taganrog-Süd. Kühl advised that he had arranged to move the 60 He 111s of I., II. and III./KG 27, I. and III./KG 55 and I./KG 100 presently at Novocherkassk north-east to Stalino, where they would join the 30–35 Heinkels already there, with around 30 others available at Saki and Odessa. Kühl also advised that the crews of the He 111-equipped KGr.z.b.V. transporter units lacked observers and radio operators, but that their pilots were 'very good'. Milch issued instructions that the 'He 111H-11, H-14 and H-18 aircraft must be armed with five or six machine guns', indicating that such variants were already arriving, or about to, and in recognition of the increasing danger from Soviet fighters.[46]

Von Beust commented that he considered any attempt to bring in more He 111s to the alternative field at Voroshilovgrad to be 'of no use at present since there is no equipment for servicing them'. The field there was only able to carry out minor repairs and, in any case, the Germans found that the Italian units based there were a 'great burden. They won't clear any of the hangars'. Nevertheless, Milch had ordered 50 new Heinkel crews to be made ready as a reserve pool.[47] Eight He 177s also ventured out to drop supplies, but because of poor visibility they all had to turn around without completing their mission.

That night von Beust told Fiebig over the telephone that 'The aircraft which landed at Stalingrad today have not returned; their fuel tanks have been completely drained'. Fiebig then asked, 'How many aircraft are out today?',

O.Qu./Qu.'(VI)   Gefechtsstand, den 19.1.1943 **12**   KTB

Einsatz der zur Luftversorgung eingesetzten
Verbände am 19.1.1943

	Ist	am Platz	einsatz= bereit	eingesetzt	erfüllt	noch im Einsatz
Ju 52 I./K.G.z.b.V.1	51	13	1	1	1	0
II./K.G.z.b.V.1	39	12	0	1	0	0
K.G. z.b.V. 9	55	7	0	0	0	0
K.G. z.b.V. 50	36	10	5	5	3	0
K.G. z.b.V. 102	33	4	1	1	1	0
K.G. z.b.V. 172	49	9	1	0	0	0
K.G. z.b.V. 500	67	28	0	0	0	0
K.G. z.b.V. 700	33	6	1	1	0	0
K.G. z.b.V. 900	43	12	2	2	1	0
	386	**101**	**14**	**12**	**6**	**0**
He 111 I./K.G.55	21	12	3	5	4	
Nowo= tscher- kask III./K.G.55	20	9	3	5	5	
I./K.G.100	21	12	5 8	15	15	
I./K.G.27	26	6	5 2 }	12	9	
II./K.G.27	15	4	2)			
III./K.G.27	18	15	7	19	19	
	121	**58**	**24**	**56**	**52**	
He 111 II./K.G.53	22	22	6	8	1	4
Woro= schilow= grad III./K.G.4	34	21	6	2	0	2
K.G. z.b.V. 5	46	13	2	2	2	
K.G. z.b.V. 20	13	13	3	4	1	3
K.G. z.b.V. 23	17	16	2	3	0	1
	132	**85**	**19**	**11**	**5**	**10**
He 177 I./F.K.G.50	25	14	1	1	0	0
Fw 200 K.G. z.b.V.200	23	19	2	3	2	0

Verteiler:

Feldmarschall
Chf d. Genst.
O.Qu.
O.Qu./Qu.1(VI) zgl.KTB
V.O. Ob.d.L.

MAJOR i. Genst.

'Operations of the Deployed Units for Air Supply 19.1.1943' – a strength return issued by the Quartermaster of *Sonderstab Milch*. The column headings are *Ist* = actual [total] strength; *am Platz* = on the airfield; *einsatzbereit* = operationally ready; *eingesetzt* = deployed; *erfüllt* = completed; *noch im Einsatz* = still out on operation. Note the disparities between total strength and aircraft on the field, and between aircraft on the field and aircraft operationally ready.

to which he was told, 'There are eight aircraft in the air at the moment who have reported that no runway lights can be seen'.

Also on this day (19 January), Major Erich Thiel, a Knight's Cross-holder and *Gruppenkommandeur* of III./KG 27, together with Hauptmann Karl Mayer,

Staffelkapitän of 9./KG 27, were ordered by VIII.*Fliegerkorps* to visit Gumrak and to report on what they found there in regards to day and night landing visibility, groundcrew organisation, the state of equipment and the possibility of replacement if needed. 6.*Armee* command staff interpreted this initiative more as an attempt to reconcile differences between the Army and the Luftwaffe.[48] Just getting to Gumrak with a small formation of He 111s, however, was challenging, as Thiel reported, and his description offers insight into the almost hopeless conditions facing the supply crews by this stage:

A first take-off in the early morning had to be interrupted over the Don due to bad ice conditions. Visibility was zero and the narrow landing strip at Gumrak would not have allowed me to land. I approached the field above the clouds, received perfect bearing and was told that the cloud base was 400 m below. When I broke through, the cloud base was 2,400 m, and I kept the flight together for a stronger defence in case of any enemy aircraft. The field can be easily seen from 1,500–2,000 m, with its surfaced runway, wrecks and numerous bomb and artillery craters. The landing strip was covered by snow. Shortly after landing, the field was attacked and fired upon by ten enemy fighters. However, these aircraft did not dare to go below 800–1,000 m because of the light anti-aircraft defence. At the same time the field was covered with enemy artillery fire. I had just shut the engines down when the attack commenced on my aircraft.

Bomb craters on the runway, which have prevented many landings, particularly at night, are caused by fragmentation bombs and show up as flat craters which can only be regarded as reed holes. However, their discolouring effect on the snow makes them appear as if they are wide craters. Enemy artillery fire is capable of concentrating on aircraft a few minutes after their landing. Whenever weather conditions are favourable the enemy guards the sky, forcing us to fly in formation, and when the formation has to be broken up for landing, this can lead to heavy losses. In my opinion it is impossible for Ju 52/3ms to approach, or at least possible only in bad weather. Fighter attacks on parked aircraft are carried out constantly, but have no particular effect.

There is a total of 13 damaged aircraft on the field. The width of the runway is therefore reduced to 80 m. Particularly an obstacle for night landings is an Me 109 at the end of the runway which can be very dangerous for overloaded aircraft and inexperienced crews. The unloading detail for my aircraft had not arrived by 2200 hrs, although I had landed at 1100 hrs. Also refuelling could not take place due to artillery fire. Conclusion: from an air-technical point of view the field condition is acceptable for day landings, but night landings can only be carried out by very experienced crews.

The runway lights were not always in operation since the field was subject to enemy bombings. These are carried out by enemy nuisance raiders (U-2), which are able to observe the field undisturbed at low altitude and make out any movement on the ground in the clear moonlight. They can observe the landing of an aircraft and destroy it with fragmentation bombs. The destruction of an aircraft on the runway obstructs any further landings for that night because the groundcrews would be held down by the enemy, thereby making it impossible to clear away the wreck. The unloading area is too small to take care of any greater landing or unloading activity. Crews report repeatedly that unloading teams were not present, and that they themselves had to unload the aircraft; unloaded goods were piled up, often without being guarded, and stolen by roaming soldiers until they were cleared away.

Thiel then met with Paulus and his senior commanders. At one point Paulus commented to the Luftwaffe officer, 'If no landings take place it will mean the death of the army. It is too late now anyway'. Thiel later returned to his aircraft, which, in the meantime, had been badly damaged by Soviet artillery fire and the mechanics killed. It had been neither unloaded nor refuelled. Another KG 27 aircraft had also been damaged by shell fire. Thiel eventually got out of the pocket aboard a Ju 52/3m carrying 20 wounded men. Panic had broken out among the soldiers, and they had rushed the aircraft, afraid that they might not make it aboard.[49]

Understandably, the relief felt at being flown out of the pocket – *escaping* it – was considerable; one officer who left Gumrak on board a He 111 in mid-January carrying important documents for army group headquarters found that as the Heinkel climbed above the cloud and into bright sunshine it felt as if he 'had been reborn'.[50]

A truly shocking report was issued by Schulz on the 19th which reveals in a 'snapshot' the appalling reality of just how staggeringly low aircraft readiness was. In fact, if Schulz's figures are accurate, it is amazing that any airlift was being achieved at all. The nine Ju 52/3m *Gruppen* assigned to the operation, which comprised I. and II./KG.z.b.V.1 and KGr.z.b.V.9, 50, 102, 172, 500, 700 and 900, had a total strength of 386 aircraft. Of this total, 101 – or less than a third – were at the front airfields. Of these machines, just 11 were classified as *einsatzbereit* or operationally ready, beyond 12 aircraft which had been deployed on the previous operation. Put another way, that was a readiness level of just 2.84 per cent of total strength, or 10.8 per cent of aircraft available on the supply airfields.

The He 111 grouping at Novocherkassk (I. and III./KG 55, I./KG 100 and I., II. and III./KG 27) had 58 aircraft on the field, 24 of which were operationally ready, or 41.3 per cent, while at the Voroshilovgrad grouping (II./KG 53, III./KG 4 and KGr.z.b.V.5, 20 and 23), of 85 aircraft on the field, 19 were operationally ready, or 22.35 per cent. Just one of I./FKG 50's troublesome He 177s was ready of 14, and two of 19 Fw 200s of KGr.z.b.V.200.

During the evening of 19 January Fiebig reported to Milch by telephone that of 23 He 111s that went out, nine had succeeded in landing at Gumrak, ten were still out and four had turned back; of six Ju 52/3ms that went out, two turned back and four had landed. The single He 177 which went out turned back, with Oberleutnant Lawatschek experiencing another mishap when the tail assembly of his Heinkel collapsed during landing at Kirovograd, having caught the hangar roof. The aircraft took off the next day for Zaporozhye, but it crashed on landing there, killing four of its crew. No Fw 200s were committed. According to Fiebig:

Two aircraft remained at Gumrak because of damage from artillery. Five other He 111s were lost as a result of damage from shell fire. For today, 22 He 111s, 8 Ju 52s and 8 Fw 200s are ready to take off. Because of bad weather at the advance airfields, night missions will not start before midnight. Tonight, a landing path will be set up with 10 tank lights. The light radio beacon and direction finder are in operation tonight; the heavy radio beacon is not.[51]

Milch responded:

If there is only light artillery fire at Gumrak field tonight, the aircraft are to land. If the artillery fire is heavy, the supplies are to be dropped.

Von Richthofen was becoming irritated and losing patience with the intrusion of Milch and his staff into his mobile headquarters, as well as Milch poking, what he saw, as an unqualified and inexperienced nose into operational affairs which simply resulted in precious time being lost. He wrote on the 20th:

For every item for which one really only has two minutes of time, you need several hours. In addition to that is the congestion in the train which has not been fitted out to cater for all these shiny personalities. I simply cannot stand by anymore and listen to all the waffle and the many drawn-out discussions. Things that are understood are chewed through six times and, in fact, things wouldn't happen at all if they weren't done like they had been previously.[52]

One of the things that was still being 'chewed over' was the deployment of gliders. In this regard although Milch continued to champion their usage to augment the air supply operation, circumstances conspired against such plans. In a discussion with Milch during the evening of the 20th, however, Oberst Petersen advised that with the shifting westwards of the supply bases, the ageing Do 17E/P tow-aeroplanes needed for the DFS 230s no longer had the range to reach Stalingrad. Furthermore, the towing of Go 242s by He 111s and Me 321s by pairs of He 111s could only take place safely in daylight if fighter escort was available and at night, without the need for instrument flying, only when there was moonlight, good visibility and scattered cloud. And according to Petersen, the huge, six-engined Me 323 (the powered version of the Me 321) could only be used 'under conditions of certain loss', since the type's range was no longer adequate either.

But Milch was like a dog with a bone. Whilst he conceded that no Me 323s should be sent for missions to the pocket, he pressed ahead with arrangements to bring in the smaller DFS and Gotha gliders operating with combined Bf 109 and Bf 110 escort. He also still believed that unpowered Me 321s could be towed under moonlight, and in this regard efforts for Gigants to join the airlift had already been attempted as early as 10 January, when two of the huge gliders left southern Germany for Stalino towed by five-engined He 111 Zwilling tugs on what was to prove a futile exercise. One of the craft, piloted by Unteroffizier Fritz Hübsch of *Sonderstaffel* (GS) 4, took off from Lechfeld, in Bavaria, on what Hübsch described as 'an extremely risky mission'. The Me 321 was loaded with 20 tons of supplies, and must have made for a spectacular sight as it was hauled into the air by a Zwilling. It was a journey of more than 1,000 km to Minsk, and from there to Zhitomir, on the first stage of the journey to Stalingrad, but because of the appalling weather the glider was forced to stay on the ground at Zhitomir, where it remained until after the German pocket had been overrun. Yet Hübsch's effort to reach Stalingrad in an Me 321 would not be the only attempt over the coming month.[53]

Milch told Oberstleutnant Christian at the *Luftwaffenführungsstab*, 'We want to use cargo gliders, convoying them under the protection of long-range single- and twin-engined fighters. It is particularly important that Bf 109s with auxiliary fuel tanks be brought in as quickly as possible'.

A meeting took place in the train on the 20th between an irritated Milch and the Chief Engineer of *Luftflotte* 4, Generalingenieur Dr.-Ing. Weidinger.[54] Milch asked him, 'How is the poor state of readiness on the part of the Ju 52 units to be explained?' Weidinger replied, 'The units are not controlled effectively by their commanders. The commanders do not push things sufficiently. The technical officers are evidently not equal to the task'. Milch responded, 'I will replace Oberst Morzik with a more energetic officer so that the Ju 52 units may finally be brought under firm control. Measures for increasing readiness are already underway. Thirty senior maintenance men for Ju 52s are being brought out from Germany by the Quartermaster General via Krakow'.

But if Milch had read *Luftflotte* 4's readiness report of the day before, he would have seen the comment appended by Schulz's staff:

> As a result of the low level of operational readiness of the Ju 52 units due to the cold and enemy bombing attacks, only a small number could be deployed on the night of 18 January.[55]

It seems, however, that events overtook Milch's decision-making, which he had actually made the previous day. In accordance with his request to von Manstein, at some point during the 20th, army commanders on the Donets defensive line warned that enemy tanks could break through and turn towards the field at Voroshilovgrad, and therefore the field should be evacuated of He 111s. This was enough for Fiebig, and he ordered von Beust to make preparatory arrangements to pull his units back to Konstantinovka, although for the time being Voroshilovgrad would continue to operate. As for other units, some Ju 52/3ms would still use Sverevo as a forward base, such as those from II./KG.z.b.V.1, but all other aircraft would operate from further back at Taganrog and Makeyevka. In any case, all aircraft needing more than 24 hours of repair work went back to Taganrog.

In terms of the airlift command, however, perhaps inevitably a sense of 'too many cooks in the kitchen' had developed, and Fiebig had begun to feel sidelined:

Milch's assignment to the supply operation has still not brought about any clear line of action. Everything is in a state of confusion because he does not have any capable staff. Orders are given directly to the *Lufttransportführers* without informing us; we don't receive any orders.

He advised von Richthofen of his feelings, with the net result that he was relieved of his responsibility for the airlift and returned to overseeing combat operations of VIII.*Fliegerkorps*. Fiebig's supply staff was duly assigned to the *Sonderstab Milch*. Fiebig seemed to be pragmatic about this:

It is hard for me to give up my job, but it is not in the interests of the situation as a whole to have three staffs working. There must be one clear organisation, in order to exert a direct effect on all the units concerned.[56]

To try to avoid the discord over the readiness and functionality of Gumrak, a small team assembled by Morzik and led by Major Ernst Maess, the *Gruppenkommandeur* of I./KG.z.b.V.1, flew into the pocket to carry out an inspection and assessment of a proposed new landing site at Stalingradskaya. Fiebig had his doubts. 'In case of emergency they are supposed to be taken out. I don't believe that. I think they are being sacrificed'. He would be proved wrong.

During daylight hours on the 20th, 53 He 111s had been sent out from Stalino, Novocherkassk and Voroshilovgrad, along with two He 177s (although 17 aircraft did not complete the mission), and more were slated to go to Stalingrad that night. However, attrition was continuing to gnaw away at the Luftwaffe's efforts: three Ju 52/3ms, at least one known to have been from KGr.z.b.V.700 which had landed at Gumrak, were forced to remain in the pocket from the night operation because of damage inflicted by enemy artillery and taxiing accidents. Shortly before midnight He 111s of I./KG 100 made two supply runs to Gumrak and brought back wounded with them. However, the He 111H-16 of Oberleutnant Georg Puff of 2./KG 100 failed to return and was posted missing.[57] Altogether that night, *Luftflotte* 4 carried out a total of 113 sorties, of which 31 aircraft landed in the pocket, 43 air-dropped supplies, 23 were shot down by anti-aircraft fire or destroyed and 16 were still out or unaccounted for.[58]

In a tetchy conversation with Oberstleutnant Christian, calling on behalf of the *Führer* who wanted to know whether a second field was being established in the pocket to increase supply volume, Milch responded:

Gorodishche is being considered, but there is a shortage of manpower to set it up. Large quantities of supplies are being flown in, but we are afraid that it is not all being picked up and distributed.

Please tell the *Führer* that there is not a man who is not giving his utmost to the supply operation. What our people are accomplishing here is more than has ever been done before in this respect in this war.

As testament to that, on the night of 21–22 January – the last night Gumrak remained in German control – 59 He 111s went out from Novocherkassk and 15 from Voroshilovgrad, with 21 landing fully laden.[59] Even 14 Ju 52/3ms managed to land. The other aircraft, as well as five Fw 200s, air-dropped. No fewer than 355 wounded were brought back.[60] Next morning, 6.*Armee* signalled an urgent requirement for around 60 tons of light field howitzer ammunition. Such ammunition was stored in Rostov. In order to maximise available aircraft, Milch ordered that those Ju 52/3ms not capable of flying to the pocket were to ferry the ammunition from Rostov to Sverevo, and from there *Kesselklar* Junkers would fly it to Stalingrad. The ammunition would also be flown in He 111s from Rostov direct to Stalingrad, and on return these machines would land at Novocherkassk, which was still in German hands – just.

On the morning of 22 January Milch spoke personally with Major Coelestin von Zitzewitz, OKH Liaison Officer to 6.*Armee*, who had received orders to fly out of the pocket in order to report to Hitler and Zeitzler. Zitzewitz gave a stark summary of conditions in the pocket, although much of it Milch was already well aware of:

> The physical condition of the troops in the pocket has deteriorated sharply during the past few days. The troops have practically no ammunition. It must also be taken into account that Gumrak will probably be lost today. The supply is threatened because as a result of the shortage of fuel and the snowdrifts, the supplies dropped are not picked up. There are scarcely any tanks which are still useable because they have been standing idle too long as a result of the shortage of fuel. Gorodishche airfield can no longer be considered for landing as the main line of resistance is now at that point. A new airfield at Stalingradskaya is in preparation.

Milch attempted to spin a gloss over what was a dreadful situation, promising the imminent arrival of large-capacity cargo gliders, additional dropping points and long-range escort fighters. But this cut little ice with Zitzewitz, who told the Generalfeldmarschall that the minimum requirement for 100,000 men per day was 200 tons, comprising 100 tons of food, 60 tons of ammunition and 20 tons of fuel and miscellaneous supplies, but, in any case, 'there was scarcely a healthy man left; everyone has suffered frostbite at least'.[61]

Meanwhile, a copy of Major Thiel's report on his visit to the pocket landed on von Manstein's desk. The army group commander was unconvinced by it, and told Milch so, not particularly aiding Luftwaffe–Army relations. 'Major Thiel apparently takes a very negative attitude', von Manstein commented to Milch by telephone on the morning of the 21st, 'and shows an inclination to consider that the existing difficulties cannot be eliminated'.

A short time later, Major von Zitzewitz reached the *Führerhauptquartier* at Rastenburg, and was ushered in to meet Hitler, Zeitzler and Schmundt. As he had done with Milch the previous day, he spoke plainly:

> My *Führer*, I feel bound to tell you that there is no point in your appealing to the troops to fight to the last round, firstly, because they are no longer physically capable of doing so, and secondly, because they haven't got a last round to fight with![62]

36 The fuselage of Fw 200C-3 Wk-Nr.0049 F8+FW of 1./KGr.z.b.V.200 broke when the aircraft landed at Zaporozhye, having been overloaded at Sslawenskaya on 12 February 1943. (Goss Collection)

37 Ju 290A-1 Wk-Nr.0152 SB+QB at Stalino in January 1943 with its hydraulic, rear *Trapoklappe* loading ramp lowered. (EN Archive)

Top and Above 38 and 39 The impressive sight of one of the two Ju 290s to reach Stalino for the airlift operation. Five Fw 200 Condors of KGr.z.b.V.200 can also be seen in the background. (EN Archive)

40 Major Kurt Schede, seen centre saluting, commander of the
He 177-equipped I./FKG 50. (Goss Collection)

41 Marked with the unit's emblem on its nose, this He 177A-1 of I./FKG 50 awaits its
next mission after being cleared of snow in Russia in early 1943. (EN Archive)

42 Anti-shipping ace Major Heinrich Schlosser succeeded Kurt Schede as commander of I./FKG 50 in January 1943. (Goss Collection)

43 Oberleutnant Adolf Spohr of I./FKG 50 was a highly qualified instructor pilot who, earlier in the war, had instructed at training and blind-flying schools in France and Germany. (Ruiz Collection)

44 Go 242 gliders are visible just beyond the nose of a Ju 290 at Stalino. (EN Archive)

45 The bleak scene at Zaporozhye-Süd in the winter of 1942–43 as two He 177s are prepared for another mission. (EN Archive)

46 Amidst the freezing conditions of the Russian winter of 1942–43, mechanics remove a protective tarpaulin from the starboard engine of a He 177A-1 belonging to I./FKG 50. (EN Archive)

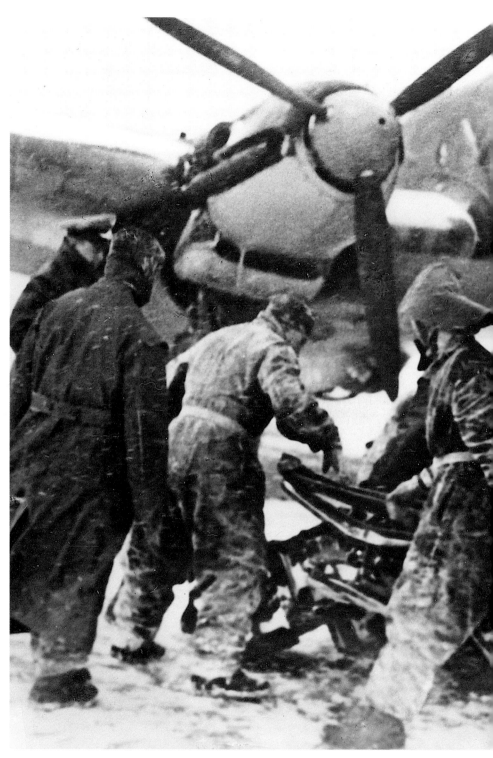

47 Groundcrew battle wintry conditions whilst preparing a He 111 for
the supply run to Stalingrad. (Author's Collection)

48 Reichsmarschall Göring (left) and Generalfeldmarschall Erhard Milch, the man who was despatched to 'rescue' and energise the airlift at Stalingrad. He failed. (EN Archive)

49 With its fuselage door open and what appears to be a crewman and sack in the doorframe, possibly ready for an air-drop, a grimy Ju 52/3m, 1Z+KY, of 14./KG.z.b.V.1 passes low overhead. (EN Archive)

50 A Ju 52/3m makes a low-level air-drop. (EN Archive)

51 A large supply crate intended for air-dropping awaits fixing to the external centreline mounts of a He 111. (Author's Collection)

52 A soldier uses all his strength to pull a heavy air-drop container from deep snow using one of its parachute lines. (Author's Collection)

53 A Ju 52/3m apparently photographed after having been attacked by Soviet fighters during the supply operation at Stalingrad. (EN Archive)

54 Watched by a ground-controller, three He 111s of KG 27 taxi out in a flurry of snow. (Author's Collection)

55 A He 111 is guided in over packed snow. (Goss Collection)

56 Following an attack by the VVS, a wrecked He 111 and other debris litter the frozen expanse of one of the supply airfields. (Goss Collection)

57 Forlorn soldiers from 6.*Armee* march away from the ruins into Soviet captivity following the battle of Stalingrad. (ullstein bild via Getty Images)

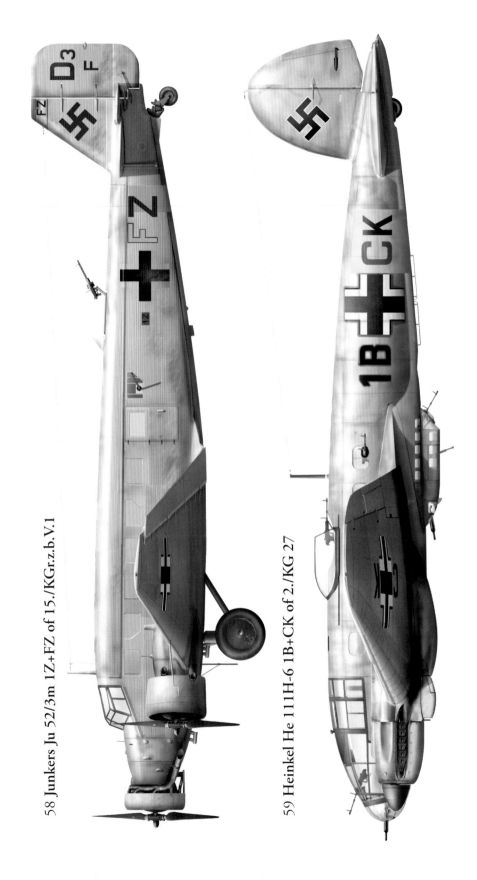

58 Junkers Ju 52/3m 1Z+FZ of 15./KGr.z.b.V.1

59 Heinkel He 111H-6 1B+CK of 2./KG 27

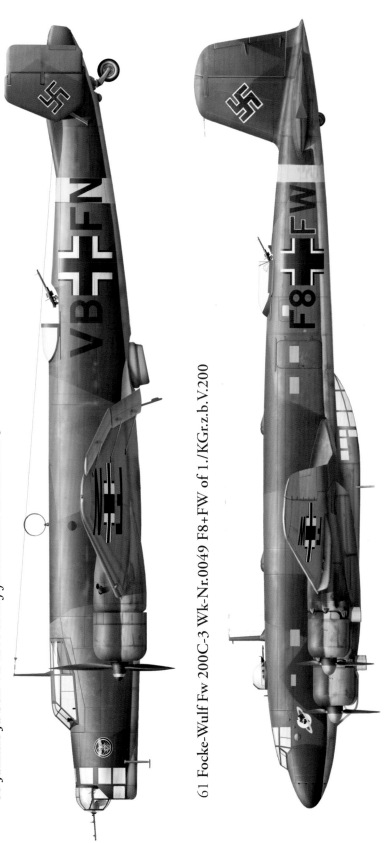

60 Junkers Ju 86E VB+FN of *Luftflottennachrichtenschule* 3

61 Focke-Wulf Fw 200C-3 Wk-Nr.0049 F8+FW of 1./KGr.z.b.V.200

62 Heinkel He 177A-1 E8+HK of I./FKG 50

63 Junkers Ju 290A-1 Wk-Nr.0152 SB+QB

⁶⁴ *Mischlastabwurfbehälter 1000*

(Mixed load air-drop container)

Maximum Loaded Weight: Approx 1,000 kg
(empty with parachute = 280 kg)
Loading: 720 kg ammunition and other supplies
(usable capacity 420 ltr)
Dimensions: 3,174 x 660 mm

Wooden construction with metal frame; for dropping at low-level around 100 m. High-altitude drops possible at over 1,000 m.

Direction of flight and drop
←

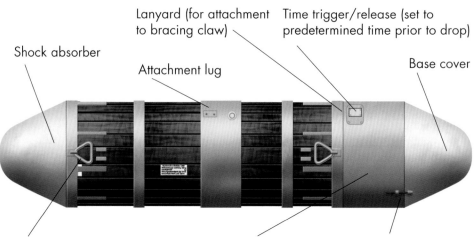

Lanyard (for attachment to bracing claw)

Time trigger/release (set to predetermined time prior to drop)

Shock absorber

Attachment lug

Base cover

Locking bracket

Parachute holder

Emergency pulley (bind into the emergency pull hook)

Inscription on the container:
Mixed load drop container 1000
Maximum permissible payload
700 kg
Payload .... kg
Dropping speed 350 km/h
Drop height: Not less than 200 m

The container is opened by removing the locking brackets. Press in the screws in the upper part of the bolt with a screwdriver or a coin and turn them 90 degrees, then pull out the bolt.

Meanwhile Pickert, who had been ordered by Milch on the 19th to travel to East Prussia to brief Hitler and Göring on the situation at Stalingrad, and on the airlift, had arrived at Berlin's Silesian Station, having flown into Berlin-Staaken. As he waited on the freezing platform for the nightly train to Rastenburg, a railway police sergeant called him to the station guard room and handed the Luftwaffe general the telephone receiver. Pickert listened to what he was told, gave his understanding and replaced the receiver:

> New situation. No departure. I am greatly worried about the situation in the East. It has grown worse since I left![63]

Pickert kicked his heels for 48 hours, both irritated and uncertain as to what to do. After two days, and with no further instructions, he telephoned Major Bernd von Brauchitsch, Göring's adjutant, to find out what he *should* do. He was advised that his planned report was no longer required because 'the situation had changed'.[64] Furthermore, the Reichsmarschall could see no value in his report. Pickert was both upset and furious. He later told Milch that the Luftwaffe troops at Stalingrad 'had certainly earned the right to have a report made on their behalf to the Commander-in-Chief of the Luftwaffe', but Milch simply told Pickert that 'as a soldier he was only supposed to do his duty, and not to express criticism'. Pickert was promptly sent off to oversee the air defence of the Taman Peninsula.

Late on 21 January, the strip at Gumrak, which had been pounded by *Katyusha* rockets, effectively ceased operations and was captured by infantry from the Soviet 65th Army the next day. The 500 German wounded who had been left at the field hospital there listened helplessly to the engines of Soviet tanks as they rumbled through the snow close by, heading east along the railway line, closer to the ruins of Stalingrad.

As predicted by von Zitzewitz, plans to utilise Gorodishche airfield as an alternative had to be abandoned because it lay in the path of the ground-fighting, and so an optimistically titled 'auxiliary airfield' was hastily prepared at Stalingradskaya, five kilometres south of Gorodishche, a site closer to the city. Kühl recounted:

> Only the most experienced crews were authorised to land there [which at least minimised losses through accidents]. With snow at a depth of 50 cm, it was not possible to harden the surface properly with a steamroller. Consequently, some aircraft only travelled 50 m along the 'runway' before ploughing to a stop. The greatest difficulty was on take-off, especially at night. The Heinkel crews themselves set about laying out two flare paths, but this comprised just a few lamps which quickly became lost in the snowdrifts. Despite such efforts, the number of aircraft lost as a result of crashes and accidents due to shell craters was comparable to Gumrak. Twenty-two He 111s landed at Stalingradskaya during its brief period of operation.[65]

Five of these aircraft and one Ju 52/3m crashed and remained in place, but their crews were flown out on board their comrades' machines. The frozen snow that lay over the runway was bordered by many craters which were potentially lethal to aircraft attempting to taxi. The brief statement on *Luftflotte* 4's daily report for the night of 21–22 January said it all:

> Supply during the night of 21–22 January was performed under the most difficult weather conditions (50 m cloud base and heavy icing on the Ju 52s, which experienced more than 3 cm ice accumulation). They could only be used in the first part of the night.
>
> The new Stalingradskaya airfield went into operation on 22 January. Despite good unloading organisation, difficulties arose as a result of the poor quality of the ground (snowdrifts, bumps, bomb craters).[66]

Despite all the meteorological adversity, and with the loss of Gumrak, according to Milch's diary, 'Supply aircraft are being sent out in the greatest possible numbers' presumably to air-drop.

There were 339 aircraft in total reported on the supply airfields on the 22nd – an increase of 31 machines on the figure reported on the 16th.[67] During daylight, aircraft went out from Zaporozhye (two He 177s), Stalino (six He 111s and two Fw 200s), Konstantinovka (four He 111s), Sverevo (22 Ju 52/3ms) and Novocherkassk (45 He 111s). Twenty-three aircraft landed in the pocket. One of these was the He 111 flown by Unteroffizier Peter Adrian of III./KG 55, which left Novocherkassk at 0905 hrs on the 22nd to land at Stalingradskaya at 1045 hrs. Flight engineer Unteroffizier Michael Deiml described the scene that greeted them:

> There, a very sad sight met our eyes. In the icy temperatures of -30°C and lower, we met our soldiers, lightly clad in uniforms of thin material, starving, frozen together and almost motionless. Unloading the provisions containers and bread sacks, a still able Flak captain said that he wanted to give his will, which he had in his overcoat pocket, to the last machine to land. Next day, on our last landing, he was nowhere to be seen. During this stop we had to leave the propellers turning since there was no machine available to warm the engines up. In addition to the provisions, we took fuel from our tanks for the vehicles at the airfield which had run dry. Of the many wounded present, we could only fly a few out with us since we had to take the five men of an aircraft shot down in the pocket. We left at 1125 hrs and landed at Novocherkassk 90 minutes later.[68]

Altogether, 151 wounded troops were lifted out of the pocket that day.

The Stalingrad historiography includes stories of women's fur coats, condoms, Christmas trees and other useless items being dropped into the pocket, thus taking up precious transport space and burning aircraft fuel. The management of goods was, at times, questionable: items such as fresh meat and canned vegetables were often sent out, but these contained high water content which increased weight (not to mention the tins). More use of dehydrated food concentrates should have been considered, which were available to parachute units and U-boat crews, but which were rarely seen in the pocket. Given the abundant availability of snow-water in the fortress, this was a mystifying omission. On one occasion, Milch claimed to have blocked an excessive delivery of fishmeal into the pocket as a result of pre-flight inspections. He sent the consignment back with orders to have the supply officer hanged.[69]

Another absurd commodity arriving for onward delivery to Stalingrad were bones on the basis that they could be used to make a form of the clear French broth, *Bouillon*. 'This was absolute stupidity', recalled Dr. Heinrich Potthoff, 'as *Bouillon* possesses little nourishment and on top of that, bones took up space and weight in the transports. At Tatsinskaya the transport of bones was firmly rejected'.[70] But as Pickert has remarked in a post-war article, 'The fact that the para-dropped goods now and then contained foolish and unnecessary items is undisputed, but this was an exception which should not be overestimated'.[71]

Conversely, von Richthofen and Dr. Potthoff were involved in an innovative plan to build an experimental 'dry bread facility' at Rostov in which bread could be dried out, leaving a minimal water content and thus reducing weight. On delivery, the bread was rehydrated. The process was successful, but the available facility was simply too small to produce anywhere near the quantities needed.[72]

Late on the 21st, Generalingenieur Dr.-Ing. Weidinger reported the following aircraft reserves in the workshops:

158 Ju 52/3ms
20 of which can go out immediately
59 of which will be ready in three days
54 of which will be ready in 3-14 days
41 of which will not be ready for more than 14 days
3 returned to Germany

131 He 111s
11 of which can go out immediately
37 of which will be ready in three days
42 of which will be ready in 3-14 days
34 of which will not be ready for more than 14 days
7 returned to Germany

Eighty more specialist Ju 52/3m mechanics had also arrived from Germany.

Among those men returning from the pocket on 22 January was Major Ernst Maess of I./KG.z.b.V.1, whom Fiebig believed, incorrectly, would never get back. But what he reported made for grim listening. The new field at Stalingradskaya was, according to Fiebig's account of the *Gruppenkommandeur's* report, 'not very good'. Indeed, on the 22nd, six supply aircraft crash-landed there because of the deep snow and concealed bomb craters. Furthermore, there was only one fuel bowser available to take on fuel from the aircraft tanks. However, Maess had much praise for the ground organisation set up at Gumrak by Oberleutnant Pfeil 'in so far as this was possible under the poor conditions'. Maess reported that:

The unloading was above reproach and was executed quickly. Air-drop containers which fell somewhat away from the target were not used and were lost since they could not be moved because of the shortage of motor fuel and because of the exhaustion of the unloading squads.

When Maess reported to 6.*Armee*, Paulus simply commented, 'Whatever help you are bringing us is too late. We are lost. Our people have no strength left'. Furthermore, when it came to Maess' impressions of 6.*Armee*, the Luftwaffe was accused of not having complied with the *Führer's* promise. Maess painted a desperate picture of the dying soldiers, stating 'They consider themselves as dead already'.[73]

As far as flights to Stalingradskaya were concerned, Milch noted that 'the field is full of holes filled with drifted snow, so that night landings must reckon with heavy losses. Tonight there will be only dropping operations'.

On 22 January the *Lufttransportführer Stalino* and his units relocated to Zaporozhye to become the *Lufttransportführer Zaporozhye*. Here, Major Willers' sphere of command embraced I./FKG 50 under Major Schlosser, whose operations he had to coordinate, as well as the local Luftwaffe workshop detachment, a group of mechanics flown in from Lufthansa, a small detachment of civilian fitters from Focke-Wulf and an assigned army motor transport unit comprising 26 vehicles.

Morzik made sure that Willers received good cooperation from the administration staff of the joint Luftwaffe/Army supply office at Zaporozhye. This worked well, and Willers was assigned an efficient army liaison officer. The latter ensured that Willers received notification of the numbers of wounded to be expected ahead of each aircraft returning from the pocket, and the appropriate vehicles were always made ready. Fortunately, as well, the airfield infrastructure was far superior to those at the other fields: engines could be serviced or changed in the shelter of a hangar, while personnel were quartered in nearby stone buildings with doors and glass in the windows. The teams from Lufthansa and Focke-Wulf made up for the poor levels of training exhibited by the mechanics and technicians from IV./KG 40. The runway was considered by Willers to be 'perfect'.

The five Fw 200s of 2./KGr.z.b.V.200 had finally reached Zaporozhye from Staaken on 21 January. The most common examples of damage to the Condors in Russia occurred to their oil coolers and shock absorbers (caused by oil leakage and the expulsion of compressed air). This latter problem could not be easily rectified until the availability of the aircraft jacking machine, which finally arrived on 19 January because the Ju 52/3m in which it was loaded had been stuck at Radom having suffered damage itself. Attempts to raise collapsed Condors using makeshift, but potentially dangerous, scaffolding and hoists had failed because of the strong prevailing winds on exposed airfields.[74]

Two He 177s of IV./KG 40 were assigned to bolster I./FKG 50, but when these aircraft reached Russia, the net result was that they required almost full-time servicing and repair and only managed one day of airlift operations to Stalingrad.

Meanwhile, more new 'giants' were arriving in the shape of two further Me 321 cargo gliders, each being towed by a pair of He 111s to Makayevka, but Fiebig cautioned Milch that their use at Stalingrad would be 'completely impossible' as there was no level area of the necessary 800–1,000 m in length on which they could land. Milch seemed impervious to Fiebig's warnings.

On the 22nd, Paulus signalled Hitler via OKH:

> Rations exhausted. Over 12,000 unattended wounded in the pocket. What orders should I give to troops who have no more ammunition and are subjected to mass attacks supported by heavy artillery fire?

Hitler responded:

> Surrender is out of the question. The troops will defend themselves to the last. If possible the size of the fortress is to be reduced so that it can be held by the troops still capable of fighting.[75]

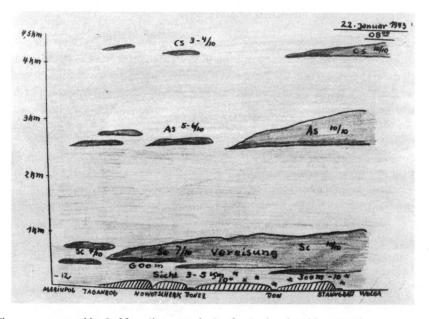

The report prepared by *Luftflotte* 4's meteorologists for *Sonderstab Milch* at 0800 hrs on 22 January 1943 – the day that Paulus advised that 6.*Armee*'s rations were exhausted. 3-4/10th cirrostratus and 5-6/10ths altostratus cloud is shown between 4,000–4,500 m and 2,500 m, respectively, over Taganrog and Novocherkassk, increasing to 10/10ths from the Don to the Volga. Heavy icing covered almost the whole route from Taganrog to Stalingrad and the Volga, with visibility at 3,000–5,000 m over the Donets, falling to just 300 m, and decreasing to ten metres over Stalingrad. Snow was also forecast over the Don and the approach to Stalingrad. This report illustrates how varied the weather could be on the airlift route.

In reviewing operations for the night of 22–23 January, *Luftflotte* 4 stated:

> During the night, the delivery of supplies was severely hampered by snowfall and freezing rain in the take-off area. Supply had to be broken off around 2300. When the weather improved in the take-off area, only the best crews could be deployed. No deployment possible for Ju 52 units because of cloud over Sverevo.

During the 23rd, 25 He 111s flew to Stalingrad from Novocherkassk, 11 from Stalino and 12 from Konstantinovka, while six He 177s managed to get airborne, four of which air-dropped and two turned back (again no Ju 52/3ms flew as there was low cloud and icing at Sverevo). By this stage no effort was made to recover supplies from wrecked aircraft on the ground.[76] The dichotomy between the Luftwaffe's reports and those of 6.*Armee* is highlighted by a message sent by the latter to *Heeresgruppe Don* at 0630 hrs in which it was advised that 'No supplies landed'.[77] But *Luftflotte* 4's daily report states that 8.1 tons of supplies and ammunition were delivered, as well as 9.5 cbm of fuel. Seventy-eight wounded were evacuated.[78] This, despite the fact that there was snow and occasional artillery fire directed at the landing grounds.

Milch duly called Christian and told him:

> A great number of aircraft were sent out to the new Stalingradskaya airfield today (81 altogether, of which 26 are reported as having landed so far). Because of the bad condition of the field, many aircraft crashed on landing, but in spite of that the field is still usable. The weather conditions were unfavourable for the mission.[79]

The crew of Unteroffizier Adrian of II./KG 55 made their last flight to land in the pocket on 23 January. They were one of the 26 aircraft to land at Stalingradskaya.[80] Taking off from Novocherkassk at 0725 hrs, their He 111 put down just under two hours later at 0920 hrs. It was to be a frightening experience, as Unteroffizier Michael Deiml recalled:

> While unloading the bread sacks, we suddenly came under fire from Russian fighters. I jumped out of the aircraft at once and replied with an MG 15. Luckily, neither our aircraft nor its crew, nor any of the wounded lying around us, were hit. Whilst we were there the Russians did not try again. In great haste we finished unloading the bread sacks and suddenly heard a dull thump. Looking towards the direction from where the noise had come, we saw a headless soldier falling near the rotating propellers of the port engine. There was blood on the undercarriage left side, but no other remains visible. Two military police collected and identified the body. Despite the emotion we all felt, we had to unload the rest of the cargo as quickly as possible, for we had to reckon on renewed air attacks by the Russians.

We rolled out to the airstrip with eight wounded aboard. Very many of them, including those we had seen the day before, we had to leave behind in the pocket. Before we took off, Adrian said I should get out and bend one of the elevators at the rear to stop it jamming. It had been damaged on landing by hitting frozen snow standing 30–40 cm high. After opening the entry flap on the lower fuselage I got down, went to the rear of the aircraft and bent the elevator back into shape. While I was doing this, a wounded man stole into the aircraft through the open flap. When I followed him inside he looked at me in agitation, as if fighting for his life, his eyes begging me to let him leave with us. I can never forget that look. Although we were already loaded to the limit, I let him into the interior and said nothing to Unteroffizier Adrian about the additional wounded man. As a result of all these events we had been at the airfield for 90 minutes, and left for our return flight at 1045 hrs. During our short stay at Stalingradskaya we saw no other German aircraft.[81]

It is possible that this was the aircraft which Joachim Wieder, an intelligence officer with 6.*Armee*, has described as 'the last supply aircraft filled to overflowing with wounded'.[82]

While the final aircraft landed in the pocket, two He 177A-1s flew out from Zaporozhye to air-drop supplies. They were flown respectively by the *Staffelkapitän* of 2./FKG 50, a pre-war Lufthansa pilot and veteran of the *Legion Condor* in Spain, Hauptmann Hans-Joachim Dochtermann, and Oberleutnant Adolf Spohr on what was probably his second, but last, mission in Russia. The poor weather meant that the two bombers flew close together on their outward course, but broke up over Stalingrad and then descended through thick cloud. In a subsequent letter to Spohr's widow, Gerda, the following month, Dochtermann described the unfortunate outcome of the mission:

Through the intercom system I told your husband we would carry out the mission individually. We had then to fly at 200–300 m through a very strong and accurate anti-aircraft barrage. Just before the drop, your husband's aircraft emerged from the clouds a few metres away from us. But then quickly we lost each other again due to the bad weather and reduced visibility. After the drop, your husband reported that he could only fly with three engines, and didn't want to be distracted at that moment. I gave him my return flight course and had no further radio communication with him. When I landed at the operational base, I immediately asked my radio operator if he had heard any radio traffic from the other aircraft, which he answered affirmatively. At our command post I was also informed that the aircraft had reported, and that it should already have been about 100–200 km from our base. We had no concerns that your husband would not arrive during the next hour, as I also came back on only three engines. Unfortunately, we waited in vain!

After no news had arrived after two days, every command headquarters was requested to initiate investigations about the whereabouts of the aircraft.

Given the vast expanses and distances in Russia, this involved considerable natural difficulties, so that no search results were advised before our withdrawal. However, there is at least the possibility that something will be found during the spring season, as the aircraft must have been over our territory based on our calculations.[83]

Sadly, neither Adolf Spohr, who had recently become a father, nor his crew were ever found.

That day, as the headquarters of *Luftflotte* 4 pulled back more than 100 km west along the coast of the Sea of Azov from Taganrog to Mariupol, Soviet forces broke through the western perimeter of the pocket and 6.*Armee's* defence fell apart as it withdrew 'the southern part of the fortress to prepared positions on the edge of the city'.[84]

17

Fading Signals

24 January–2 February 1943

At around 2200 hrs on 23 January, General Hube's liaison officer to *Heeresgruppe Don* relayed to the headquarters of *Luftflotte* 4 the depressing news that:

> The western front of the fortress has been pushed back following heavy fighting. Two pockets have thus been formed. The northern pocket includes the Gorodishche and tractor plant areas, the southern pocket, and the southern part of the municipal area of Stalingrad.[1]

This being the case, Milch wanted to use He 111s and He 177s to carry out both bombing missions against enemy concentrations on the 'western front' of what was still being termed optimistically a 'fortress' and to drop supplies in order 'to provide relief and to boost morale'. Although the He 177s could indeed be employed as bombers, they had been found to be totally unsuited to the transport role during the 20 supply sorties the aircraft had completed to date.

Bearing in mind that the first four aircraft that managed to fly over the fortress on the 24th were unable to see the ground through the fog and wintry gloom, even when flying at very low altitude, Milch's intention was optimistic given that the 'front' was now just west of Gorodishche. Nevertheless, for the next four days, the He 177s bombed targets around the city with 250-kg and 500-kg bombs, as well as one mission carried out along with Ju 88s of KG 51 in which 128 SD 50 anti-personnel bombs were dropped by five He 177s in the Pitomnik area. Further bombing operations were carried out, as well as the occasional reconnaissance mission for He 111s dropping supplies, but these resulted in additional losses accruing.

In a depressing illustration of the severe wear and tear that the transport units had suffered, that day *Luftflotte* 4 reported 308 Ju 52/3ms on strength, of which 51 were operational, and 355 He 111s, of which just 55 were operational.[2] Generalingenieur Dr.-Ing. Weidinger reported to Milch the following situation with regard to Ju 52/3ms:[3]

> 30 available at Sverevo
> 21 available at Taganrog-West

25 not flight-ready at Sverevo, of which 21 repairable

73 not flight-ready at Taganrog-West, of which:

    23 ready in 24 hours

    38 ready in three days

    12 ready in 14 days

    (149 aircraft in total, of which 51 available immediately)

Plus: 144 available in *Luftgau* area

    15 immediately ready for collection

    50 ready for collection in three days

    34 ready for collection in 3–14 days

    42 ready for collection in more than 14 days

    5 not available in other areas

    13 under repair in the Reich

    Total of 308 aircraft immediately available for supply

The following figures applied to the He 111s:

Immediately available at **Novocherkassk**	18
Available after 24 hrs	17
Unavailable (flight ready)	14
Immediately available at **Konstantinovka**	23
Available after 24 hrs	6
Available in three days	21
Immediately available at **Stalino**	14
Unavailable (flight ready)	7
Available after 24 hrs	11
Available within 1–24 hrs	28
Available	55
Unavailable	104

Supply operations on the morning of the 24th were almost completely paralysed by the weather, although throughout the day a single Fw 200, three He 111s and three Ju 52/3ms succeeded in making air-drops over the ruined city area in daylight and through clouds while being fired at by Russian anti-aircraft guns. Because of the heights of the buildings, however, it was impossible to fly at low altitude, and the Ju 52/3ms were forced to drop their supplies from altitudes of 50–80 m above the ruins, but at least the new types of supply sacks were equipped with parachutes. However, frequently loads had to be dropped by hand by pushing them through fuselage doors or out of bomb-bays, although communication from fore to aft in an aircraft over the location and timing of a drop was often difficult. Even a slight error in dropping accuracy could cause supplies to land some distance from the intended drop-point. Furthermore,

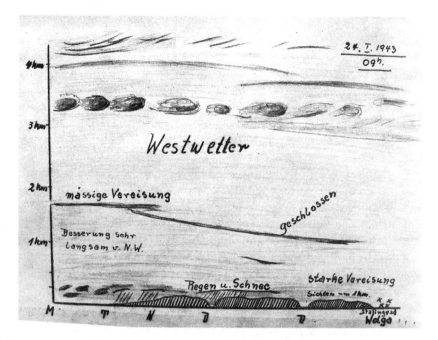

The report prepared by *Luftflotte* 4's meteorologists for *Sonderstab Milch* at 0900 hrs on 24 January 1943. The weather was prevailing from the west, with severe airborne icing at 2,000 m, but with conditions slowly expected to improve from the north-west. There was also rain and snow at 250 m, with more icing over the terrain approaching Stalingrad and the Volga. The weather effectively brought a halt to airlift operations.

100-kg aerial delivery sacks proved too unwieldy for dropping, whereas the 50-kg type was more practical.

One alarming hazard experienced by crews attempting to drop parachute-equipped containers was when the parachute opened prematurely *inside* the aircraft during flight. This would happen during the low-speed approach to the drop point by a He 111 when its bomb-bay doors were open in readiness for dropping. Even pulling the emergency release lever would fail to free a container because the force of the airstream into the opened chute resulted in it becoming caught in the bomb-bay. Occasionally, a Heinkel's flight engineer would be able, with some difficulty and with a considerable amount of energy, to cut the lines to the parachute. Major Uhl of KGr.z.b.V.5 warned that close attention had to be paid to ensuring that parachutes were properly secured within the supply containers, particularly in the case of containers that had seen repeated use.[4]

Meanwhile, Göring bombarded Milch with telegrams, and Hitler had called early that morning wanting to know the latest situation. 'He was hoping for a miracle', Milch recorded, 'But I saw no chance'.

By the end of daylight, another 20 He 111s, seven Ju 52/3ms and three Fw 200s had made it to Stalingrad despite 'the very worst weather conditions' according to Fiebig. Six aircraft dropped supplies over the city, but their crews were unable to identify any drop points. With the arrival of darkness, operations were discontinued because of the lack of radio guidance, heavy icing and low cloud.

Despite temperatures of -20°C, which made pre-flight preparation very challenging, He 111s commenced flights to the pocket in formation because of clearing skies from 0230 hrs on the 25th, dropping supplies over the southern outskirts of Stalingrad. The bombers ran into strong VVS nightfighter opposition and anti-aircraft fire, but escaped without loss. However, the clear weather meant that the slower, less defensible Ju 52/3ms and Fw 200s were limited to night-flying. Contact between the two pockets had been severed and the 'frontlines' were now very fluid, and thus hard to identify from the air. On the ground, the northern pocket had contracted further under enemy pressure and the German remnants were now holding out in the Dzerzhinsky Tractor Factory.

During daylight hours (on 25 January) and in improved weather, 28 He 111s were sent out, 14 of which had returned safely by 1845 hrs, while nine were forced to turn back and five were still out by that time. Probably on account of the low serviceability figures, one formation of seven Heinkels was assembled from aircraft drawn from different *Geschwader*. In a He 111 of 2./KG 27 one member of the crew recalled how:

> In bright sunshine and without fighter escort, we flew east. Over a wide, swampy area to the south-east of Stalingrad, which was crossed by the many tributaries of the Volga, we intended to descend to air-drop altitude. However, we were greeted by intense Flak so that we were forced to turn away, our formation scattered.

But as the German bombers turned back to the west, they were suddenly engaged by VVS fighters and once more closed up for defence:

> As a result of our fierce defensive fire, the Russians left us unmolested. But it became clear that daylight operations were no longer possible.[5]

Three Fw 200s were forced to turn back for the same reasons. No drop markers or combat activity was observed on the ground in either pocket.

That night, Oberst Wolf-Dietrich Wilcke, the fighter ace and illustrious *Geschwaderkommodore* of JG 3, made his timely arrival at Milch's new command centre at Mariupol to discuss fighter operations over Stalingrad. Wilcke had been awarded the Swords to his Knight's Cross with Oak Leaves on 23 December and his personal victory tally stood at 156 enemy aircraft shot down. He had arrived as the commander of a small, composite fighter force, hastily assembled from just six Bf 109G-2s of *Stab*/JG 3 and five Bf 110G-2s drawn from I./ZG 1, all fitted with long-range tanks which Milch had badgered Jeschonnek and Christian for. They had eventually relented, despite pressure for fighters on the northern sector of the Russian Front. 'There will be a long-range fighter mission over Stalingrad tomorrow', Milch told his staff confidently. 'The single-engined fighters will engage the enemy in the air and the twin-engined fighters will attack the occupied airfields'.[6]

It seems from surviving records in Milch's diary that by this point there was a tacit acceptance that the end in Stalingrad was imminent. On the 25th, 6.*Armee* requested the Luftwaffe to drop only food, as ammunition was no longer required because there were no longer enough guns left with which to fight.[7]

At the headquarters of *Luftflotte* 4 the decision was taken to divert any DFS 230 and Me 321 cargo gliders that were not required for the air supply operation or any powered aircraft that were not 'in a good enough condition for missions to the pocket' to the *Luftflotte*, which, under orders from Göring, would deploy them in aid of 1.*Panzerarmee* in its move out of the Caucasus from Krasnodar to Kerch and Mariupol. Aside from anything else, the trains on which these craft had arrived needed to be unloaded and freed up for the carriage of supplies. Furthermore, the idea of sending out little Fi 156 Storch fitted with long-range tanks to airlift 'specially designated individual soldiers' from the fortress was abandoned for various practical reasons.

Over the night of 25–26 January, 75 aircraft took off for the pocket – 27 He 111s from Novocherkassk, 12 from Konstantinovka, nine from Stalino and a single Heinkel from Makejewka, along with 21 Ju 52/3ms from Sverevo and five Fw 200s from Stalino. Forty-five aircraft completed the mission, dropping 45 tons of supplies, although fog had set in at Sverevo from 2300 hrs resulting in only 21 Ju 52/3ms being able to fly. Nevertheless, Fiebig thought the night's operations had, in the main, 'worked out well'.[8] But Milch, as ever, wanted more: 'Every crew must fly at least one mission today, since we have more crews available than aircraft', he told Hauptmann Heinz-Günter Amelung, a veteran Stuka pilot and Knight's Cross-holder who had been seconded to his staff from *Luftflotte* 4, on the morning of the 26th. 'If Sverevo continues to have fog and Novocherkassk is clear, the Ju 52/3ms should take off from there'. Milch also wanted the Junkers loaded with the new air-drop sacks that had arrived.

During the morning of the 26th Weidinger advised that 31 Ju 52/3ms were ready at Sverevo, to which another 34 had been ferried in and were being checked and prepared. There were in total 96 Ju 52/3ms and 47 He 111s operationally ready. Milch was unimpressed, and in an irate telephone conversation an hour later vented his anger at Morzik on the previous night's performance:

Milch:	'Of 62 Ju 52/3ms which were fit for service, only 21 were sent out and ten of them turned back. Why?'
Morzik:	'After the aircraft had been standing at Sverevo for a short time, the engines would not start because of the cold.'
Milch:	'I demand that missions operate very differently tonight. Every pilot who turns back without adequate reasons will be court-martialled. Ninety-eight Ju 52s are ready for missions today.'
Morzik:	'There are 66 Ju 52s on the field at present, 26 of them suitable for missions. Yesterday there were only 41 aircraft which were suitable for missions to the pocket, and 21 of them were used.

	The other 20 had ignition trouble caused by the sudden change in the weather.'
Milch:	'The He 111 units send out many more aircraft (last night they sent out 51 sorties with 47 serviceable aircraft), and it is no easier for them. I demand that tonight everything humanly possible be done. I have the impression that some of the commands are not functioning properly. It is also absolutely incomprehensible to me that Major Maess can be sent into the fortress.'
Morzik:	'Except for Major Maess, all commands are functioning properly.'
Milch:	'I do not fail to comprehend the difficulties of your improvised operation, and I realise perfectly that losses are inevitable in rendering assistance to our hard-fighting comrades in 6.*Armee*. I hope that you are a stern and strict commander.'

After returning to the Reich in February, Milch told attendees at one of his production conferences that the Ju 52/3m units were hopeless at improvising and that he had to 'club some sense into them'. He arranged more accommodation, and enforced upon them the need to use the correct cold-start procedures – about which many of the crews arriving from North Africa were ignorant – and if they did not do so, the threat was execution.[9]

Morzik was given some credence when Major Johannes Planert, a flight engineering officer from the staff of *Luftflotte* 4 who had 'received the assignment of increasing mechanical preparedness of the Ju 52 units at Sverevo and of assisting the *Lufttransportführer* at Sverevo' returned to Mariupol that evening from the base where he made an independent assessment of the situation affecting the aircraft there. He reported to Milch:

Ju 52s have difficulty in taking off because of the deep snow. Crystals form in the carburettors [after take-off]. Several mechanics have suffered frostbite because of the intense cold. There is only one very small building for the heating trucks. The servicing personnel for the heating trucks do not have adequate winter clothing.

Thirty minutes later, Hauptmann i.G. Hans-Theodor Meffert, the efficient Operations Officer at VIII.*Fliegerkorps*, informed Milch that 69 aircraft were so far ready for the forthcoming night's operation, 21 of them Ju 52/3ms, but that combined combat and transport missions by He 111s would not be possible because of a lack of dropping equipment.

But all this activity was becoming academic because of events taking place on the ground. During the day, after fighting elements of the German VIII.*Armeekorps* near Aleksandrovka, the Soviet 62nd Army captured the Mamayev-Kurgan and its 13th Guards Rifle and 284th Rifle Divisions linked up with armoured units of the 21st Army. In doing so, they cut what remained of the German pockets in two and separated them irrevocably. The northern pocket, some 11 km x 14 km in size, was held by what remained of XI.*Armeekorps* around the tractor works, while the southern pocket was held by 6.*Armee* headquarters and the remnants of IV.,VIII. and LI. *Armeekorps* and XIV.*Panzerkorps*. The landing site at Stalingradskaya was also lost in the process. Russian artillery continued to fire at the already shattered ruins still held by the Germans, while tanks simply drove through weaponless Wehrmacht units, crushing exhausted men in their foxholes, dugouts, trenches and bunkers.

Now even the Heinkels were unable to land, and it was only *Mischlastbehälter* that could be used to drop supplies.[10] However, this method came with a number of difficulties: prearranged drop areas were often hard to identify at times of poor visibility, and although the plan was to assist air-drops by using coloured recognition fires lit in the north and south pockets, frequently the troops on the ground had no means by which to sufficiently mark the drop zone; wind blew containers off course; they became buried in snow, meaning the ground troops could not locate them; a lack of horses and vehicle fuel in the pocket together with the mens' weakened condition meant that searching for, and transporting, the containers was challenging; and containers were often damaged, as were their contents. 6.*Armee* repeatedly asked the Luftwaffe when air-dropping *Mischlastbehälter* to drop parachutes with red identification canopies, but still they came with white ones, which were next to useless against the snow.[11] In an attempt to improve air-drop accuracy, the senior Luftwaffe signals officer in the pocket, Major Freudenfeld, completed work on a drop site in the southern pocket on the 26th.[12]

However, because of the proximity and strength of the Russian anti-aircraft batteries, only once was an air-drop conducted in *Staffel* strength in daylight. Sorties thus became restricted to clear-weather night-flights, and while the Soviet guns were also active at night, except for times when fog and haze obscured the fires, drops were generally effected successfully, adjusting well to the changing parameters of the *Kessel* as a result of the rapidly changing battle situation – another testimony to the skill of the aircrews. It was also usual for He 111s to have to make two approach runs over the drop area to ensure maximum accuracy and Ju 52/3ms, four.[13] Also, once a Heinkel had released its containers, its crew would then throw out further smaller, individual parcels from the aircraft's *Bola* – the ventral gun gondola.

Somewhat surprisingly, prospects for the night of 26–27 January were handsomely exceeded with no fewer than 142 serviceable aircraft undertaking 144 supply sorties (104 He 111 sorties with 80 serviceable aircraft; 35 Ju 52/3m sorties with 57 serviceable aircraft; five Fw 200 sorties with five serviceable aircraft), although 19 turned back. The aircraft dropped 3.96 tons of ammunition, 98.5 tons of general supplies and just under a ton of medical supplies.[14] This was the case because of improved weather, the dropping area in the northern pocket was clearly marked and recognised, and a radio marker also provided guidance intermittently. Of particular note was that Oberst Kühl, the *Lufttransportführer* at Novocherkassk, achieved 65 sorties with just 24 serviceable aircraft.

Despite this effort, Fiebig remained gloomy, if not realistic:

> If only all the supplies dropped could be found. But that is impossible in those ruins on Red Square, the pioneer barracks and the tractor plant. Only a fraction of the supplies will be found. One cannot expect any more.[15]

Indeed, as the German-held territory shrank in size under enemy pressure, it became inevitable that more and more containers landed in territory taken by the Russians. The extent of recovery of containers by German groups in this final period is not known.[16]

Meanwhile, resources were being stretched to the limit: von Richthofen had been agitating for more He 111s to be released from airlift operations in order to be returned to combat duty, where they were badly needed to aid Hoth's 4.*Panzerarmee* which was being pushed back to Rostov. 'Things can only get better when the bulk of the forces are freed up from Stalingrad (He 111)', he noted on the 26th. 'The intention of the Russians to scratch together all their forces in order to enable a breakthrough south of Rostov and to exert pressure on *Heeresgruppe* A is abundantly clear'.[17]

The following day (27th) Hitler issued instructions that 30 He 111s were to be deployed by *Luftflotte* 4 in support of the right flank of 4.*Panzerarmee* – but only for one day.[18] This was just as well, as besides the Russians and the weather, the Luftwaffe supply operation's other continual 'enemy' was availability and serviceability. As an example, on the 27th, the force assigned to the air supply of 6.*Armee* was as follows:

He 111 Total available	= 230
Of which: on the airfields	= 154
Still on operations	= 38
Available for immediate supply operations	= 19
On the airfields, but not available	= 97
On rear area airfields	= 71
In the Reich	= 5
Ju 52/3m Total available	= 331
Of which: on the airfields	= 210
On operations in rear areas	= 17
Available immediately at Taganrog	= 19
On operations from Sverevo	= 4
Available immediately at Sverevo	= 36
On the airfield, but not available at Taganrog	= 105
At Sverevo	= 29
On rear airfields	= 121
In the Reich	= 0
He 177 Total available	= 24
Of which: on the airfields	= 18

Still on operations	= 4
Available for immediate supply operations	= 0
On the airfield, but not available	= 14
On rear area airfields	= 1
In the Reich	= 5
Fw 200 Total available	= 22
Of which: on the airfields	= 20
Still on operations	= 2
Available for immediate supply operations	= 1
On the airfield, but not available	= 17
On rear area airfields	= 1
In the Reich	= 1

At the morning conference of *Sonderstab Milch* on the 27th, Fiebig was aware of the growing enmity between Milch and Morzik, the latter being one of the Luftwaffe's most experienced and capable transport commanders. He reiterated his faith in Morzik as *Lufttransportführer* of the Ju 52/3m units at Sverevo and told Milch, 'A great deal has been done. Sverevo has the best airfield commander. When they were at Tatsinskaya, they did everything possible; at that time they would send out more than 100 aircraft at night'. But Milch was unconvinced – he made the point that 'there remains the fact that on one day 31 serviceable aircraft were brought fresh from Taganrog and that then only a total of 21 aircraft were sent out'.

Sometime after the battle of Stalingrad, on 12 February, a weary and irate Morzik wrote to Hauptmann Meffert at VIII. *Fliegerkorps* expressing his frustration at the way the Ju 52/3m units had been organised throughout the airlift. He offered some practical advice based on his experience in other operations, such as at Demyansk, and in doing so provided a revealing insight into what may have been perceived as 'meddling':

> For the execution of supply missions, such as Stalingrad, a clear, coordinated and rigorous command structure is necessary. A condition for this is that the *Gruppen* are held together as an organic whole, that they are left alone and are deployed in such a way that all superfluous burdens are eliminated. Every displacement of the *Gruppen*, or removal of their *Kommandeuren* and *Staffelkapitänen* for assignment to other tasks, endangers operational readiness, since the vital control that needs to be effected over the crews, as well as their care, will not be available because of the challenges of such deployments, particularly in the case of the z.b.V. units.

The use of different *Kommandeuren* for day and night operations as a doctrine of operational leadership during the Stalingrad airlift destroyed the organisation of the *Gruppen* and took away responsibility from their *Kommandeuren*. The pulling apart of individual *Gruppen* onto two airfields (i.e., advance detachments and follow-on detachments) did not allow the *Kommandeuren* to properly supervise the elements of their *Gruppen* and made overall leadership more difficult for them (such as the issuing of orders, situational awareness, care and reporting). The assembling of nine *Gruppen* on one airfield certainly simplified the issuing of orders, but led to the complete overcrowding of the airfield, billeting problems and, connected to that, a lack of vehicles for transporting crews and technical personnel, as well as difficulties in obtaining an understanding of the technical situation.[19]

By comparison with the effort made by the Ju 52/3m units, on the morning of the 27th, 50 He 111s, representing most of the strength of KG 55, had managed to get airborne without needing a heating truck after applying the correct cold-start procedure, in spite of an outside temperature of -15°C. Furthermore, the *Kommodore*, Oberst Dr. Kühl, had personally flown 65 sorties during the airlift by this point.[20]

In his efforts to support von Manstein, von Richthofen was a little happier:

> It's cold. A very strong wind. In the evening comes the decision that the He 111s are freed up for missions south-east of Rostov. I had previously exerted pressure for this, as otherwise, the *Heeresgruppe* would stand no chance in holding out. It appears that gradually those up above have come to recognise the situation.[21]

Yet over and above the need for supporting *Heeresgruppe Don*, over the night of 27–28 January, 116 aircraft, comprising 80 He 111s, 33 Ju 52/3ms and three Fw 200s, took off for the Stalingrad pockets, of which 87 had reported completing their mission by midday on the 28th.[22] They dropped 83 tons of supplies, including 74 tons of food, 7,000 litres of fuel and 2.5 tons of ammunition. That day Milch agreed to allow the crews some rest, some of whom had been flying transport and bomber missions day and night for weeks.

Petersen reported to Milch that to date seven He 177s of I./FKG 50 had been destroyed by fire. 'It is a question of principle whether their missions should continue under these circumstances'.

Milch and General Hube – the latter had not returned to the pocket and was working as an army liaison officer to Milch – each sent a request to Hitler via Christian to make a night flight to Stalingrad to gain a personal understanding of operations. Their requests were refused.

In a night mission mounted on 28–29 January, 125 aircraft went out, of which 111 reached the pocket to drop 111.6 tons of supplies – mainly food, but including 3.76 tons of ammunition, just over a ton of medical supplies, 1,000 litres of fuel and a radio transmitter.[23] One Ju 52/3m failed to return. Initially, 6.*Armee* signalled from the southern pocket in the city to advise that only three tons of food and one container with fuel were found, but this was later corrected. In fact, all supplies dropped were found, short of 20 tons. Operations were assisted by improved radio guidance from the fortress, and dropping points were easy to spot in the southern pocket, but less so to the north. This was, of course, encouraging, but Fiebig remained cautious: 'It should help them to find more of the dropped containers. But will it work out amongst those ruins?'[24] Christian admitted to Milch that:

This is another indication of the precision with which the supplies are dropped, and of the fact that the supplies dropped previously actually landed in the fortress but were not properly picked up.

To date, losses incurred on transport missions to the pocket to 28 January amounted to 330 aircraft, and in terms of aircrew, 791 men had been lost to 26 January. Availability and serviceability continued to be a problem: of 340 apparently 'available' Ju 52/3ms on the 29th, 208 were at the supply airfields, of which just 46 were at immediate readiness at Taganrog and Sverevo. Forty-four He 111s were at immediate readiness out of 151 on the airfields.

During the afternoon of the 29th, Fiebig flew by Storch to Konstantinovka, where he met with Oberstleutnant von Beust, ostensibly running the composite *Lufttransportführer Beust*. In this capacity, in addition to KG 27, von Beust oversaw the activities of the He 111 bombers of II./KG 53 that had been brought in as emergency transports, as well as the He 111 transports of KGr.z.b.V.20 and the recently formed KGr.z.b.V.23. Fiebig was able to discuss operations with the respective commanders of these units – Oberstleutnant Hans Schulz-Müllensiefen, Major Hermann Schmidt and Oberstleutnant Karl-Heinz Schellmann. 'A mixed unit', Fiebig noted, 'but it works. They fly their ten different types of He 111 as well as they can'.[25]

By late January I./FKG 50 had lost three of its He 177s, with two more posted as missing. On the 28th, one Heinkel returned from operations damaged by fighters, having taken 18 hits to its control surfaces, ventral gondola and propeller, yet it still managed to make it back to Kalinovka. However, only around 13 bombing sorties had been mounted by 30 January, when Milch requested the Luftwaffe *Führungsstab* by teleprinter that the remaining He 177s be withdrawn immediately as a result of 'six bad accidents within 14 days'.

On the 31st, Major Schlosser drafted a report on the performance of the He 177 in Russia. He accepted that while the Heinkels had proved themselves as fast, heavy bombers, their Achilles' heel were their volatile engines, which had resulted in the loss of five aircraft, or a casualty rate of 26 per cent.

The problem by this point was that still more He 111s and He 177s were needed for combat operations against Soviet ground forces. Milch called Christian early on the morning of the 29th requesting a 'definite decision as to how many He 111s could be diverted from the airlift to combat assignments'. Of 211 Ju 52/3ms at the advanced fields, 72 were operationally ready, while of 133 available He 111s, 61 were immediately ready for operations, with 40 more projected as being available within 24 hours. That night, Göring stepped in with an order that the following day (30 January), the tenth anniversary of Hitler's seizure of power, 'all He 111s were to be used for supply missions' – and this at a time when some Heinkels were flying without bomb racks to which containers could be attached because *Luftflotte* 4 needed them for conventional bombing operations elsewhere.[26]

In a further blow for the survivors at Stalingrad, however, during late January, as the Russians advanced against the Don, the He 111 units were forced to commence pulling out of Novocherkassk back to Taganrog. The flight distance to the pocket now increased to 420 km, and thus the chances of any continuous and meaningful air supply began to fade.[27]

Over the night of 29–30 January, 151 aircraft took off for Stalingrad, of which 132 were able to drop 113.03 tons of general supplies including food, three tons of medical supplies, 16.95 tons of ammunition and 100 litres of fuel. Crews saw fires raging in the southern pocket. The view at the morning conference of *Sonderstab Milch* on the 30th was that air supply of the southern pocket would only be carried out that night if it was requested, as it was now considered possible that the defence in that sector might collapse imminently. Supplies were still reaching XI.*Armeekorps* to the north on the 30th, which radioed *Heeresgruppe Don* to confirm that despite the aircrews being deprived of good visibility, 1,300 kg of bread, 70 kg of vegetables, a quantity of meat concentrates, 323 kg of spread for bread, 43 kg of chocolate and 55 kg of Destro-energin had been dropped by He 111s and recovered.[28]

Continuing his tour of the transport *Gruppen*, Fiebig was back in the Storch to fly to Novocherkassk, where he met with Oberst Kühl on the 30th, and then on to Sverevo to talk with Morzik:

> I also spoke with the *Gruppenkommandeure* about the situation and about their missions and thanked them for their performance. My heart was overflowing, and yet still more had to be demanded of them on behalf of our comrades in the pocket.[29]

Meanwhile, to coincide with the anniversary of 30 January, Milch attempted a propaganda stunt and ordered that 'German fighters must be over Stalingrad' that day. When Oberst Wilcke attempted to protest that the Bf 109s and Bf 110s were not capable of the task, Milch overrode him, proclaiming 'No objections will be tolerated'. Furthermore, if possible, He 111s were to carry out a bombing mission of enemy positions shortly before, although this was overruled by Göring's edict that all He 111s were to be used for supply runs. Regardless, Milch warned that the reputation of the Luftwaffe – and especially that of its fighter arm – with the army was at stake.

Milch's tiny fighter force of five Bf 110s from I./ZG 1 and nine Bf 109s from JG 3 was at Rovenki, in eastern Ukraine, some 55 km south of Voroshilovgrad, but Oberst Petersen had warned that there was very deep snow there, and that the take-off runway, only 30 x 600 m, was affected by frequent crosswinds:

> The condition of the field in general is very bad. It is not suitable for a fighter escort unit. The capability of the workshops is very limited because there have been so many evacuations. Only one heating truck was in operation there when it was visited.

There is evidence from a British radio intercept that it was intended to 'transfer the escort unit Wilcke at once to Stalino owing to conditions of inadequacy of Rovenki airfield', but it appears that this did not happen.[30]

At 1900 hrs on the 29th, seven Bf 109s were reported as operationally ready, but Oberleutnant Eduard Tratt, the *Staffelkapitän* of 1./ZG 1, who was an experienced *Zerstörer* pilot with more than 20 victories and a recipient of the Knight's Cross, advised that the Bf 110s could not be deployed, as two of the machines had 1,475 hp Daimler-Benz DB 601B-type engines, while the other three had 1,050 hp A-type engines, meaning the latter were some 100 km/h slower. According to Milch, however, 'That is not true. Everything is to be sent out regardless of consequences, and I want a detailed report sent to me afterwards'.

On the morning of the 30th, six of the Bf 109s and five Bf 110s, all fitted with auxiliary tanks, took off for Stalingrad under the overall command of Oberleutnant Tratt. Reaching the city at 1045 hrs, they flew a patrol for 30 minutes, without seeing any enemy aircraft, before turning for home. On the way back, two VVS fighters were encountered and apparently shot down. As Rovenki came into sight, Tratt's Bf 110G-2 suffered engine failure and crashed into a snowdrift on the airfield. Tratt was injured and his radio operator killed.[31]

Wilcke advised that a second mission planned for the following day could not take place as no further auxiliary fuel tanks were available, the others having been used and expended. Milch dismissed this problem: the tanks would arrive tomorrow and the mission would be flown. But the reality was that all the fighters were worn out. Despite Milch demanding that both Bf 109s and Bf 110s be made ready for further operations, aside from an abortive, supposedly 'long-range' sortie by two Bf 109s over the Don on the 31st, they were quickly transferred to the command of *Luftflotte* 4 to be used for air defence over the airfields at Rostov and Novocherkassk.

As the day progressed, reports filtering in to Mariupol from Stalingrad became ever more bleak. By 1245 hrs, it was understood that air-drops over the Square of the Fallen Fighters (known to the Germans as Red Square) in the ruins of the city, where 6.*Armee's* battle headquarters continued to hold out, were no longer possible, while the situation at the Pioneer Barracks west of *Stalingrad 1-i* (the Central Railway Station) was unknown. Drops at the tractor plant to the north were 'apparently possible'. Only a short time later, however, the conclusion was that with the situation in the southern pocket not clear, collapse 'was probable within a very short time'.

But during the night of 30–31 January, of 120 available transport aircraft, 89 fulfilled their sorties to what remained of the pockets, dropping 103 tons of supplies. The Heinkel units operated from Novocherkassk, Konstantinovka and Stalino, the Ju 52/3ms from Sverevo and four Fw 200s went out from Zaporozhye. Two He 111s failed to return, one having been shot down by a Russian fighter, one crashed, and one was posted missing, along with a Ju 52/3m and an Fw 200.[32] Most dropped their loads in the northern pocket because the drop-point was again easily recognisable. In the southern pocket, the perimeter of which was no longer identifiable, there was only some haphazard firing of flare signals and very severe fires burning.[33] Around 40 Russian guns were reported at Orlovka, to the north-west of the city, aimed at the northern pocket. From the drop points, XI.*Armeekorps* was able to collect 180 kg of bread, 1,700 kg of meat concentrate, 35 kg of vegetables, 220 kg of spread for bread, 50 kg of chocolate and 6 kg of energy tablets.[34]

At his new headquarters, Fiebig listened to the *Führer's* 30 January commemoration speech, as well as others made by Göring and Goebbels:

> They say openly how things stand and what is at stake. The people know it. They have to steel themselves to accept this and to recover from it – the worst blow we have ever received.[35]

In the cold cellar of the vast, bomb-shattered *Univermag* (State Department Store) off the Square of the Fallen Fighters, Oberst Wilhelm Adam sat with Generaloberst Paulus, hungry and shivering on camp-beds, listening to the speeches from Berlin on a wireless set under candlelight. Both men were experiencing some discomfort from minor wounds they had received to their heads, and Paulus was also ill from dysentery. According to one account the commander of 6.*Armee* had suffered a nervous breakdown and was in 'a state of near-collapse'.[36] As the wireless reception faded and crackled alongside the occasional, muffled thump of a shell in the streets above them, Adam bristled with contempt at what he heard:

> I was overcome with disgust as I listened to the fat Luftwaffe marshal. But my anger at Hitler's unscrupulous riff-raff grew, that after his shameless betrayal, they now expected those of us still alive to listen to our own obituaries.[37]

Von Richthofen simply noted in his diary, 'The drama comes to a close'.[38]

But as a last, almost perverse act on this day of Nazi stage management, the *Führer* promoted Paulus to Generalfeldmarschall. Hitler's gambit was most likely based on the fact that no German field marshal in history had surrendered, and that, as such, the loyal Paulus would choose to take his own life rather than go into captivity, being the first to bring shame to such an exalted appointment. But Paulus was under no illusions. 'This is just an order to commit suicide', he told Schmidt. He apparently later remarked to one of his generals, 'I have no intention of shooting myself for this Bohemian corporal'.[39]

Above the cellars at street level, where all that remained of the *Univermag* were its stone staircases leading upwards to nothing but winter sky, the last German *Igelstellung* around the army headquarters had been reduced to a ring of just 300 m by 1900 hrs. That would shrink further over the coming hours as the Russians came ever nearer, street-by-street. At that point, the German 'defence' of Stalingrad was fragmented into three groupings: some 50,000 men of XI.*Armeekorps* under General der Infanterie Karl Strecker holding out to the north around the tractor plant and its associated village to the west, VIII.*Armeekorps* west of the railway and

6.*Armee*'s headquarters around the Square of the Fallen Fighters. But a few hours later, General Schmidt sent a signal to *Heeresgruppe Don*:

> The remains of 6.*Armee* closely confined in the three fortresses still hold some built-up areas west of the railway station and south of the water works. IV.*Armee*-Korps no longer exists. XIV.*Panzerkorps* has surrendered. No information concerning VIII. and LI.*Armeekorps*. Final collapse cannot be delayed for more than 24 hours.[40]

Among his last acts before he surrendered to the Russians, Paulus sent a delayed signal to Hitler, which Schmidt had drafted for despatch at midday the day before:

> On the anniversary of your accession to power, 6.*Armee* sends greetings to its *Führer*. The Swastika flag still flies over Stalingrad. Should our struggle be an example to present and future generations never to surrender, even when hope is gone, then Germany will be victorious. *Heil, mein Führer!*[41]

But the centre of Stalingrad now belonged almost entirely to the troops of Lt Gen Mikhail Stepanovich Shumilov's 64th Army who had been systematically flushing out those buildings and cellars which contained the last vestiges of German resistance with grenades and flame-throwers. Then, following an intense mortar and artillery bombardment during the morning, Red Army soldiers closed in on the *Univermag*.

At 0615 hrs on 31 January, 6.*Armee* signalled *Heeresgruppe Don*, 'The Russians are at the door. We are preparing to destroy papers and radio equipment'. Forty-five minutes later, under a white flag, Oberst Adam climbed up the steps from the basement of the *Univermag* followed by a gaunt Field Marshal Paulus. It was the moment of surrender. The first thing Adam noticed was how captured German soldiers in the square appeared 'ragged, in thin greatcoats over shabby uniforms, as lean as rakes, emaciated, exhausted figures with hollow cheeks and stubbled faces' while the Soviet troops were 'well kempt, vigorous, in wonderful winter clothing'.[42]

Some minutes later, a second signal was transmitted from the last personnel in 6.*Armee*'s basement. 'We are destroying papers and radio equipment.'[43] It was the last signal to be received from 6.*Armee*. Paulus and his staff were then driven off to Shumilov's headquarters.

'The last radio messages have come in', noted Fiebig later. 'It is goodbye and regards to those at home. The enemy is at the door'. From this point, the He 111 bomber units assigned to the airlift would revert back to their usual combat role. 'It was a necessary step', Fiebig wrote.[44]

At Milch's morning conference at 1000 hrs on the 31st, in something of an understatement, an army officer on Hube's staff advised that the southern pocket had 'splintered'. 'The last groups still fighting there were overcome', he told the assembled officers. There had also been attacks and breakthroughs into the northern pocket from the south and south-west, where Strecker's group was running low on food and ammunition. Milch was undeterred – perhaps in denial even. The air-drops would continue for as long as possible; *Luftflotte* 4 had 98 Ju 52/3ms and 60 He 111 transports ready for operations out of a total of 393 aircraft on the supply fields (a readiness rate of 40.20 per cent).[45] While he conceded that the 'retreating troops will not receive radio equipment', they were to receive dye for colouring the snow, as well as 'emergency winter equipment' – whatever that meant. He also ordered that any spare He 111 bombers should strike the Russian guns at Orlovka using 250-kg to 1,000-kg bombs. He wanted the bombers to receive escort from the Bf 109s, but this idea had to be abandoned as there was now a greater need for fighter protection of the supply bases. [46]

XI. *Armeekorps*, which, for the time being, continued to fight on in the north, signalled that a landing site would be usable on the 1st, with 'auxiliary' lighting and a flare path set up, but the *Korps* also asked that regular lighting equipment be brought in together with a technician for setting it up.

During the night of 31 January–1 February, 109 aircraft, comprising Ju 52/3ms, He 111s and Fw 200s, flew to Stalingrad, with 89 of them dropping 72 tons of food, ammunition, fuel and medical supplies over the northern pocket. The crews were aided by a large illuminated triangle and a Swastika laid out in red lights in the snow. Nothing could be recognised in the southern pocket except for a few isolated, last-ditch skirmishes.[47]

'The weather does not make things too difficult any more', Fiebig wrote optimistically in his diary on the 1st. 'I have the impression that a change to spring weather is in the offing. The weather is steadier, milder and there is less fog and ice. We must wait and see'.[48]

At the morning conference on the 1st, Schulz reported that there were sufficient supplies to allow air-drops to continue for up to 80 days. With what must have been a heavy heart and a sense of failure, Milch instructed Schulz to release the stocks to the army and, in exchange, to obtain the release of the army trains for Luftwaffe usage. He then addressed the assembled officers and staff:

> The forwarding of aerial delivery food packs to the supply points is to be halted and preparations made for taking them back. A final decision will be made on 3 February, as soon as the fate of the fortress becomes clear.

He also instructed that no further supplies should be sent to Sverevo, where there were five days of reserves remaining. All shipments of aircraft repair equipment by rail were to cease in favour of urgently needed supplies, as there were still around 200 Ju 52/3ms available to make flights.[49]

At the *Wolfschanze*, Major Gerhard Engel, Hitler's army adjutant, recorded, 'We are all imagining how it is ending at Stalingrad. The *Führer* was very depressed, looking everywhere for errors and negligence'.[50] At 1725 hrs, *Heeresgruppe Don* relayed Hitler's latest order to XI. *Armeekorps*. It was familiar in its blend of psychological arm-twisting and terseness:

I anticipate that the northern pocket at Stalingrad will hold out to the last. Every day, every hour, which is won thereby is of decisive advantage to the rest of the front.

In response, around four hours later, the *Korps* signalled that the enemy had made deep incursions into the west of the vast tractor plant and to the south-west of the *Barrikady* ordnance factory. Under assault, the *Korps* had sustained severe losses and some of its units had been 'torn to pieces'. It expected to cease resistance the following day when all its ammunition had been expended.[51]

During the night of 1–2 February, the Luftwaffe sent out a force of 116 aircraft, including 82 Ju 52/3ms and eight Fw 200s. They flew to the northern pocket, where 82 aircraft dropped 98 tons of supplies comprising 64 tons of food and 34 tons of ammunition.[52] Twenty-five aircraft turned back as a result of smoke and fog over the city from 0100 hrs. The dropping areas were clearly visible up to 2400 hrs, but after that the smoke from heavy Soviet artillery fire obscured the ground. The aircrews observed many fires. The crews of the last He 111s to fly to Stalingrad reported that it was no longer easy to determine the perimeter of the pockets. Fire was raging in the north-western corner of the tractor plant and there were signal flares of all colours being fired up from the ruins. Their general impression was that the remaining German positions were 'at the point of extinction'.[53]

They were not wrong. At 0700 hrs in the suddenly clear, sunlit morning of the 2nd, XI.*Armeekorps* signalled that it expected Russian troops to arrive within an hour. The *Korps* would destroy all its weapons in anticipation. A further signal came at 0840 hrs:

The XI.*Armeekorps* has carried out its duty with its six divisions to the very last. Heil to the *Führer*! Long live Germany!

Apart from a garbled transmission just under an hour later, that was the last to be heard of Strecker's *Korps*.

At his morning conference, Milch instructed that a further formation of eight He 111s be sent to Stalingrad to determine whether the presence of any German troops could be detected. Crews were to make immediate reports by radio. Three codewords would be agreed to denote each of the following scenarios:

a 'Our troops can still be seen. I am dropping my load.'
b 'There is reason to believe that our troops are still active. I am dropping my load.'
c 'Nothing more can be seen. It is pointless to drop anything.'

Among the aircraft making the last flights over Stalingrad on 3 February was a He 111 from 9./KG 27. One of its crew remembered how:

With a cloud base of 100 m, we lost course and only regained our bearings when we came across the wreck of a ship in the frozen Volga. We now flew at a height of around 100 m over the Volga in a south-westerly direction towards Stalingrad.

The Luftwaffe crews observed how Red Army tanks and trucks were swarming around the city, while 'For many kilometres, the miserable remnants of the 6.*Armee* are dragging themselves into captivity. The Russians will have taken the supplies we air-dropped'. As Russian anti-aircraft batteries opened fire from the steep west back of the river, the Heinkels turned for home.[54]

Following a request from Milch, a lone aircraft from 2.(F)/*Aufklärungsgruppe* Ob.d.L. (2.*Staffel* of the Luftwaffe High Command's Reconnaissance Group) carried out a reconnaissance mission over Stalingrad. At around midday the pilot radioed *Luftflotte* 4 advising that he could see no more signs of fighting in the city.[55]

At 1900 hrs, VIII.*Fliegerkorps* reported that the crews of the first three aircraft from the eight that had been despatched to Stalingrad had not seen anything, the pilot of the fourth thought he may have seen something and the fifth had observed lights – possibly intended as a dropping point – and so the pilot had released his load at that spot. They had taken with them 3.5 tons of ammunition, 500 litres of fuel and 2.2 tons of general supplies.[56] VIII.*Fliegerkorps'* Chief of Staff, Oberstleutnant Lothar von Heinemann, asked Milch whether a second wave of He 111s should take off. Milch instructed that they should do so. By 2000 hrs there was still no word from the remaining aircraft in the first wave. Milch told Fiebig by telephone that:

> Ju 52s are to be kept in readiness, but they are not to be sent out until the situation is clarified. Relay the reports of the returning crews to me immediately. *Heeresgruppe Don* has no new reports.

Ninety minutes later Fiebig called Milch with news from the other returning crews:

> Outlines of the pocket can no longer be recognised. No artillery fire observed. An enemy column is working its way into what was formerly the pocket from the north-east, from the bank of the Volga River. The head of the column is about at the former dropping point.

Milch told Fiebig not to despatch any more Ju 52/3ms or Fw 200s. In the meantime Fiebig was 'to be reassigned to *Luftflotte* 4 tomorrow for a new mission'.

At 2252 hrs, Milch telephoned Rastenburg. His call was answered by a major on the staff, to whom he said with an air of finality:

> The aircraft which were over Stalingrad tonight did not observe any ground combat. There was a Russian horse-drawn column at the tractor plant. Even crews who believed that they still saw something admitted, upon questioning, that their observations were uncertain. The first 12 supply aircraft have

returned. Sixteen more are still out. Ju 52s will no longer be sent, but will be turned over to *Luftflotte* 4 instead for new transport assignments.

That evening, Milch decided that transport operations by Ju 52/3ms and Fw 200s would cease permanently and the aircraft be made available for other commitments, probably in support of 1.*Panzerarmee*'s withdrawal from the Caucasus and 17.*Armee*'s advance from the Kuban towards the Taman Peninsula.

By the cessation of the airlift there had been some changes and consolidation in unit organisation under Milch's tenure: I./KG 100, II./KG 27, I./FKG 50 and KGr.z.b.V.105 had been withdrawn in order to replenish their crews and aircraft; III./KG 4 had been removed from supply runs to operate as an air-towing unit; KGr.z.b.V.21 was absorbed into KG 55; the eight surviving He 111s of 15./KG 6 were taken on by II./KG 53; and a small number of aircraft from KGr.z.b.V.OBS were absorbed into KGr.z.b.V.5. The remaining organisation was as follows:[57]

Lufttransportführer Sverevo
    I. and II./KGr.z.b.V.1
    KGr.z.b.V.9
    KGr.z.b.V.50
    KGr.z.b.V.102
    KGr.z.b.V.172
    KGr.z.b.V.500
    KGr.z.b.V.700
    KGr.z.b.V.900

Lufttransportführer Novocherkassk
    Stab, I. and III./KG 55
    I. and III./KG 27

Lufttransportführer Konstantinovka
    Stab/KG 27
    II./KG 53
    KGr.z.b.V.20
    KGr.z.b.V.23

Lufttransportführer Stalino
    KGr.z.b.V.5

Lufttransportführer Zaporozhye
    KGr.z.b.V.200

In an example of the chasm of ignorance which existed between the authorities in the Reich and the military reality at Stalingrad, in early February as 6.*Armee* entered its death throes, Professor Wilhelm Ziegelmayer, a leading army nutritionist, flew into southern Russia with a team of experts to explore in more depth the feasibility of the supply, preparation and consumption of food concentrates on a mass scale in the Stalingrad pocket. The arrival of Ziegelmayer and his staff, however well intended, was a source of bemusement, as Heinrich Potthoff recalled:

> Not a few of us found it incomprehensible that the OKW had not given thought much earlier to the mass production of concentrates, and that they had not made preparations to do so. The practical result of the meeting with Professor Ziegelmayer was not very promising. We had to explain the reality of the situation at Stalingrad to him. The daily calorific quantity at the middle of January per head was estimated to lie at the most at 400, or significantly below that! At that level, the fighting capability in the *Kessel* was hardly great. Professor Ziegelmayer and his team were told the necessary: how things really stood was not known to them before.[58]

As the Red Army advanced across the former 'fortress', so its soldiers came upon many harrowing scenes such as at that at Gumrak, where they found piles of frozen corpses dropped off stretchers or planks by German personnel. 'Themselves weak', as Wilhelm Adam has written, 'the medical orderlies no longer wanted to hack out graves for the dead in the hard-frozen ground. And there were no more explosives available'.[59]

Thankfully, at last, the battle of Stalingrad was over.

18

The Reckoning

The Wehrmacht had indeed broken Stalingrad, but in the process it had broken itself.

ROBERT M. CITINO, *DEATH OF THE WEHRMACHT:*
THE GERMAN CAMPAIGNS OF 1942

The Stalingrad airlift lasted 71 days, and in those 71 days Germany's military grip on the Soviet Union weakened irretrievably. The airlift attempt failed, which lead, in turn, to a chain of subsequent events (including the loss of an entire army) that, arguably, saw the collapse of German strategic aims in southern Russia from early 1943. The loss of 6.*Armee*, amidst the frozen wastes, was perceived by the German public not only as a military defeat but also as an act of abandonment; it had a devastating effect on the nation's morale. Stalingrad could not be hidden, forgiven, or justified militarily, or morally – even by Joseph Goebbels and the Reich ministry of Public Enlightenment and Propaganda.

It was the first time a Prussian or German field army had been encircled and effectively destroyed since 1806. Of around 364,000 men who approached Stalingrad at the height of *Blau* in the summer of 1942, only some 91,000 starving and sick survivors limped into Soviet captivity in the final three days of the battle. More than 150,000 Axis soldiers, most of them German, had been killed or wounded during the fighting in and around the city.[1] The collapse of German resistance at Stalingrad freed up several Soviet armies to be deployed elsewhere against a badly shaken German front.[2] For the first time, Hitler's judgements as a leader had come under question. 'The Russian was not dead, as Hitler and Göring had continued to assume in November 1942', opined Heinrich Potthoff. 'From the debacle of the first Russian winter of 1941–42, they had learned nothing'.[3]

Von Manstein claimed to have attempted, repeatedly, to persuade Hitler, or even Jodl, to visit southern Russia in order to gain an understanding of the situation facing German forces there for themselves, but to no avail. When von Manstein visited Hitler on 5 February 1943, the latter apparently admitted, 'I alone bear the responsibility for Stalingrad'. He further stated that he 'could perhaps put some of the blame on Göring' as a result of the Reichsmarschall presenting him with an inaccurate picture of the Luftwaffe's capability, but as his appointed successor, Hitler deemed that it would not be politic to charge Göring with such a responsibility.[4] Whatever the case, Göring never really fell foul of Hitler publicly over Stalingrad.[5] Yet, while von Manstein was of the opinion that Göring was 'solely responsible' for the decision to proceed with the airlift, he also felt it was Hitler's duty to 'examine the declaration made by Göring'.[6]

However to attribute the airlift as the *cause* of the German collapse would be an oversimplification which ignores the ill-advised, hasty and increasingly desperate decisions that overruled common sense, practicalities, logistics and weather, as well as the reluctance of 6.*Armee* to effect a breakout in order *to save itself* while it was still able to do so.

Of course, it is facile for an author to hypothesise with the benefit of nearly 80 years' comfortable hindsight. It is also impossible to reach balanced or nuanced conclusions which accommodate the various views of the German supreme political and military commands, the airlift commanders and organisers, and the senior commanders within 6.*Armee*. So, in keeping with the aim of this book, we shall focus on the air perspective.

Fritz Morzik places the *cause* resolutely on the shoulders of Paulus and Schmidt:

> The Commander-in-Chief and Chief of Staff of the Sixth Army showed by their rigid demands for air-supply that they had no conception whatsoever of the limitations in performance which the military situation and weather conditions imposed on the air transport units.[7]

In other words, they displayed intransigence and ignorance. When Major Thiel met with Paulus and Schmidt in the pocket on 19 January, Paulus, in a hostile mood, mentioned the Luftwaffe's 'betrayal' of the army. Yet Fiebig had already warned him in no uncertain terms on 21 November, and again on the 22nd, of the impossibility of sustaining the Army by airlift. It seems this had slipped from the minds of both Paulus and his Chief of Staff.

The transport and bomber units of *Luftflotte* 4 had done their utmost to supply the men of 6.*Armee*. Between 24 November and 3 February they had flown 8,350 tons into the pocket, or an average of 116 tons per day, including 1,648 cbm of fuel, 1,122 tons of ammunition, 2,020 tons of rations and 129 tons of miscellaneous supplies. The peak delivery (reached on 7 December) was 362.6 tons. An estimated 24,900 wounded and sick men were evacuated, at a cost of 488 aircraft and 1,000 airmen.[8]

Just about everything was against the Luftwaffe transport force: the appalling Russian winter and the accidents it caused (which increased attrition), the VVS and Soviet anti-aircraft batteries, as well as a lack of a permanent, efficient and safe base infrastructure, high losses with inadequate replacement levels, insecure and unreliable routes and methods of supply and support – even the wrong variants of aircraft. The result was that the Luftwaffe paid a very high price to save an army that did not attempt to save itself.

For his part, Morzik attributed the following reasons as to why, from the outset, it should have been clear that an adequate air supply operation could not be sustained for any great period:

1 The size of the encircled force.
2 The small amount of supplies that 6.*Armee* had on hand at the time of encirclement.
3 The inadequacy of the main supply airfields, the distances to and from the pocket and the lack of the necessary technical support services.
4 The inadequate supply routes to the supply bases.
5 The eventual forced abandonment of the supply bases.
6 Adverse seasonal weather.
7 The lack of sufficient air transport capacity actually able to reach Stalingrad at any given time – not simply a question of available aircraft.
8 The duration of the supply operation.
9 Lack of escort fighters and sufficient Flak defence for take-off and landing fields.[9]

The last fundamental, and vital, item is especially valid: most of the time air superiority was missing during the Luftwaffe's attempt to supply Stalingrad. As one senior USAF officer has commented, this missing element 'turned an incredibly challenging mission from the outset into, quite simply, an impossible task. The lack of air superiority forced key tactical adjustments that produced rippling effects throughout the German air mobility enterprise supplying the Sixth Army'.[10]

It seems that despite any personal enmity between Milch and Morzik, Milch did, in fact, share the latter's views of 6.*Armee*'s 'rigid demands', for when he flew to Hitler's headquarters at the end of the airlift and told the *Führer* that had he been in command of 6.*Armee*, he would have disobeyed orders and broken out. Not surprisingly, Hitler was displeased at such a view, and told Milch he would have reprimanded him seriously had that been the case, but Milch responded that the sacrifice of a field marshal would have been of little consequence set against the lives of 300,000 men.[11]

Milch was also forthright in his views to Hitler's senior military adjutant, General Rudolf Schmundt, during a visit by the latter to *Heeresgruppe Don* and Mariupol on 28 January. As the disaster of Stalingrad drew to its apocalyptic conclusion, Milch told Schmundt that he believed, in future, mobile warfare should be avoided in winter, as both losses in men and materiel could be expected to be too high. And yes, one can wonder why it took the crisis of Stalingrad for an aviator, businessman, commander and minister like Milch to recognise this, let alone to recall the historic precedent of Napoleon and 1812. He also stated that the formation of large pockets should be avoided, as 'air supply can never be completely assured, especially during seasons of bad weather'.[12] A lesson learned.

Fiebig and Pickert echoed the views of Milch when they listed the principle reasons why they felt the airlift had failed:[13]

1 By October, which Fiebig viewed as being the appropriate time, no decision had been taken by the Wehrmacht to go into winter positions.
2 No measures – or only belated ones – had been taken against early visible enemy offensive preparations in front of the Italian Eighth and Romanian Third and Fourth Armies and elsewhere along the Don which had been observed and reported by the Luftwaffe in early October.
3 The decision to hold the *Festung* at Stalingrad without surrendering at least some territory gained in the Caucasus.
4 No order to 6.*Armee* to break out was issued in mid-December when 4. *Panzerarmee* was in the Myschkova sector.
5 A flawed understanding of air-supply capacity which overlooked weather, the battle situation and the inability to utilise certain airfields at key times.
6 The right to take fully unencumbered decisions was withdrawn from most commanders to Army Group-level.
7 A false understanding of Soviet and Axis strengths.
8 No supreme command representative arrived to gain a personal and accurate assessment of the true situation. This also applied to the Luftwaffe in respect to air supply capability and performance.

Heinrich Potthoff, who oversaw the medical aspects of *Luftflotte* 4's activities during the airlift, supported Fiebig and Pickert. He felt that:

Special thanks is owed to the transport crews, and also to the good cooperation within the *Luftflotte* staff under the leadership of von Richthofen. However, as in the previous winter of 1941–42, we had not been paid a visit by any of the prominent leaders in the OKW anywhere near the front. On human and psychological grounds, it would have been useful and beneficial if they had witnessed personally and learned of the misery and the awful conditions experienced by the troop units at the front, in the army and Luftwaffe field hospitals, as well as at the assembly and transport points for the sick and wounded. The wounded, the sick, the doctors and the medical services would have recognised and appreciated such an initiative. But it was not the case. However, we were grateful for the exemplary support provided by the Luftwaffe ground support units on the airfields.[14]

Göring's bulky shadow falls across Stalingrad, and his actions (or inaction?) affected events in one way or another. Yet one is left with the impression that Stalingrad, and Hitler's continual calls for him to explain what he saw as the Luftwaffe's shortcomings, were, in reality, just an inconvenience to Göring which had to be dealt with and then brushed away. In the same way he prioritised a shopping trip to Paris at the time Hitler was demanding a supply commitment by the Luftwaffe from Jeschonnek in November 1942, on 12 December, with the airlift well underway and *Wintergewitter* freshly launched, Göring's priority was to attend a gala performance of Wagner's *Die Meistersinger von Nürnberg* at the reopening of the Berlin State Opera House which had been damaged by RAF bombs the previous year. Armaments minister Albert Speer was one of many guests of the Reichsmarschall that evening, and despite the sense of occasion, the glittering splendour and dress uniforms, he was aware that 'Göring knew that the fate of the army encircled in Stalingrad hung on his promise'. Speer also claimed that the event pricked at his own conscience: 'The jovial plot of the opera painfully contrasted with the events at the front, so that I kept chiding myself for having accepted the invitation'.[15]

However, Göring gave an ill-informed, spontaneous and irrational pledge to Hitler that 'his' Luftwaffe (as he was proud of calling it) could supply 6.*Armee*, and he stuck by that pledge well into December. The truth was that he had little idea of what tonnage could be delivered daily, and of precisely what it took to organise a large-scale airlift. He did not consult his transport specialists, nor did he take into account the fact that a large element of the transport arm was committed in the Mediterranean and North Africa. Yet, as Commander-in-Chief, his word to the Luftwaffe was final. Göring, therefore, must bear some of the responsibility for the failed airlift. And as von Rohden comments, 'Nothing would have changed in this regard if Göring had been pressured by Hitler to make such a promise'.[16]

Von Rohden assigns the remaining responsibility to Hitler: 'He was the "Supreme Commander", and as such bore the final decision and thus his share of responsibility'. Yet in his analysis, while acknowledging the extreme authoritarian nature of Hitler's command system, von Rohden also balances this by recognising that history will judge, rightly or wrongly, fairly or unfairly, the senior figures and staff of the OKW and the Luftwaffe – men such as Keitel, Jodl, Zeitzler, Jeschonnek, Milch, von Richthofen, Fiebig, Morzik and Schulz – for not sufficiently and uncompromisingly advancing, as von Rohden describes it, 'the hopelessness of supply'.[17]

In an interview with Johannes Fischer in March 1969, Milch stated that while the airlift was taking place Göring told his senior staff officers that if it failed he expected *them* to take the blame. Furthermore, in a lecture given in 1949, Hans-Georg Seidel, the Luftwaffe's former Quartermaster General, stated that Göring intended to court-martial him and Jeschonnek in the wake of Stalingrad in order to demonstrate publicly that 'guilty parties' had been found and punished. Göring was also desperate to prove to Hitler that 'his' Luftwaffe had done everything in its power to supply 6.*Armee* – something which the army had very much doubted in December 1942 and January 1943, and told Hitler so.[18]

Probably anticipating Göring's search to find the 'culprits' responsible for the 'failure' of the airlift, even with the operation still in progress, Fiebig met with two senior Luftwaffe legal functionaries on 26 January 1943 in order to issue an official statement as a 'determination of events'. In the document, he reaffirmed his sworn position that he had clearly informed Paulus and Schmidt that he deemed an airlift on the scale requested by 6.*Armee* to be an impossibility.[19]

In fairness to von Richthofen and Fiebig, regardless of their professionalism and endeavour, *Luftflotte* 4 was a large command geared primarily towards *combat* operations which was suddenly forced to manage a large-scale air-supply operation – a mission which needed specialist organisers with logistics skills and experience, able to act independently and with authority. Von Richthofen moved as quickly as he could, but it was all a kneejerk reaction.

On 10 February 1943, a few days after the airlift had drawn to an end, von Richthofen flew to East Prussia, where he met with Göring at his hunting lodge on the Rominter Heath. That evening, von Richthofen dined with Göring, and the two men apparently spoke plainly to each other. Göring asked the air fleet commander to be frank, and admitted that at the beginning of the air-supply operation, which he assumed would be only temporary, it had been he who had 'generated optimism and had supported the *Führer* in his decision to hold out'. Göring also blamed the collapse of Italian forces on the Don for what had become a catastrophe. According to von Richthofen:

> I stressed that it would serve no purpose simply to use abusive language at the army, army group and air fleet commanders on-the-spot. One must either have trust in them or replace them. If one is not able to replace them, one has to force oneself to trust them, and if one is not able to do that, one has to go there and form a picture of the situation for one's self.

Von Richthofen further told Göring that he believed 'a general leadership crisis exists, and that at the present time, no one knows what they want or what should be done.' He stressed that there needed to be trust between commanders and their subordinates, and that:

> . . . plans are made looking far into the future, and such plans should be adhered to. The theories about the conduct of the winter war in Russia, which are always announced beforehand, have certainly been correct, but when it comes down to carrying them out, action has been taken that is not in accordance with these entirely correct theories, but rather, actions that are much more impulsive.[20]

This must have been intended as a thinly veiled reference to Hitler's shifting of strategic objectives during *Blau*. According to von Richthofen, Göring accepted what he said, and the two men parted company, amicably, well after midnight. The following morning, von Richthofen travelled to Rastenburg, where he reported to Hitler in the company of Göring. The Luftwaffe general was respectful, but candid, as was Hitler. The *Führer* asked von Richthofen his opinion of von Manstein:

> I said to him that I held him to be the best tactician and leader that we have among the fighting forces. However, from some source or other, the *Führer*

seems to be strongly influenced against von Manstein. The Reichsmarschall blew the same horn. I have serious grounds to believe [and there are indications in support of this] that this position emanates from Keitel and Jodl, who fear the competition. I also told the *Führer* that von Manstein, like all other army commanders, is really only interested in operations and tactics, and that an energetic hand in the organisation of the rear services, evacuation and care matters, unit organisation, the inspection of rear areas and so on, is lacking.

Having got the ear of Hitler by this stage, and with Göring still in the room, von Richthofen ventured the key question of who was responsible for promising 6.*Armee* a daily supply of 500 tons:

I had previously asked the Reichsmarschall the decisive question of who had been really responsible for the optimism at Stalingrad, and who had promised those who were encircled there a daily air supply of 500 tons. The Reichsmarschall continually admitted that he had supported the *Führer's* optimism. This was considered justified prior to our offensive forces having to bolster the Italian sector of the front. With regard to the 500 tons, the Reichsmarschall was of the view that this could only have been the result of a misunderstanding. I asked the *Führer* directly, and mentioned that the deployment of 6.*Armee* was simply not comprehensible. He admitted that he had promised them the 500 tons, supposedly without the knowledge of the Reichsmarschall, with the proviso, however, that this would only be possible if the supplies situation did not deteriorate. Due to the bad weather and the forced abandonment of the forward airfields, his promise could not, of course, be fulfilled.[21]

Of course, as has been evidenced in this book, even if the Luftwaffe had been in a position to maintain an airlift of significant assistance to 6.*Armee* – for example, deliveries of 500 tons per day – it is unlikely the Army's predicament could have been improved. Soviet pressure around the pocket would have increased until the exhausted forces trapped within it would eventually, and inevitably, have given up. This was aside from the fact that by early 1943, as German forces in southern Russia were forced to pull back ever further westwards, supply and contact with the pocket would have become ever more slim, and challenging, and then physically impossible.

In his post-war memoir, Heinrich Potthoff echoed the likely thoughts of all those who experienced Stalingrad when he wrote:

Those responsible for the debacle did not set an example. For those they had sentenced to die, they were no shining example at all. As leadership personalities, they stayed well away from the firing line. My experiences in and around Stalingrad were the most awful of my life, especially my professional life as a doctor, military doctor and soldier.[22]

Poignantly, Major Hans-Jürgen Willers, the commander of KGr.z.b.V.200, recalled how:

> At the end of the Stalingrad operation, the members of my *Gruppe* asked that no requests for medals or decorations be put forward for Stalingrad, and I granted this request.[23]

★ ★ ★

Events at Stalingrad did not arrest the Wehrmacht's dependency on Luftwaffe airlift support.

By early February 1943, 1.*Panzerarmee* had been pulled back in a long, hard retreat, under bitterly cold temperatures and with the enemy chasing it all the way, into the southern Ukraine to join *Heeresgruppe Don*. This left 17.*Armee* retreating towards the Taman Peninsula and isolated in the Kuban with some 350,000 men and 2,000 artillery pieces. Instead of being bottled up there, with its back to the Sea of Azov, such a force could have been much better utilised in the main line. Hitler, however, decided that the *Armee's* position on what was to become known as the Kuban bridgehead should be held, as it was considered to be a strong spot from which to tie down large Soviet forces and to keep open a route to the Caucasus' oil fields. In addition, he hoped to deny the Russians the use of Novorissisk, the port to the south of the bridgehead.[24] Furthermore, supplies were reasonably plentiful, and they could be replenished by using air transport that had been ordered by Milch and flown in for the Stalingrad airlift but not utilised. Paradoxically, however, on 17 January, the Chief of Staff of 17.*Armee* had written to OKW and advised, 'The Commander of 17.*Armee* still believes that it would be best to move all the forces to the north. Otherwise we'll have to go through a second Stalingrad'.[25]

On 29 January 1943, VIII.*Fliegerkorps*, battered and in need of reinforcement, was assigned the task of coordinating the air supply of the Kuban bridgehead.[26] Transports, and a small force of bombers, would fly in supplies of food, fuel, ammunition and horse fodder over the Straits of Kerch. The fodder was for the small Alpine horses which were used by the mountain troops in the encircled area.[27] On their return flights, the transports would take out the wounded and other key personnel, as well as carrying supplies of copper to Zaparozhye.[28]

Even before January was out, a sizeable fleet of transport aircraft had been assembled on airfields in the Crimea at Saki, Sarabus, Bagerowo and Kerch so as to keep 17.*Armee* supplied. There were Fw 200s from KGr.z.b.V.200 and five *Gruppen* of Ju 52/3ms, to which was added the DFS 230 gliders and mixed types of tow aircraft from LLG 1 that Milch had so ardently championed at Stalingrad. Joining this force were the Go 242 gliders and their He 111 tugs from Major Werner Richers' I./LLG 2, as well as He 111 Zwillings and Me 321s of GS-*Kommando* 2 alongside aircraft from 17./LLG 1.[29]

To organise the operations of the Ju 52/3m units, two *Lufttransportführer* were appointed: in overall charge of the operation was Oberst Morzik, based at Mariupol-West, and under his direction Oberstleutnant Adolf Jäckl, based initially at Taganrog-West but moving shortly to Samorsk, who would oversee the day-to-day execution.[30] Jäckl was a former World War I aviator and an experienced transport officer who served in the Mediterranean and the Balkans.[31] He coordinated the activities of the airfield staffs and workshops and controlled matters associated with operational readiness and serviceability. He arranged that aircraft available for immediate operations, or available within 48 hours, were to remain on operational airfields, while those assessed as not fitting that level of readiness were to be sent immediately to Cherson for repair.[32]

Once again, as with the Stalingrad operation, conditions on the landing grounds were harsh, and the *Gruppen* battled on despite a lack of heating equipment and adequate winter clothing. Although it was cold, it was not cold enough for runways in the Kuban to freeze permanently, and they softened during the day, allowing landings only in the early morning and late afternoon.[33] Morzik recounted, quite realistically, that comparatively, in the Kuban/Crimea, the Ju 52/3m was restricted in what it could do:

> The feasibility of air supply operations from a rear area with medium and light transport aircraft will no doubt always be limited by the range of action of the aircraft concerned. Range, fuel consumption and speed must always remain reasonably proportional to the load which can be transported and thus to the prospects of fulfilling the purpose of the mission. For example, the employment of a Ju 52 to carry two tons of supplies over a route of four or five hours' duration (approximately 800 km, assuming a flight speed of 170–180 km/h) can hardly be considered profitable. Even if the Ju 52 continues its mission by means of a series of shorter flights within the target area, the time factor alone would prevent an increase of more than two, or at best four, tons in the total volume of supplies which it could handle on one day. For this reason, the Ju 52 is inevitably forced to select take-off airfields lying as close as possible to the area to be supplied.

As such, Morzik argued, even during the relatively short duration of the *Lufttransporteinsatz Krim*, the above factors 'decidedly favoured the employment of the Fw 200' as a long-range transport aircraft. The Focke-Wulf's higher speed and greater fuel capacity made the flight length fairly irrelevant, and its greater cargo capacity was a distinct advantage.[34]

On 2 February, von Richthofen noted:

> He 111 units have been freed up from Stalingrad. They will be relocated to operational airfields and reorganised and made ready for tasks or alternatively deployed immediately. During the evening Ju 52 forces will also be freed up for transport duties in the Kuban region.[35]

This initiative saw VIII.*Fliegerkorps* being able to call additionally upon Major Hermann Schmidt's KGr.z.b.V.20, which arrived from Denpropetrovsk in early February, and the Heinkels of Oberstleutnant Karl-Heinz Schellmann's KGr.z.b.V.23, which transferred from Konstantinovka to Saki at the same time.[36]

Supply operations over the Kuban, which commenced at the end January, were very challenging. In the cold and icy conditions, the sheer numbers of aircraft operating in the take-off and landing areas (at Timoschewskaya, Slawjanskaya, Wyschestebliwskaya, Tamanskaya and Krasnodar) demanded the greatest skill on the part of both the tug and glider pilots. On Hitler's direct orders, the airfield at Tamanskaya was to be 'developed with all resources', incorporating two wide runways.[37] However, as the harsh winter weather gradually thawed, the mud came, presenting even more operating difficulties, although the ice in the Kerch Straits began to melt.[38] Nevertheless, more demands from the *Führer* himself came to the effect that Slawjanskaya was to be 'proofed against mud to the maximum extent by making use of army personnel, the civil population, broken down vehicles, rubble etc'.[39]

The field at Slawjanskaya was held by the Germans up to 17 March, when it was finally evacuated. Between 29 January and 17 March 1943, He 111s flew 291 sorties there, most of them as tug flights. This was far less than the number of sorties made by the Ju 52/3m units, but it was still a significant and vital contribution.[40] Up to 30 March, the transports flew in almost 13,000 tons of supplies, horse fodder and ammunition. Approximately 85,000 German and Romanian troops, as well as Cossacks, were lifted out of the Kuban, including more than 29,000 wounded, but as April arrived, it became possible to supply 17.*Armee* by sea, allowing many of the transport *Gruppen* to pull out of the area and return to Germany for rest and re-equipping.

By the end of April, however, 17.*Armee* was forced to yield ground in the face of heavy Soviet attacks aimed at the bridgehead. However, by late May, the German ability to repel the Soviet thrusts in the Kuban prompted the Red Army's North Caucasus Front to end its long-running offensive aimed at Krasnodar, having lost more than 66,000 troops killed and more than 173,000 wounded in fierce fighting. Although 17.*Armee* was isolated, Hitler ordered that the Crimea was to be held at all costs; once again the *Transportverbände* – and in a large measure, the Ju 52/3m – had made this situation possible. The Junkers transports would continue to fly into the area until late 1943.

Indeed, the Luftwaffe would continue to fly supply operations until the end of the war, for example over the Crimea between November 1943 and May 1944, and in the final battles over the Eastern Front from late 1944. During the latter campaigns, designated 'fortresses' at Budapest, Breslau and Glogau were resupplied, while on the Western Front, air-drops were undertaken for the isolated German garrisons holding out in ports on the Atlantic coast in France from the summer of 1944 through to May 1945.

★ ★ ★

Fritz Morzik was promoted to Generalmajor in October 1943. During the final stages of the war he was appointed Chief of Air Transport of the

Wehrmacht, but by this time this was very much an 'on paper' function only and he had few resources to manage. His main objective seems to have been to use whatever aircraft he had to move German troops and civilians west, away from the Soviet advance. Morzik was taken prisoner by US forces in May 1945 and remained in captivity until 30 June 1947. In the post-war years he continued to take an active role in the old comrades' associations of the *Transportverbände*. He died at the age of 93 on 17 June 1985.

In the wake of the airlift at Stalingrad, **Wolfram von Richthofen** was promoted to Generalfeldmarschall – at 47, he was the youngest officer to hold that rank in the German armed forces. In the summer of 1943 he was sent to Italy, where he took command of Luftwaffe forces in that theatre. In October 1944 he suffered a brain tumor and died at Bad Ischl, in Austria, while in American captivity on 12 July 1945.

Erhard Milch returned to Germany after the airlift and diligently and energetically continued his work as Secretary of State, overseeing aircraft production and development at the RLM, but he fell out of favour with Hitler and Göring in the summer of 1944 at what they perceived as Milch's misrepresentations on the development of the Me 262 jet. He was forced to resign from the RLM and suffered another car crash. Stripped of all his offices, Milch languished at home until the German surrender. He served seven years in prison on charges related to deportations, slave labour and criminal medical experiments and was released on 28 June 1954. Milch subsequently found employment in industry with the aviation division of Fiat and the Thyssen Steel Company. He died on 25 January 1972 after a short illness.

Wolfgang Pickert was awarded the Knight's Cross on 11 January 1943 for his service in support of 6.*Armee* at Stalingrad. Promoted to Generalleutnant in November of that same year, he subsequently led Flak formations with distinction in Normandy and the Ardennes. Pickert was promoted to General der Flakartillerie in March 1945, but surrendered to US forces in the Ruhr Pocket on 8 May 1945. He remained in captivity until 5 January 1948. Pickert died at Weinheim on 19 July 1984.

Karl-Heinrich Schulz was also decorated with the Knight's Cross, receiving his award on 9 June 1944 for his service in support of German forces during the heavy fighting in the Caucasus. From 23 April 1945, he held the dubious accolade of being the Luftwaffe's last Chief of Operations Staff, but by then the Luftwaffe was a spent force. Less than two weeks' later he surrendered to the Allies and spent the next two years in captivity. Schulz died on 28 July 1986.

After Stalingrad, **Martin Fiebig** took command of X.*Fliegerkorps* and was also appointed overall commander of Luftwaffe forces in Greece and the Balkans (*Luftwaffenkommando Süd-Ost*). In February 1945 he was appointed commander of II.*Fliegerkorps* (later *Luftwaffenkommando Nord-Ost*),responsible for the air defence of north-east Germany and for supporting the forces of *Heeresgruppe Vistula*. On 8 May 1945, Fiebig was able to surrender to British forces, but he was later handed over to the Yugoslavians, who tried him for his role in bombing raids on Belgrade in which some 1,700 civilians were killed. He was found guilty of war crimes and hanged in Belgrade on 24 October 1947.

Appendix 1

Supply Performance and Tonnage/Delivery

To compile a conclusive summary of aircraft deployment, tonnage delivery and wounded evacuation with any accuracy or certainty for the Stalingrad airlift is impossible. All the known documentary and credible published sources at the time of writing vary and contradict to some extent. These sources are also limited in number.

Often cited is the list included by Generalmajor Wolfgang Pickert, commander of 9.*Flak-Division* in the pocket, in his *Tagebuch* or *Notizbuchaufzeichnungen 25.6.1942–23.1.1943* (Notebook Records). The list includes a figure for the number of aircraft per day that actually reached the pocket, together with daily fuel, ammunition, food and miscellaneous tonnage delivery figures from 25 November 1942 to 11 January 1943, but the origins of the list – and therefore its accuracy – are not known. However, according to this list, in the 48 days in the aforementioned period, a daily average of 102 tons was delivered, comprised of 34.4 cbm of fuel, 21.5 tons of ammunition and 42.0 tons of other supplies. This resulted in an average lift of 1.539 tons per aircraft – not even the two-ton capacity of a Ju 52/3m. There was a daily average of 520 personnel airlifted out of the pocket. In the aforementioned period, the Luftwaffe flew 3,196 supply sorties to Stalingrad.

The surviving papers of the *Sonderstab Milch* contain various lists detailing aircraft deployment and losses, and daily tonnage figures, as well as a selection of block graphs showing transport performance, wounded evacuation, aircraft loss figures, daily weather conditions and air temperature at the supply bases, and sketches of meteorological conditions over the supply base areas and Volga region. The Milch papers also include very detailed daily performance logs, commencing from 16 January 1943 (the day Milch arrived in Russia), which are broken down into day and night operations and then further by the numbers of aircraft sorties classified as *erfüllt* (fulfilled/completed) by aircraft type and out of each supply base. This is augmented by numbers of failed/aborted sorties, aircraft shot down or listed as missing, as well as aircraft which were *noch im Einsatz* ('still out') at the time of the report, and then split between landings and air-drops. Tonnage figures are shown by fuel,

		Versorgung der Armee seit 25.11.42-11.1.43				
tum	Maschinen	Betriebs- stoff cbm	Munition to	Verpflegung to	Sonsti- ges to	Verwundet
.11.	34	36	28		-	330
	37	42	28	-	-	290
	12	24	-	-	-	200
	39	33	29	7	1	430
	39	23	16	-	2	490
	71	69	35	-	1	660
.12.	56	44	32	-	-	530
	28	12	24	4	-	200

general supplies and ammunition. Unfortunately, these logs are too extensive and detailed to include fully here.

However, the issue is that they conflict with other data in the Milch papers.

Another 'snapshot' source is the tabular graph produced for the 'Von Rohden Collection', a collection of material assembled under the direction of General Herhudt von Rohden, the former Chief of Staff of Luftflotte 4 during the time of the airlift and latterly head of the Luftwaffe's 8.Abteilung (Historical Section) in the OKL, in connection with his preparation of an official history of the Luftwaffe during World War II. Von Rohden began assembling the material and writing his history during the course of the war, but at the end of hostilities he was directed by the USAAF to complete his work with the assistance of other former senior Luftwaffe officers. He prepared a graph showing daily tonnage performance aligned with key events, such as the losses of Pitomnik and Gumrak, and key phases such as the Soviet Uranus offensive. This graph was later included on page 100 of von Rohden's book Die Luftwaffe Ringt um Stalingrad, published in 1950.

A useful attempt to present an abridged overview of aircraft commitment, tonnage figures and wounded evacuation was made by former German Luftwaffe officers and personnel from the USAF Historical Division based at Karlsruhe in the 1950s as part of what became known as the 'Karlsruhe Project'. This was a major investigative and research initiative into the history of the Luftwaffe which continued the work of von Rohden, who died in 1951. The data was drawn from the Fiebig, Pickert and Milch Tagebuch, as well as occasional information from the Kriegstagbuch of the OKW and von Rohden's own figures. At the time of writing, this table can be found in various files at the Bundesarchiv-Militärchiv in Freiburg (see for example ZA 3/111 Sammelakte mit Abschriften Luftversorgung Stalingrads). It calculates

Gruppe I c　　　　　　　　　　　　　　　　　18.1.1943

Luftversorgung 6.Armee

1) Nachteinsatz 16./17.1.:　32 He 111 Nowotscherkassk
　　　　　　　　　　　　　　　　(30 erfüllt /Abwurf/, 1 nicht
　　　　　　　　　　　　　　　　　　erfüllt, 1 noch im Einsatz)
　　zugeführt:　　　　　　　0,3 cbm Betriebsstoff
　　　　　　　　　　　　　　21,0 t　Verpflegung
　　　　　　　　　　　　　　10 He 111 Woroschilowgrad
　　　　　　　　　　　　　　　　(9 erfüllt /Abwurf/, 1 vermisst)
　　zugeführt:　　　　　　　4,2 t Verpflegung
　　　　　　　　　　　　　　0,7 cbm Betriebsstoff
　　　　　　　　　　　　　　7 Ju 52　(4 erfüllt /Abwurf/, 2 nicht
　　　　　　　　　　　　　　　　　　erfüllt, 1 vermisst)
　　zugeführt:　　　　　　　8 t Verpflegung

2) Tageinsatz 17.1.　　　　10 He 111 (8 erfüllt /3 Landung, 5 Abwurf/,
　　　　　　　　　　　　　　　　　　1 nicht erfüllt, 1 noch im Eins.)
　　zugeführt:　　　　　　　2,8 cbm Betriebsstoff
　　　　　　　　　　　　　　4,0 t Verpflegung
　　zurück:　　　　　　　　11　　Verwundete
　　　　　　　　　　　　　　36　　Mann
　　　　　　　　　　　　　　11 He 111 Nowotscherkassk (5 erfüllt, 4 nicht
　　　　　　　　　　　　　　　　　　erfüllt, 2 noch im Einsatz)
　　zugeführt:　　　　　　　0,8 cbm Betriebsstoff
　　　　　　　　　　　　　　5,3 t Verpflegung
　　　　　　　　　　　　　　0,2 t sonstiges Gut
　　zurück:　　　　　　　　37　　Verwundete

3) Vorläufige Gesamtversorgungsleistung vom 16.1.1700 Uhr - 17.1.1700 Uhr
　　　　　　　　　　　　　　46,2 t

4) Bemerkungen zum Einsatz:　Infolge Artl.- und Bombentrichter und Flug-
　zeugbrüchen in der Nacht keine Landung in Gumrak möglich.

5) Nachmeldungen:
　　Tageinsatz 14.1.　　　　8 He 111 noch im Einsatz = erfüllt, 3 Flz.
　　　　　　　　　　　　　　　　　　am Rückflug abgeschossen.
　　zugeführt:　　　　　　　6,25 t Munition
　　　　　　　　　　　　　　4,2 cbm Betriebsstoff
　　zurück:　　　　　　　　34　　Verwundete
　　Nachteinsatz 14./15.1.:　6 Ju 52 Ssalsk noch im Einsatz = 3 erfüllt
　　　　　　　　　　　　　　　　　　3 nicht erfüllt.
　　zugeführt:　　　　　　　4,4 cbm Betriebsstoff
　　　　　　　　　　　　　　2　　t sonstiges Gut
　　zurück:　　　　　　　　13　　Verwundete
　　Tageinsatz 15.1.　　　　11 He 111 noch im Einsatz = 8 erfüllt,
　　　　　　　　　　　　　　　　　　2 nicht erfüllt, 1 vermisst.
　　zugeführt:　　　　　　　7,6 t Munition
　　　　　　　　　　　　　　6,2 cbm Betriebsstoff
　　　　　　　　　　　　　　6　　t Verpflegung
　　zurück:　　　　　　　　61　　Verwundete
　　Nachteinsatz 15./16.1.　4 Ju 52 Ssalsk noch im Einsatz = 1 erf.
　　　　　　　　　　　　　　　　　　3 nicht erfüllt.
　　zugeführt:　　　　　　　2,2 cbm Betriebsstoff
　　zurück:　　　　　　　　14　　Verwundete
　　　　　　　　　　　　　　1 Ju 52 Swerewo noch im Einsatz = 1 erfüll
　　zugeführt:　　　　　　　0,4 cbm Betriebsstoff
　　　　　　　　　　　　　　1,2 t Verpflegung

K　4612

that a total of 6,591 tons was delivered over 70 days from 25 November, with a daily average of 94.16 tons – 205.84 tons below 6.*Armee*'s subsistence figure of 300 tons. The highest daily average period (137.7 tons) was achieved during the ten days from 12–22 December, while the lowest was over the two days of 22–23 January (45 tons) after the loss of Gumrak, when Stalingradskaya was used briefly.

In his study *Die deutschen Transportflieger im Zweiten Weltkrieg* (160), Morzik states the following totals as being delivered, although he gives no timeframe:

Fuel 1,648 cbm
Ammunition 1,122 tons
Food 2,020 tons
Misc. 129 tons
Wounded, sick and other personnel flown out = 24,910

Finally, in his peerless study of Stalingrad from 1974, Manfred Kehrig presented another tabular compilation of aircraft, tonnage and evacuation numbers (see Kehrig, *Stalingrad – Analyse und Dokumentation einer Schlacht*, *Anlage* 14, pp. 670–671), for which he credits 'TB Pickert' – in other words, the aforementioned Pickert *Tagebuch*. Kehrig's data was also used in the official German account, *Germany and the Second World War, Volume VI, The Global War* published in 2001 (p. 1150).

The problem is that in reviewing all these sources, one runs into, perhaps inevitably, numerous differences, variations and contradictions within them. For example, if one takes 25 November 1942, Pickert gives a figure of 34 aircraft used (*eingesetzt*) for this day (24-hour period?), whereas a list in the Milch papers states 33 aircraft as *eingesetzt* and *erfüllt*. Kehrig states 31 aircraft. Pickert states that 36 cbm of fuel and 28 tons of ammunition were prepared (if not loaded), while a figure of 66 tons total is quoted in Milch. Depending on density, 36 cbm of fuel would equate to approximately 26–31 tons, which, when added to the other supplies that day, would give a maximum of circa 59 tons. Kehrig states 44 cbm of fuel and ten tons of ammunition.

As a random further example, on 16 December Pickert states that 93 aircraft completed the mission, Kehrig states 92 and Milch 94 (25 Ju 52/3ms, 65 He 111s and four Ju 86s). Pickert lists a figure of 79 cbm of fuel, 22 tons of ammunition, 25 tons of supplies and four tons of miscellaneous goods (probably medical), while Milch gives a combined figure of 93 tons.

There is other somewhat confusing data. On 3 December, for example, the Karlsruhe table states *Keine LV, Eisregen-Schnee-Nebel* ('No air supply, freezing rain, snow, fog'), yet on the same table (and as seen below), 24 aircraft are shown as having gone out, carrying 36 cbm of fuel, 25 tons of ammunition, three tons of food and three tons of medical supplies. The assumption, therefore, is that these figures actually denote *prepared* supplies only. Similar anomalies occur on 14 and 15 December.

With this being said, I am basing the appended table on the 'Karlsruhe' table which is, in turn, based on Pickert and Milch, with additional elements from von Rohden, but the above factors should be borne in mind.

The daily weather summaries are quoted from BA-MA ZA4/459 (Karlsruhe Document Collection).

Date	Key events	A/C[1]	F (cbm)[2]	A[3]	F[4]	O/M[5]	CT[6]	W-O[7]	Notes
25.11		34	36	28	–	–		320	
26.11		37	42	28	–	–		290	
27.11		12	24	–	–	–		220	
28.11		39	33	29	7	1		430	
29.11		39	23	16	–	2		490	
30.11		71	69	35	–	1		660	
1.12		56	44	32	–	–		530	
2.12		28	12	24	4	–		200	
3.12		34	36	25	3	3		450	
4.12		63	51	50	16	5		710	
5.12		28	18	65	–	–		110	
6.12		44	23	42	1	3		260	
7.12		130	87	77	10	1		670	
8.12		104	52	119	8	1		790	
9.12		9	10	10	–	–		30	
10.12		64	24	35	9	1		470	
11.12		130	38	106	12	5		510	
12.12		55	24	73	10	1		280	
13.12		60	34	37	12	2		620	
14.12		69	63	29	5	2		230	
15.12		44	56	23	4	3		560	
16.12	Russian 'Little Saturn' offensive	93	79	22	25	4		610	
17.12		36	47	2	21	1		470	
18.12		31	12	3	41	3		280	
19.12		154	32	4	245	8		1,010	
20.12		144	32	5	162	9		1,220	
21.12		120	32	52	150	8		850	
22.12		33	22	37	23	1		230	
23.12		12	87	29	31	3		650	
24.12	Tatsinskaya	–	–	–	–	–		30	
25.12		–	–	–	–	–		–	
26.12		43	1	2	66	–		250	
27.12		69	8	–	71	1		580	
28.12		56	2	1	35	1		500	
29.12		86	63	2	60	5		830	
30.12		118	52	3	79	3		980	
31.12		152	65	10	162	5		980	
1.1.43		92	63	31	118	10		860	

Date	Key events	A/C[1]	F (cbm)[2]	A[3]	F[4]	O/M[5]	CT[6]	W-O[7]	Notes
2.1		–	–	–	–	–		–	
3.1		85	3	4	45	2		550	
4.1		144	62	–	167	2		1,220	
5.1		60	8	4	45	2		610	
6.1		40	8	2	42	5		190	
7.1		50	17	4	53	1		480	
8.1		44	18	2	35	1		300	
9.1		109	43	7	90	10		760	
10.1		126	43	10	110	2		940	
11.1		79	50	5	76	10		466	
12.1		51					61.7		Figs ex Milch, but Kehrig states 35 a/c; 16 cbm F, 11 t A, 35 t F and 2 t O/M cbm F, 30.5 t A, 32 t F and 1.5 t O/M
13.1		69					224.5		
14.1		74					65.2		Figs ex Milch, but Kehrig states 72 a/c; 56 cbm F, 30.5 t A, 32 t F and 1.5 t O/M
15.1		56					105.1		Figs ex Milch, but Kehrig states 61 a/c; 25 cbm F, 31 t A, 48 t F and 2 t O/M
16.1		39					68.5		
17.1		61					52.9		
18.1		42					24.1		
19.1		70					60.8		
20.1		57					52.2		Figs ex Milch, but Kehrig states 31 a/c; 14 cbm F, 0.5 t A, 17 t F
21.1	Gumrak lost	108					99.4		
22.1	Stalingradskaya opens	69					93.2		
23.1		78					80.4		
24.1		7					12.4		
25.1		21					13.0		
26.1		52					46.3		
27.1		124					103.4		

Date	Key events	A/C[1]	F (cbm)[2]	A[3]	F[4]	O/M[5]	CT[6]	W-O[7]	Notes
28.1		87					83.1		
29.1		111					108.7		Figs ex Milch, but Kehrig states 108 a/c; 1 cbm F, 4 t A, 99 t F and 1.5 t O/M
30.1		130					128.0		
31.1		89					118.0		
1.2		89					73.9		
2.2		82					98.0		
2.3		10					7.0		

In terms of the He 111 force, 2,566 sorties were flown to the Stalingrad pocket (37.73 per day), of which 2,260 (33.23 per day) were unloaded (91 per cent). They supplied:

General supplies, including food	1,541.14 tons (22.66 tons each day)
Ammunition	767.50 tons (11.28 tons each day)
Other supplies	99.16 tons (1.45 tons each day)
Total	2,407.80 tons (35.40 tons each day)

Additionally, a total of 1,111.02 cbm of fuel (16.33 cbm per day) was delivered (1,111.02 cbm fuel = 887.00 tons).

In total for the above goods, the He 111 units supplied 3,294.80 tons, or an average of 48.45 tons per day.

The He 111 units flew 9,208 personnel (all ranks) out of the pocket (135.41 each day).[8] In addition, they flew out 533 bags of mail and 2,369 empty air-drop containers.[9]

NOTES

1 Aircraft which have completed the mission (for 25.11.42 to 11.1.43 BA-MA ZA 3/111; for 12.1. to 2.2.43 BA-MA RL 30 /3).
2 Fuel (BA-MA ZA 3/111).
3 Ammunition (BA-MA ZA 3/111).
4 Food and general supplies (BA-MA ZA 3/111).
5 Other supplies and medical (BA-MA ZA 3/111).
6 Combined commodity total from Milch (BA-MA RL 30 /3).
7 Wounded airlifted out (BA-MA ZA 3/111).
8 BA-MA/ZA 3/644, Kühl, *Erfahrungsbericht Stalingrad*.
9 BA-MA/ZA 3/644, Kühl.

Appendix 2

'Karlsruhe Project' Supply Overview

This graph shows the performance of the airlift, broken down into the key phases, along with the respective tonnages. At no time did the Luftwaffe ever even approach 6.*Armee*'s daily subsistence figure of 300 tons.

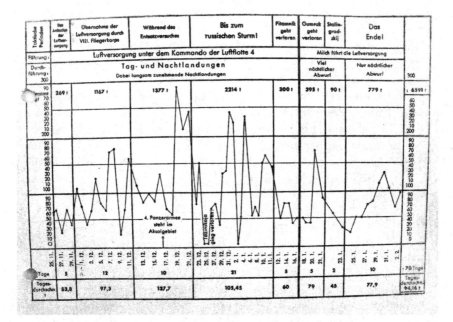

Appendix 3

KG 55 and KGr.z.b.V.5 Delivery and Evacuation Figures

KG 55				KGr.z.b.V.5
	29/11/42 to 16/1/43	17/1/43 to 3/2/43	Total	28/11/42 to 3/2/43
Available Aircraft	1,766	800	2,566	?
Mission Completed	1,548 92 per cent	712 89 per cent	2,260	?
Total Losses	53	6	59 (two per cent)	9
Delivered Supplies	1,245.61 tons	295.53 tons	1,541.14 tons	250.3 tons
Ammunition	722.55 tons	45.04 tons	767.50 tons	198.6 tons
Misc.	90.85 tons	8.31 tons	99.16 tons	12.45 tons
B4 Fuel	576.36 cbm	32.97 cbm	609.07 cbm	539.0 cbm
Otto Fuel	379.36 cbm	79.99 cbm	459.35 cbm	329.8 cbm
Diesel	41.6 cbm	-	41.6 cbm	-
Soldiers flown in	-	-	-	75
Wounded Out	8,605	556 + 47 other pers.	9,208	1,255 + 75 other pers.
Empty Containers	2,229	140	2,369	859
Post In/ Sacks Out	437	96	533	3.5 tons

Total non-fuel = 2,407.89 tons
Total fuel = 1,110.02 cbm (888.01 tons)
Grand total = 3,295.9 tons

Appendix 4

Aircraft Losses during Stalingrad Airlift for Period 24/11/42 to 31/1/43

(based on Milch *Tagebuch*):

Ju 52/3m	266
He 111	165
Ju 86	42
Fw 200	9
He 177	5
Ju 290	1

TOTAL   488

Total loss	= 166
Missing	= 108
Crashed beyond repair	= 214

TOTAL   = 488

Losses as percentage of total number of missions flown per type:

He 177	= 26 per cent
Ju 86	= 21 per cent
Ju 52	= 10 per cent
Fw 200	= 9.7 per cent
He 111	= 5.5 per cent

The losses were equivalent to five *Geschwader* or greater than one *Fliegerkorps*.

Losses in flying personnel = approximately 1,000 men

Sources and Bibliography

ARCHIVE, UNPUBLISHED AND MISCELLANEOUS SOURCES

Air Council, *The German Air Force in Maps and Diagrams 1939–43*, Air Publication 3038, November 1943

Air Division, Control Commission for Germany, British Element, *A Study of the Supply Organisation of the German Air Force 1935–1945*, June 1946

Bundesarchiv (Abt. Militärarchiv), Freiburg (BA-MA)

RL 7/483: *Die Luftflotte 4 bei Stalingrad und am Kaukasus 1942/43 (Entwurfsunterlagen aus dem Projekt von Rohden) – Gen.Maj. Herhudt von Rohden*, 11/1/56

RL 8/55: *Unterlagen des VIII.Fliegerkorps (Anl.Bd. z. KTB) vom 5/10/42–22/2/43*

RL 10/153: *Kampfgruppe z.b.V.5: Erfahrungsbericht über den Einsatz in die Festung Stalingrad in der Zeit vom 28.11.42 bis 3.2.1943*, Major Fritz Uhl, 9/2/43

- *Luftversorgungsführer VIII.Fliegerkorps, Nr.70/43: Besondere Anordnungen für die Luftversorgung der Festung Stalingrad*, 6/1/4 (additionally annotated and based on same document issued by *Gen.Kdo. VIII.Fliegerkorps*, Ia Nr.4200/42, 30/11/42) and *Gen.Kdo. VIII.Fliegerkorps, Quartiermeister* Nr.5970/42, *Besondere Anordnungen für die Versorgung (Anlage 1 zu , Ia Nr.4200/42*, 7/12/42

RL 30/2: *Versorgungsmeldungen Luftflotte 4 und Sonderstab; Einsatzbereitschaft smeldungen; Skizzen zur Wetterlage*

RL 30/3: *Sonderstab Generalfeldmarschall Milch*, 1943

ZA 3/111: *Sammelakte mit Abschriften 'Luftversorgung Stalingrads'*, incl:

Schulz, Generalmajor a.D. Karl Heinrich, *Luftversorgung Stalingrad (21/11/42–1/2/43), ohne Datum*

Greffrath, *Die Luftversorgung Stalingrads (Gesamtüberblick)*, no date

Zahlenangaben zur Luftversorgung Stalingrad (25/11/42–2/2/43), ohne Datum

ZA 3/458: *Die Luftversorgung Stalingrads (Gesamtüberblick)*, Ausarbeitung von Greffrath

- *Erfahrungsbericht über die Luftversorgung der Festung Stalingrad*, Ausarbeitung von General der Panzertruppe Hube
- *Die Luftversorgung Stalingrads, Bericht ohne Titel von Fritz Morzik*

ZA 3/459: *Versorgung Stalingrads durch Lufttransportführer Willers in Stalino und Saporoshje*, Ausarbeitung von Major a.D. Willers, mit Anlagen (see chapter endnotes for individual documents)
  - Briefe von Oberst i.G. a.D. Lothar von Heinemann betreffs der Luftversorgung von Stalingrad, c) *Vorbereitung der Übernahme der Führung der Versorgung für die 6. Armee durch den Stab des VIII. Fliegerkorps. Die Beurteilung der Lage abgestimmt auf die Versorgungsaufgabe 'Luftversorgung Stalingrads'*
  - Brief von General der Flakartillerie a.D. Wolfgang Pickert an Generalmajor a.D. Hans Dörr betreffs der Luftversorgung Stalingrads
  - *Der Kampf um den Versorgungs-Flugplatz Tazinskaja (Aus einer Studie der 8. Abt. des Generalstabes der Lw. Aus dem Jahre 1944 'Einsatz und Führung der B.O. während rückläufiger Bwegungen')*: attached to *Stalingrad* (Aus einem Brief von Gen.a.D. Pickert an die Studiengruppe Geschichte des Luftkrieges vom 10/4/58)
  - *Zahlenangaben zur Luftversorgung Stalingrad (25/11/42–2/2/43)*
ZA 3/460: *Stalingrad 1942/1943*: Brief Erhard Milchs an General a.D. Hermann Plocher betreffs der Luftversorgung Stalingrads vom 10/6/56
ZA 3/644: *Luftversorgung Stalingrad und Festung Sewastopol*
  - *Kampfgeschwader 55 Kommodore (Kühl): Erfahrungsbericht über den Versorgungseinsatz für die 6. Armee in Festung Stalingrad vom 29/11/42– 3/2/43* (see also RL 10/106)
  - *Lufttransportführer Oberst Morzik, Nr. 509/43: Erfahrungsbericht Stalingrad, 12/12/43*
Fiebig, General.Lt., *Tagebuch v. Nov. 1942*, 8. Abt. records as contained on AHB.6 microfilm, Tin 28, IWM London. Translation also available in von Rohden Collection, Karlsruhe Collection, AFHRA, Maxwell AFB, as *Personal Diary of Maj. Gen. Fiebig, 25 Nov. 1942 to 2 Feb. 1943 re Stalingrad Airlift, RSI document translation*, Foreign Docs, Br.AUL 3-4074-12
Hozzel, Brigadier General (ret.) Paul-Werner, *Recollections and Experiences of a Stuka Pilot 1931–1945*, Battelle Institute, 1978
Imperial War Museum, London (IWM)
  AHB.6 microfilm, Tin 21, 8. Abt., *Der Einsatz der Luftflotte 4 im Jahre 1942*
Library and Archives Canada/Bibliothèque et Archives Canada: Department of National Defence, Directorate of History and Heritage: lac reel T-2419 (microfilm of AHB.6 copies of *Luftflotte* 4 operational daily summaries for air supply to Stalingrad 17.1.1943-3.2.1943), accessed at https://heritage.canadiana.ca/view/oocihm.lac_reel_t2419
Luftflotte 4 vor Stalingrad unter Gen. Obst Fhr. v. Richthofen (author collection)
National Archives and Records Administration, T-321, R.G. No. 242, Roll 179, *Kriegstagebuch Sonderstab Genfm. Milch, Anlagenband 3, 15/1–3-2/43*
Pabst, Hauptmann Herbert, *Russian Diary – 1942* (via Pegg)

Pickert, Wolfgang, *Aufzeichnungen des Generalmajor Pickert, Kommandeurs der 9. Flak-Division und General der Luftwaffe bei der 6. Armee aus der Zeit vom 25. VI. 42-23. I. 43*, 8. Abt. records as contained on AHB.6 microfilm, Tin 28, IWM London. Translation also available in von Rohden Collection, Karlsruhe Collection, AFHRA, Maxwell AFB, Foreign Docs, Br.Rpt. M-410/49, AUL M-34852-C

Potthoff, Dr. Heinrich, *Russland (Luftflottenarzt 4) Oktober 1942-April 1943: Meine Tätigkeiten bei Luftflotte 4 in Russland 1942/43 — Stalingrad — Winter* (Götz Frhr. von Richthofen)

Richthofen, Generalfeldmarschall Dr.-Ing. Wolfram Frhr. von Richthofen, *Tagebuch* 1942 and 1943 (via Götz Frhr. von Richthofen)

UK National Archives, Kew (TNA)

AIR 20/7701: *Extracts of Reports of Führer Conferences held on 12/12/42, 1/2/43 and 4/3/43*, (AHB 6 Translation No. VII/44, 25.9.1947)

AIR 20/7702: German Air Historical Branch (8. Abt), 25 March 1944, *The Use of Transport Aircraft in the Present War* (AHB 6 Translation No. VII/69, 30th April 1948)

Government Code and Cypher School: Signals Intelligence Passed to the Prime minister, Messages and Correspondence:

HW1/1152

HW1/1154

HW1/1166

HW1/1169

PUBLISHED ARTICLES AND THESES

Akins, Willard B., Maj., *The Ghosts of Stalingrad*, US Army Command and General Staff College, Fort Leavenworth, 2004

Bieber, Helmut, *50 Jahre nach Stalingrad*, Jägerblatt, Köln, Nr.2 XLII, Mai/ Juni 1993

Brunhaver, John Steven, *Lifeline from the Sky — The Doctrinal Implications of Supplying an Enclave from the Air*, Air University Press, Maxwell Air Force Base, Alabama, June 1996

Coyle, Captain (P) Harold W., *Tatsinskaya and Soviet OMG Doctrine*, Armor, Vol XCIV., No. 1, January-February 1985

Donoho, Capt. James H., *An Analysis of Tactical Military Airlift*, Air Force Institute of Technology, Air University Air Education and Training Command, September 1997

Ebener, Kurt, *Nur zwei Mann der I. und II. /JG 3 "Udet" kamen aus Sowjetrußland zurück: Erinnerung an die Platzschutzstaffel Pitomnik*, Jägerblatt, Köln, Nr.1 XLII, Februar/März 1993

Fischer, Johannes, *Über den Entschluß zur Luftversorgung Stalingrads Ein Beitrag zur militärischen Führung im Dritten Reich*, Militaergeschichtliche Zeitschrift, Vol.6, No.2, 1969

General Fritz Morzik 90 Jahre Alt, Jägerblatt, Köln, Nr.1 XXXI, Februar/März 1982

Grechko, Andrei, *Battle for the Caucasus*, Progress Publishers, Moscow, 1971

Hayward, Joel S.A., *Seeking the Philosopher's Stone – Luftwaffe Operations during the Drive to the South-East, 1942–1943*, University of Canterbury
- *Stalingrad: An Examination of Hitler's Decision to Airlift*, Airpower Journal, Spring 1997

Heywood, Anthony, *Stalingrad – The Greatest Allied Victory?*, Military History Monthly, May 2019

Keen, Richard David, *Half A Million tons and a Goat: A Study of British Participation in the Berlin Airlift – 25 June 1948–12 May 1949*, Thesis submitted for the degree of Doctor of Philosophy to the School of Humanities in the University of Buckingham, September 2013

Lower, Major Roy W., *Luftwaffe Tactical Operations at Stalingrad 19 November–02 February 1943*, Air Command and Staff College, Air University, Maxwell AFB, 1987

Pickert, Wolfgang, *The Stalingrad Airlift: An Eyewitness Commentary*, Aerospace Historian, Vol.18, Winter, December 1971

Salmi, Col. Derek M., *Behind the Light Switch: Toward a Theory of Air Mobility*, Air University Press, Maxwell AFB, August 2020

Thyssen, Major Mike, *A Desperate Struggle to Save a Condemned Army – A Critical Review of the Stalingrad Airlift*, A Research Paper Presented to the Research Department Air Command and Staff College, Maxwell Air Force Base, Alabama, March 1997

Vaughan, David K. and James H. Donoho, *From Stalingrad to Khe Sanh: Factors in the Successful Use of Tactical Airlift to Support Isolated Land Battle Areas*, Air and Space Power Chronicles, Maxwell AFB Database on-line. http://www.airpower.maxwell.af.mil/airchronicles/cc/vaughan.html (accessed 15 August 2003)

Weber, Dr. Theodore, *Reflections on the Air Supply of Encircled Units*, Flugwehr und -Technik, Switzerland, October 1951 (translated and digested by the *Military Review*, April 1952)

Zamansky, Dan, *How were German air force resources distributed between different fronts in the years 1941 to 1943 and what are the implications of this case study for understanding the political economy of the period?*, December 2016 at https://www.ww2.dk/Luftwaffe%20Research.html and https://web.archive.org/web/20190828095325/http:/www.ww2.dk/Dan%20Zamansky%20-%20The%20Study.pdf

PUBLISHED BOOKS

Adam, Wilhelm and Rühle, Otto, *With Paulus at Stalingrad*, Pen and Sword Books, Barnsley, 2015

Antill, Peter, *Stalingrad 1942*, Osprey Publishing, Oxford, 2007

Balke, Ulf, *Kampfgeschwader 100 'Wiking' – Eine Geschichte aus Kriegstagbüchern, Dokumenten und Berichten 1934–1945*, Motorbuch-Verlag, Stuttgart, 1981

Barbas, Bernd, *Die Geschichte der II. Gruppe des Jagdgeschwaders 52 – Offizielle Ausgabe der Traditionsgemeinschaft JG 52*, self-published, Germany, undated

Beevor, Antony, *Stalingrad*, Viking, London, 1998

Bekker, Cajus, *The Luftwaffe War Diaries*, Macdonald & Co., London, 1968

Below, Nicolaus von, *At Hitler's Side – The Memoirs of Hitler's Luftwaffe Adjutant*, Greenhill Books, London, 2001

Bergström, Christer, *Stalingrad – The Air Battle: 1942 through January 1943*, Midland Publishing, Hinckley, 2007

Bergström, Christer, and Mikhailov, Andrey, *Black Cross-Red Star – The Air War over the Eastern Front: Volume 2, Resurgence, January–June 1942*, Pacifica Military History, Pacifica, 2001

Bergström, Christer; Dikov Andrey and Antipov, Vlad, *Black Cross-Red Star – Air War over the Eastern Front: Volume 3, Everything for Stalingrad*, Eagle Editions, Hamilton, 2006

Bergström, Christer, *Black Cross-Red Star – Air War over the Eastern Front: Volume 4 – Stalingrad to Kuban*, Vaktel Books, Eskilstuna, 2019

Bock, GFM Fedor von, *The War Diary 1939-1945*, Schiffer Publishing, Atglen, 1996

Boog, Horst, *Die deutsche Luftwaffenführung 1935–1945: Führungsprobleme, Spitzengliederung, Generalstabsausbildung*, Deutsche Verlags-Anstalt, Stuttgart, 1982

Boog, Horst et al., *Germany and the Second World War: Volume IV – The Attack on the Soviet Union*, Clarendon Press, Oxford, 1998

Burdick, Charles and Jacobsen, Hans-Adolf, *The Halder War Diary 1939–1942*, Greenhill Books, London, 1988

Busch, Reinhold (ed.), *Survivors of Stalingrad – Eyewitness Accounts from the Sixth Army, 1942–43*, Frontline Books, Barnsley, 2012

Carell, Paul, *Hitler's War on Russia: The Story of the German Defeat in the East*, George C. Harrap, London, 1964
    - *Scorched Earth: Hitler's War on Russia Volume 2*, George C. Harrap, London, 1970

Chuikov, Marshal Vasili Ivanovich, *The Beginning of the Road – The Story of the Battle for Stalingrad*, MacGibbon & Kee, London, 1963

Citino, Robert M., *Death of the Wehrmacht – The German Campaigns of 1942*, University Press of Kansas, Lawrence, 2007

Cooper, Matthew, *The German Air Force 1933–1945 – An Anatomy of Failure*, Jane's Publishing, London, 1981

Die Wehrmachtberichte 1939–1945, Band 2 1.Januar 1942 bis 31.Dezember 1943, Gesellschaft für Literatur und Bildung, Köln, 1989

Diedrich, Torsten, *Paulus – Das Trauma von Stalingrad: Eine Biographie*, Ferdinand Schöningh, Paderborn 2009

Dierich, Wolfgang, *Kampfgeschwader 51 'Edelweiss' – The History of a German Bomber Unit 1939–1945*, Ian Allan, Shepperton, 1975
- *Kampfgeschwader 55 'Greif' – Eine Chronik aus Dokumenten und Berichten 1937–1945*, Motorbuch Verlag, Stuttgart, 1994

DiNardo, Richard L., *Germany and the Axis Powers – From Coalition to Collapse*, University Press of Kansas, Lawrence, 2005

Engel, Major Gerhard, *At the Heart of the Reich: The Secret Diary of Hitler's Army Adjutant*, Greenhill Books, London, 2005

Erickson, John, *The Road to Stalingrad – Stalin's War with Germany: Volume 1*, Weidenfeld & Nicolson, London, 1977
- *The Road to Berlin – Stalin's War with Germany: Volume 2*, Weidenfeld & Nicolson, London, 1983

Eriksson, Patrick G, *Alarmstart East: the German fighter pilot's experience on the Eastern Front 1941–1945*, Amberley Publishing, Stroud 2020

Fleischer, Wolfgang, *German Air-Dropped Weapons to 1945*, Midland Publishing, Hinckley, 2004

Forsyth, Robert, *Heinkel He 111 – An Illustrated History*, Classic Publications, Manchester, 2014
- *Junkers Ju 52 – A History: 1930–1945*, Classic Publications, Manchester, 2014

Forczyk, Robert, *Demyansk 1942–43 – The frozen fortress*, Osprey Publishing, Oxford, 2012
- *Stalingrad 1942–43(1) – The German Advance to the Volga*, Osprey Publishing, Oxford, 2021
- *Stalingrad 1942–43(2) – The Fight for the City*, Osprey Publishing, Oxford, 2021

Glantz, David M., *The Battle for Leningrad 1941–1944*, University Press of Kansas, Lawrence, 2002

Glantz, David M. with House, Jonathan M., *The Stalingrad Trilogy Volume 1: To the Gates of Stalingrad – Soviet-German Combat Operations April–August 1942*, University Press of Kansas, Lawrence, 2009
- *The Stalingrad Trilogy Volume 2: Armageddon in Stalingrad – September–November 1942*, University Press of Kansas, Lawrence, 2009
- *The Stalingrad Trilogy Volume 3: Endgame at Stalingrad – Book One: November 1942*, University Press of Kansas, Lawrence, 2014

- *The Stalingrad Trilogy Volume 3: Endgame at Stalingrad – Book Two: December 1942–February 1943*, University Press of Kansas, Lawrence, 2014

Goerlitz, Walter, *Paulus and Stalingrad*, The Citadel Press, New York, 1963

Gundelach, Karl, *Kampfgeschwader 4: Eine Geschichte aus Kriegstagebüchern, Dokumenten und Berichten 1939–1945*, Motorbuch Verlag, Stuttgart, 1978
- *Die deutsche Luftwaffe im Mittelmeer 1940–1945 Band 1*, Peter D. Lang, Frankfurt-am-Main, 1981

Hardesty, Von, *Red Phoenix – The Rise of Soviet Air Power 1941–1945*, Smithsonian Institution Press, Washington, D.C., 1982

Haupt, Werner, *Army Group North: The Wehrmacht in Russia 1941–1945*, Schiffer Military History, Atglen, 1997
- *Army Group South: The Wehrmacht in Russia 1941–1945*, Schiffer Military History, Atglen, 1998

Hayward, Joel S. A., *Stopped at Stalingrad – The Luftwaffe and Hitler's Defeat in the East, 1942–1943*, University Press of Kansas, Lawrence, 1998

Hinsley, F. H. (et.al), *British Intelligence in the Second World War – Volume 2*, Her Majesty's Stationery Office, London, 1981

Homze, Edward L., *Arming the Luftwaffe*, University of Nebraska Press, Lincoln, 1996

Irving, David, *The Rise and Fall of the Luftwaffe – The Life of Erhard Milch*, Weidenfeld & Nicolson, London, 1973
- *Göring – A Biography*, Macmillan, London, 1989
- *Hitler's War*, Focal Point, London, 2002

Kaiser, Jochen, *Die Ritterkreuzträger der Kampfflieger, Band 1*, Luftfahrtverlag Start, Bad Zwischenahn, 2010
- *Die Ritterkreuzträger der Kampfflieger, Band 2*, Luftfahrtverlag Start, Bad Zwischenahn, 2011

Kehrig, Manfred, *Stalingrad – Analyse und Dokumentation einer Schlacht*, Deutsche Verlags-Anstalt, Stuttgart, 1979

Keitel, Wilhelm, (ed. Gorlitz, Walter; trans. Irving, David), *The Memoirs of Field Marshal Keitel*, William Kimber, London, 1965

Kershaw, Ian, *Hitler – 1936–1945: Nemesis*, Allen Lane, The Penguin Press, London, 2000

Kössler, Karl and Ott, Günther, *Die großen Dessauer: Junkers Ju 89, Ju 90, Ju 290, Ju 390 – Die Geschichte einer Flugzeugfamilie*, Aviatic Verlag, Planegg, 1973

Kozhevnikov, M. N., *The Command and Staff of the Soviet Army Air Force in the Great Patriotic War 1941–1945*, Moscow, 1977 (translated and published in association with the USAF)

Kurowski, Franz, *Luftbrücke Stalingrad – Die Tragodie der Luftwaffe und der Untergang der 6. Armee*, Kurt Vowinckel-Verlag, Berg am See, 1982

Manstein, Field Marshal Erich von, *Lost Victories*, Arms and Armour Press, London, 1982

Mawdsley, Evan, *Thunder in the East – The Nazi-Soviet War 1941–1945*, Hodder Arnold, London, 2005

Megargee, Geoffrey P., *Inside Hitler's High Command*, University of Kansas Press, Kansas, 2000

Melvin, Mungo, *Manstein – Hitler's Greatest General*, Weidenfeld & Nicolson, London, 2010

Möbius, Ingo and Huß, Jürgen, *Stille Adler – Die Ritterkreuzträger der Transportflieger 1940–1945*, Eigenverlag Ingo Möbius, Chemnitz, 2019

Morzik, Generalmajor a.D. Fritz, *USAF Historical Studies No. 167: German Air Force Airlift Operations*, USAF Historical Division, Aerospace Studies Institute, Arno Press, New York, 1961

Morzik, Fritz (ed. Hümmelchen, Gerhard), *Die deutschen Transportflieger im Zweiten Weltkrieg*, Bernard & Graefe Verlag, Frankfurt am Main, 1966

Muller, Richard: *The German Air War in Russia*, The Nautical and Aviation Publishing Company of America, Baltimore, 1992

Müller, Rudolf, *Ikarus – Ein Fliegerleben*, Verlag Dr. Neufang, Gelsenkirchen-Buer, 1979

Murawski, Marek J., *Objective: the Caucusus! The Luftwaffe operations in the southern sector of the Eastern Front: May–August, 1942* [Sic] Kagero Publishing, Lublin, 2011

Murray, Williamson, *Luftwaffe*, George Allen & Unwin, London, 1985

Pawlas, Karl W., *Munitions Lexikon Band 3: Deutsche Bomben*, Journal-Verlag Schwend, Schwäbisch-Hall, 1977

Pegg, Martin, *Transporter: Volume One – Luftwaffe Transport Units 1939–1943*, Classic Publications, Hersham, 2006

Plocher, Gen.Lt. Hermann, *The German Air Force Versus Russia, 1942*, USAF Historical Division, Arno Press, New York, 1966

Preston Chaney Jr., Otto, *Zhukov*, David & Charles, Newton Abbot, 1972

Prien, Jochen and Stemmer, Gerhard, *Messerschmitt Bf 109 im Einsatz bei der Stab und I./Jagdgeschwader 3*, Struve-Druck, Eutin, 1997
  - *Messerschmitt Bf 109 im Einsatz bei der II./Jagdgeschwader 3*, Struve-Druck, Eutin, 1996

Probert, Air Cdre H.A., (ed.), *The Rise and Fall of the German Air Force 1933–1945*, Arms and Armour Press, London, 1983

Rohden, Hans-Detlef Herhudt v., *Die Luftwaffe ringt um Stalingrad*, Limes Verlag, Wiesbaden, 1950

Schlaug, Georg, *Die deutschen Lastensegler-Verbände 1937–1945 – Eine Chronik aus Berichten, Tagebüchern, Dokumenten*, Motorbuch Verlag, Stuttgart, 1985

- *Die II. Kampfgeschwader zur besonderen Verwendung 1 1938-1943 unbenannt in II. Transportgeschwader 1: Geschichte Einer Transportflieger-Gruppe im II. Weltkrieg*, Kameradschaft ehemaliger Transportflieger, Ronnenberg/ Hannover, 1989

Schmoll, Peter, *Nest of Eagles – Messerschmitt Production and Flight-Testing at Regensburg 1936–1945*, Classic Publications, Hersham, 2009

Schramm, Percy E., *Kriegstagebuch des Oberkommandos der Wehrmacht, 1942 – Teilband I, Teilband II* and *1943, Teilband I*, Bernard & Graefe Verlag, München, 1982

Schröter, Heinz, *Stalingrad*, Michael Joseph, London, 1958

Seaton, Albert, *The Russo-German War 1941–45*, Arthur Barker, London, 1971

Speer, Albert: *Inside the Third Reich*, Weidenfeld & Nicolson, London 1970

Suchenwirth, Richard, *USAF Historical Studies No. 189: Historical Turning Points in the German Air Force War Effort*, USAF Historical Studies, USAF Historical Division, Aerospace Studies Institute, Arno Press, New York, 1968

Supf, Peter, *Das Buch der deutschen Fluggeschichte: Band 2*, Drei Brunnen Verlag, Stuttgart, 1958

Sydnor Jr., Charles W., *Soldiers of Destruction: The SS Death's Head Division 1933–1945*, Guild Publishing, London, 1989

The Fatal Decisions – Six decisive battles of the Second World War from the viewpoint of the vanquished, (Richardson, William and Freidin, Seymour [ed.]), Michael Joseph, London, 1956

Völker, Karl-Heinz, *Die Deutsche Luftwaffe 1933–1939 – Aufbau, Führung und Rüstung der Luftwaffe sowie die Entwicklung der deutschen Luftkriegstheorie*, Deutsche Verlags-Anstalt, Stuttgart, 1967

Waiss, Walter, *Chronik Kampfgeschwader Nr. 27 Boelcke, Band IV, Teil 3: 1/1/42– 31/12/42*, Helios Verlags- und Buchvertriebsgesellschaft, Aachen, 2005
- *Chronik Kampfgeschwader Nr. 27 Boelcke, Band V, Teil 4: 1/1/43–31/12/43*, Helios Verlags- und Buchvertriebsgesellschaft, Aachen, 2007

Warlimont, Walter, *Inside Hitler's Headquarters 1939–45*, Weidenfeld & Nicolson, London, 1964

Weal, John, *Osprey Aircraft of the Aces 25 – Messerschmitt Bf 110 Zerstörer Aces of World War 2*, Osprey Publishing, Oxford, 1999

Wieder Joachim, and von Einsidel, Heinrich Graf, *Stalingrad – Memories and Reassessments*, Arms and Armour Press, London, 1998

Zhukov, Georgi K., (Salisbury, Harrison E. ed.), *Marshal Zhukov's Greatest Battles*, Macdonald, London, 1969

Ziemke, Earl F. and Bauer, Magna E., *Moscow to Stalingrad: Decision in the East*, Military Heritage Press, New York, 1985

Ziemke, Earl F., *Stalingrad to Berlin: The German Defeat in the East*, Dorset Press, New York, 1985

ON-LINE RESOURCES

The Luftwaffe and *The Heer* by Gareth Collins and Michael Miller at Axis Biographical Research (accessed 2021 at http://www.oocities.org/~orion47/index2.html)

The Luftwaffe, 1933–1945 at www.ww2.dk, also incorporating *Luftwaffe Officer Career Summaries* by Henry L. deZeng IV and Douglas G. Stankey and *Luftwaffe Airfields 1935–1945* by Henry L. deZeng IV

The Stalingrad Airlift at www.stalingrad.net

Notes

PREFACE

1 Phillips, Major Thomas R., ed., *Roots of Strategy – A Collection of Military Classics*, John Lane the Bodley Head, London, 1943, pp. 219–20 and p. 230.

2 Villars, Duke Claude Louis Hector (1653–1734), Marshal of France.

3 See, for example, Bullock, Alan, *Hitler – A Study in Tyranny*, Konceky & Konecky, New York, 1962, p. 805; also Fest, Joachim C., *Hitler*, Weidenfeld & Nicolson, London, 1974, pp. 157, 319, 331 and 666.

4 Brunhaver, *Lifeline from the Sky – The Doctrinal Implications of Supplying an Enclave from the Air*, p. 15.

1. THE MAN FOR THE MOMENT

1 Mawdsley, p. 125 and Forczyk, *Demyansk*, pp. 23–32.

2 Glantz, *Leningrad*, p. 184.

3 Halder, p. 600.

4 Muller, pp. 62–63.

5 Morzik, p. 143.

6 Halder, p. 601.

7 Boog et al., pp. 738–40 and Seaton, p. 246 and Haupt, *Army Group North*, p. 123.

8 Forczyk, *Demyansk*, p. 53.

9 Boog et al., p. 742.

10 Haupt, p. 124.

11 Boog et al., p. 742.

12 Mawdsley, p. 125.

13 Carell, *Hitler's War on Russia*, p. 398.

14 Seaton, p. 245.

15 Haupt, p. 123.

16 Beevor, p. 40.

17 Adam and Rühle, p. 6.

18 Forczyk, p. 10 and Snydor, p. 214.

19 Haupt, p. 124.

20 Akins, p. 18.
21 Forczyk, p. 53.
22 Boog et al, p. 744.
23 Forczyk, p. 11.
24 For Morzik's career, various sources include, *General Fritz Morzik 90 Jahre Alt*, Jägerblatt, Köln, Nr.1 XXX1, Februar/März 1982; Supf, *Das Buch der deutschen Fluggeschichte: Band I,* p. 643 and *Band II,* pp. 132, 180 and A9; Möbius and Huß, *Stille Adler – Die Ritterkreuzträger der Transportflieger 1940–1945*, pp. 44–45; Morzik, *German Air Force Airlift Operations,* p. xxiii; Richard Meredith, *Phoenix – A Complete History of the Luftwaffe 1918–1945: Volume One – The Phoenix is Reborn 1918–1934,* Helion & Co., Solihull, 2015, various pages.

2. DANGEROUS PRECEDENTS

1 Akins, p. 20.
2 Morzik, p. 150; and Bekker, p. 276.
3 Forczyk, p. 53.
4 Morzik and Hümmelchen, p. 127.
5 Morzik and Hümmelchen, p. 8; and Möbius & Huß, pp. 10 and 54.
6 Morzik, p. 148.
7 www.ww2.dk/Airfields%20-%20Russia%20and%20Ukraine.pdf (accessed July 2021).
8 Bekker, p. 276.
9 Bekker, p. 276.
10 Bergström, *Black Cross-Red Star – The Air War over the Eastern Front: Volume 2* [hereinafter BC/RS], p. 86; see also by Bergström, *Hans-Ekkehard Bob*, AirPower Editions, Crowborough, 2007, p. 49.
11 Morzik, p. 152.
12 Morzik, p. 167.
13 Morzik and Hümmelchen, p. 133; and Morzik, p. 154.
14 Morzik and Hümmelchen, p. 138; and Morzik, p. 162.
15 Bergström, BC/RS Vol. 2, p. 96.
16 Forczyk, p. 54.
17 Morzik and Hümmelchen, p. 134; and Morzik, p. 155.
18 Morzik and Hümmelchen, p. 130; and Morzik, p. 149.
19 Morzik, p. 157.
20 Forczyk, p. 54.
21 Erickson, *The Road to Stalingrad*, p. 324.
22 Bergström, BC/RS Vol. 2, p. 88.
23 Boog et al., p. 745.
24 Halder, p. 608.
25 Bekker, p. 277; Morzik and Hümmelchen, p. 133; and Morzik, p. 154 and pp. 163–64.
26 Beevor, p. 44.

27 Snydor, p. 219.
28 Snydor, p. 221.
29 Bergström, BC/RS Vol. 2, p. 85; and Morzik and Hümmelchen, p. 128.
30 Bergström, BC/RS Vol. 2, p. 88.
31 Morzik (p. 173-A) claims five aircraft were destroyed, but Bergström quotes four based on *Generalquartiermeister der Luftwaffe* returns (BC/RS Vol. 2, pp. 88 and 222). OKL pressure, see Forczyk, p. 56.
32 Von Rohden cited in Muller, p. 63.
33 Gundelach, *Kampfgeschwader 4*, pp.167–68.
34 Bergström, BC/RS Vol. 2, p. 98.
35 Forczyk, p. 55.
36 Morzik and Hümmelchen, p. 145; and Forczyk, p. 55.
37 Boog et al., p. 747.
38 Forczyk, p. 11.
39 Bergström, BC/RS Vol. 2, p. 94.
40 Erickson, p. 332.
41 Bergström, BC/RS Vol. 2, p. 95.
42 Forczyk, p. 11.
43 Akins, p. 26.
44 Erickson, p. 381.
45 Morzik and Hümmelchen, p. 145; and Morzik, p. 172 – but there is a slight discrepancy in these two sources. In Morzik and Hümmelchen the period is stated as 19.2 to 18.5, while in Morzik's later account, it is stated as 18.2 to 19.5.
46 Forczyk, p. 55.
47 Forczyk, p. 56.
48 Forczyk, p. 56.
49 Morzik, p. 172.
50 Gundelach, p. 172.
51 Forczyk, p. 11.
52 Carell, pp. 399–400.
53 Morzik, p. 142.
54 Morzik and Hümmelchen, p. 145; and Morzik, p. 172.
55 Morzik, pp. 171–72.
56 Forczyk, p. 56.
57 Morzik, p. 175.
58 TNA/AIR 20/7702, 8.Abt., *The Use of Transport Aircraft in the Present War*, 25/3/44.
59 Pickert, *The Stalingrad Airlift: An Eyewitness Commentary*, p. 183.

3. THE *FÜHRER* DIRECTIVE

1 Von Below, p. 145.
2 Kershaw, p. 505.
3 Irving, *Hitler's War*, p. 486.
4 Kershaw, pp. 505–06 and 967.

5 Irving, p. 486.
6 Beevor, p. 62.
7 Warlimont, p. 230.
8 Megargee, p. 176.
9 Halder, p. 612.
10 Warlimont, p. 231.
11 Warlimont, p. 231.
12 Von Rohden, RL 7/483: *Die Luftflotte 4 bei Stalingrad und am Kaukasus 1942/43 (Entwurfsunterlagen aus dem Projekt von Rohden)*, p. 1.
13 Hayward, *Seeking*, p. 386.
14 Hayward, *Stopped*, p. 18.
15 Hayward, *Seeking*, p. 387.
16 Citino, p. 157.
17 Megargee, p. 177; and Ziemke and Bauer, pp. 287–89.
18 Hayward, *Seeking*, p. 388.
19 Seaton, pp. 266 and 269.
20 Citino, p. 163.
21 Warlimont, p. 231.
22 Citino, p. 153.
23 IWM/8.Abt., *Gliederung des Heeres und der Luftwaffe am 1.7.1942* and *Der Einsatz der Luftflotte 4 im Jahre 1942*, AHB.6 microfilm, Tin 21.
24 Bergström, BC/RS Vol. 3, p. 19.
25 Murawski, p. 29.
26 Muller, p. 86.
27 Glantz with House, *To the Gates of Stalingrad*, p. 131; Citino, pp. 162 and 166; and Adam and Rühle, p. 37.
28 Murawski, p. 29.
29 Beevor, p. 67.
30 Clemens, Graf von Podewils from *Don und Volga* cited in Beevor, p. 75.
31 TNA/HW1/693 CX/MSS/1147/T20, 3/7/42.
32 Beevor, p. 73.
33 Haupt, p. 147.
34 Hayward, *Stopped*, p. 128.
35 Plocher, p. 213.
36 Adam and Rühle, p. 26.
37 Adam and Rühle, p. 26.
38 Adam and Rühle, p. 27.
39 Von Bock, p. 520.
40 Glantz with House, p. 167.
41 Von Bock, p. 526.

4. THE DECISIVE FACTOR?

1 Overy cited in *The Oxford Companion to World War II*, OUP Oxford, pp. 362–63.

2 Zamansky, p. 8.

3 Zamansky, p. 10.

4 Probert, 152 and Air Council, *GAF in Maps and Diagrams*, p. 14.

5 Akins, p. 10.

6 Donoho, p. 22.

7 Control Commission for Germany, *A Study of the Supply*, pp. 178–79.

8 See Gen.St. der Lw.,Nr.3244/38,7.11.1938 cited in Völker, p. 170.

9 Homze, p. 172.

10 Völker, p. 189.

11 Homze, pp. 227–30.

12 TNA/HW1/608.

13 TNA/AIR40/2037.

14 IWM/AHB.6:Von Rohden: *Der Luftkrieg im Osten 1941*

15 Suchenwirth, p. 32.

16 Suchenwirth, p. 33.

17 Morzik and Hümmelchen, 7; Morzik, p. 7; and Akins, p. 13.

18 TNA/AIR20/7702.

19 Air Council, *GAF in Maps and Diagrams*, p. 76.

20 Akins, pp. 10–11.

21 Suchenwirth, p. 35.

22 TNA/AIR20/7702.

23 Morzik and Hümmelchen, p. 112; and Morzik, p. 125.

24 Gundelach, *Die deutsche Luftwaffe im Mittelmeer 1940–1945 Band 1*, p. 354.

25 Gundelach, p. 377.

26 Pegg, p. 79.

27 Probert, p. 153; and Pegg, p. 82.

28 Pegg, pp. 79 and 82.

29 Air Council, *GAF in Maps and Diagrams*, p. 48.

30 Morzik and Hümmelchen, p. 150; and Morzik, p. 178.

31 TNA/AIR20/7702.

5. 'THE GREAT DAY'

1 Von Richthofen's arrival at Mariupol is based on his *Tagebuch*, photographs taken at the time and other documents in the author's possession.

2 Von Rohden, RL 7/483: *Die Luftflotte 4 bei Stalingrad und am Kaukasus 1942/43 (Entwurfsunterlagen aus dem Projekt von Rohden)*, p. 1.

3 Von Richthofen, 20/7/42.

4 Air Division, Control Commission for Germany, British Element, *A Study of the Supply Organisation of the German Air Force 1935–1945*, p. 249.

5 Hayward, *Seeking*, p. 388.

6 Bergström, Dikov and Antipov, *BC/RS: Vol. 2*, p. 48.

7 Muller, p. 87.

8 Von Rohden, RL 7/483, p. 7.

9 Hayward, *Stopped*, p. 145; and Boog et al., p. 982.

10 Muller, p. 87.

11 See Peter Hoffmann, *Hitler's Personal Security*, pp. 226–29; R. Raiber, *The Führerhauptquartiere* in *After the Battle*, No. 19, 1977, pp. 48–49; and *Wehrwolf: Hitler's Headquarters in Ukraine* at https://war-documentary.info/wehrwolf-hitlers-headquarters/ (accessed 8/9/21)

12 Keitel, pp. 182-183; and Irving, *Hitler's War*, p. 507.

13 Boog et al., p. 982.

14 Pickert, *The Stalingrad Airlift: An Eyewitness Commentary*, p. 183.

15 Ziemke and Bauer, p. 388.

16 Heywood, p. 23.

17 Akins, p. 39.

18 Kozhevnikov, p. 82.

19 Boog et al., p. 981; and Beevor, pp. 97–98.

20 Halder, p. 641.

21 Citino, p. 227.

22 Boog et al., p. 981.

23 Karl Lang from *Geschichte der 384. Infanterie-Division 1942–1944: zur Erinnerung an die gefallenen und vermißten Kameraden*, Rodenkirchen, 1965, quoted in Haupt, p. 157.

24 Müller, p. 153.

25 Beevor, p. 87.

26 Adam, p. 27.

27 Boog et al., pp. 984–85.

28 Citino, p. 227.

29 Adam, p. 32.

30 Ziemke and Bauer, p. 364.

31 Von Rohden, RL 7/483, p. 3.

32 Halder, p. 646.

33 Muller, p. 88.

34 Von Richthofen, 23/7/42.

35 Hozzel, p. 88–89.

36 Ziemke and Bauer, p. 360.

37 Beevor, p. 88.

38 Hozzel, pp. 91–92.

39 Halder, p. 649.

40 Ziemke and Bauer, p. 365.

41 Halder, p. 649.

42 Hinsley, F. H. (et.al.), pp. 99–100.

43 Beevor, p. 93.

44 Bergström, Dikov and Antipov, p. 59.

45 Bergström, Dikov and Antipov, p. 60.

46 Adam, p. 29.

47 Wolfgang Pickert, *Aufzeichnungen des Generalmajor Pickert* [etc], 25/7/42.

48 Citino, p. 225.
49 Glantz and House, *To the Gates of Stalingrad*, p. 261; and Beevor, pp. 84–85.
50 Plocher, p. 222.
51 Glantz and House, p. 286; and Chuikov, p. 51.
52 Von Richthofen, 28/8/42.
53 Von Richthofen, 6/8/42; and Plocher, p. 222.
54 Hayward, *Stopped*, pp. 185–87.
55 Von Richthofen, 10/8/42.
56 Von Richthofen, 15/8/42.
57 Adam, p. 48.
58 Von Richthofen, 19/8/42.
59 Bergström, Dikov and Antipov, p. 65.
60 Plocher, pp. 230–32.
61 Adam, p. 55.
62 Plocher, p. 233.
63 Von Rohden, p. 12; and Plocher, p. 233.
64 Pabst, p. 81.
65 Glantz and House, p. 322.
66 Plocher, p. 231; Schröter, p. 34; Glantz and House, p. 344; Brunhaver, p. 8; and Adam, p. 56.
67 Glantz and House, p. 334; and Hayward, p. 187.
68 Muller, p. 89.
69 Hayward, p. 187.
70 Pabst, p. 82.
71 Beevor, p. 107; and Haupt, p. 164.
72 Prien and Stemmer, *Messerschmitt Bf 109 im Einsatz bei der II./Jagdgeschwader 3*, p. 167.
73 Beevor, p. 112.
74 Pabst, pp. 83–84.
75 Von Richthofen, 25/8/42.
76 Adam, pp. 59–61.
77 Balke, pp. 118–19; and Bergström, Dikov and Antipov, p. 134.
78 Adam, p. 61; Beevor, p. 113; and Irving, p. 516.
79 Von Richthofen, 28/8/42.
80 See Jeremy Dixon, *Luftwaffe Generals – The Knight's Cross Holders, 1939–1945*, Schiffer Publishing, Atglen, 2009, pp. 197–98.
81 Von Richthofen, 30/8/42.

6. RUBBLE AND FIRE

1 Erickson, *The Road to Stalingrad*, p. 387.
2 Glantz, *To the Gates of Stalingrad – Soviet-German Combat Operations April–August 1942*, p. 380.
3 Beevor, pp. 117 and 123; and Irving, *Hitler's War*, p. 517.

4 Plocher, pp. 234–35.

5 Plocher, p. 238.

6 Hozzel, pp. 97–98.

7 Beevor, p. 141.

8 Pabst, p. 89.

9 Müller, p. 154.

10 Ziemke and Bauer, p. 392; and Hayward, *Stopped*, p. 193.

11 Von Richthofen, TB 13/9/42.

12 Erickson, p. 404.

13 Adam, *With Paulus at Stalingrad*, p. 67; and Beevor, p. 141.

14 Kozhevnikov, M. N., p. 89; and Hardesty, p. 102.

15 Pabst, pp. 98–100.

16 Hozzel, pp. 98–99.

17 Von Richthofen, 16/9/42.

18 Hayward, p. 195.

19 Adam, p. 69.

20 Erickson, pp. 405–07.

21 Boog et al., p. 1087.

22 Pabst, p. 100.

23 Pabst, p. 101.

24 Megargee, p. 180.

25 Halder KTB cited in Leach, Barry A., 'Colonel General Franz Halder' in Correlli Barnett (ed.), *Hitler's Generals*, London, 1989, p. 121.

26 Halder, p. 670.

27 Pabst, pp. 105–06.

28 Beevor, p. 147.

29 Chuikov, p. 152.

30 Chuikov, p. 162.

31 Pabst, p. 109.

32 Irving, p. 522; and Kershaw, p. 536.

33 Adam, p. 84.

34 Ziemke and Bauer, p. 397.

35 Boog et al., p. 1090.

36 Erickson, p. 416.

37 Boog et al., p. 1097.

38 Chuikov, p. 180.

39 Hayward, p. 210.

40 Chuikov, p. 180.

41 Beevor, p. 193.

42 From Doerr, Hans, *Der Feldzug nach Stalingrad: Versuch eines operativen Überblickes*, 1955, cited in Chuikov, p. 182; and Hayward, p. 210.

43 Hozzel, pp. 100–01.

44 Erickson, p. 436.

45 Von Richthofen, 14/10/42.

46 Hozzel, p. 101.
47 Pabst, p. 110.
48 Pickert, 15/10/42.
49 Hayward, p. 199.
50 Pickert, 9/9/42 and 7/10/42.
51 Pickert, 17/10/42.
52 Pickert, 19/10/42.
53 Von Richthofen, 19/10/42.
54 Adam, p. 85.
55 Von Below, p. 156.
56 Boog et al., p. 1094.
57 Beevor, pp. 209–11.

7. *URANUS*

1 Adam, p. 83.
2 Glantz and House, *Endgame at Stalingrad, Book One*, p. 22.
3 Zhukov, p. 166.
4 Preston Chaney Jr., p. 229.
5 Zhukov, p. 165.
6 Erickson, *The Road to Stalingrad*, p. 453.
7 Preston Chaney Jr., p. 230; and Glantz and House, p. 26.
8 Zhukov, p. 168; and Glantz and House, p. 43.
9 Erickson, p. 459.
10 Citino, p. 292.
11 Erickson, p. 459.
12 Erickson, p. 462.
13 Beevor, p. 227.
14 In *Endgame at Stalingrad, Book One*, David M. Glantz and Jonathan M. House explain how the post-war historiography on *Uranus* has been 'obscured by vanity and self-interest' and also 'warped by the political shifts within the USSR', including Krushchev's de-Stalinisation programme of the early 1960s (p. 20). These authors have also exhaustively analysed and assessed the various agendas and positions taken by Soviet writers, including Zhukov, as well as drawing on reliable archival material. I have shaded my text largely on their conclusions.
15 Citino, p. 292; and Beevor, p. 226.
16 Glantz and House, p. 168.
17 Adam, p. 83.
18 Von Richthofen, 12/11/42.
19 Pickert, *The Stalingrad Airlift*, p. 183.
20 Plocher, p. 247.
21 Von Richthofen, 16/11/42.
22 Adam, p. 83.

23 Adam, p. 88.
24 Carell, *Hitler's War on Russia*, p. 580.
25 Engel, p. 140.
26 Adam, pp. 91–92.
27 Beevor, p. 245.
28 Seaton, p. 314; Ziemke and Bauer, p. 468; and Beevor, p. 245.
29 Glantz and House, p. 199.
30 DiNardo, pp. 151–52.
31 Carell, p. 582.
32 Boog et al., pp. 1123–24; and Hayward, *Stopped*, p. 228.
33 Von Richthofen, 19/11/42.
34 Pickert, 19/11/42.
35 DiNardo, p. 153.
36 Ziemke and Bauer, p. 470.
37 Seaton, pp. 315–16.
38 Boog et al., p. 1126; Carell, *Hitler's War on Russia* pp. 586–87; and Ziemke and Bauer, p. 473.
39 Carell, p. 583.
40 Brunhaver, p. 8.
41 Erickson, p. 469.
42 Hayward, p. 231; and Salmi, p. 28.
43 Glantz and House, p. 364.

8. 'IMPOSSIBLE'

 1 For Hitler's movements on 7 November, see Toland, *Hitler* (BCA, 1997), p. 723; Gilbert, *Second World War* (Weidenfeld & Nicolson, 1989), p. 375; Fest, *Hitler* (Weidenfeld & Nicolson, 1974), p. 663, and Warlimont, p. 271.
 2 Megargee, p. 183.
 3 Zeitzler in *The Fatal Decisions*, pp. 117–18.
 4 Engel, p. 141.
 5 Irving, *Göring – A Biography*, p. 367, although Irving states the conference was in 'Berlin', whereas other sources state Carinhall.
 6 Morzik, p. 180.
 7 For background on the decision to airlift I have drawn primarily on Hayward, *Stalingrad: An Examination of Hitler's Decision to Airlift* and *Stopped at Stalingrad*, pp. 234–46.
 8 Kehrig, p. 163.
 9 Akin, p. 32.
10 Dierich, *Kampfgeschwader 51 'Edelweiss'*, pp. 74–75.
11 For Fiebig's biography see www.airhistory.org.uk/rfc/Kagohl3-diary.html; James S. Corum, *Wolfram von Richthofen – Master of the German Air War*, 2008, p. 91, and Kaiser, *Die Ritterkreuzträger der Kampfflieger, Band 1*, p. 35.

12 Fiebig, Br.B.7/43, 26/1/43.
13 Von Richthofen, 21/11/42; see also Irving, *Göring*, p. 368 and *Hitler's War*, p. 540.
14 Fiebig, Br.B.7/43, 26/1/43.
15 TNA/HW1/1152, CX/MSS/1728/T13, 25/11/42.
16 Pickert, 22/11/42.
17 Schröter, p. 101.
18 Hayward, *Decision*, p. 28.
19 OB HGr B an OKH/Chef GenStdH vom 23/11/42, betr. Zurücknahme der 6. *Armee*, cited in Kehrig, *Stalingrad, Dokument 9*, p. 561; the text also appears in Schröter, pp. 98–99.
20 Pickert, *The Stalingrad Airlift*, p. 184.
21 Hayward, *Decision*, p. 30. The implication is that the instructions to von Seidel and Langemeyer were issued by telephone, however Morzik cites a manuscript by Plocher (Morzik, pp. 202 and 396) which states Göring held a 'conference' on 23/11/42. This cannot have taken place that day.
22 Morzik, p. 202.
23 Irving, *Göring*, p. 368 and *Hitler's War*, p. 541.
24 BA-MA: ZA 3/460: *Stalingrad 1942/1943: Bericht über eine Auskunft über Görings Stalingrader Zusage durch Generaloberst Loerzer (Befragung Hamburg-Othmarschen, 16 April 1956 durch Prof. Dr. Richard Suchenwirth, Karlsruhe)*.
25 Fischer, p. 8.
26 BA-MA: ZA 3/111: *Sammelakte mit Abschriften 'Luftversorgung Stalingrads'*, Suchenwirth to Körner (*Befragung am 19.9.1955 in München*), Karlsruhe, 30/9/55.
27 Fleischer, p. 193.
28 Irving, *Göring*, p. 369; and Hayward, *Decision*, p. 31.
29 Obst. i.G. Kurt von Greiff, Chef der 1.(Führungs-) Abt. der Lw.Gen.St., cited in Plocher, pp. 275 and 384.
30 Carell, *Hitler's War on Russia*, p. 591. See also Kehrig, *Dokument 10*, Paulus an Hitler vom 23/11/42, betr. Notwendigkeit des Ausbruches der 6. *Armee*, vom 23/11/42.
31 Beevor, p. 273.
32 Von Below, p. 159.
33 Hayward, *Decision*, p. 29.
34 Zeitzler in *The Fatal Decisions*, p. 132.
35 Kershaw, p. 544.
36 Kehrig, p. 562, *Dokument 11*, Führerentscheid vom 24/11/42, betr. Halten der Stel lungen der 6. *Armee* und Ensatzstoss. FS OKH GenStdH/Op. Abt. (I/SB) Nr. 420 960/42 gKdos Chefs. vom 24/11/42, 0140 Uhr, aufgenommen bei AOK 6 um 0830 Uhr
37 Von Richthofen, 24/11/42.
38 Zeitzler, p. 132; see also Fischer, p. 10.
39 Hayward, *Decision*, p. 29.

40 Glantz and House, *Endgame at Stalingrad, Book Two*, p. 4.

41 Boog et al., p. 1127.

42 Glantz and House, *Endgame at Stalingrad, Book One*, p. 413.

43 Von Richthofen, 25/11/42.

44 Schramm, *Kriegstagebuch des Oberkommandos der Wehrmacht, 1942, Teilband II*, p. 1019.

10. 'THE COST IN BLOOD WILL BE HIGH'

1 BA-MA ZA 3/111: Schulz, *Luftversorgung Stalingrad (21/11/42–1/2/43)*.

2 Plocher, p. 316.

3 Signal from *Luftflotte* 4 to I.Flak-Korps, Ia Op.Nr.5013/42, 27/11/44; and also Kehrig, p. 289.

4 See Axis Biographical Research and Peter Kilduff, *Germany's First Air Force 1914–1918*, London 1991.

5 Kehrig, p. 28.

6 deZeng IV, *Luftwaffe Airfields 1935–1945* at www.ww2.dk; Morzik, p. 197 and Bergström, *BC/RS Vol. 4*, p. 46.

7 Kehrig, p. 289; and Möbius and Huß, pp. 67–70.

8 TNA/HW1/1166, CX/MSS/1739/T28, 27/11/42; and Morzik (Airlift), p. 199.

9 TNA/HW1/1166, CX/MSS/1739/ T28, 27/11/42; deZeng IV, *Luftwaffe Airfields 1935–1945* at www.ww2.dk; and Bergström, *BC/RS Vol. 4*, p. 46.

10 Signal from *Luftflotte* 4 to I.Flak-Korps, Ia Op.Nr.5013/42, 27/11/44; also Kehrig, p. 289; Von Rohden, p. 26; and Akins, p. 35.

11 Kaiser, *Die Ritterkreuzträger der Kampfflieger, Band 1*, p. 49.

12 Von Richthofen, 26/12/42.

13 BA-MA/ZA 3/644a, Kühl, *Erfahrungsbericht Stalingrad* and BA-MA/RL 10/153: Uhl, *Kampfgruppe z.b.V.5*, 9/2/43.

14 Plocher, p. 282.

15 Plocher, p. 277.

16 Morzik and Hümmelchen, p. 153.

17 BA-MA ZA 3/111: Schulz.

18 BA-MA ZA 3/111: Schulz.

19 Hinsley et al., p. 109.

20 Akins, p. 36.

21 Bekker, p. 282.

22 Thyssen, p. 11; and Akins, p. 37.

23 BA-MA ZA 3/111: Schulz; and Plocher, p. 283.

24 Zamansky, *How were German air force resources?*, December 2016.

25 Murray, p. 149; and Keen, p. 96.

26 BA-MA ZA 3/111: Schulz.

27 Morzik and Hümmelchen, p. 153; and Morzik, p. 183.

28 Plocher, p. 281.

29 Boog, Horst, p. 1152.
30 Brunhaver, p. 9.
31 Pickert, Wolfgang, *The Stalingrad Airlift*, p. 184.
32 Salmi, p. 33.
33 Brunhaver, p. 12.
34 Kehrig, p. 286.
35 Von Manstein, p. 307.
36 Signal from *Luftflotte* 4 to I.*Flak-Korps*, Ia Op.Nr.5013/42, 27/11/44.
37 Kehrig, p. 296.
38 Thyssen, p. 9.
39 Morzik, p. 190.
40 Von Richthofen, 24/11/42.
41 Eriksson, p. 99.
42 Von Richthofen, 25/11/42. Pickert states 34 aircraft flew 28 tons of ammunition and 36 cbm of fuel. If this was the case, then the fuel must have weighed 47 tons, which would seem excessive.
43 Wieder and von Einsiedel, *Stalingrad – Memories and Reassessments*, p. 56 (reproduced with kind permission of Orion Publishing Group through PLSclear).
44 For airfields see deZeng IV, *Luftwaffe Airfields 1935–1945*, Plocher, pp. 306–09; Morzik, pp. 195–96; Akins, p. 39; and Brunhaver, p. 13.
45 Plocher, p. 307.
46 BA-MA ZA 3/459 *Zahlenangaben zur Luftversorgung Stalingrad (25/11/42–2/2/43)*: composite figures based on *Tagebuch* Fiebig, Pickert, Milch, *Kriegstagebuch des OKW* and data from von Rohden.
47 Kehrig, p. 286.
48 BA-MA ZA 3/111: Schulz.
49 Von Richthofen, 28/11/42.
50 Potthoff, *Russland (Luftflottenarzt 4) Oktober 1942–April 1943*.
51 Kehrig, p. 282; and Morzik and Hümmelchen, p. 157.
52 Plocher, p. 282.
53 Morzik, pp. 188–89.
54 Potthoff, p. 15.
55 Fiebig, 29/11/42.
56 Von Richthofen, 29/11/42; and Dierich, *Kampfgeschwader 55 'Greif'*, p. 433.
57 BA-MA RL 8/55: Gen.Kdo VIII.*Fliegerkorps* Quartiermeister: *Besondere Anordnungen des Quartiermeisters für die Luftversorgung der Festung Stalingrad* (Anlage 2 zu. Gen.Kdo.VIII.Fl.Korps, Ia Nr.4200/42, 30/11/42).
58 TNA/HW1/1166, CX/MSS/1739/ T28, 27/11/42.
59 Fiebig, 27/11/42.
60 In *The Fatal Decisions* [pp. 140–46], Zeitzler is vague as to the dates of the two situation conferences he had with Hitler in which Stalingrad was discussed. See also Fischer, f/n 17, 11 of *Uber den Entschluß zur Luftversorgung Stalingrads*. Professor Joel S. A. Hayward has concluded

that this latter meeting would probably have taken place on the 27th [Hayward, *Stalingrad: An Examination of Hitler's Decision to Airlift*, p. 32]. In his diary, von Richthofen states Göring was still in Paris on the 25th, as does Irving in *Hitler's War* [p. 542]. Given it would have taken two days to travel from Paris to Rastenburg, the 27th would seem likely.

61 Schramm, *Kriegstagebuch des Oberkommandos der Wehrmacht, 1942 – Teilband II*, p. 1031.

62 *The Fatal Decisions – Six decisive battles of the Second World War from the viewpoint of the vanquished*, pp. 144–46.

63 Pickert, 27/11/42; and Schröter, p. 109.

64 Plocher, pp. 268–69.

65 LK AK Nr.603/43, 25/11/42 contained in Kehrig, p. 564 (Dokument 15). English translation in Wieder and von Einsiedel, pp. 290–91.

66 Plocher, p. 228-29.

67 Plocher, p. 284.

68 BA-MA/RL 10/153: Uhl, *Kampfgruppe z.b.V.5*, 9/2/43.

69 Plocher, p. 283; and Prien & Stemmer, *Messerschmitt Bf 109 im Einsatz bei der Stab und I./Jagdgeschwader 3*, pp. 246–48.

70 BA-MA/RL 10/153: Uhl, *Kampfgruppe z.b.V.5*, 9/2/43.

71 Pickert, 29/11/42.

72 Von Manstein, p. 315.

73 Cited in Melvin, p. 300.

74 Fiebig, 26/11/42.

75 BA-MA ZA 3/459 *Zahlenangaben zur Luftversorgung Stalingrad (25/11/42–2/2/43)*; and Morzik and Hümmelchen, p. 160.

76 Plocher, p. 283.

77 Beevor, p. 292.

11. 'A HARD AND DANGEROUS WAY FOR THE MEN TO EARN THEIR BREAD'

1 Beevor, p. 278; Adam, p. 115; Fiebig, 11/12/42; and Plocher, p. 286.

2 Kozhevnikov, p. 98.

3 Kurowski, p. 100; and Bekker, p. 284.

4 Von Richthofen, 30/11/42.

5 Pickert, 30/11/42.

6 BA-MA/ZA 3/644a, Kühl, *Erfahrungsbericht Stalingrad*.

7 BA-MA/ZA 3/644a, Kühl.

8 Pickert, *The Stalingrad Airlift*, p. 184.

9 Morzik, p. 189.

10 BA-MA/ZA 3/644a, Kühl and ZA 3/111: Schulz, *Luftversorgung Stalingrad (21/11/42–1/2/43)*.

11 Kehrig, p. 287.

12 Von Rohden, p. 28.

13 Morzik and Hümmelchen, p. 157.

14 TNA/AIR 40/1977.
15 Plocher, p. 284.
16 Fiebig, 2/12/42.
17 Bergström, *Stalingrad – The Air Battle*, p. 93.
18 Hardesty, p. 110; and Bergström, *BC/RS Vol. 4*, p. 53.
19 Kehrig, p. 297.
20 Balke, Ulf, *Kampfgeschwader 100 'Wiking'*, p. 127.
21 Potthoff, *Russland*, p. 12.
22 Glantz & House, *The Stalingrad Trilogy Volume 3: Endgame at Stalingrad – Book Two: December 1942–February 1943*, pp. 164–65.
23 Pickert, 2–3/12/42.
24 Fiebig, 3/12/42.
25 Fiebig, 4/12/42.
26 BA-MA/ZA 3/644a, Kühl.
27 Kozhevnikov, p. 98.
28 Bergström, *BC/RS: Volume 4*, p. 54.
29 Kozhevnikov, pp. 98–99.
30 Plocher, p. 284; and Fiebig, 5/12/42.
31 Von Richthofen, 5/12/42.
32 Pickert, 5/12/42.
33 BA-MA/ZA 3/644a, Kühl.
34 Akins, p. 37.
35 BA-MA/ZA 3/644a, Kühl.
36 BA-MA ZA 3/111: Schulz.
37 Akins, pp. 45–46.
38 Bekker, p. 284.
39 BA-MA ZA 3/111: Schulz.
40 BA-MA/ZA 3/644a, Kühl.
41 Pawlas, pp. 324–25; Fleischer, p. 193; and BA-MA ZA 3/111: Schulz.
42 BA-MA/RL 10/153: Uhl, *Kampfgruppe z.b.V.5*, 9/2/43.
43 Akins, p. 51.
44 BA-MA ZA 3/111: Schulz.
45 BA-MA ZA 3/111: Schulz.
46 Beevor, p. 280.
47 Zeitzler in *The Fatal Decisions*, p. 148.
48 Balke, p. 128.
49 BA-MA ZA 3/111: Schulz, *Luftversorgung Stalingrad (21/11/42–1/2/43)*; see also Thyssen, p. 10.
50 Plocher, p. 284.
51 Bergström, *Stalingrad – The Air Battle*, p. 94.
52 Potthoff, *Russland*.
53 Plocher, p. 285; and von Richthofen, 8/12/42.
54 Bergström, *Stalingrad – The Air Battle*, p. 95.
55 Von Below, p. 161.

56 Bergström, *BC/RS, Vol. 4*, p. 58.
57 Fiebig, 7–8/12/42; and *Luftwaffe Airfields 1935–1945* by Henry L. deZeng IV.
58 *Die Wehrmachtberichte 1939–1945, Band 2 1.Januar 1942 bis 31.Dezember 1943*, p. 389.
59 Von Richthofen, 8/11/42.
60 Potthoff, *Russland.*
61 Fiebig, 9/12/42; Plocher, p. 285; and Bergström, *BC/RS, Vol. 4*, p. 58.
62 Fiebig, 9/12/42.
63 Beevor, p. 281.
64 Pickert, 9/12/42.
65 Bergström, *Stalingrad – The Air Battle,* p. 95.
66 Barbas, p. 338.
67 Weal, p. 81.
68 Thyssen, p. 15.
69 Fiebig, 11/12/42.
70 BA-MA/ZA 3/644a, Kühl, *Erfahrungsbericht Stalingrad.*
71 BA-MA/RL 10/153: Uhl, *Kampfgruppe z.b.V.5,* 9/2/43.
72 BA-MA/ZA 3/644a, Kühl, *Erfahrungsbericht Stalingrad.*
73 Feldgericht des VIII.*Fliegerkorps*, Br.B.Nr.7/45, 26/1/43 in Fiebig TB.
74 Morzik and Hümmelchen, p. 160.
75 Bergström, *Stalingrad – The Air Battle*, p. 98.
76 I have based this on information in Bernd Barbas' *Die Geschichte der II. Gruppe des Jagdgeschwaders 52*, pp. 111–12 and 338, as well as the account in Christer Bergstrom's *Black Cross-Red Star – Air War over the Eastern Front:Volume 4 – Stalingrad to Kuban*, p. 60.The latter credits logbooks and interviews, although the figures for the numbers of transports engaged and shot down varies in Kozhevnikov, p. 99 and *The Soviet Air Force in World War II – The Official History* (ed. Wagner, 1974), p. 143.
77 Melvin, p. 301; and von Manstein, p. 329.

12. 'THE *FÜHRER* WAS APPALLED'

1 For *Wintergewitter* see Seaton, pp. 326–27; Melvin, pp. 301–07; Ziemke, pp. 63–65; Erickson, pp. 10–11; Citino, p. 300; Hayward, *Stopped*, p. 262; and Plocher, p. 287.
2 Von Manstein, p. 327.
3 Schramm, *Kriegstagebuch des Oberkommandos der Wehrmacht, 1942 – Teilband II*, p. 1067.
4 Kehrig, p. 329 and pp. 586–87 (Dokument 28); also Hayward, *Stopped*, p. 264.
5 Schramm, p. 1104.
6 Von Richthofen, 11/11/42.
7 Boog, Horst et al., p. 1154; and Erickson, *The Road to Berlin*, p. 11.

8 Von Manstein, p. 327.

9 Boog, Horst et al., p. 1148.

10 Warlimont, p. 285.

11 Boog, Horst et al., 1155.

12 Boog, Horst et al., p. 1155–56.

13 Seaton, p. 328; and Glantz with House, *The Stalingrad Trilogy Volume 3: Endgame at Stalingrad – Book Two*, p. 227.

14 Adam, p. 137; and Beevor, pp. 284 and 306.

15 Bekker, p. 284.

16 Morzik and Hümmelchen, p. 160.

17 TNA/AIR20/7701: *Extracts of Reports of Führer Conferences held on 12/12/42, 1/2/43 and 4/3/43*, (AHB 6 Translation No.VII/44, 25/9/47).

18 Fiebig, 16/12/42; and Balke, p. 133.

19 Glantz with House, p. 235.

20 Plocher, p. 287.

21 Fiebig, 16–18/12/42; and Balke, *Kampfgeschwader 100 'Wiking'*, p. 133.

22 Müller, p. 154.

23 Plocher, p. 309.

24 Schröter, p. 184.

25 Wieder and von Einsiedel, *Stalingrad – Memories and Reassessments*, pp. 52–53 (reproduced with kind permission of Orion Publishing Group through PLSclear).

26 Wieder and von Einsiedel, *Stalingrad – Memories and Reassessments*, p. 56 (reproduced with kind permission of Orion Publishing Group through PLSclear).

27 Schröter, p. 185.

28 BA-MA ZA 3/111: Schulz, *Luftversorgung Stalingrad (21/11/42–1/2/43)*.

29 Adam, p. 152; and Wieder and von Einsiedel, p. 51.

30 Ziemke, p. 64.

31 Von Manstein, p. 333.

32 Goerlitz, p. 255.

33 Adam, p. 143.

34 See von Manstein, p. 334. However, Goerlitz, in *Paulus and Stalingrad*, in a footnote on p. 255, states that, post-war, Schmidt maintained that this was '. . . of course, a figure of speech. During a discussion on the inadequacy of the supplies being flown, he did, in fact, say something to the effect that if Sixth Army were kept adequately supplied it could probably hold out till Easter'. See also Seaton, p. 329; Plocher, p. 289; Adam, pp. 142–43; and Beevor, pp. 299 and 309.

35 Pickert, 19/12/42.

36 Glantz with House, p. 291.

37 Von Richthofen, 18/12/42.

38 Boog, Horst et al., p. 1156.

39 Seaton, pp. 329–30; and Ziemke, p. 64.

40 Fiebig, 19/12/42.
41 Pickert, 19/12/42.
42 Potthoff, *Russland*, p. 33.
43 Von Richthofen, 19/12/42.
44 Glantz with House, p. 302; and Plocher, p. 291.
45 Fiebig, 20/12/42.
46 Von Rohden, p. 40.
47 Von Richthofen, 21/12/42.
48 Thyssen, p. 14.
49 Fiebig, 21/12/42.
50 Pickert, 21/12/42.
51 Hayward, *Stopped*, p. 271.

13. 'GENERAL, WE MUST GET OUT OF HERE!' DISASTER AT TATSINSKAYA

1 Glantz with House, *The Stalingrad Trilogy Volume 3: Endgame at Stalingrad –
   Book Two*, p. 238.
2 Von Richthofen, 22/12/42; and Kehrig, p. 491.
3 BA-MA ZA 3/459: *Der Kampf um den Versorgungs-Flugplatz Tazinskaja
   (Aus einer Studie der 8.Abt. des Generalstabes der Lw. Aus dem Jahre 1944
   'Einsatz und Führung der B.O. während rückläufiger Bwegungen').*
4 BA-MA ZA 3/459: *Der Kampf um den Versorgungs-Flugplatz Tazinskaja*;
   and Coyle, p. 35.
5 Hayward, p. 271.
6 Fiebig, 23/12/42.
7 Ziemke, pp. 68–69.
8 Coyle, p. 34.
9 Erickson, *The Road to Berlin*, p. 18; and Glantz with House, p. 240.
10 Akins, p. 44.
11 Plocher, p. 293.
12 BA-MA ZA 3/111: Schulz, *Luftversorgung Stalingrad (21/11/42–1/2/43).*
13 BA-MA ZA 3/111: Schulz.
14 BA-MA/ZA 3/644a, Kühl, *Erfahrungsbericht Stalingrad.*
15 Thyssen, p. 15.
16 BA-MA/ZA 3/644, Morzik, *Erfahrungsbericht Stalingrad.*
17 BA-MA/ZA 3/644a, Kühl.
18 See Goerlitz, pp. 275–76: reproduced AHQ teleprinter signal, HQ,
   Heeresgruppe Don to Chief of the General Staff, Army HQ, No.421026/42,
   23/12/42.
19 Coyle, p. 35.
20 BA-MA/RL 10/153: Uhl, *Kampfgruppe z.b.V.5,* 9/2/43.
21 Plocher, p. 349.
22 BA-MA/ZA 3/644, Morzik.
23 Plocher, p. 350.

24 BA-MA/ZA 3/644a, Kühl.

25 BA-MA/ZA 3/644a, Kühl.

26 Fiebig, 23/12/42.

27 Schramm, *Kriegstagebuch des Oberkommandos der Wehrmacht, 1942 – Teilband II*, p. 1182; see also Carell, *Scorched Earth – Hitler's War on Russia Volume 2*, p. 120.

28 Carell, *Scorched* Earth, p. 116; and Fiebig, 23/12/42. For JG 3, see Prien and Stemmer, *Messerschmitt Bf 109 im Einsatz bei der Stab und I./Jagdgeschwader 3*, pp. 498 and 516, and *Messerschmitt Bf 109 im Einsatz bei der II./Jagdgeschwader 3*, pp. 174 and 176.

29 Glantz with House, p. 240.

30 Carell, *Scorched Earth*, p. 118.

31 Erickson, p. 19.

32 BA-MA ZA 3/459: *Der Kampf um den Versorgungs-Flugplatz Tazinskaja.*

33 Akins, p. 42.

34 Bemerkung Nr.11978/42, 30/12/42 quoted in BA-MA ZA 3/459: *Der Kampf um den Versorgungs-Flugplatz Tazinskaja.*

35 Plocher, p. 294.

36 Akins, p. 43.

37 The events of 24 December at Tatsinskaya are based on Fiebig's *Tagebuch*. Von Rohden in *Die Luftwaffe ringt um Stalingrad* (pp. 46–50) evidently bases his account on the same source, as does Kurowski in *Luftbrücke Stalingrad*, pp. 81–87. See also Plocher, p. 294, and Glantz with House, p. 240.

38 Von Richthofen, 24/12/42.

39 Plocher, p. 295.

40 Kehrig, p. 491.

41 Schlaug, *Die II. Kampfgeschwader zur besonderen Verwendung 1 1938–1943*, p. 158.

42 Pickert, 24/12/42.

43 Bieber, p. 55.

44 Erickson, p. 18; and Glantz with House, p. 240.

45 Von Richthofen, 24/12/42.

46 Haupt, p. 221; and Beevor, pp. 314–15.

47 Fiebig, 25/12/42.

48 Von Richthofen, 25/12/42.

49 Plocher, p. 294.

50 Zhukov, p. 187; and Erickson, p. 20.

51 Von Manstein, p. 351.

52 Fiebig, 26/12/42.

53 Erickson, p. 21.

54 Kurowski, p. 98; von Richthofen, 24/12/42; and Morzik, p. 191.

55 Balke, p. 134.

56 Beevor, p. 316.

57 Boog, Horst et al., p. 1159.
58 Fiebig, 27/12/42.
59 Von Richthofen, 28/12/42.
60 Engel, p. 146.
61 Möbius and Huß, p. 70.
62 Boog et al., p. 1160.
63 Ebener, p. 12.
64 Lower, pp. 29–30.
65 Erickson, p. 22; and Glantz with House, p. 240.
66 Morzik and Hümmelchen, p. 158; and Morzik, p. 190.
67 Hinsley et al., p. 111.
68 Kehrig, p. 488.
69 Fiebig, 29/12/42.
70 Ziemke, p. 73.
71 Melvin, pp. 306–07.
72 Haupt, p. 205.
73 Carell, p. 126.
74 Zhukov, p. 188.
75 Balke, p. 134.
76 Bergström, *Stalingrad – The Air Battle*, p. 106.
77 Ebener, p. 12.
78 Schramm, *1942 – Teilband II*, p. 1200; Goerlitz, p. 79.
79 Haupt, p. 223.
80 Waiss, *Chronik Kampfgeschwader Nr.27 Boelcke, Band IV, Teil 3*, p. 173.
81 BA-MA/RL 10/153: Uhl, *Kampfgruppe z.b.V.5*, 9/2/43.
82 BA-MA/RL 10/153: Uhl.
83 Boog et al., p. 1159.
84 Adam, p. 163.
85 Fiebig, 21/12/42.
86 Boog et al., p. 1159.
87 Boog et al., p. 1159.
88 Adam, p. 165.
89 Schlaug, pp. 158–59.
90 Ziemke, p. 73; and Kehrig, p. 492.
91 Beevor, p. 318; Ziemke, p. 73; and von Manstein, p. 349.
92 Kurowski, p. 100.
93 Von Richthofen and Fiebig TBs, 1/1/43.
94 Plocher, p. 296; and Kehrig, p. 491.
95 deZeng IV, *Luftwaffe Airfields 1935–45 Russia* at www.ww2.dk.
96 Plocher, p. 298.
97 Salmi, p. 33.
98 BA-MA ZA 3/111: Schulz.
99 BA-MA ZA 3/111: Schulz; and Plocher, p. 299.
100 Balke, p. 134.

101 Fiebig, 5/1/43.
102 Waiss, *Chronik Kampfgeschwader Nr. 27 Boelcke, Band V, Teil 4*, pp. 25 and 27.
103 Pickert, 5/1/43.
104 Schlaug, p. 161.
105 Fiebig, 7/1/43.
106 Balke, p. 135.
107 Akins, p. 52.
108 Adam, p. 166.
109 Fiebig, 7/1/43.
110 Balke, p. 135.
111 Fiebig, 8/1/43.
112 Von Richthofen, 8/1/43.

14. THE GIANTS OF STALINGRAD

1 Fiebig, 8/1/43.
2 See ADI(K) Report No.377/1945: *The Life and Work of Oberst Petersen*, 22/8/45. For the Fw 200 early history see Chris Goss, *Osprey Combat Aircraft 115 – Fw 200 Condor Units of World War 2*, Osprey Publishing, 2016 and *Focke-Wulf Fw 200 – The Condor at War 1939–1945*, Classic Publications, 2017.
3 Unless noted otherwise, all information related to the activities of Willer and KGr.z.b.V.200 is from BA-MA ZA 3/459: *Versorgung Stalingrads durch Lufttransportführer Willers in Stalino und Saporoshje*, Ausarbeitung von Major a.D. Willers, mit Anlagen. This file includes the reports by the *Gruppe's Staffelkapitäne* and details of individual missions.
4 BA-MA ZA 3/459: Schulte-Vogelheim, *Erfahrungsbericht über den Einsatz der 1./K.G.z.b.V.200 vom 2/1-2/2/43, 8/2/43.*
5 BA-MA ZA 3/459: Kuchenmeister, *Erfahrungsbericht über die Zeit der 2./K.G.z.b.V.200 vom 8/1/-2/2/43, 8/2/43.*
6 BA-MA ZA 3/111: Schulz, *Luftversorgung Stalingrad (21/11/42–1/2/43)*
7 BA-MA ZA 3/459: Kuchenmeister
8 See Budraß, Lutz, *Flugzeugindustrie und Luftrüstung in Deutschland 1918–1945*, Droste Verlag, Düsseldorf, 1998, pp. 388 and 485.
9 Kössler and Ott, *Die großen Dessauer: Junkers Ju 89, Ju 90, Ju 290, Ju 390 – Die Geschichte einer Flugzeugfamilie*, various pages.

15. 'NO HEARTS BEAT STRONGER'

1 Glantz with House, pp. 432–33; and Beevor, pp. 326–27.
2 Ziemke, p. 76; Seaton, p. 332; and Glantz with House, pp. 438–39.
3 Balke, p. 135.
4 Plocher, p. 323.
5 Fiebig, 10/1/43.
6 Fiebig, 11/1.43.
7 Pickert, 11/1/43.

8   BA-MA/RL 10/153: Uhl, *Kampfgruppe z.b. V.5*, 9/2/43.

9   BA-MA/ZA 3/644, Kühl, *Erfahrungsbericht Stalingrad*.

10 BA-MA/RL 10/153: Uhl.

11 BA-MA/ZA 3/644, Morzik, *Erfahrungsbericht Stalingrad*.

12 deZeng IV, *Luftwaffe Airfields 1935–45 Russia* at www.ww2.dk.

13 Lower, *Luftwaffe Tactical Operations at Stalingrad 19 November–2 February 1943*, p. 31.

14 Bergström, *Stalingrad – The Air Battle*, p. 117; and *BC/RS Vol. 4*, p. 155.

15 Pickert, *Tagebuch*.

16 Pickert, *Tagebuch*.

17 Morzik and Hümmelchen, p. 160.

18 Pickert, 13/1/43; and *Eyewitness Commentary*, p. 185.

19 Fiebig, 13/1/43.

20 Warlimont, *Inside Hitler's Headquarters*, p. 284.

21 BA-MA/ZA 3/644, Kühl.

22 Fiebig, 12/1/43.

23 Adam, p. 175; and Beevor, p. 359.

24 Busch, Reinhold (ed.), p. 11.

25 Schlaug, *Die II. Kampfgeschwader zur besonderen Verwendung 1 1938–1943*, p. 164.

26 Kössler and Ott, pp. 151–55.

27 BA-MA ZA 3/459: *Versorgung Stalingrads durch Lufttransportführer Willers in Stalino und Saporoshje*.

28 BA-MA ZA 3/459: Willers, *Erfolgsbericht der K. G. z. b. V. 200 über Versorgung der Festung Stalingrad*, 31/1/43.

29 BA-MA ZA 3/459: Kuchenmeister, *Erfahrungsbericht über die Zeit der 2./K. G. z. b. V. 200 vom 8/1–2/2/43*, 8/2/43.

30 Fiebig, 14/1/43.

31 Fiebig, 14/1/43; and Beevor, p. 359.

32 Pickert, *The Stalingrad Airlift*, p. 184.

33 BA-MA ZA 3/459.

34 Fiebig, 14/1/43.

35 Schlaug, *Die deutschen Lastensegler-Verbände 1937–1945 – Eine Chronik aus Berichten, Tagebüchern, Dokumenten*, p. 127.

36 Von Richthofen, 14/1/43.

37 Fiebig, 14/1/43.

38 BA-MA ZA 3/111: Schulz, *Luftversorgung Stalingrad (21/11/42–1/2/43)*.

39 Morzik and Hümmelchen, p. 156.

40 Schlaug, *Die deutschen Lastensegler-Verbände 1937–1945*, p. 128.

41 Kehrig, p. 516.

42 Milch, 18/1/43.

43 Schlaug, *Die II. Kampfgeschwader zur besonderen Verwendung 1 1938–1943*, p. 164.

44 Schlaug, p. 164.

45 Plocher, p. 299.

46 Plocher, p. 314.

47 Plocher, p. 315.

48 Plocher, pp. 313–14.

49 Plocher, p. 323.

50 Milch, 18/1/43.

51 Plocher, p. 308.

52 Plocher, p. 318.

53 Irving, *Rise & Fall*, p. 184.

54 Schramm, *Kriegstagebuch des OKW, 1943, Teilband I*, p. 42.

55 Prien Stemmer, *Messerschmitt Bf 109 im Einsatz bei der Stab und I./Jagdgeschwader 3*, p. 256; and Fiebig, 16/1/43.

56 Müller, p. 155.

57 Pickert, 15–16/1/43.

58 Glantz with House, p. 487.

16. COMETH THE HOUR

1 The Hugo Junkers Home Page (http://hugojunkers.pytalhost.com/ju _home.htm).

2 Irving, *Rise and Fall*, p. 26.

3 Milch, 15/1/43; and v.Rohden, p. 74.

4 Potthoff, *Russland*.

5 Milch, 16/1/43; and Kehrig, p. 523.

6 BA-MA/RL 30/3: *Sonderstab Milch Ia*, 16/1/43.

7 Fiebig, 16/1/43.

8 Fiebig, 16/1/43.

9 Kehrig, p. 517.

10 Thyssen, p. 13.

11 Milch, 18/1/43.

12 Akins, p. 48; and Milch, 18/1/42.

13 Morzik and Hümmelchen, p. 160.

14 Fiebig, 17/1/43.

15 Milch, 17–18/1/43.

16 Milch, 17/1/43 and BA-MA RL 30/2 *Sonderstab Einsatzbereitschaftsmeldungen*.

17 Irving, pp. 186–87.

18 Potthoff, *Russland*.

19 Von Richthofen, 17/1/43.

20 BA-MA RL 30/2 *Übersicht über die voraussichtlich zur Verfügung stehenden Lastensegler und Schleppflugzeuge, Sonderstab Milch*, 16/1/43.

21 BA-MA ZA 3/111: Schulz, *Luftversorgung Stalingrad (21/11/42–1/2/43)*.

22 Eriksson, pp. 99–100.

23 Prien and Stemmer, *Messerschmitt Bf 109 im Einsatz bei der Stab und I./Jagdgeschwader 3*, p. 256.

24 Milch, 18/1/43.

25 Fiebig, 17/1/43.

26 Fiebig, 17/1/43.

27 Plocher, p. 317.

28 Fiebig, 17/1/43; and Balke, p. 135.

29 BA–MA/RL 10/153: Uhl, *Kampfgruppe z.b.V.5*, 9/2/43.

30 BA–MA/ZA 3/644, Kühl, *Erfahrungsbericht Stalingrad*.

31 Milch, 17/1/43.

32 Schramm, *Kriegstagebuch des OKW, 1943, Teilband I*, p. 47.

33 BA–MA RL 30/2.

34 Morzik and Hümmelchen, p. 159.

35 Milch, 17/1/43.

36 Von Richthofen, 18/1/43.

37 BA–MA RL 30/2.

38 Irving, p. 189.

39 Milch, 18/1/43; and Irving, p. 188.

40 Private letter dated 18/1/43 supplied by Javier Ruiz of the Spohr family.

41 Von Richthofen, 17/1/43.

42 BA–MA ZA 3/459: *Versorgung Stalingrads durch Lufttransportführer Willers in Stalino und Saporoshje*, Ausarbeitung von Major a.D. Willers, mit Anlagen.

43 Plocher, p. 299; and von Below, p. 162.

44 Fiebig, 19/1/43.

45 Pickert, 19/12/42.

46 Milch, 19/1/43.

47 Milch, 19/1/43.

48 Craig, p. 350.

49 Thiel report in Milch TB.

50 Beevor, p. 367.

51 Milch, 19/1/43.

52 Von Richthofen, 20/1/43.

53 Schmoll, p. 104.

54 Milch, 20/1/43.

55 BA–MA RL 30/2 Luft.fl.4 Nr.636/43, 19/1/43.

56 Fiebig, 21/1/43.

57 Balke, p. 136.

58 Glantz with House, p. 507.

59 Akins, p. 51.

60 BA–MA RL 30/2.

61 Milch, 21/1/43.

62 Goerlitz, p. 83.

63 Pickert, 21/1/43.

64 Pickert, 22–23/1/43.

65 BA–MA/ZA 3/644, Kühl.

66 BA–MA RL 30/2 Luft.fl.4 Nr.636/43, 22/1/43.

67 Kehrig, p. 524.

68 Busch, Reinhold (ed.), p. 13.

69 Irving, p. 190; and Thyssen, p. 17.

70 Potthoff, *Russland*.

71 Pickert, Wolfgang, *The Stalingrad Airlift*, p. 184.

72 Potthoff, *Russland*.

73 Fiebig, TB 22/1/43.

74 BA-MA ZA 3/459: Kuchenmeister.

75 Ziemke, p. 78.

76 Plocher, p. 324.

77 *Funkspruch an Heeresgruppe Don, 0630 Uhr, AOK 6, Ia, 23/1/43* quoted in Glantz with House, p. 517.

78 BA-MA RL 30/2.

79 Milch, 22/1/43.

80 Kehrig, p. 523.

81 Busch, pp. 13–14

82 Wieder and von Einsiedel, p. 102.

83 Private letter dated 20/2/43 supplied by Javier Ruiz of the Spohr family.

84 Glantz with House, p. 518.

17. FADING SIGNALS

1 Milch, 23/1/43.

2 Von Rohden, p. 101.

3 Milch, 24/1/43.

4 BA-MA/RL 10/153: Uhl, *Kampf Gruppe z.b.V.5*, 9/2/43.

5 Waiss, *Chronik Kampfgeschwader Nr.27 Boelcke, Band V, Teil 4*, p. 48.

6 Milch, 25/1/43; and Weal, p. 81.

7 Ziemke, p. 78.

8 Fiebig, 26/1/43; and BA-MA RL 30/2.

9 Irving, p. 189.

10 Thyssen, p. 10.

11 Beevor, p. 374.

12 Akins, p. 53.

13 Morzik (Airlift), p. 194; and Plocher, p. 324.

14 BA-MA RL 30/2.

15 Fiebig, 27/1/43.

16 BA-MA/ZA 3/644a, Kühl, *Erfahrungsbericht Stalingrad*.

17 Von Richthofen, 26/1/43.

18 Milch, 28/1/43.

19 BA-MA/ZA 3/644, Morzik, *Erfahrungsbericht Stalingrad*.

20 Von Rohden, p. 102.

21 Von Richthofen, 27/1/43.

22 Milch, 28/1/43.

23 BA-MA RL 30/2 S.Stab Milch Nr.67.43, 29/1/43.

24 Fiebig, 29/1/43.

25 Fiebig, 29/1/43.

26 Milch, 30/1/43.

27 BA-MA ZA 3/111: Schulz, *Luftversorgung Stalingrad (21/11/42–1/2/43)*.

28 Milch, 30/1/43.

29 Fiebig, 30/1/43.

30 TNA/AIR40/1982.

31 Plocher, p. 322; and Bergström, *BC/RS Vol. 4*, p. 163.

32 BA-MA RL 30/2 S.Stab Milch Nr.78.43, 31/1/43.

33 Fiebig, 31/1/43.

34 NARA, T-321, R.G.No.242, Roll 179, XI.AK an H.Gr.Don Ia, 31.1. and Milch, 31/1/43.

35 Fiebig, 30/1/43.

36 Schröter, p. 248.

37 Adam, pp. 206–07.

38 Von Richthofen, 30/1/43.

39 Adam, p. 212; Goerlitz, p. 82; Beevor, p. 381; and Glantz with House, p. 560.

40 Schröter, p. 252; and Glantz with House, pp. 559 and 673, f/n 74.

41 Glantz with House, p. 553; and Adam, p. 206.

42 Adam, p. 214.

43 Ziemke, p. 79.

44 Fiebig, 31/1/43.

45 Kehrig, p. 524.

46 Milch, 31/1/43.

47 Plocher, p. 329.

48 Fiebig, 1/2/43.

49 Milch, 1/2/43.

50 Engel, p. 147.

51 Glantz with House, p. 564.

52 BA-MA RL 30/2 S.Stab Milch Nr.88.43, 1/2/43.

53 Fiebig, 2/2/43.

54 Waiss, *Chronik Kampfgeschwader Nr.27 Boelcke, Band V, Teil 4*, p. 63.

55 Milch, 2/2/43; and Beevor, p. 396.

56 BA-MA RL 30/2 S.Stab Milch Nr.92.43, 3/2/43.

57 BA-MA RL 30/2 S.Stab Milch Ia Nr.92.43, 2/2/43.

58 Potthoff, *Russland*.

59 Adam, p. 184.

18. THE RECKONING

1 Hayward, *Examination*, p. 21.

2 Akins, *The Ghosts of Stalingrad*, p. 61.

3 Potthoff, *Russland*.

4 Von Manstein, p. 365.

5 Suchenwirth, p. 108.

6 Plocher, p. 276.

7 Morzik and Hümmelchen, p. 152; and Morzik, p. 181.

8 Morzik and Hümmelchen, p. 160; and Thyssen, p. 7.

9 Morzik and Hümmelchen, p. 165; and Morzik, p. 200.

10 Salmi, p. 32.

11 Irving, *Milch*, p. 196.

12 Milch, 28/1/43.

13 Fiebig, 16/1/43; and Pickert, *The Stalingrad Airlift*, p. 185.

14 Potthoff, *Russland*.

15 Speer, p. 249.

16 Von Rohden, pp. 25–26; and Fischer, 16.

17 Von Rohden, p. 26.

18 Fischer, pp. 58–59; and Plocher, p. 274.

19 Fiebig, Feldgericht des VIII.Fl.K., Br.B.Nr.7/43, 26/1/43.

20 Von Richthofen, 10/2/43.

21 Von Richthofen, 11/2/43.

22 Potthoff, *Russland*.

23 BAMA ZA 3/459: Willers, *Versorgung Stalingrads durch Lufttransportführer Willers in Stalino und Saporoshje*.

24 Morzik, p. 203.

25 Grechko, p. 261.

26 BA–MA/RL8/55.

27 Morzik, p. 213.

28 BA–MA/RL8/55; and Pegg, p. 68.

29 BA–MA/RL8/55.

30 BA–MA/RL8/55 (Gen.Kdo.VIII.Fl.K., Qu/Ib. Nr.150/43, 30/1/43).

31 deZeng and Stankey (Officer Career Summaries).

32 BA–MA/RL8/55 (Gen.Kdo.VIII.Fl.K., Qu/Ib. Nr.150/43, 30/1/43).

33 Pegg, p. 69.

34 Morzik, p. 217.

35 Von Richthofen, 2/2/43.

36 Schlaug, *Die deutschen Lastensegler-Verbände 1937–1945*, p. 135; and www.ww2.dk.

37 UKNA/HW1/1360.

38 Pegg, p. 69.

39 UKNA/HW1/1360.

40 Schlaug, *Lastensegler-Verbände*, p. 138.

Index

Note: page numbers in **bold** refer to illustrations, tables and captions. All materiel is German unless otherwise stated.